THE SCIENCE OF
GARDENING

THE SCIENCE OF
GARDENING

The hows and whys of successful gardening

Professor Peter Jones

THE CROWOOD PRESS

First published in 2011 by
The Crowood Press Ltd
Ramsbury, Marlborough
Wiltshire SN8 2HR

www.crowood.com

© Peter Jones 2011

British Library Cataloguing-in-Publication Data
A catalogue record for this book is available from the British Library.

ISBN 978 1 84797 242 2

Front cover: (top left) lower surface of a sage leaf (×500), showing hairs to reduce water loss; (top right) the fern *Dryopteris wallichiana*; (bottom right) lower surface of a mint leaf (×60) showing round scent glands; (bottom left) fennel, sage, mint and lavender, all native to dry habitats. **Back cover:** (left) chains of spores (×500) of the cocksfoot powdery mildew fungus on an infected leaf of the grass cocksfoot; (right) part of a woodland garden, showing *Hosta sieboldiana* 'Elegans' and the shuttlecock fern, *Matteucia struthiopteris*.

Frontispiece: *Primula viallii*.

Typeset by Servis Filmsetting Ltd, Stockport, Cheshire
Printed and bound in Malaysia by Times Offset (m) Sdn Bhd

Contents

Chapter 1   Understanding Plant Structure and Names   7

Chapter 2   Selecting the Right Site for a Plant   27

Chapter 3   Choosing the Specimen and Preparing the Site   51

Chapter 4   Soil, Water and Nutrients   63

Chapter 5   Pruning and Training Garden Plants   103

Chapter 6   Managing Pests, Diseases and Weeds   123

Chapter 7   Propagating Plants   149

Chapter 8   Colour in the Ornamental Garden   185

Chapter 9   Productivity in the Kitchen Garden   213

Glossary   241

Index   255

CHAPTER 1

Understanding Plant Structure and Names

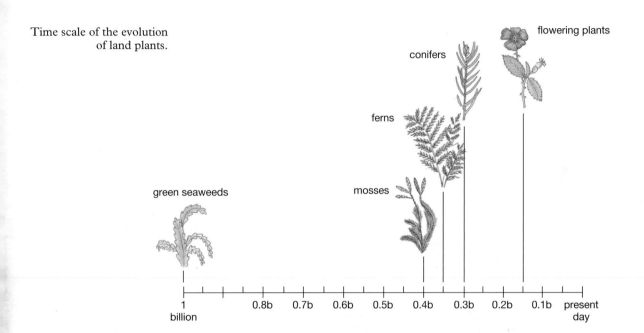

Time scale of the evolution of land plants.

green seaweeds

mosses

ferns

conifers

flowering plants

| 1 billion | 0.8b | 0.7b | 0.6b | 0.5b | 0.4b | 0.3b | 0.2b | 0.1b | present day |

The study of describing, identifying and naming plants is called plant taxonomy. This involves an understanding of how plants evolved, how plants are constructed and organized, and what plant names means – all valuable topics for gardeners to appreciate.

THE ORIGIN OF PLANTS

Life on earth started about four billion years ago with single-celled bacteria, and for nearly two billion years these were the only life forms. Today

Campanula portenschlagiana self sown into a limestone wall.

bacteria are still the dominant organisms on the planet, making up more than 90 per cent of the total weight of all living organisms (biomass) – about 80 billion tonnes. The actions of the earliest bacteria changed the chemistry of the atmosphere, water and land. As a result, more advanced organisms, like plants and animals, found a home.

About 3.7 billion years ago one group of bacteria, the cyanobacteria, evolved a process called photosynthesis, which we now usually associate with plants. In this process the energy from sunlight is trapped by coloured pigments and powers a chemical reaction which converts carbon dioxide and water into sugars and oxygen (Chapter 4). The sugars contain the sunlight energy stored as chemical energy, which living organisms can use where and when they need energy to grow or make new chemicals.

At that time most life existed in the waters of the planet. The first plants were the green algae, which evolved from photosynthetic bacteria 1–2.5 billion years ago. Modern-day algae range in size from single-celled microscopic organisms (though still much larger than bacteria) to giant seaweeds.

The land was inhospitable because of low concentrations of oxygen in the air, drying winds, high temperatures and high levels of damaging ultraviolet (UV) light. A side effect of the evolution of photosynthesis was that the oxygen concentration in the atmosphere rose, and as a consequence conditions on land started to become more suitable for life. Oxygen molecules (which are made of two oxygen atoms combined: O_2) in the upper atmosphere were acted on by sunlight to produce a layer of a new molecule (ozone: O_3), which absorbed UV rays from the sun. This made life on the planet's surface much more attractive.

The first land plants appeared about 0.4 billion years ago and were ancestors of modern-day mosses and liverworts, followed by the ferns and horsetails (at 0.35 billion years ago), then the seed plants, starting with cycads and conifers (from about 0.3 billion years ago) and finishing with the flowering plants. The latter first appeared around 0.13 billion years ago, yet within 40 million years (a blink of an eye, in evolutionary terms) flowering plants were the most common and diverse group of plants on earth.

THE STRUCTURE OF FLOWERING PLANTS

The vast majority of our garden plants are members of the flowering plant group of seed plants. Even grasses and broad-leaved trees like oak are flowering plants, although they don't have brightly-coloured flowers. Because they are wind pollinated, these plants have no need for colourful flowers to attract an animal to transfer pollen from one flower to another to carry out pollination. Garden plants that are not flowering plants include the conifers (such as pine, yew and ginkgo) and the ferns, while mosses are common weeds, particularly of lawns.

The Cell

The basic unit of all plants (and all other organisms) is the cell. Some algae are made up of just one cell, but each garden plant is made of millions, if not billions, of cells connected together. Remarkably, the structure of the cell of plants from all different groups, from the alga to the orchid to the oak, is similar.

Each plant cell is surrounded by an outer strengthening wall, made up of the most common chemical in the world, the carbohydrate cellulose. Animal and bacterial cells have no such cell wall. Inside the plant cell wall is a membrane through which the cell controls which chemicals move in or out of the cell. This membrane wraps around a watery material, the cytoplasm, where most of

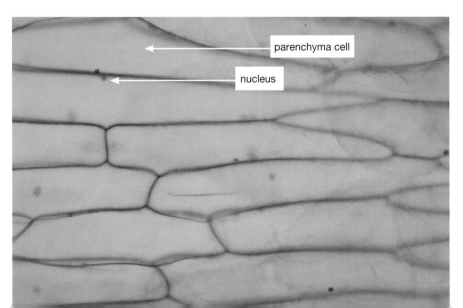

A micrograph of epidermis from an onion bulb, showing parenchyma cells.

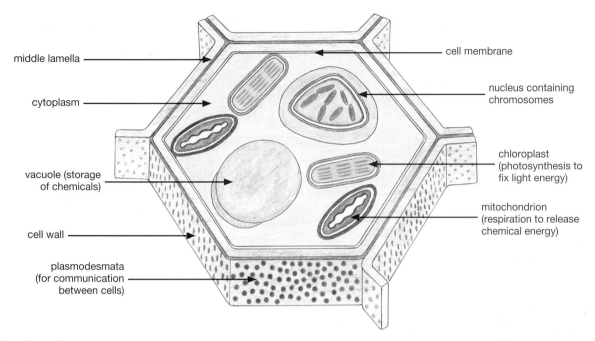

The plant cell.

the chemical reactions of the cell take place. In the cytoplasm are a number of membrane-bound packages known as organelles.

The membranes are made largely of fats (or lipids), which do not dissolve in water. Anyone who cooks will recognize that fats and water do not mix, with fat globules floating as separate entities in a water-based stock. The design of the membrane-bound organelles allows each one to do a particular job within the cell.

The control centre of each cell is the nucleus. This organelle contains the cell's chromosomes, each of which is a linear piece of the genetic material DNA or deoxyribonucleic acid (Chapter 7). Dotted along each chromosome are genes, lengths of DNA which are the factors which control inherited traits such as flower colour and disease resistance. Every cell of a plant contains the same chromosomes and genes, with the exception of the sex cells, pollen and ovules.

Another plant organelle is the plastid, of which there are several different types. Each leaf cell contains more than 100 chloroplasts, where the first phase of photosynthesis takes place. Chloroplast membranes contain lipid-soluble pigments involved in photosynthesis, like the green chlorophylls and the yellow carotenoids (Chapter 4). In red, orange or yellow coloured plant organs, like fruits (such as sweet peppers, tomatoes and sweetcorn), roots (like carrots), or flowers (such as marigold and daffodils), the pigments are carotenoids, and the plastid is known as a chromoplast.

Uniquely, sea slugs are marine animals which contain working chloroplasts which they harvest and store from the algae they eat.

While plastids are only found in plants, another organelle, the mitochondrion, is found in plants, animals and bacteria. The mitochondrion carries out the release of the chemical energy stored in sugars by the process of respiration (Chapter 4). Mitochondria are present in all cells, with large numbers per cell.

Another important organelle unique to plant cells is the vacuole, which is a membrane-bound sac where the plant cell stores many of the water-soluble chemicals it makes. These include pigments like the red, blue and purple anthocyanins found in most petals, many fruits such as blackberries, and leaves with red or purple tints in the autumn.

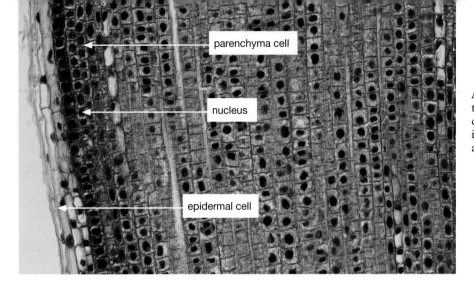

A micrograph of a thin cross-section of a daffodil root tip, showing individual cells, each with a dark nucleus.

parenchyma cell

nucleus

epidermal cell

Many defence chemicals, which help the plant protect itself against would-be attackers, are stored in the vacuole. When an animal chews a leaf or seed for example, the vacuole membrane breaks down and the contents are released. The animal gets a mouthful of a distasteful or even toxic chemical.

Plant cells are grouped into three basic cell types, each with a different function. Most cells in a plant are called parenchyma. These are the least specialized cells, and their main function is to carry out chemical reactions and to store the chemical products. For example, photosynthesis in leaf cells and food storage in potato tubers both take place in parenchyma cells.

Collenchyma cells have thicker cell walls than parenchyma cells, and their function is to provide support plus flexibility to growing parts of the plant. Collenchyma cells are grouped into strands just under the epidermis in young shoots and in leaf stalks (or petioles). The stringy parts of celery

and rhubarb are strands of collenchyma, and what we eat are the enlarged petioles.

The third type of plant cell is sclerenchyma, which also provides support like collenchyma, but this time along with rigidity. This applies to parts of the plant which have stopped growing. Here, the cells have thick cell walls, but stiffness is increased by combining the cellulose with a second plant chemical, lignin, to form lignocellulose. Wood is basically made up of lignocellulose, so it is particularly important in woody plants, but non-woody plants also produce lignocellulose and hence sclerenchyma.

Eventually sclerenchyma cells die, but their rigidity means that they continue to provide support even after death. Sclerenchyma fibres are commonly found in groups in leaves and stems, providing support, and for millennia have been exploited by mankind for rope and fabric from plants like flax, New Zealand flax (phormium) and hemp. From a gardener's perspective, these fibres

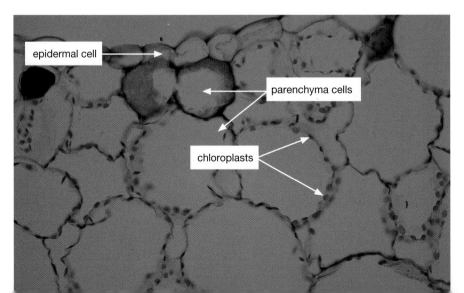

A micrograph of a thin cross-section through a kalanchoë leaf, showing chloroplasts within each parenchyma cell.

epidermal cell

parenchyma cells

chloroplasts

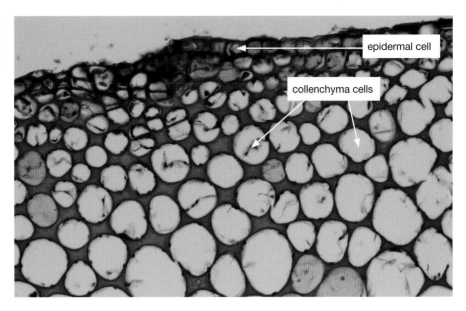

A micrograph of a thin cross-section of a sunflower stem, showing collenchyma with varying amounts of thickening.

also make plants like phormiums wind tolerant. Shorter groups of sclerenchyma cells, known as sclereids, confer hardness to nutshells and seed coats as well as providing the gritty mouthfeel of pears and supplying one type of fibre in our diet.

Tissues and Organs

When two or more of these three cell types combine together, they can form specialized tissues within the plant – such as the outer tissue on all parts of the plant surface (the epidermis), the vascular tissue which transports water, sugars etc around the plant, and the ground tissue which makes up the bulk of the plant.

The epidermis covers the entire plant body, and with its waxy cover or cuticle it provides protection from drying out and from attackers. The epidermis is made up largely of parenchyma, which can form outgrowths like hairs. Thorns (technically speaking, prickles) of the rose bush and blackberries are rigid outgrowths of the epidermis, containing sclerenchyma. True thorns, like those on hawthorn and blackthorn, are modified side shoots, and are characteristically found at the nodes, where a leaf attaches to the stem.

In turn, the different tissues combine to produce specific plant organs – primarily stems, leaves (together comprising the shoots) and roots.

A micrograph of a thin cross-section through a leaf, showing sclerenchyma, collenchyma and parenchyma.

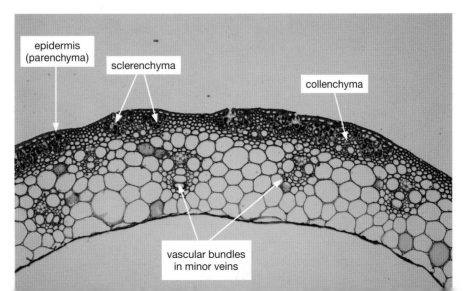

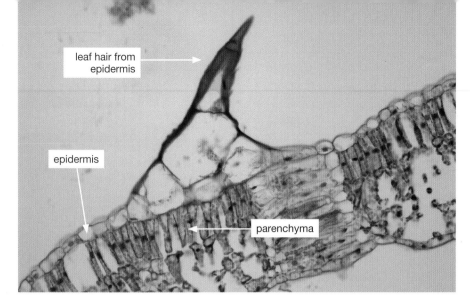

A micrograph of a thin cross-section through a privet leaf, showing a leaf hair developing from an epidermal cell.

Surprisingly flowers (and the fruits they form) are actually modified shoots.

These various parts of the plant, looking and acting very differently, are all derived from the same basic unit, the plant cell. How does this happen? Cells in a leaf and a root of one plant, for example, contain the same genes (on average, approximately 15,000 genes in each cell) but look completely different. This is because leaf genes, such as those responsible for making the green pigments (chlorophylls), are only switched on in leaf cells in the light, while these genes are switched off in root cells, with root genes being switched on instead.

Mutualism

The evolution of land plants needed so many adaptations that on several occasions nature took a short cut, employing beneficial micro-organisms like bacteria and fungi to carry out certain jobs for the primitive plants. We now know that plastids and mitochondria, for example, contain small chromosomes of their own, suggesting that, in the dim and distant past, these organelles were living organisms. The organelle chromosomes exist as DNA circles rather than the linear DNA found in the nucleus of plants and animals; circular DNA is characteristic of the chromosomes of bacteria.

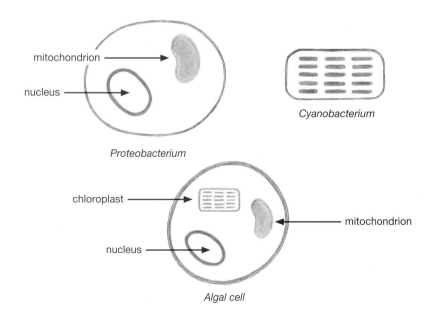

Evolution of the first plant cell.

The reason for the presence of DNA in plastids and mitochondria is that they evolved from free-living bacteria which took up residence in plant cells. Both the bacteria and the plant cell benefited from this association. The plant cell gained the abilities to photosynthesize and to respire, so that it could make all the chemicals it needed, while the bacteria gained protection.

This type of mutually beneficial arrangement is known as a mutualism. After billions of years of mutualism, plastids and mitochondria are no longer able to survive on their own, but they retain most of their DNA, a reminder of their previous independence.

Another plant-microorganism mutualism was involved in the evolution of the root system, soon after plants started to colonize the land. The modern-day counterparts of the earliest plants, the algae and mosses, have no root system for taking up water and dissolved nutrients from the soil, so are restricted to aquatic (algae) or damp (mosses) environments. Mosses need to take up water over their entire body, so they are small, rarely more than 20cm tall.

The first root system appears to have evolved when plants entered into associations with micro-organisms, this time fungi. Fungi have a root-like system, the mycelium, which acts both as an anchor and as a rudimentary system for taking up chemicals and water. The white network you see over the surface of rotting wood is an example of fungal mycelium, composed of individual strands, or hyphae.

As a result of this mutualism (known as a myc-orrhiza, meaning 'fungus-root') primitive plants gained the ability to take up water and other chemicals from the soil while the fungal partner, which cannot photosynthesize, was provided with sugars from its host.

Beneficial mycorrhizal fungi living within root systems increase the efficiency of the uptake of water and of hard-to-get nutrients such as phosphorus (Chapter 4). Most of the mushrooms and toadstools you find in the woods in the autumn are the fruiting bodies of mycorrhizal fungi, such as the fly agaric, the highly poisonous white-spotted red toadstool, beloved of children's book illustrators, which associates with the roots of birch trees.

The fruiting bodies of mycorrhizal fungi associated with the roots of silver birch.

Vascular Plants

From the ferns onwards, plants became known as vascular plants because they possessed an internal transport system akin to our own blood system. This vascular system has two components. Water, and the dissolved nutrients it contains, travels up from the roots in xylem, which is largely dead sclerenchyma cells fulfilling both transport and support functions. On the other hand, chemi-cals produced in plant cells (assimilates), such as sugars and proteins, travel from the leaves in all directions around the plant in the phloem, which consists of living cells of both the parenchyma and collenchyma cell types.

The phloem and xylem combine together to form vascular bundles, which run continuously from the roots to the stem and leaves, where the leaf veins and midrib contain the vascular bundles. Protective spines around the edges of leaves of plants like holly are actually the ends of major leaf veins, while cactus spines are modified leaves, formed by the reduced petiole and midrib. When you slice a stick of celery, the small circles visible on the cut surface are the vascular bundles.

One of the major adaptations which plants needed to evolve in order to colonize dry land was

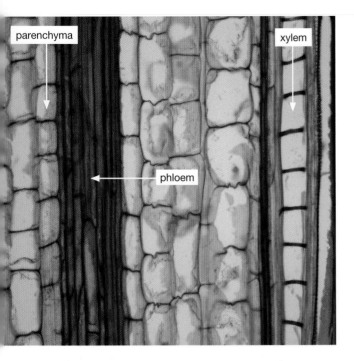

parenchyma

xylem

phloem

A micrograph of a thin longitudinal section down a sweetcorn stem, showing xylem and phloem.

The spines of a cactus are the hardened remains of the mid-rib and main veins of leaves.

to minimize water loss through the leaf or stem – this was achieved by the outer cell layer of the organ (epidermis) being coated with a waxy water-proof layer known as the cuticle (waxes are lipids).

As a result, pores (stomata), mostly in the lower epidermis of leaves, are the main route by which plants can control the movement of water vapour out of the plant, by changing the shape of kidney-shaped guard cells to close or open the stomata. This is important because stomata also control the movement of CO_2 (carbon dioxide) in and O_2 (oxygen) out of the leaf during photosynthesis.

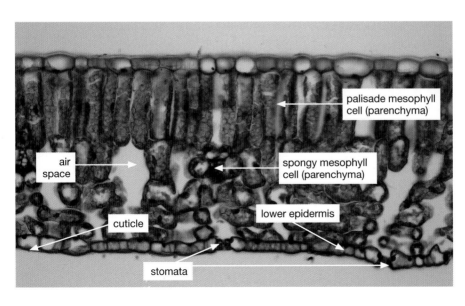

A micrograph of a thin cross-section through a privet leaf, showing stomata in the lower epidermis.

palisade mesophyll cell (parenchyma)

air space

spongy mesophyll cell (parenchyma)

cuticle

lower epidermis

stomata

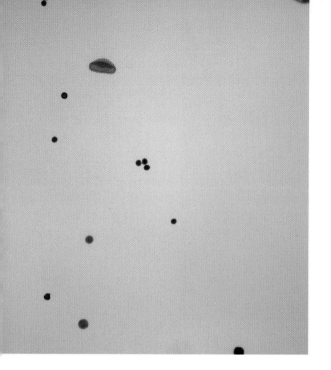

A mixture of wind-dispersed pollen grains (small and light) and insect-dispersed pollen grains (large and sculpted).

Plant Reproduction

The most primitive plants, the algae and mosses, and to a lesser extent the ferns, depend on water to transport the male sex cells to the female ones to achieve sexual reproduction. The conifers exchanged a reliance on water to transport the sex cells for one requiring wind, developing male and female cones.

The main advance made by the flowering plants was achieved by replacing the cones of conifers with brightly coloured and scented flowers which attracted insects (in the first instance) to accidentally move pollen (which the insects used as food) from flower to flower to achieve fertilization. This was less random and more efficient than reliance on wind or water. There was also a change from producing large numbers of small light pollen grains for wind dispersal to large sculpted pollen grains to attach to insects.

The typical flower includes four organs, arranged in concentric circles or whorls. Starting with the green sepals on the outside, protecting the flower bud, the next whorl is that of the petals. The third whorl consists of the male sex organs, the stamens, made up of the anther producing pollen and attached to the flower by a filament.

Finally, the female sex organ, the innermost whorl, is the carpel, consisting of the stigma on which the pollen lands, then the style and finally the ovary, containing the ovules. It is the stigmas and styles of the saffron crocus which are harvested to make saffron, the most valuable spice in the world, for cooking. When fertilized, the ovules become the seeds and the ovary develops into the fruit in most plants. Flowers are said to have a superior ovary where the petals attach below the ovary, while those like daffodils, where the petals attach above the ovary, have an inferior ovary.

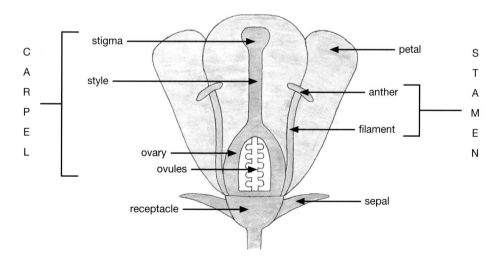

The structure of a typical flower.

Flowers of a magnolia, which resemble the first flowers on the Earth.

The first flowers, resembling those of modern-day magnolias and waterlilies, were large and flattened, with thick petals, to attract the first insects which would have been wingless, probably resembling modern-day beetles. The evolution of insects mirrored the increasing biodiversity of flowering plants. Insects were attracted to flowers by offers of a nutrient-rich food, which would have been excess pollen in the more primitive plants, but this was replaced in more advanced plants by sugar-rich nectar from specialized organs in the flowers known as nectaries.

To ensure that the visiting insect went to a different flower of the same species (to achieve cross-pollination), the flowers evolved to attract a specific type of pollinator, by using specific combinations of colour, scent and shape (Chapter 8). As the animal kingdom developed, plants evolved to attract birds and mammals as pollinators, though most animal-pollinated plant species still use insects. For example, the pineapple sage, with red flowers, a long narrow flower tube and no scent, evolved to attract hummingbirds.

The second adaptation by the flowering plants occurred later, where the seeds had the protection of developing within a fruit. This was a major improvement on the naked seeds carried in cones found in most conifers. In the most advanced of the conifers, like yew, the ovary develops into a red fruit or aril, but the black seed is attached inside an opening of the fruit rather than being completely enclosed within the fruit. Interestingly,

Flowers of the hummingbird-pollinated pineapple sage.

A developing magnolia fruit, resembling the cone of a conifer.

in the fruit by chewing them, so many plants have designed their fruits and seeds to make them attractive to birds. Because birds, unlike most mammals, have colour vision but no sense of smell, ripe fruits containing seeds for birds to disperse tend to be brightly coloured but unscented.

But this still does not stop mammals from trying to eat fruits designed for birds. Producing fruits high up on the plant tends to favour birds, but plants also use chemical tricks to deter animals. One of these is to incorporate into fruits or seeds chemicals which are distasteful or even poisonous, but which are active against mammals only. Some of our most poisonous fruits, like deadly nightshade and mistletoe, contain mammal-specific toxins so they are meant to be eaten by birds.

Other plants allow the fruit to be eaten by mammals but then protect the enclosed seeds. If you crush apple seeds between your teeth you will detect a flavour of bitter almonds as hydrogen cyanide is released. Animals feeding on fallen apples tend to spit out or swallow the seeds whole. Another strategy is the production of large numbers of small seeds in the fruit, as in the tomato, so that when the fruit is eaten by a mammal, at least some seeds will escape undamaged.

modern-day relatives of some of the earliest flowering plants, such as magnolia, produce a cone-like fruit resembling those of the conifers.

The fruits of flowering plants are adapted to disperse seeds from the parent plant, reducing potential competition between parent and offspring plants. The ovary walls of fruits of maples and sycamores form a wing to aid wind dispersal. As with pollination, however, a more efficient dispersal system evolved involving the use of an appropriate animal.

Again, each plant would 'advertise' for the appropriate dispersal agent, usually mammal or bird, but sometimes insect, by using a combination of fruit colour and scent. The reward for the disperser is a tasty treat usually in the form of a nutrient-rich fruit, but the seeds must survive the fruit being eaten and then dispersed by being spat out or excreted unharmed onto the ground.

Unlike birds, mammals can damage the seeds

INTRODUCTION TO PLANT NAMES

So far, all the plant names I have cited have been the so-called common ones, like deadly nightshade and apple. However, every keen gardener will be aware that plants (and animals) actually have a second type of name, generally known as the scientific, Latin or botanical name, but officially called the binomial ('two names'). This is basically a two-part name which is printed in italics or underlined if handwritten. You will already be familiar with a number of binomials which are used in fairly general conversation: *Homo sapiens* (humans), the carnivorous dinosaur *Tyrannosaurus rex* (*T. rex*), and the gut bacterium *Escherichia coli*, usually abbreviated to *E. coli*, in news stories about food poisoning and contamination of water.

But why are binomials needed? Even among people speaking the same language, there can be

A flower of the English bluebell, *Hyacinthoides non-scripta*.

several common names for the same species, such as monkey puzzle tree and Chilean pine for *Araucaria araucana*, while the European white water lily, *Nymphaea alba*, has fifteen common English names and over 100 common German ones. On the other hand, the name 'bluebell' has been used for more than forty different plant species, such as *Hyacinthoides non-scripta* in England, *Sollya heterophylla* in Australia, *Campanula rotundifolia* in Scotland and species of *Mertensia, Polemonium, Muscari* or *Phacelia* in North America. Finally, for most of the plants in the world there is no common name.

The main advantage of using binomials is that, as a result, all over the world there is one consistent unique name given to each species, which is clearly not the case with common names. The binomial is written largely in Latin, not only the language of scholarship but also a dead language, so that the words do not change over time.

Development of the Naming System

By the early eighteenth century, attempts were being made to give each plant a unique descriptive Latin name. As more plants were named, these names became longer and more tortuous in order to distinguish them from one another. The clove pink was known as *Dianthus floribus solitaries, squamis calycinus subovatis brevissimis, corollas crenatis,* meaning 'Dianthus with solitary flowers, with very short, inverted egg-shaped scaled calyces and crown-shaped corollas'.

All this changed in 1753 when a Swedish doctor and keen naturalist, Carl von Linné, working in the bulb-growing centre of the world in Holland, introduced a two-name system for each plant in his book *Species Plantarum*. He was an amateur botanist, the first person to grow bananas in Europe, and apparently regarded the banana, rather than the apple, as the forbidden fruit in the Garden of Eden. (von Linné is usually referred to by his Latinized name, Carolus Linnaeus.)

In Linnaeus's binomial system, the clove pink (which evolved into the carnation) became *Dianthus caryophyllus*. The first name is the genus (akin to the surname) while the second name is the species ('first name') of the plant. Species of the genus *Dianthus*, such as *Dianthus caryophyllus, D. knappii (*the yellow-flowered species) or *D. barbatus* (sweet William) therefore are all closely related but distinct.

Linnaeus himself eventually named more than 9,000 plant species using his binomial system, and ever since then the person who first describes a new species receives the honour of naming it. His binomial system has continued to be the basis of plant taxonomy (the science of plant identification and naming), and the system proved so successful that it was extended to include animals and micro-organisms.

Structure of the Binomial System

Genus names can provide some information on the plant, such as *Erodium* (heron's beak, after the shape of this plant's fruit) and *Geranium* (crane's beak). *Trillium* has three (tri-) of each flower part, such as petals.

The genus can also commemorate a person (although no one can name a plant after themselves). The genus *Tradescantia* is named after the two John Tradescants, father and son, influential gardeners and plant hunters for King Charles I. The origins of *Captaincookia*, a plant endemic to New Caledonia, are fairly obvious. The Dutch botanist Jan Gronovius named the twinflower from Lapland *Linnaea borealis* after his friend Linnaeus, who contributed to the official self-deprecating description: 'lowly, insignificant, disregarded, flowering but for a brief space.... From Linnaeus who resembles it'.

Species names, on the other hand, can be regarded as adjectives qualifying the nouns of the genus names, and can provide some useful information on the plant itself. Examples of traits described in species names include:

- **Colour:** *nigra*: black; *alba*: white; *flava*: pale yellow; *lutea*: deep yellow; *caerulea*: blue; *rubra*: red; *coccinea*: scarlet; *aurea*: golden; *virens*: green; *mutabilis*: the flower colour changes as the flower ages.
- **Habit:** *nana, nanum, minima*: very small; *major*: tall; *humile, procumbens, prostrata, horizontalis*: low growing; *fastigiata*: erect; *fruticosus*: shrub-like; *arborescens*: tree-like; *patens*: spreading; *repens, reptans*: creeping; *caespitosa*: tufted.
- **Leaf character**: *incana*: downy; *hirsuta*: hairy; *mollis*: softly hairy; *glauca*: blue-grey waxy; *angustifolia*: narrow; *brevifolia*: short.
- **Habitat**: *sylvestris*: woodland; *borealis*: forest; *pratensis*: meadows; *rivale*: by streams; *montanus, alpinus*: mountains; *uliginosa*: damp place; *arvensis*: crop field.
- **Uses:** *officinalis*: used in medicine; *esculentum*: good to eat; *oleracea*: used in kitchen garden.
- **Flowering time**: *praecox*: early spring; *vernalis*: spring; *aestivalis*: summer; *autumnalis*: autumn.

Leycesteria formosa, for which one common name, Elisha's tears, sounds like the genus name (Lie-sus-*tee*-re-uh).

Species names can also be used to commemorate individuals. One or two 'i's at the end of a species name indicates that it is named after a man, like *Clematis jackmannii*, or *Lilium henryi* (celebrating the great Irish plant collector Augustine Henry). The suffix 'iae' signifies that the name commemorates a woman, such as the beautiful lily with shell-pink flowers *Lilium mackliniae* (named after June Macklin by her husband, the renowned plant hunter Frank Kingdon-Ward). Plant binomials are sometimes playful, such as the species name of *Kalanchoë mitejea* (an anagram of *je t'aime*).

Increasingly, gardeners refer to plants by their genus names. Some garden plants are only known by their genus name, such as rhododendron, clematis and hydrangea (they have no common name), while some genus names like dierama (rather than Angel's fishing rods) and aquilegia (Granny's bonnets) are quietly taking over from the common names.

Some Problems with Binomials

There is still scope for confusion with binomials. The Christmas rose *Helleborus niger* (from the Latin *niger*: black) has white flowers; the species name refers to its black roots. The marigold relative *Tagetes minuta*, which is sometimes recommended to be grown to deter root-eating nematodes, can grow to more than six feet tall; *minuta* refers to its small flowers.

The binomial of the garden plant nasturtium is *Tropaeolum majus*, while the genus name *Nasturtium* belongs to unrelated plants like watercress (*N. officinale*). The popular indoor bulb amaryllis is actually the tender species *Hippeastrum* from tropical South America, while the related genus *Amaryllis* includes both hardy (such as *Amaryllis belladonna*) and tender bulbs from South Africa.

Pronunciation of binomials should follow the rules of Latin. For a genus or species name with three syllables or more, the stress should be placed on the syllable third from the end, while for a two-syllable word it should be on the first syllable. For example:

Hydrangea is pronounced hy-DRAN-jee-uh.
Kniphofia (red-hot poker) is pronounced
ni-FOE-fee-a.
Clematis should be CLEM-uh-tiss.

In English a number of plant genus names have been deliberately mis-pronounced over the years to avoid giving offence to the more sensitive gardeners. So *Fuchsia* (named after one of the three founding fathers of botany, Leonhart Fuchs) should therefore not be pronounced fee-OO-shi-a nor should the genus of pine trees, *Pinus*, be pronounced PEYE-nus.

One of the frustrating aspects of plant taxonomy for gardeners is that names can change, as research reveals new similarities or differences between plants, or someone finds that a plant had been given a different name before the current one was first used. A wide range of plants with large daisy-shaped flowers in late summer and autumn used to be grouped under the genus *Chrysanthemum*, but it has since been split into at least twelve distinct genera, including *Xanthophthalum*, *Agyranthemum*, *Dendranthema* and *Leucanthemum,* although the florists' chrysanthemum has recently been returned to the genus *Chrysanthemum.*

Tomato, *Lycopersicon esculentum* (with the intriguing translation 'the edible wolf-peach') has long been known to be related to potato, *Solanum tuberosum*. Recently, it has been moved to the same genus as potato and has been renamed *Solanum lycopersicum.*

Species and Hybrids

Within a genus, there are somewhere between one and several hundred species, all of which can be traced back to a common ancestor. Over time, different populations of the ancestor became adapted to the different conditions under which they lived, and as a result these populations diverged more and more from one another. Some populations even became physically separated, by the flooding of landbridges at the end of an Ice Age, by the appearance of mountains or by the moving apart of continents.

Eventually, the populations, which started off as the same species, will have diverged so much that they can no longer produce fertile hybrids between one another. This might be because they have developed different flower colours or shapes and are pollinated by different animals. They might have adapted to live in different habitats or to flower at different times, so that pollen from one population is never transferred to a flower of the other population.

For example, two evening primrose species, *Oenothera breviceps* and *Oe. clavaeformis*, grow together but do not form hybrids because they flower at different times, either early morning (*Oe. breviceps*) or late afternoon (*Oe. clavaeformis*), so that different bees pollinate each species. In yet other cases, cross-pollination does occur between the populations, but the hybrid seeds either die or produce sterile plants.

Any of these so-called 'reproductive isolation barriers' which prevent the two populations from producing a fertile hybrid means that the two populations are now separate species within the same genus. This process is called speciation.

In the garden, however, sterility is not the problem it is in the wild, and sterile inter-specific hybrids (hybrid between two related species) can be propagated vegetatively, without seed. The hybrid winter aconite *Eranthis* × *tubergenii* 'Guinea Gold' (*E. cilica* × *E. hyemalis*) is sterile but can be propagated asexually by underground tubers. An '×' between the genus and species names indicates that the species is an inter-specific hybrid.

Sterility can actually be a useful trait in garden

Digitalis x *mertonensis*, an inter-specific foxglove hybrid.

plants. The sterile hybrid laburnum, *Laburnum* × *waterii* 'Vossii', does not produce the poisonous seeds characteristic of fertile laburnum cultivars, making it particularly appropriate where there are young children around. Sterility in plants also usually means that the plants flower for a longer-than-usual period, as they do not receive the signal from the developing seeds to stop flowering (Chapter 8).

Artificial (man-made) inter-specific hybrids can be fertile, as with *Digitalis* × *mertonensis*, a perennial hybrid foxglove, with flowers the colour of crushed strawberries. It is a hybrid between the perennial creamy yellow-flowered *Digitalis grandiflora* and our native biennial purple foxglove, *Digitalis purpurea*.

Many inter-specific hybrids have been produced accidentally or deliberately in gardens because the reproduction isolation barriers have broken down. The hybrid dogwood *Cornus* 'Norman Hadden' was first found as a chance seedling in the woodland at West Porlock, and is a hybrid between *C. nuttallii* from North America and *C. kousa* from Japan. Deliberate inter-specific hybrids are particularly common among the orchids, where in the wild the complex flower structure prevents all but the specific pollinator from gaining access, but this barrier is readily breached by the plant breeder (Chapter 8).

An '×' before the genus name means that the plant is a hybrid between plants from two different but related genera. For example, a cross between plants of the related genera *Tiarella* and *Heuchera* resulted in the production of plants of a hybrid genus, × *Heucherella*. Another well-known inter-generic hybrid found in gardens is × *Fatshedera lizei*, a hybrid between Japanese fatsia, *Fatsia japonica* 'Moseri', and Irish ivy, *Hedera hibernica*. As species from different genera are less closely related than are species from the same genus, inter-generic hybrids are almost always sterile. Again, inter-generic hybrids are particularly common among orchids.

Sub-species, Varieties and Cultivars

Under the binomial system many plants actually have three Latin names. The third name (also written in italics, starting with a lower-case letter) results from splitting a species into several sub-groups, referred to as either varieties or sub-species. These sub-groups may arise during speciation, but they have diverged from one another less than different species have. Populations in the mountains, for example, tend to be shorter in height than lowland populations, as a protection against high winds, and they are later flowering, because the lower temperatures delay the appearance of pollinators, than related populations in the lowlands, but these are still capable of cross-pollination and producing fertile hybrids.

If the two populations are geographically isolated as well as looking distinct, they are referred to as sub-species, as long as the differences can be inherited through seed. The popular foliage plant New Zealand flax *Phormium tenax* has more than twenty-five sub-species. Tea is produced from leaves of *Camellia sinensis,* with China tea coming from *C. sinensis sinensis* and most Indian teas from *C. sinensis assamica.*

If the populations are not from different areas, the term variety is used. For example, the genus *Brassica* includes all the cabbage relatives, such as cauliflower, broccoli and Brussels sprout. The wild cabbage, *Brassica oleracea,* is still found around the Mediterranean. Over the past 4,000 years or so, natural mutants of *B. oleracea* have been recognized and selected for use as speciality vegetables. The single physical differences between these different closely related crops mean that they are described as varieties of *B. oleracea,* including cabbage (*B. oleracea* var. *capitata* or *B. oleracea capitata*), cauliflower (*B. oleracea* var. *botrytis),* Brussels sprout (*B. oleracea* var. *gemmifera*), broccoli (*B. oleracea* var. *italica*) and kale (*B. oleracea* var. *acephala*).

These are varieties of *B. oleracea* rather than different species, shown by the ease with which hybrids can be made by crossing two of these varieties together, such as the broccoflower (*italica* × *botrytis*) which has green florets (a trait inherited from broccoli) in a rounded head (from cauliflower).

A different *Brassica* species, *B. rapa,* has been domesticated to produce a wide range of vegetable crops, like turnip and Chinese cabbage. Of the latter, there are two sub-species of *B. rapa* from different areas of China which have been selected to become different crops. *B. rapa* ssp. *pekinensis* is whitish and known as won bok, while *B. rapa* ssp. *chinensis* is greener and leafier and known as pak choi, used in stir fries and the Korean pickled cabbage dish, kimchi.

Occasionally, a fourth Latin name can be used to describe a plant. This is known as a form and usually refers to a simple difference such as flower or leaf colour or plant habit, such as *Brassica oleracea* var. *capitata* f. *rubra,* or red cabbage.

The final element of the scientific name of a garden plant may be its cultivar name (short for *culti*vated *va*riety). While a variety is a natural variant of the plant, a cultivar is a garden form of the plant that has been selected deliberately by a gardener or plant breeder. Most people would call the rose 'Peace', for example, a rose variety but, as we have seen, the term variety has been commandeered by botanists for a different meaning, hence the evolution of the much-maligned term cultivar. Many garden plants are wild species, sub-species or varieties, such as *Salvia patens* and *Lilium martagon.* A new cultivar may arise as a result of collection in the wild of a specimen of a plant with new features, such as *Corydalis flexuosa* 'Purple Leaf', or as a result of a breeding programme, such as *Rosa* 'Peace', or by selection of a spontaneous mutant (sport), such as *Rosa* 'New Dawn', a repeat-flowering mutant of *Rosa* 'J.W. Flett', which flowers only once in the season.

Many cultivars have several different names or synonyms. The potato cultivar Up to Date had more than 200 synonyms. Many cultivars developed in other countries are known by two names, in different languages: *Penstemon* 'Andenken an Friedrich Hahn' became popular in Britain only when it was marketed as 'Garnet'. Some of the translations were none too accurate: *Rosa* 'Cuisse de Nymph Êmue' is known as 'Maiden's Blush' in English, a delicate translation of the more literal 'Thigh of an Aroused Nymph'.

A cultivar must be distinct from all other cultivars of that species and must be able to be propagated true-to-type, by seed or by clonal propagation (Chapter 7), so that all the offspring

WRITTEN BINOMIALS

A reasonable analogy for the binomial is the use of car names. For the Ford Focus, the genus (or marque) is Ford and the species (or model) is Focus. There are several closely related species or models such as Ford Ka or Ford Mondeo. Ford Focus Cabriolet would be a variety of Ford Focus.

In writing, a binomial follows a set of spelling and grammar rules.

Genus (plural: genera)
Written in italics.
Starts with a capital letter, for example *Brassica*.
After the full name has been stated, subsequently the genus name can be abbreviated to the initial. Hence *T. rex* for *Tyrannosaurus rex*.

Species (plural: species)
Written in italics.
Starts with a lower-case letter, for example *Brassica oleracea* (wild cabbage).
Species names may vary slightly, for example *alba* and *albus* both mean 'white' but following the rules of Latin grammar, *alba* refers to a female noun, and *albus* to male.

Sub-species
Written in italics.
Starts with a lower case letter.
Abbreviated to 'ssp.', for example *Brassica rapa* ssp. *chinensis* (pak choi).

Variety
Written in italics.
Starts with a lower case letter.
Abbreviated to 'var.', for example *Brassica oleracea* var. *capitata* (cabbage).

Form
Written in italics.
Starts with a lower case letter.
Abbreviated to 'f.', for example: *Brassica oleracea* var. *capitata* f. *rubra* (red cabbage).

Cultivar
Not in italics
Each word starts with a capital letter, in single quotation marks.
For example: *Brassica oleracea* var. *capitata* 'Greyhound'.
This style of presentation replaces the earlier *Brassica oleracea* var. *capitata* cv. Greyhound, which is still found in some gardening books, with 'cv.' the abbreviation for cultivar.

Family
Not in italics.
Starts with a capital letter.
Ends in the suffix –aceae, for example Asteraceae (daisy family) or Brassicaceae (cabbage family).

A good tool for checking the Latin name of a plant when you know its common name (or vice versa) is www.gardenworld.co.uk/latin-convertor.asp.

resemble each other. Some garden plants exist where individuals are very similar but not identical, though the differences are not sufficient to permit calling each one a different cultivar. These are known as groups, as in the purple New Zealand flax group (*Phormium tenax* Purpureum Group) and the pendulous ginkgo group (*Ginkgo biloba* Pendula Group).

Family

So far we have looked at several different ranks of plant taxonomy. Different sub-species of the same species (such as *B. rapa pekinensis* and *B. rapa chinensis*) are more closely related than different species of the same genus (like *B. oleracea* and *B. rapa*). We can also determine how closely related different genera are by seeing if they belong to the same family.

Following recent name changes, the names of all plant families now end in the suffix -aceae, such as Brassicaceae (the cabbage family), Poaceae (the grass family) and Asteraceae (the daisy family). Each family name is now based on a genus typical of that family, such as *Brassica* in the Brassicaceae.

The Asteraceae is the largest plant family, containing 1,317 genera, with a total of approximately 21,000 species, while other large families include the Orchidaceae (orchid family) with 795 genera and 17,500 species, and the Poaceae with 737 genera and almost 8,000 species. At the other extreme, the Morinaceae contains only one genus *Morina*, which includes the attractive *Morina longifolia* with thistle-like leaves and flowers which change colour.

In some cases, it is easy to recognize family traits. Members of the Brassicaceae, for example, largely have flowers with four petals in the shape of a cross, while most of the members of the Asteraceae have daisy-like flowers. Species from the Apiaceae, like cow parsley, fennel and hogweed, have large numbers of small individual flowers arranged in flat branched heads known as umbels. This family also contains most of the plant species that taste of aniseed, like fennel, dill and chervil. Plants in the bean family (Fabaceae), like runner beans, white clover and wisteria, have pea-shaped flowers and pod-like fruits. The old family names tended to emphasize these physical similarities, with the Brassicaceae being known as the Cruciferae and the Apiaceae being the Umbelliferae

Genera from the buttercup family, the Ranunculaceae, include *Helleborus*, *Anemone* and *Clematis*. At first sight, the flower shapes of these three genera would not seem so similar, but among oriental hellebores, some cultivars where the nectaries are turned into petals are known as anemone-flowered hellebores, while the Christmas rose *Helleborus niger* 'Washfield Star' produces flowers similar in shape to those of a clematis.

In addition to looking similar, members of the same plant family can have other characteristics in common. Most plants of the Fabaceae ('legumes') fix nitrogen gas from the air, with the aid of beneficial bacteria in their roots, and turn it into nutrients a plant can use (Chapter 4). As a result they tend to be shallow-rooted because they do not need to hunt for soil nitrogen, so are vulnerable to drought, while trees in this family, such as *Acacia*, are susceptible to being blown over.

Sometimes, plants which look similar and may even have similar common names may be only distantly related. The common name autumn crocus, for example, is applied to plants of the genus *Colchicum* from the Amaryllidaceae (amaryllis) family (with six stamens per flower), while the true crocus belongs to the genus *Crocus* of the

A typical flower head, or umbel, of a member of the Apiaceae family.

A typical flower (runner bean) of a member of the pea family, Fabaceae.

iris family, the Iridaceae (with three stamens per flower).

Why does it matter? The main value for gardeners of knowing the family a garden plant belongs to is that some pests and pathogens only attack members of the same family (Chapter 6), such as the late blight fungus attacking potato and tomato, both members of the Solanaceae. This is the reasoning behind crop rotation in the vegetable garden to help control soil-borne pests and diseases (Chapter 9).

Monocots and Dicots

Among the flowering plants, two broad groups can be distinguished: the monocotyledons (monocots) and dicotyledons (dicots). The names identify an important distinguishing feature: dicot seedlings have two cotyledons (seed leaves) while monocots have but one.

It is widely held that the first flowering plant was a dicot. Today 80 per cent of plants are dicots, including all trees and shrubs which are flowering plants. Although limited in number, monocots are important to gardeners, with grasses, including bamboos and lawn species, most bulbs and orchids being included under this banner.

Dicots have vertical root systems, often with tap roots, compared to the more shallow fibrous roots of monocots. Dicots also have a netted or reticulate pattern of leaf veins, while monocots have parallel veins, and have numbers of flower parts such as petals in multiples of four or five, compared to three in monocots.

The different root systems of monocots explains why lawn grasses in a lawn turn brown during summer drought as the plants become dormant to escape drought stress, while dicot lawn weeds (broad-leaved weeds) like daisy (*Bellis perennis*) or self-heal (*Prunella vulgaris*) remain green.

Comparison of the leaf vein patterns of dicots (left: reticulate, *Brunnera* 'Jack Frost') and monocots (right: parallel, *Hosta sieboldiana* 'Elegans').

CHAPTER 2

Selecting the Right Site for a Plant

Each plant species is adapted to the environmental factors occurring at its place of origin, such as bright sun or shade, heavy soil or light, winter frost or summer heat. An understanding of this will help you to identify the plants best-suited to the climate and micro-climate of your garden, so that the plants thrive with little input from you.

WHERE DO OUR PLANTS COME FROM?

It is estimated that there are 420,000 different plant species worldwide, many of which have not even been named. Gardeners in western Europe have access to approximately 90,000 different cultivated plants, including wild species and sub-species, as well as garden cultivars. More than 85 per cent of our plants come from warmer parts of the world, primarily Asia, southern Africa and North America.

The diversity of plants found in different parts of the world is due to global phenomena such as the movements of continents and the appearance and disappearance of ice sheets. Members of the same genus can be found in distant, physically unconnected countries. Of the oaks, scarlet oak (*Quercus coccinea*) is found on the east coast of North America, pedunculate oak (*Q. robur*) over most of western Europe and *Q. semecarpifolia* in the Himalayas. This demonstrates that these areas were once connected, allowing species to migrate long distances across these areas over landbridges that existed between now-separate

The blue-grey leaves of *Hosta sieboldiana* 'Elegans' are an adaptation to the dry conditions occurring under deciduous woodland.

continents, before geological plates shifted and sea levels rose to cut them off. The presence in Ireland of the so-called Lusitanian flora normally associated with Spain and Portugal, such as the strawberry tree, *Arbutus unedo*, and St. Daboec's heath, *Daboecia cantabrica*, suggests that a landbridge once connected Ireland with northwest Iberia.

Another factor affecting plant biodiversity was the action of ice during the various Ice Ages. The presence of ice sheets scraped away the vegetation from the areas they covered. When the ice retreated as the weather warmed up, these bare sites were then re-vegetated by plants spreading northwards from refuges that had been warmer, usually more southerly areas on the same land mass which had not been covered with ice.

The last Ice Age, from 18,000 to 10,000 years ago, eliminated the flora of Britain, Ireland and much of mainland Europe, covering Europe as far south as the Mediterranean. In China and Japan, however, the ice cap covering the temperate latitudes of the northern hemisphere stopped expanding at a site much further north than in Europe, so that many plants survived the Ice Age, leading to a very diverse flora. As a result, temperate China provided masses of plants suitable for growing in European gardens, such as *Clematis*, *Meconopsis*, *Rhododendron* and *Lilium*, with probably one-quarter of all garden plants in Europe coming from China. In the sub-tropical regions of Asia, the lower temperatures during the growing season at high altitude meant that a wide diversity of plants suitable for temperate gardens have been collected from the mountains between China and India. The Himalayas, in particular, became one of the richest sources of plants for our gardens.

The flora of North America also survived the

ravages of the ice reasonably well, moving south-wards then returning northwards when the ice melted. As a result, the temperate plant biodiversity of North America is much higher than that in Europe, where the area bordering the Mediterranean is richest in different plant species. As a result, related species of magnolia flourish on the Asian and American continents but are represented only by fossil remains in Europe. Many of the plants native to Australia are endemic (unique to that country) because Australia separated from all the other continents at least 120 million years ago.

NATURAL PLANT DISTRIBUTION

All plants have a particular natural distribution, namely the habitats where they live in the wild. To understand this requires an introduction to plant ecology – the study of the interaction between plants and the environment – which will explain how the living (biotic) and non-living (abiotic) factors within an ecosystem determine which species can live there.

Each plant species has a particular fundamental niche. This represents the potential range of conditions under which that species can live, such as soil type, light levels, rainfall and temperature minima and maxima.

Probably the most important environmental factor for determining whether a plant can grow in a particular ecosystem is whether it can withstand the major stress period during the year in that site. In temperate parts of the world, this stress period refers to either the cold winter in, for example, western Europe, or the hot dry summers of, say, Mediterranean Europe.

Although the ability of a plant to withstand stress is commonly referred to as 'tolerance', from a plant physiology point of view that is not the most appropriate term. There are actually three different methods which plants can use to with-stand stress, of which only one (the least common one) is tolerance:

- Stress escape: the plant escapes the stress period by becoming dormant during that period, such as the winter-dormant deciduous trees in Europe;
- Stress avoidance: the plant is growing during the stress period but manages to avoid the stress itself (say, drought) by having very long roots to access what little water is available, such as the deep tap root of bear's breeches, *Acanthus mollis;*
- Stress tolerance: here, the plant is growing dur-ing the stress period and is exposed to the stress itself but is able to withstand the stress with mini-mal damage by, for example, accumulating high levels of protectant natural chemicals such as anti-oxidants.

Of all the strategies for coping with stress, escape is the one most widely used by garden plants. Seeds, deciduous trees and shrubs and herba-ceous perennials all resort to dormancy. When dormant, twigs of deciduous trees such as willows, maples and dogwoods can be immersed in liquid nitrogen at –196°C and re-thawed and stimulated to produce leaves without showing any signs of damage. However twigs of the same species in the summer would be killed by exposure to mild frost temperatures (about –5°C), because they would not have switched on their cold-stress defences.

Consider the niche of the European native plant

Different ways that plants withstand stresses

	Plant is growing during stress period	Plant is exposed to stress	Plant suffers stress damage
Stress escape	No	No	No
Stress avoidance	Yes	No	No
Stress tolerance	Yes	Yes	No

The lesser celandine, *Ranunculus ficaria*.

Ranunculus ficaria, the lesser celandine, several selections of which have become garden cultivars, such as 'Brazen Hussey'. Its fundamental niche over the active period February to May includes aspects of soil type (acid free-draining soil), light levels (from dappled shade to full shade) and seasonal temperature range (from −12°C to + 24°C). That represents an environment like that found in the deciduous woodland ecosystem of western Europe.

But the lesser celandine will have to share that ecosystem with other plant species, and their fundamental niches will overlap to some extent. Because no two species can occupy exactly the same niche in the same ecosystem for long (one will always compete out the other), the different species will each reduce their realized (or actual) niche until there is no competition.

In deciduous woodland, where the leaves on the tallest trees (canopy trees) fall in autumn and re-emerge in mid- to late spring, the groundflora are adapted to take advantage of the early spring window of opportunity before the tree leaf canopy cuts out most of the sunlight from reaching the floor of the woods.

Some plants do this by being geophytes, which grow quickly from bulbs (like bluebells), rhizomes (such as wood anemone) or tubers (like *R. ficaria*). Others, like some ferns, are slow-growing evergreen plants which can take advantage of any period when there is sufficient light and warmth to grow. Among the geophytes of the woodland floor, the active growth periods are different to minimize competition, with wood anemone flowering in March, lesser celandine in April and bluebell in May.

Competitive ability relates to how well the plant in question can use natural resources when growing with other plants in the same area. The main resources are light, water and nutrients. If there are sufficient nutrients (at least 400kg nitrogen per hectare) and water (at least 600mm net precipitation each year) to support its growth, a deciduous tree would be the most competitive plant type in western Europe because of its size. It would win any competition for light, by shading all neighbouring plants, and would be able to extract more water and nutrients from the soil by having a very extensive root system, as well as being able to escape the winter cold by becoming dormant.

Climate and Plant Distribution

The two most important climatic factors affecting the distribution of wild plant species are the seasonal range of temperatures and rainfall. The factor most responsible for determining these factors at a particular site is latitude.

There are three major climates, each occurring in both the northern and southern hemispheres, which differ in terms of seasonal temperatures.

• Low-latitude or tropical climates, near the equator, tend to be warm all year round, because temperature is controlled by tropical air masses from the equator.

- Mid-latitude or temperate climates, including most of Europe, North America and much of Asia, where temperature is affected by both tropical (warm) and polar (cold) air-masses, have evenly distributed seasons of winter and summer.
- High-latitude or polar climates, such as Canada and Scandinavia, where temperature is affected largely by polar air-masses, characteristically have long cold winters and short milder summers.

There are also three types of climate based on precipitation, including both rain and snow. Rainfall over an area is affected by the direction of prevailing winds and by the local geography. If the prevailing wind travels over oceans before it reaches land, it absorbs water vapour. The warmer the air, such as winds from tropical air masses, the more water vapour can be absorbed.

If the warm air mass reaches a barrier, such as cold air in temperate climates, or a mountain, the warm air rises over the barrier. Warm air is lighter than cold because the molecules are less tightly packed, allowing more space for water vapour. As it rises, the air cools and is unable to hold as much water vapour, which turns first into clouds and then condenses as rain. Thus, areas to the windward side of mountains or on the coast where prevailing winds make landfall tend to be wet, while leeward sites (in a 'rainshadow') or areas where the prevailing winds have crossed a landmass will be dry. In temperate areas in the northern hemisphere, most winds are from the west, so rain is heaviest on western coasts or west-facing mountain slopes.

Terrestrial Biomes

When the three rainfall levels are superimposed on the three temperature types, a total of nine different climate types are recognized. Because climate determines the dominant types of plants in an ecosystem, there are nine different terrestrial ecosystem types. Each of these ecosystem types is called a terrestrial biome, with characteristic plants.

In a biome, plant species, often unrelated, living at similar latitudes (north or south) on different continents look similar because they have adapted in similar ways to similar conditions. This phenomenon by which similar evolutionary pressures result in unrelated plants looking similar to one another is known as convergent evolution. An example would be evergreen drought-avoiding shrubs with spiny waxy leaves, living under deciduous woodland in temperate climates, such as common holly (*Ilex aquifolium*) in Europe, *Olearia paniculata* in New Zealand and *Mahonia* spp. in Asia and North America.

Deciduous woodland is the dominant biome not only in western Europe but also in the eastern United States (as witnessed by the famous autumn colours of New England), Oceania and coastal Japan – all areas where the soil is rich, water is plentiful and winters are cold.

Further north, where the soil is poorer and water supply is less because the ground is frozen for much of the year, the dominant species are evergreen drought-avoiding conifers, and the biome is the Northern coniferous forest or taiga.

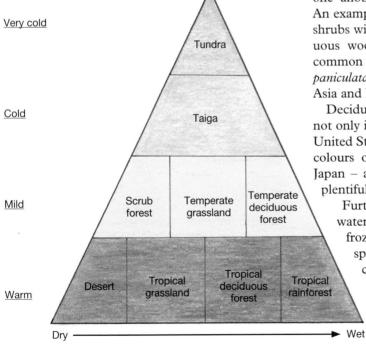

Climate and biomes.

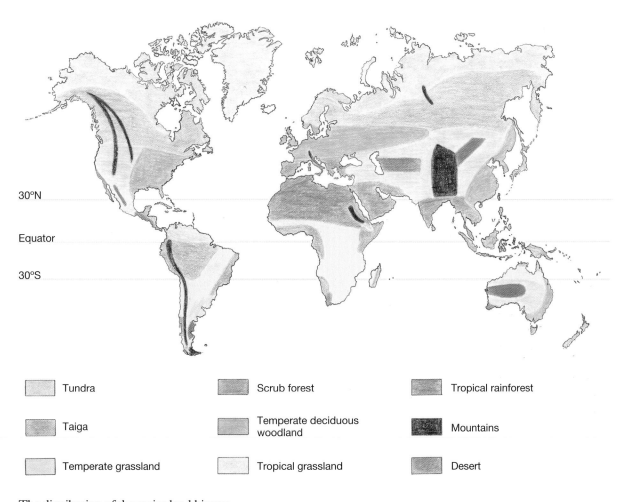

The distribution of the major land biomes.

Tundra

Taiga

Temperate grassland

Scrub forest

Temperate deciduous woodland

Tropical grassland

Tropical rainforest

Mountains

Desert

Whereas the east coast of North America, with plentiful rain and rich soils, is dominated by deciduous woodland, further inland, in the midwest, low rainfall, nutrient-deficient soils and grazing by large animals prevent the growth of trees, so that the prairies are dominated by grasses and herbaceous perennials. This is part of the temperate grassland biome.

On the south-west coast of North America, damp winters, hot dry summers, nutrient-poor soils and regular fires (a so-called Mediterranean-type climate) allow evergreen drought-tolerant shrubs to grow and thrive, interspersed by grasses, bulbs and annuals. This is part of the scrub forest biome, found in California and Mexico, as well as Chile, South Africa and parts of Australia.

Although the biome concept is a valuable tool for looking at the distribution of plants, it does not tell the whole story. Although deciduous woodland is the characteristic ecosystem of western Europe there are many natural and semi-natural areas of Britain and Ireland where the vegetation is not woodland. This situation comes about when one or more environmental factors prevent the development of woodland.

In areas where rainfall is heavy and the underlying bedrock is not limestone but rather an acid rock such as granite or sandstone, the soil will become acidic and oxygen-poor. Both of these characteristics make it difficult for soil bacteria to recycle nitrogen and other plant nutrients (Chapter 4), so the soil becomes deficient in

Stabilized sand dune vegetation in Barleycove, Co. Cork in Ireland. The low water and food reserves of the sandy soil and grazing by rabbits prevent taller plant species taking over.

nitrogen and cannot support the growth of trees. The largest (and most competitive) plants which can colonize these acidic areas are woody shrubs like gorse (*Ulex europaeus*) and heathers such as *Calluna vulgaris* and *Erica cinerea*.

These plants have evolved to cope with nitrogen-poor conditions by entering into mutualisms with micro-organisms which help the plants get the nutrients they need. Gorse is a legume and has nitrogen-fixing bacteria living in nodules in its roots, while the heathers, like most members of the Ericaceae, have associations with specialist ericoid mycorrhizal fungi.

Old hay meadows which receive little or no fertilizers have a rich flora including perennial grasses, annual (field poppy, cornflower) and herbaceous perennial dicots such as purple loosestrife, scabious and ox-eye daisy. The one hay harvest each year cuts through the growing point of tree and shrub seedlings, killing them and preventing the progression to woodland. In some ecosystems, a similar effect is achieved naturally, for example by the grazing activity of rabbits on the South Downs of southern England, resulting in short grassland, or by feral goats on the limestone pavements of the Burren in Co. Clare in Ireland. The surviving plant species are adapted to grazing by having their growing points near or below soil level

GARDEN PLANTS AND THE WORLD'S BIOMES

Most of the plants in our gardens in Britain and Ireland come from just three temperate terrestrial biomes: temperate deciduous woodland, scrub forest and temperate grasslands. All three of these climates are characteristic of mid-latitude areas, and the prevailing seasonal temperature extremes are broadly similar to those in western Europe.

The Deciduous Woodland

Environment and Distribution

This biome is characterized by wet cold winters (which represents the main stress period) and moist warm summers. Examples are found in western Europe, eastern US, and coastal parts of China, Japan and Australia.

Plant Characteristics

The dominant plants are slow-growing but long-lived tall deciduous trees with a broad crown, like oak and sycamore, which are known as canopy trees. Plants living under the canopy trees are adapted to winter cold and summer shade and

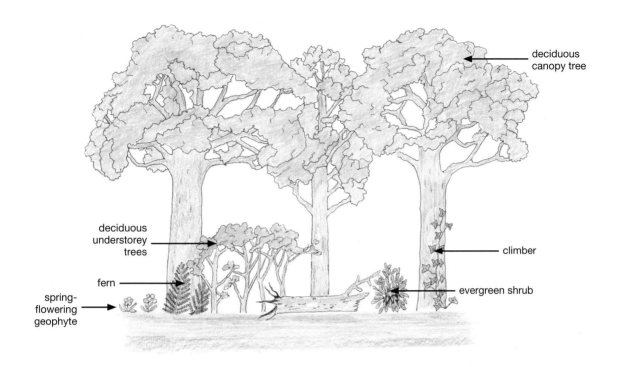

deciduous canopy tree

deciduous understorey trees

climber

fern

evergreen shrub

spring-flowering geophyte

The structure of a deciduous woodland.

drought, the latter caused by the trees stopping rain reaching the soil, much of which is taken up by the tree roots.

A second layer of smaller shorter-lived but faster-growing deciduous trees, known as the understorey tree layer, grows under the canopy trees. These species, such as hazel and mountain ash (*Sorbus* spp.), produce leaves earlier in spring than the canopy trees, to absorb spring sunshine. These trees are distinct from the fast-growing deciduous pioneer trees like birches and poplars, which are adapted to colonize bare areas where canopy trees have fallen.

Under the tree layers are the shrubs which tend to be slow-growing evergreen species like holly and laurel, with waxy shiny leaves which help to minimize water loss through the leaves. Under the shelter of the deciduous trees, these evergreen shrubs need to retain their leaves to ensure that they capture as much light as possible. Protection from wind damage and frost under the trees helps them retain their leaves.

At the edges of woodland or in clearings, climbing plants use twining stems (honeysuckle), adventitious roots (ivy) or modified leaves called tendrils (black bryony) to climb trees and get access to the sun without having to invest resources in producing wood tissue like the trees and shrubs.

Part of the ground flora of a deciduous temperate woodland, with geophytes and ferns.

The lowest layer of plants is the groundflora layer consisting of herbaceous non-woody flowering plants which die back in the autumn, and ferns and mosses which tolerate shade and grow slowly on the woodland floor.

Many of the plants within the deciduous woodland biome are geophytes which flower in spring, before the leaf canopy of the trees blocks out most of the light, then escape summer drought and winter cold by dying back. To achieve such rapid growth, these plants need large food reserves, which are made the previous year and stored in the form of bulbs, corms and rhizomes. The trigger for flowering in these plants is the rising temperatures in springtime. As global warming takes hold, these spring-flowering plants are tending to flower earlier.

Deciduous Woodland Plants for the Garden

Canopy trees include pedunculate oak and sycamore (from western Europe), liquidamber, liriodendron, oaks and sugar maples (eastern US) and the Japanese horse chestnut in Asia. These species do well in full sunlight and are good competitors.

On the other hand, given their natural habitat, understorey trees can grow in shady as well as sunny sites in gardens. Good examples include magnolias (from Asia and the US), silverbells (*Halesia* spp. from the US and *Styrax* spp. from Japan), dogwoods (such as *Cornus kousa* from China), flowering cherries, crabapples, mountain ash and *Amelanchier lamarckii* from the US. Such

Silver birch, *Betula pendula*, a pioneer tree from temperate deciduous woodland, with an upright growth habit.

trees characteristically have a spreading canopy, adapted to absorb as much as possible of the light that penetrates through the canopy layer.

Fast-growing deciduous trees with a much more upright growth habit, such as silver birch, are pioneer species. As a result, they do best in sunlit sites and do not respond well to being shaded by other trees, so are best grown as individuals or as small groves of the same species.

Magnolia species are under-storey trees from temperate deciduous woodland, with spreading canopies.

Leaves of *Asarum europaeum*, an evergreen native of the taiga biome.

Understorey evergreen shrubs with shiny waxy leaves are well suited to shady or dry conditions in the garden as these conditions resemble those under a deciduous woodland. Examples include *Sarcococca, Skimmia, Camellia, Mahonia* and *Ilex*. The shiny appearance of these leaves also helps to brighten up a shady site in the garden, as does the winter flowering (*Sarcococca* and *Mahonia*) and fruiting of these species. Early flowering is an adaptation to the period when light levels have increased after canopy trees have shed their leaves.

Most garden climbing plants are adapted to woodland edge conditions, which explains the usual instruction in gardening books to plant clematis, honeysuckle and so on with their roots shaded and their heads in the sun.

Many of the non-woody garden plants suitable for shady sites originated from the herbaceous and geophyte groundflora of the deciduous woodland biome. These include wood anemone (*Anemone nemorosa*) and lily-of-the-valley (*Convallaria majalis*) from Europe; hostas, *Deinanthe caerulea*, herbaceous primulas, arisaemas, corydalis, dicentras and *Kirengishoma palmatum* (Asia); and trilliums and erythroniums (North America).

By their nature, these understorey plants are adapted to partially shaded sites, sheltered from the wind. Leaves of these woodland plants are adapted to absorbing efficiently the small amount of light which reaches them and so tend to be quite large (hostas and arisaemas) and thin. These characteristics also explain their sensitivity to wind damage. To grow these understorey species in gardens, important conditions include shelter from the wind, some shade in high-light areas and a soil

with a high organic matter content, to aid water retention. Such a soil will also provide nutrients (woodland species are adapted to quite nutrient-rich soils and generally respond well to feeding).

Evergreen flowering plants adapted to shade, such as wild gingers (*Asarum* spp.) and *Hepatica* spp., are usually native to particularly dense woodland, such as that dominated by beech (whose shallow roots create a very dry soil) or maples, or even to the coniferous forests of the taiga.

The Scrub Forest

Environment and Distribution

Closer to the equator lie scrub forest areas, with the Mediterranean-type climate of cool damp winters and hot dry summers. The summers are the main stress period in this biome, and fires occur regularly. In the northern hemisphere the scrub forest is found in coastal regions of southern Europe (where it is called maquis or garrigue), southern and central parts of California and Mexico (chaparral), and in the southern hemisphere on the Chilean coast, western and south Australia and the Cape region of South Africa (fynbos).

This biome is also favoured for growing vines for wine making, at latitudes at 30–50°N in the Old World and 30–50°S in the New World. The land south of Perth in western Australia, for example, is regarded as having a 'terroir' very similar to that of Bordeaux in France. The soil is generally free-draining and nutrient poor.

Scrub forest is by far the smallest biome, but it is second only to the tropical rainforest in terms of biodiversity, containing up to 20 per cent of all known plant species. Indeed, the scrub forest of the Cape Floral Kingdom of South Africa is the second richest place on the planet for plants, with 1,300 species per 10,000 km², after 4,000/10,000 km² for the South American rainforest, in first place, and about 80/10,000 km² for the UK. The scrub forest is one of the major contributors to our garden flora.

Plant Characteristics

Such dry conditions generally do not support the growth of trees, so the dominant vegetation is small drought-avoiding evergreen shrubs and sub-shrubs, with either inrolled or leathery leaves to reduce water loss. Sub-shrubs, such as lavender, have a woody framework which produces new growth from the branch tips every year. These herbaceous branch ends die back to the old wood in the autumn. Evergreen woody plants are well suited to the short growing season in the scrub forest biome.

Non-woody, perennial plants in the scrub forest can escape drought and high temperatures in the summer by becoming dormant ('aestivation' in the summer, as opposed to 'hibernation' in the winter). This happens in their native habitats with geophytes like ornamental onions (*Allium* spp.) and tulips, as well as herbaceous perennials such as *Salvia farinacea*, *Verbena bonariensis* and *Agastache* spp.

Dormancy in scrub forest species is triggered by environmental factors such as long days (for onions), drought and high temperatures. Under these conditions, scrub forest annuals like *Eschscholtsia californica* die as stress takes hold in the summer, surviving to the next year as seeds.

Plant density is often quite low, with individual plants being well spread out. This is due, at least in part, to the fact that many plants in this biome produce chemicals, known as allelochemicals, which inhibit the seed germination or growth of neighbouring plants, even sometimes of the same species, to reduce competition.

Evergreen scrub forest native species avoid the effects of drought and heat by having long tap roots to gather water from deep in the soil, as in *Foeniculum vulgare* (fennel). Others minimize water loss from the leaves by storing water in succulent leaves, as in *Portulaca grandiflora* (moss-rose) or small-leaved *Hebe* spp., or by having tough leathery wax-covered leaves, as with *Ceanothus* spp. (Californian lilac), or small leaves, such as *Thymus vulgaris* (thyme), *Spartium junceum* (Spanish broom) or *Leptospermum* spp. (tea tree) to reduce the amount of sunlight, and hence heat, absorbed.

Since the leaf is covered with a thick waterproof layer of waxes (cuticle), the stomata, mostly on the underside of the leaf, are the main ports through which water vapour exits the leaf and CO_2 enters the leaf for photosynthesis. Unfortunately, for every molecule of CO_2 entering, 200 molecules of water vapour are lost, because the air inside the leaf is damper than the outside air and moisture

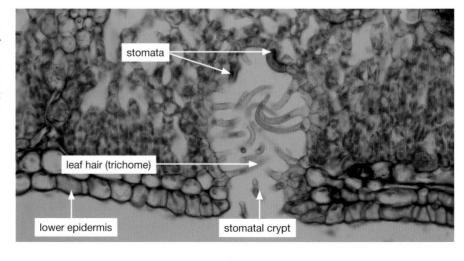

A micrograph of a thin cross-section through a leaf of *Nerium oleander* (oleander), an evergreen shrub adapted to the scrub forest biome in the Mediterranean, showing sunken stomata with hairs to trap moist air.

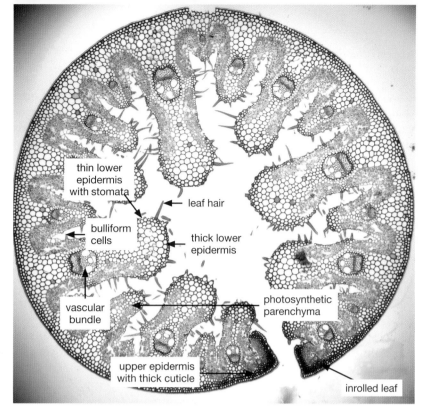

A micrograph of a thin cross-section of a leaf of *Ammophila arenaria* (marram grass), adapted to dry sand dune conditions. The leaf rolls inwards as a result of collapse of bulliform cells, so that moist air is trapped, reducing water loss.

thin lower epidermis with stomata

leaf hair

bulliform cells

thick lower epidermis

vascular bundle

photosynthetic parenchyma

upper epidermis with thick cuticle

inrolled leaf

moves down a gradient from wet to dry. Closing the stomata to stop water escaping also stops transpiration, the main strategy for cooling the plant, and photosynthesis, which provides the energy for growth. In the absence of cooling, upper leaves of plants exposed to strong sunlight even in mild summers can heat up to 50–55°C for hours on end.

Many plants native to the scrub forest biome exhibit adaptations so that the stomata can open to take in CO_2 while minimizing loss of water. Hairs on the leaf surface, as in *Artemisia* spp., trap moist air around the stomata so that no gradient occurs between the inside and outside of the leaf.

A similar strategy involves the inrolling of leaves

Melianthus major, the honey bush, a native of the scrub forest biome in South Africa. Note the glaucous foliage, resulting from a heavy wax deposit to minimize water loss.

Verbascum bombyciferum, a mullein, native to Turkey. Note the leaf hairs that trap moisture.

into needle-like structures, as in *Santolina chamae-cyparis* and the blue-grey leaves of *Festuca glauca*, so that the stomata are situated in a pocket of still moist air. If you put these leaves in water, they will flatten out. This rolling of grass leaves under drought conditions is helped by having large thin-walled cells (bulliform cells) either side of the mid-rib, which act as hinges for the leaf.

Other adaptations are designed to reduce leaf temperatures and hence the need for transpiration and water loss.

Some plants from this biome have silvery leaves as a result of waxes (*Eschscholtsia californica* and *Melianthus major*) or hairs to reflect sunlight and to prevent water loss through the leaf epidermis.

In another cooling mechanism, volatile chemicals, which form strong-smelling vapours in warm air, evaporate from the plants. The combustible nature of these volatiles may also help trigger the regular fires which fashion the vegetation characteristic of this biome. (The common name for *Dictamnus faxinella* from the Mediterranean scrub forest, for example, is 'burning bush'.)

Flowering date in scrub forest native plants can occur either side of the summer drought stress period, with the main flowering periods being winter/spring, as with the Algerian iris, *Iris unguicularis*, and winter heliotrope, *Petasites fragrans*; late spring/early summer, as with *Ceanothus* spp.; and late summer/autumn, such as with South African plants like nerines, kniphofia and schizostylis.

The regular occurrence of fires in scrub forest ecosystems requires the plants to adapt to surviving these conditions. Seeds of a number of South African scrub forest natives, like the restios, are actually stimulated to germinate by chemicals in smoke (Chapter 7). Some of the scrub forest trees and shrubs, such as *Acacia* spp., produce underground fire-resistant lignotubers from which they can re-sprout after the fire. Indeed, burr-wood pipes are made from the lignotubers of the Mediterranean heather *Erica arborea*, which can withstand temperatures as high as 700°F.

Scrub Forest Plants for the Garden

Scrub forest plants are ideally suited to dry gardens and gravel gardens, where the gardener intends not to water. On the other hand, judicious watering can extend the flowering season of many of the annual and non-woody perennial species.

Examples of garden shrubs originating from the scrub forest biome include spring- or early summer-flowering evergreen shrubs with small leathery leaves such as *Buxus*, *Olea*, *Ceanothus*, *Cytisus* and *Cistus*. Sub-shrubs from the scrub forest include lavenders, *Zauschneria californica*, *Santolina* spp., *Perovskia* spp. and *Euryops pectinatus*.

Many of the evergreen plants in the herb garden are native to this Mediterranean-type climate, including thyme, rosemary (both sub-shrubs), oregano, sage and mint. These plants have tough aromatic leaves.

Herbaceous perennials from this biome for the dry garden tend to flower from late summer onwards, after the drought is over, and include *Salvia* spp. (*S. farinacea, S. guarantica, S. patens*), *Nepeta*, *Cleome*, *Agastache*, *Achillea*, *Phygelius*, *Penstemon barbatus*, *Kniphofia* spp. and *Gaura lindheimeri*.

Early summer-flowering hardy annuals, such as *Eschscholtsia* (California poppy), *Phacelia*, *Gilia*, *Scaveola*, *Clarkia* (godetia), *Coreopsis*, *Zinnia*, *Amaranthus*, *Cosmos* and annual penstemons all originate from the scrub forest biome. Given the short flowering period of scrub forest annuals before they perish in their native habitat as a result of drought, it is not surprising that they produce large individual flowers (*Eschscholzia*, *Clarkia*) or inflorescences (*Gilia*, *Amaranthus*) of brilliant hues in order to attract pollinators to generate seeds for the next generation.

Many of the early spring- and autumn-flowering geophytes (such as bulbs) that we grow in our gardens originate from this biome, including *Narcissus*, *Tulipa*, *Cyclamen*, *Crocus*, *Iris*, *Amaryllis*, *Crinum*, *Nerine*, *Muscari*. Unlike the geophytes from the deciduous woodland, like bluebell, where flowering is triggered by rising temperatures at the end of the winter stress period, the main trigger of flowering of scrub forest geophytes is moisture.

Most winter- and spring-flowering bulbs from the scrub forest biome exploit the moisture from the winter rains (and spring snow melt for the high-altitude species). They produce leaves and flowers together, and include *Iris unguicularis*,

Foliage of *Arum italicum* 'Marmoratum'.

tulips, crocus, narcissus and grape hyacinths. On the other hand, autumn-flowering bulbs, such as *Nerine bowdenii, Colchicum* spp. and *Cyclamen hederifolium*, have naked flowers, with the leaves appearing later. Many scrub forest geophytes produce attractive leaves from autumn to spring, in order to build up food reserves for flowering the next year after the summer drought, and this makes them very useful garden plants. Examples include *Cyclamen hederifolium* and *Arum italicum* 'Marmoratum'. With *C. hederifolium*, leaf production occurs almost overnight, being stimulated by falling temperature and daylength.

Most of the garden plants from the South African scrub forest biome were collected from high-altitude sites so are not tender when grown in western Europe, but problems can still arise. The dormancy of South African geophyte species such as *Crocosmia, Nerine* and *Gladiolus* is broken by short periods of exposure to low temperatures, with gladiolus corms requiring only 24 hours at 0–5°C. This results in the early spring appearance of foliage of these species and makes them vulnerable to frost damage in the colder winters of western Europe and North America.

Many species from the scrub forest biome behave quite differently in European gardens than in their native habitat. Many of the herbaceous perennials (especially *Salvia, Agastache, Achillea* and *Kniphofia*) and annuals (such as *Zinnia, Coreopsis, Cosmos* and *Amaranthus*) have much longer flowering seasons when grown in British gardens than in their native scrub forests, where extremes of drought and heat signal the end of flowering and the death or die-back of the plants to escape stress.

In mild temperate gardens, *Ornithogalum thyrsoides* is evergreen and flowers almost all year round in the absence of drought stress, unlike the situation in South Africa. Several of the Australian annuals such as *Correa* and *Scaeveola*, on the other hand, when grown in western European gardens will die before the end of the summer.

Because flowering in scrub forest bulbs is largely controlled by soil moisture, flowering date can be manipulated by appropriate timing of watering. Mid-summer watering of *Nerine bowdenii* will accelerate flowering, while delaying watering of Juno group *Iris* spp. from the Middle East until November will delay growth and increase the probability that the plants will survive the winter wet.

In nature, most scrub forest bulbs would undergo a distinct summer rest under dry conditions, and this should be replicated when they are grown in European gardens. These conditions are necessary for flower development within the bulb, but can be difficult to achieve in more temperate climes.

Planting bulbs in full sun would have been good advice in the past, but the increased summer rainfall in recent years over much of Ireland and Britain requires a different approach. If these bulbs, such as fritillaries, tulips, most crocus and colchicums, are planted under deciduous small trees or shrubs such as the coyote willow, *Salix exigua,* or *Spiraea* spp., which do not leaf until after the geophytes have finished flowering, the over-planting keeps the soil dry by reducing rainfall from hitting the soil and by the shrubs taking up the soil moisture in the top 15cm or so. This strategy can result in tulip species flowering in a more reliable manner year after year.

Planting bulbs near walls (ideally facing away from prevailing winds, so that the wall provides rainshadow as well as drying out the soil) also helps to keep bulbs dry in winter. Because rainfall triggers the end of the dormant period for scrub forest geophytes in nature, during the summer it is best not to water areas where these bulbs are resting in your garden.

To maximize the performance of scrub forest natives in the garden, summer conditions need to mimic the nutrient-poor dry conditions to which they are adapted. Herbs, for example, need to be grown in full sun, with a relatively nutrient-poor and free-draining soil, to achieve best flavour and to increase the chance that the plants will survive the winter. Many of the scrub forest geophytes will not thrive in heavy soils which stay wet over the winter. Over-use of fertilizers will cause excessive vegetative growth which will tend to flop.

The low plant density of the vegetation in the wild is reflected in the fact that many of the scrub forest natives, including kniphofia, lavender, santolina, cistus, dierama and the giant oatgrass *Stipa gigantea*, respond poorly to competition when they are young, so should be planted as isolated plants or to the front of a border.

The low water and nutrient content of soils in the scrub forest means that plants native to these areas often have shallow fibrous root systems restricted to the upper part of the soil, in order to capture the limited resources. Under the better conditions found in temperate gardens, species of taller shrubs and trees such as *Acacia* and *Eucalyptus* grow rapidly and can become unstable, with small root systems anchoring tall trees. Planting such species in sheltered locations is therefore important.

The Temperate Grassland Biome

Environment and Distribution

This biome is mainly restricted to the interior regions of continents, where moist air masses from the ocean are blocked by mountain ranges to the west and the south. Summers range from warm to hot, and winters cold to very cold. The resulting low rainfall prevents the dominance of trees and shrubs, and the dominant plant type is perennial herbaceous grass, combined with herbaceous perennials. Grazing by large mammals and occasional fires also act to prevent the establishment of woody plants, although the soils are quite rich.

Such grasslands are found in the mid-west of the United States ('prairie'), in Russia ('steppes') and Argentina ('pampas'), although the steppes are associated with drier regions than the pampas or prairie.

Plant Characteristics

The species dominating depend on the climatic conditions. In the US, places with higher rainfall produce the so-called tall-grass prairie, compared to the short-grass prairie which develops in the drier areas.

Garden grasses associated with this biome fall into two classes: cool-season and warm-season grasses. The latter have evolved a form of photosynthesis (termed 'C4' instead of the more usual 'C3' photosynthesis of nearly all temperate plants, including cool-season grasses) which uses carbon dioxide more efficiently, so that the stomata do not need to be open for as long. This adaptation reduces the amount of water lost and increases the efficiency with which water is used by warm-season grasses (Chapter 4).

Warm-season or C4 grasses, like *Panicum* cultivars, *Miscanthus* spp., *Schizachyrium scoparium*, *Pennisetum* spp. and the scented *Sporobilis heterolepis*, are therefore drought-avoiders, staying green over the summer, but cold-escapers, dying down for the winter. Cool-season or C3 grasses, on the other hand, which include *Stipa*, fescues and ryegrasses, are drought-escapers, dying down under summer drought conditions as occur in parts of the US, but cold tolerant, remaining green over winter. Cool-season grasses, when grown in the milder conditions of Britain and Ireland, on the other hand, stay green all year round.

In addition to the grass species, temperate grassland includes late summer-flowering herbaceous perennials, particularly members of the Asteraceae (daisy family), such as *Echinacea, Rudbeckia, Aster, Solidago, Helianthus* and *Coreopsis* spp., as well as *Monarda, Filipendula and Liatris* from North America, and *Verbena bonariensis* from South America. The high plant density found in temperate grasslands means that the perennials from this biome need to be very competitive.

Temperate Grassland Plants for the Garden

Species from the temperate grassland biome are the mainstays of the herbaceous border and, more recently, of prairie planting. They are adapted to a nutrient-rich soil and full sun, as is to be expected of plants growing in the absence of shade from trees.

The very competitive nature of the plants which dominate temperate grassland is an important trait which must be considered when mixing plants from different biomes. It is advisable not to mix grasses and herbaceous perennials from temperate grassland with the less competitive grasses from scrub forest.

Similarly, sowing seed of a mixture of cool- and warm-season grasses together can be problematic, because the warm-season species need temperatures of nearly 20°C to germinate, which means that the cool-season grasses (as well as local weeds) will have had a head start.

Furthermore, herbaceous perennials from the US temperate grassland biome will tend to outcompete similar plants from Europe. Because of their shorter growing season, these American plants grow more quickly than their European counterparts and tend to crowd out their neighbours.

Plants from Other Biomes

Another factor which must be taken into account when considering the conditions under which a plant may grow in your garden is the altitude at which it grows in its native habitat. Each 125m increase in altitude above sea-level lowers the average temperature by 1°C, which is equivalent to a northwards movement in latitude of about 0.5°.

The length of the European growing season is classified as the number of days when the temperature is greater than 6°C, so the length of the growing season decreases as the altitude increases. As a consequence, above the treeline on the mountains of Europe and the Americas, the dominant plants are evergreen perennial low-growing alpine plants. These resemble plants of the tundra, a nutrient-poor region which is classified as being *beyond* the treeline, in that the tundra occurs near sea-level at more northerly latitudes. During the last Ice Age, tundra plants retreated southwards ahead of the glaciers and found refuge in cold regions on the tallest peaks, safe from the ice sheets. When the ice receded, the plants returned northwards, leaving relatives in alpine sites as well as in the tundra.

Alpine plants are naturally small evergreen perennials, forming mats or cushions. This way of growing helps the plants gain heat by radiative warming from the rocks over which they grow. Their low growth means that their growth buds are several centimetres under the soil, protecting them from frost damage. Growth buds of taller alpines such as dwarf willows and shrubs are protected from frost by being under snow cover during the winter. Above the treeline, the growth buds of taller woody plants have no protection, so they are killed in the winter.

The leaves of alpines tend to be thick, with either woolly hairs, such as edelweiss, *Leontopodium alpinum*, or waxy surfaces which appear white, glaucous or silvery in colour. These leaf coverings are designed to reflect UV light, which increases with increasing altitude.

Because of their short (10–12 weeks) growing season, alpines tend to have disproportionately large flowers for the size of the plant, in order to attract pollinators. Given the harsh nature of the

Flowers of *Nerine bowdenii* from southern Africa.

winters at high altitudes, one would expect alpines to withstand anything a lowland European winter could throw at them, but these plants survive in their native habitat in mild, quite dry conditions under a duvet of snow and are frequently killed by the cold and (mainly) wet of a European winter spent outdoors.

A similar paradox can occur in other biomes. A rich part of the garden flora of Europe is from South Africa, leading many gardeners to consider that these plants would be of doubtful frost hardiness. But many of the South African plants which we grow in western Europe, such as *Kniphofia*, *Nerine bowdenii*, *Crocosmia* spp. and *Gladiolus* spp., were collected from the Drakensberg Mountains, a high-altitude (8–10,000 feet) location in the Cape Region, and these species are sufficiently cold hardy to withstand winters even in parts of northern England.

The native flora of the tropical grassland, taiga and the tropical rainforest biomes also provide some garden and houseplants for western Europe. Closer to the equator than the temperate grassland, the higher summer temperatures and drier winters result in tropical grassland, such as the savannah of east Africa.

From these areas come half-hardy perennial garden plants such as *Osteospermum*, *Diascia* and *Argyranthemum*, which are often grown in European gardens as annuals because of their vulnerability to winter cold and damp. As with the temperate grassland, these plants are adapted to highly competitive conditions and frequently flower best when their roots are restricted. This can be achieved by growing them in containers, especially with other vigorous plants such as ivy.

The taiga is the largest of the terrestrial biomes. Garden plants from the taiga are predominantly conifers, particularly firs and spruces. Most conifers are adapted to cold dry climates, because the Permian period when they dominated the Earth (Chapter 1) was very cold and dry. These trees withstand the extreme winters of the taiga by stress avoidance rather than the stress escape strategy of the deciduous trees further south.

To conserve water, leaves were replaced in conifers by inrolled needles with a limited surface area from which water could be lost. The inrolling, sunken stomata and thick waxy cuticles of the needles are all adaptations by conifers to avoid drought. By being evergreen, conifers can make the most of the short growing season in the far north.

Waxy needles on conifers would also deter herbivores. The most ancient conifers, such as the monkey puzzle, were present in the age of the dinosaurs, so this adaptation would have reduced feeding damage by plant-eating dinosaurs. Fossil remains of the monkey puzzle tree are jet, the black material popularized in funeral jewellery in Victorian times.

Groundflora species from the taiga grow in the year-round shade cast by evergreen conifers. These plants, such as twinflower (*Linnaea borealis*), bunchberry (*Cornus canadensis*), *Asarum europaeum* and *Hepatica* spp., are characterized by being evergreen and by flowering in early summer. These shade-tolerant evergreen woodland plants tend to have leathery leaves to retain water under such dry conditions. Flowering in taiga plants is usually triggered by water availability. A plant with such adaptations is the cast-iron plant, *Aspidistra*, a common houseplant in Victorian times, which is native to dense shady forests in China and Japan.

Many houseplants originate from tropical rainforests, where the shade under evergreen rainforests makes plants like African violets well-suited to the low light found in homes. Rainforest plants are evergreen because of the lack of a distinct stress season. There is no shortage of rainfall, with the main rain-related problem being how to shed the rain fast enough. As a consequence, the leaves of most rainforest plants hang down to a pointed end, called a drip tip. On the other hand, the low humidity in modern centrally heated homes is in contrast to the humid conditions under which such plants evolved and can therefore cause problems.

Increasingly, garden plants such as banana, gingers (*Hedychium* spp.) and cannas from the higher altitude (and therefore cooler) parts of tropical rainforest areas are being grown in gardens in western Europe, providing colour and drama late in the season.

WHICH PLANT FOR WHICH SITE?

Selecting plants appropriate for your garden means that the niche of the plant must fit within the environmental constraints of your garden. But how can you tell the appropriate site for a plant without resorting to bulky garden encyclopaedias?

So far, we have seen that plants from particular regions of the world have certain requirements.

But even if you know the place of origin of the plant, this may not give you all the information you need. *Kniphofia* spp. from South Africa and *Fritillaria imperialis* from Turkey and Iran would both seem to be candidates for the hottest driest site in your garden, yet both are natives of flood meadows and need a well-drained but moisture-retentive soil.

From its name and its dominance of the Florida everglades, you would think that the swamp cypress, *Taxodium distichum*, a deciduous conifer, would need a wet soil with standing water to give of its best. But this is an example of a plant able to occupy a specific niche to which no other tree could adapt. This beautiful tree, with wonderful autumn colour, actually does better in good quality moist but unflooded sites.

Autumn colour of the swamp cypress, *Taxodium distichum*, a deciduous conifer.

In some cases, plant species may appear very similar while originating from quite different climates, because the key environmental factor is the same. Of the two most commonly grown garden cyclamen species, *C. hederifolium* comes from the parched scrub forest areas around the Mediterranean and flowers in autumn after the summer drought, while *C. coum* is a native of deciduous woodland from eastern Europe to the Middle East and flowers in spring before the leaf canopy of the trees closes. But both can withstand dry conditions and are happy under the shade of deciduous trees.

Physical Characteristics

Many of the adaptations plants have made to their environment are reflected in physical traits, which can in turn provide some indication of the ideal garden site. These are presented as guidelines, rather than hard-and-fast rules:

Woody herbs, for example, are usually native to scrub forest areas, so herb gardens should be planted on free-draining sunny sites which are low in nutrients. Leafy herbs, such as basil, coriander and parsley, on the other hand, prefer more benign conditions.

On a shrub, evergreen leaves which are leathery dull or needle-like are characteristic of plants adapted to hot dry conditions, while glossy evergreen leaves are found on plants used to dry shade. Geophytes with upright spear-shaped leaves, like allium, gladiolus and dierama, tend to be adapted to hot dry conditions, because this leaf shape minimizes the leaf area exposed to the sun, so that they do not heat up too much.

Plants with large simple leaves are usually adapted to sheltered conditions, such as can be found in woodland. Having large leaves means that these leaves can absorb as much as possible of the limited light which reaches the forest floor. Such species include hostas, darmera and arisaemas. Woody plants which grow well in windy exposed sites tend to have narrow leaves which move in the slightest wind, such as willow and poplar.

Silvery leaves as a result of leaf hairs, or blue-grey (glaucous) leaves caused by waxes are usually

Podophyllum delavayi 'Spotty Dotty', showing the large simple leaves, held flat, which are characteristic of a shade plant.

associated with dry conditions. Dry conditions can be due to quite different environments, such as: high-alpine high-UV environments, inhabited by plants such as the woolly-leaved edelweiss, *Leontopodium alpinum*; hot dry environments like the scrub forest biome, with plants such as *Papaver nudicaule*, *Helichtotrichon sempervirens* or *Festuca glauca*; and the cool dry shade under woodland, characterized by plants like *Hosta sieboldiana* 'Elegans', *Dicentra* 'Stuart Boothman' or *Astelia chathamica*. Leaf hairs or waxes reduce the amount of water lost from the leaf via the leaf surface or the stomata.

Waxes forming the cuticle are water-repellent (hence waxed jackets!) and greatly reduce the amount of water vapour that can pass from the leaf through the cuticle. Heavy deposits of wax plates result in shiny leaves, commonly found in woodland shrubs, while wax rods result in a blue-grey colour, frequent among grasses from dry areas, like *Festuca glauca* and *Helichtotrichon*.

Plants with short leaf hairs tend to be associated with dry conditions because the hairs will absorb moisture. In European gardens these hairy plants, such as *Artemisia* 'Powys Castle', can find it difficult to survive over the winter in damp climates.

Dicentra 'Stuart Boothman', adapted to the dry shade under woodland, the waxes on the foliage minimizing loss of water through the leaves.

Under these conditions, plants with glaucous leaves have a better survival rate. Silver leaves due to waxes or hairs can be distinguished by rubbing your finger over the leaf. With a waxy leaf, the waxes will be removed showing a clear distinction between rubbed and unrubbed areas.

Rarely, leaf hairs can have different functions.

Underside of leaves of *Rhododendron* spp., showing removal of the wax layer by rubbing.

The very long hairs on leaves of *Meconopsis nepaulensis* act to keep moisture away from the leaf in the wet climate it grows in. The African violet, *Saintpaulia ionantha*, in its native habitat on very dry cliff faces in tropical rainforest, uses its fine leaf hairs to absorb moisture from the humid atmosphere, which explains why indoors this plant grows best in bathrooms and kitchens, where the air is damper; direct watering onto the leaf causes African violets to rot.

Finally, all things being equal, herbaceous or deciduous species tend to do better over a British winter than do evergreen species because they escape the cold stress. For example, herbaceous *Agapanthus* spp. or deciduous *Ceanothus* spp. tend to be more winter hardy than their evergreen relatives.

It is generally best to grow plants which suit your garden's conditions, rather than the converse, but most of us long to grow plants we know are unsuitable for our gardens. As the great plantsman E.B. Anderson once said, 'One can make a garden on anything provided one has patience and is willing to experiment'.

CLIMATE AND PLANT CULTIVATION

The plants you can grow in your garden will be limited mainly by macroclimate factors, such as minimum winter temperature and summer rainfall. Many of the non-climatic environmental factors which help determine plant distribution of wild plants can be modified to suit the plant within a garden ecosystem. Pests and pathogens which feed on the plant can be controlled (Chapter 6), while soil characteristics like drainage, nutrient content and acidity/alkalinity can be modified (Chapter 4).

In western Europe, the prevailing winds blow from the southwest. As the warm air passes over the Atlantic on its way to Europe, it picks up water vapour, which is deposited as rain when it meets land or mountains. This causes the high rainfall on the west coasts of Ireland and the UK.

High rainfall in parts of the north and west explains why gardens such as Bodnant on the

The Himalayan blue poppy, *Meconopsis betonicifolia*, which grows well in the cool, high-rainfall climate of Scotland.

windward side of Snowdonia are capable of growing rhododendrons so well, while those in western Scotland can grow woodland plants such as lilies, corydalis, primulas and blue poppies to the envy of the gardening world. The native home of many of these species is the Himalayas, where annual rainfall values are similar to those in western parts of Wales, Ireland and Scotland.

The coldest winter winds in Britain are those from the frozen expanses to the north and east, which will also be drying winds because they travel over land so do not pick up moisture. The conditions on the east coast of Essex, therefore, qualify it as a cold desert!

Within these isles, the further north you travel, you find not only that the temperature falls and the rainfall increases but light intensity also falls. There are two main reasons for this. Because the sun is never directly overhead in western Europe, sunlight hits the earth at an oblique angle. The more northerly the site, the greater the angle and hence the light is spread out over a larger area, so that less light hits a given area of land. Secondly, the higher humidity in the north creates greater cloud cover, and hence a smaller percentage of sunlight reaches the ground. In terms of gardening, this is important, as a woodland plant which

needs partial shade in southern England could be grown in full sun in the north of Scotland, as long as the other requirements (such as protection from the wind) are met.

An important feature of the climate in Britain and Ireland is the influence of the Gulf Stream (or the North Atlantic Drift). Warm water from the tropics moves northwards via the Gulf of Mexico to the waters around Scandinavia and Greenland, raising the temperature on the west coasts of Europe by some 10°C, compared to what it should be on the basis of latitude alone.

The influence of the Gulf Stream provides a mild climate which is exploited by gardeners along the southern and western coasts of Ireland and Scotland, where minimum winter temperatures range from –1°C to –6°C. In these areas, sub-tropical plants such as ornamental bananas can be kept outside all year round. In comparison, the winter temperatures of the rest of Britain and Ireland would range from –7°C to –12°C, with the northernmost parts falling to as low as –17°C.

In response to seasonal changes in temperature and daylength deciduous trees switch on their cold-coping strategies in autumn. Firstly, the trees switch on stress avoidance and tolerance genes, so

A deciduous sycamore tree in December. Note the green leaves remaining on the branches around the street light to the right.

that the tree is better able to withstand the rigours of the winter cold (cold hardening). Secondly, the trees drop their leaves to prevent water loss and wind damage over the winter.

Trees of European origin respond mainly to the shortening days in autumn, which is a more reliable indicator of season than is falling temperatures. Because of this, some deciduous trees, such as willow, some maples and birches, may retain their leaves in towns long into the winter, as a result of supplementary light from streetlamps.

Interestingly, some trees from eastern US tend to be more cold-sensitive in the milder winters of western Europe than in the colder American winters. This appears to be due to the fact that, in their native habitat, these trees recognize autumn by the falling temperatures. Unfortunately, temperature fall is less predictable in western Europe than in the US.

As a consequence, the first autumn frost may find American trees growing in Britain or Ireland in a non-hardened state. For example, sugar maple (*Acer saccharum*) and flowering dogwood (*Cornus florida*) are hardy down to −46°C in the US but can be damaged by temperatures as high as −10°C in Britain. Similar problems can also arise with plants from the taiga biome, such as

Siberian larch, which can be damaged by mild but early frosts in Britain.

Your Garden Aspect

The aspect of a garden is basically the direction into which it faces, which will affect the amount of sunlight it receives, what part of the day it receives most light and the angle of that light. To determine the aspect of your garden, stand with your back to the house wall and take the reading on a compass. If the arrow points 'south', then your garden has a southerly aspect and will receive sunlight for most of the day in the summer.

Of course, different growing surfaces in a garden will have different aspects and hence different characteristics, such as temperature and exposure to the wind. Walls which are south-facing receive the most sun and are the warmest sites, allowing early growth and flowering on plants sited there, but they also face the prevailing south-westerly winds in western Europe. North-facing walls receive the least sun, particularly in the winter, but at least they are protected from the prevailing winds. North-facing aspects can, however, be dry, because of a local rain-shadow effect. West-facing walls have the advantages of warmth and moist

Wind damage to the thin leaf tips of Japanese maple, *Acer japonicum dissectum* 'Garnet'.

winds, although winds from this direction are common. East-facing walls are probably preferable to surfaces with a westerly aspect if protection can be given from the easterly winds.

Though the least common of winds, easterlies travel across the European landmass so that they are cold and dry in winter, hot and dry in summer, and can be particularly damaging as they can sear thin-leaved plants, such as woodland species and the dissected-leaf Japanese maples, in a short time; the more dissected a Japanese maple leaf, the thinner and more sensitive it is to desiccation. A south-easterly aspect is therefore the best compromise between maximum exposure to sun and minimum to wind.

One important consideration with respect to east-facing walls is that they receive morning sun. This can be a problem in the winter when plant tissue may have frozen overnight. The dangers of frost damage are two-fold, based on the effects of freezing (how low does the temperature reach?) and thawing (how quickly does the frozen tissue thaw?).

Many woodland plants are very cold hardy, in that ice does not form within their cells even at very low temperatures (frost avoidance), but their sheltered habitat means that they are poorly adapted to rapid thawing. This is particularly true for shrubs which produce frost-sensitive organs early in the season, such as flowers in camellias,

Frost-sensitive young foliage of the tree paeony, 'Flight of Cranes'.

Foliage of *Rodgersia aesculifolia* 'Irish Bronze', growing with shuttlecock ferns, *Matteucia struthiopteris*.

flowering cherry, magnolia and early rhododendrons, or young leaves, like *Pieris forrestii* 'Forest Flame'. Such plants should not be planted on east-facing sites in frost-prone areas. as early morning sunshine brings about damage as organs thaw.

Cold air is heavier than warm air and, like water, drains to the lowest level. Because of this, cold air can accumulate in gardens in valleys and at locations at the bottom of slopes, resulting in so-called 'frost pockets' which can be damaging to a wide range of plants.

But just to show that one man's problem is another man's opportunity, it is worth noting that 93 per cent of the UK rhubarb crop is grown in a frost pocket in the Pennines in an area bordering Wakefield, Leeds and Bradford, known as the Rhubarb Triangle. Rhubarb crowns lose their winter dormancy and start to produce leaves once they have experienced a minimum number of days with temperatures of 6°C or less. The cold winters in the Rhubarb Triangle ensure that the leaves start to grow early in spring, so that the leaf stalks (the part we eat as rhubarb) will be harvested as early as possible in the season to fetch a premium price.

Careful planting of trees or shrubs can be used to provide a new micro-climate suitable for other plants. Deciduous trees, especially those late into leaf, such as *Catalpa bignonioides* 'Aurea'*, Cercis canadensis* 'Forest Pansy' and *Fraxinus excelsior* 'Aurea', are suitable for under-planting with

spring-flowering plants such as snowdrops, wood anemones and winter aconites.

Later in the season the greater humidity and protection from wind provided by the tree canopy makes the understorey an ideal site for growing beautiful woodland plants such as *Trillium, Hosta, Rodgersia, Erythronium, Sanguinaria, Tricyrtis* and *Deinanthe*, and many other plants native to deciduous woodland biomes in Europe, North America, Japan and China.

Relatively uncompetitive trees, such as pioneers like birches and ash, with deep roots (to reduce competition for water and nutrients with the groundflora) and which shed a relatively light shade, are good choices for providing sites for growing shade-loving species. On the other hand, shallow-rooted species such as beech and *Magnolia* make the under-canopy soil very dry, by reducing the amount of rain which penetrates the soil and by taking up much of that water which does reach the soil, making the establishment of groundflora vegetation difficult.

Trees and shrubs can also raise the winter temperature of the area under the canopy, providing some respite for marginally cold-tender species. Planting a frost-tender plant under a small deciduous tree or large shrub will provide protection from the worst of an air frost. This strategy is particularly appropriate for early-flowering shrubs such as camellia, *Magnolia stellata* and rhododendron, to minimize flower damage.

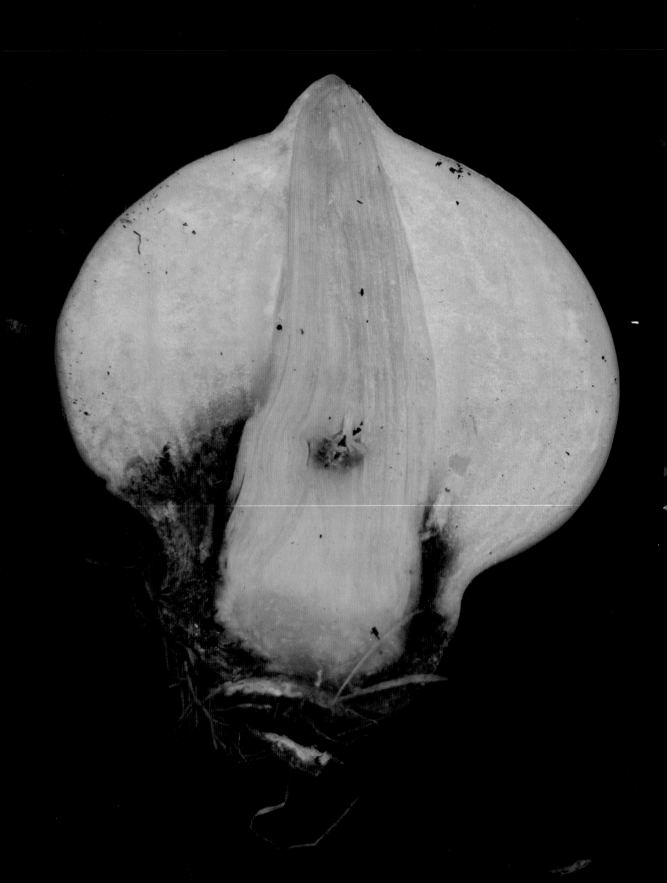

CHAPTER 3

Choosing the Specimen and Preparing the Site

Once you have identified a suitable site in your garden for a particular plant (using guidelines described in Chapter 2), it is time to consider careful selection of the specimen, preparation of the site and provision of support to get the plant off to a good start. Here we look at the science behind planting instructions, dispelling some outdated recommendations.

THE IMPORTANCE OF A GOOD ROOT SYSTEM

When choosing a plant we tend to ignore the roots, buying pot-bound plants and then planting without regard for how the roots will develop in the soil. A vigorous root system will provide not only anchorage (primarily from the older roots) and adequate supply of water and minerals to the plant (supplied largely by the younger finer roots), but, less obviously, it will also have a beneficial influence on the above-ground growth and development of the plant.

Plant growth and development is controlled by natural plant chemicals known as hormones, or plant growth substances (Chapter 5). To regulate plant growth, plant hormones include auxins, which are produced in the shoot but transported to the root system to stimulate root growth, and cytokinins, which are produced in the root and transported to the above-ground tissues where they stimulate shoot growth.

A healthy plant should have a balance between the size of the root system and the size of the

A section through a bulb of *Allium christophii*, showing the flowering shoot in miniature.

above-ground part of the plant, and this is important to bear in mind when buying a plant, especially a specimen tree.

Roots are the principal means by which plants take up water and soil nutrients. Monocot seedlings, primarily grasses and most garden geophytes (Chapter 1), produce between three and six primary roots, which then develop a fibrous root system in which it is usually impossible to identify a main root. Dicot seedlings, on the other hand, generally produce a single main root, which can develop into a swollen tap root, from which lateral roots develop to produce an extensively branched root system. Generally, the root system of dicots is deeper than that of monocots.

The roots we can see, however, are only part of the root system. The outer layer of all plant organs is the epidermis (Chapter 1). In roots, this is termed the rhizodermis. Near the tip of each root there are tiny outgrowths of the rhizodermis, known as root hairs, which contribute significantly to the ability of the root system to absorb water, even though each root hair lasts for only a few days. When the total length of roots and root hairs in a typical root system is added together, the figures can be mind-boggling. In a classic study, a single mature rye plant was reported to have a total root length of 622km. In addition, it had more than ten billion root hairs, totalling more than 10,000 km in length, with a daily increase in total length (root + root hair) of 90km.

Another way in which most plants increase their ability to take up water is by mycorrhizal associations between the roots and specific natural beneficial soil fungi (Chapter 1). It is now known that mycorrhiza are found in more than 90 per cent of plant species. Members of the Chenopodiaceae

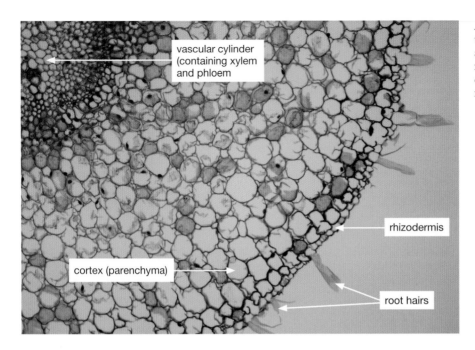

A micrograph of a thin transverse section across a broad bean (*Vicia faba*) root, showing root hairs developing from the rhizodermal layer.

(the beet family), the Caryophyllaceae (the carnation family) and the Brassicaceae (the cabbage family) tend not to support mycorrhizal associations.

There are two main classes of mycorrhizal fungi. Endomycorrhizal fungi are by far the more common and are mainly found on herbaceous plants, actually living within the root cells. Ectomycorrhizal fungi, on the other hand, are generally associated with trees and shrubs, with the fungus connected to the root, forming a sheath around it and spreading out into surrounding soil. The contribution

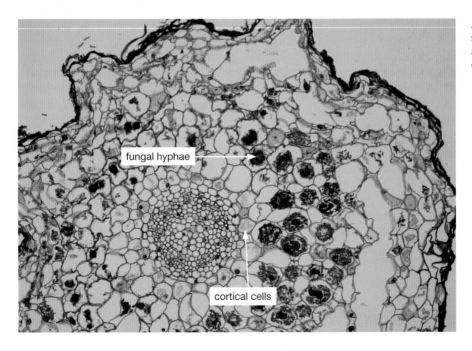

A micrograph of a thin section through a root associated with an endomycorrhizal fungus.

of mycorrhizal fungi to water uptake by a plant is even higher than that of root hairs, while they can also improve the ability of roots to harvest nutrients from the soil (Chapter 4).

PICKING YOUR PLANT

When you go to buy a plant, the main categories available are container-grown plants (including bedding and seedlings), bareroot stock and bulbs (including corms, tubers etc.). The following information also applies to transplants, where you dig up a plant and replant it elsewhere, or divisions, where you split an herbaceous perennial into several independent pieces.

Container-Grown and Bareroot Plants

The production and sale of plants in containers has increased the year-round availability of plants, particularly evergreen shrubs and trees, and specimen trees. The down-side of container-grown plants is that the plants have a limited root run and supply of nutrients, and, if left for too long, can suffer from nutrient deficiency (shown by yellowing and/or purpling of the leaves) or from being pot bound. Although short-term nutrient deficiencies can be addressed, an inadequate root system will affect the subsequent above-ground growth and performance of a plant, particularly a tree, which may not recover from this early growth check.

Check the plant carefully before you buy it. Tell-tale signs of a plant which has been in the pot for too long are old (brown) roots growing through the drainage holes and above the compost surface (young white roots are OK), or the presence of liverworts and mosses (Chapter 1) on the soil surface. Try knocking the plant out of its pot to examine the root system – good signs are some cream-coloured roots and a root system which does not wind round and round.

Bareroot plants are dug up from the open soil when they are dormant. This means that the type of plants sold in this format are largely restricted to deciduous shrubs and trees, but the range of species and varieties is greater than for container-grown plants, and they are markedly cheaper. Because the plants have been grown in the open ground, there is much less risk of root restriction but a greater risk of root damage. Avoid plants with damaged roots, but look for plants with a well-developed root system showing a radial pattern of growth, growing outwards from the centre. Once you have bought a bareroot plant, the roots must be kept damp until planted.

The greater vigour of the root system of a bare-rooted, compared to a container-grown plant, results in greater levels of cytokinin production and increased water and nutrient uptake, reflected in faster establishment and higher growth rates. Although the initial height of bareroot trees may be less than for container-grown plants, bareroot plants grow more quickly and will catch up and probably overtake the more expensive pot-grown specimens in a couple of years.

For some situations, especially for large-scale planting, bareroot plants are far superior to container-grown specimens. For a hedge or shelter belt, one- to two-year-old bareroot 'whips' would be much cheaper than pot-grown plants and would need no staking.

Annuals (including bedding plants and vegetable seedlings) are commonly sold in plastic modules with limited scope for water or nutrients. Plants grown in this way are best bought when young, as there will be less risk that the plants will have suffered from drought stress or starvation which could permanently stunt the performance of the plants. For plants with tap roots, like verbascums, sweet peas, lupins or fennel, root restriction is particularly detrimental, so seedlings or young plants grown in long pots or modules should be selected.

Bulbs, Corms, Tubers and Rhizomes

As described in Chapter 2, geophytes are plants which are adapted to live under conditions where they have to grow, flower and reproduce in a short time, before a stress period arises, such as the summer drought in the Mediterranean or the development of shade as leaves appear in deciduous woodland. To achieve this, they need to have plenty of food reserves, in the form of vegetative storage organs with growth buds from which shoots, flowers and roots can develop. These are all underground modified stems, like bulbs, corms, tubers or rhizomes.

Bulbs (such as tulips, narcissus), corms (crocus, dog's tooth violet, gladiolus) and tubers (*Anemone blanda*) are compacted underground stems with growth buds which will develop into next year's leaves, stems, roots and flowers. Bulbs are enlarged apical growth buds surrounded by numerous fleshy leaves formed from the swollen bases of last season's leaves. These are protected by scale leaves and are attached to a disc at the base (the basal plate) which is actually the compacted stem from which roots develop.

Bulbs grow by one of two different methods. In the tulip bulb, a central growth bud becomes the flowering shoot with leaves attached, after which the bulb dies. Each year, an axillary bud of one of the fleshy leaves develops into next year's bulb at the basal plate.

In the second method, illustrated by daffodil and snowdrop, the leaves and flowers develop from different parts of the bulb, so that the flowering shoot does not carry leaves. The leaves develop from the old bulb which, unlike the situation with the tulip, persists from year to year. In contrast, the flower develops from an axillary bud, with new bulbs developing from the axils of the outer bulb scales. With geophytes like the daffodil, then, the main bulb is permanent, while new bulbs also develop each year. This explains why bulbs like daffodils flower well year after year, with the flowering clump growing.

Bulbs with the tulip method of propagation, on the other hand, where the main bulb dies after flowering, tend to flower in their first year then irregularly thereafter, reflecting the time it takes for the new bulb to grow to flowering size. This phenomenon occurs for hybrid tulip cultivars but not the species, such as *Tulipa praestans, T. sprengeri, T. greigii* or *T. linifolia,* which are reliable repeat flowerers. Interestingly, the sterile Darwin hybrid tulip cultivars, such as 'Apeldoorn', are fairly reliable repeat-flowerers, maybe because there is no redirection of assimilates away from the young bulbs to developing seeds.

Corms, which are usually associated with members of the iris family or Iridaceae, differ from bulbs by having no fleshy leaves. Instead, they are composed almost entirely of stem tissue, with the exception of a small number of dead papery scale leaves covering the outside of the corm. The scale leaves are the remains of last season's leaves. In the axils of the scale leaves are the buds which will produce the flowering shoots the following year. New corms which will flower the next year form on the side or top of the previous corm, the latter situation resulting in vertical chains of corms in plants like *Crocosmia.*

Tubers (cyclamen, corydalis, dahlia, potato, tuberous begonia and some orchids) are solid swollen underground stems with growing points along the surface. Rhizomes (bearded iris, agapanthus, lily of the valley, hedychium, *Anemone nemorosa, Roscoea* spp.), although they look like roots, are actually swollen stems which grow horizontally beneath the soil surface.

Bulbs are resilient organs and can generally be bought with confidence that they will perform well when planted. Most bulbs, like ornamental onions (*Allium* spp.), tulips and daffodils, are protected by a tough protective tunic of dead scale leaves. On the other hand, the bulbs of some geophytes, like those of lilies and fritillaries, have no such protection, the bulb being composed of the naked fleshy scales. As a consequence, these bulbs can lose moisture or sustain damage readily during display in garden centres.

Lilies, in particular, are problematic in that they do not have a dormant phase. Whereas most of the garden geophytes are natives of hot dry areas such as Greece (crocus), Spain and North Africa (daffodils) and central Asia (tulips), with well-defined dormancy periods during the summer drought, lilies come largely from damp woodlands. Furthermore, lily bulbs do not arrive in the shops until after other bulbs, around late autumn, and poor weather conditions at that time can delay planting, meaning that the bulbs are stored for longer. If you need to store any bulbs for a time, unpack them and store them in damp peat to prevent dehydration.

Similarly, corms, tubers and (particularly) rhizomes are best not bought dry. The performance of *Anemone blanda* tubers can be improved by

The geophyte *Tulipa bakeri* 'Lilac Wonder', which grows from bulbs.

The geophyte *Crocus tommassinianus* 'Ruby Giant', which grows from corms.

The geophyte *Dactylorhiza maculata*, which grows from tubers.

The tubers of *Anemone blanda* can benefit from a soak in tepid water before planting.

soaking them in tepid water for an hour just before planting, but other species always perform poorly when planted as dry corms, such as dog's tooth violets, *Erythronium* spp. or tubers, like *Cyclamen hederifolium*. In the case of lilies, corms, tubers and rhizomes, therefore, it is preferable to source these from specialist growers, who will send the plants packed in moist packing material.

Otherwise, you are better off buying growing plants. This has the added advantages of being able to select desirable characters such as leaf pattern in cyclamen, and to avoid virus-infected plants, such as canna lilies infected by canna yellow mottle virus. Propagation by vegetative means, like bulbs, corms and rhizomes, unlike seed propagation, spreads virus infections (Chapter 7) which are only apparent when you can see the leaves.

Increasingly, spring-flowering geophytes such as snowdrops, winter aconites, wood anemone, dog's tooth violets and bluebells are being sold in bulk in full growth, freshly lifted from the field, a form described as 'in the green'. Most of these species do not fare well when sold as dry bulbs or corms, and 'in the green' is a cheap way of quickly establishing large colonies of woodland geophytes.

Erythronium americanum from North America.

Winter aconites, *Eranthis hyemalis.*

WHEN TO PLANT

Container-grown woody plants can be planted any time the ground is not frozen or waterlogged, although autumn and spring are still the most widely used times for planting. The two main parameters for deciding when to plant these are: when are the roots produced? and how hospitable will the conditions be, including the soil? For deciduous species, the general rule is to plant either in autumn on light soils (sufficient soil warmth and moisture to allow roots to develop) or in spring on heavy soils (to avoid the plant sitting in cold wet soil over the winter).

Evergreens are generally best planted in spring, so that they do not suffer the stresses of winter in the open ground before they have become established. For the same reasons planting of species from the scrub forest biome, such as woody herbs like rosemary and thyme, or from the temperate grassland biome, such as warm-season grasses, should be delayed until spring. Grasses, including bamboos, and evergreen monocots like iris and watsonia, generally start producing new roots from March to April and should be planted from spring to late summer.

Bareroot plants must be planted when still dormant; otherwise tissue damage can cause serious sap loss. In deciduous trees and shrubs, the plants break dormancy by responding to a combination of rising temperatures and increasing daylength in spring. Carbohydrate and protein food reserves in the roots, where they were stored over winter, are translocated in the sap to the shoots above ground. This provides the energy needed for bud break and leaf expansion.

Unfortunately, different species enter and leave dormancy at different dates, with birches breaking dormancy in February, some two months earlier than ash. Dormancy ends some two weeks before bud break is visible, by which time it can be too late to plant. If you cannot plant bareroot stock immediately, I have found that two- to three-year-old bareroot trees can be stored tied inside black bags in a cold room at around 4°C. In this way, the plants are not exposed to the environmental factors which trigger leaf growth, and will keep for at least four months without any detrimental effect before planting.

Spring-flowering bulbs and corms start to appear in shops and garden centres from August onwards. Bulbs should be planted when roots start to grow, with fritillaries planted in mid-August, most others in October, and hyacinths, lilies and tulips left until November (except the Madonna lily, *L. candidum*, which should be planted in August). Tulips can be planted as late as March; if they do not flower that year, they will the next.

TRANSPLANTING AND DIVISION

The final type of planting material to be dealt with here is transplants, where you need to move a plant within your garden or perhaps from another garden, and divisions, where a clump is split into a number of independent plants, to achieve both true-to-type propagation (Chapter 7) and regeneration of over-crowded specimens.

The extra problem to contend with here, compared with container-grown plants, is the damage suffered by the roots during transplantation. The importance of root hairs and mycorrhizal fungi, both easily damaged, to water uptake underlines the importance of maintaining moisture levels (by watering and by reducing losses).

In the past, it was recommended to transplant in winter when plants are dormant, but now it is considered that survival rate of shrubs and even quite large trees is highest when transplanting takes place between July and August. At this time, root growth is particularly vigorous and the soil is warm, allowing new roots to replace damaged ones and to take hold and establish in the new site before winter. Similar thinking is now occurring with regard to the best time to divide herbaceous perennials. If care is taken, most plants can be moved at any time of the year, though droughts and frosty weather should be avoided.

As to be expected, recently planted specimens move better than established plants, while smaller plants survive transplantation better than larger ones. For herbaceous perennials, plants with fibrous root systems transplant much better than those with taproots, such as *Verbascum*, *Digitalis* and *Echium* spp.

Oriental hellebores,
Helleborus × hybridus.

With shrubs and trees, the success of transplantation also depends on the species. Shallow-rooted plants like acers, rhododendrons, camellias, magnolias, skimmias and roses transplant reasonably easily. On the other hand, species with less fibrous and more spreading root systems, like apple and plum, often fail when transplanted because it can be difficult to preserve a large enough root system.

The rejuvenation of hardy perennials can be achieved by division. Clump-forming perennials, such as asters, corydalis, monardas, heleniums, hellebores and hostas, expand by development of new shoots at the outer edges of the clump. This often results in congestion of the shoots in the centre, where a woody core may develop. Division involves separation of the clump into independent shoots, each with its own root system, with the woody centre being discarded. As a consequence, one starving clump becomes several actively growing plants.

For grasses, bamboos and evergreen monocots, fibrous root growth starts in late spring, so division in April would be best as new shoots start to develop.

With hardy perennials, including dicot herbaceous perennials and non-grassy herbaceous monocots, the spring release of assimilates from the root reserves stimulates the formation of fine feeder roots from the larger anchor roots. This is followed by the formation of new anchor roots in mid-summer, which subsequently become storage sites for overwintering reserves in late summer and autumn. The best time to divide herbaceous perennials is June to July, after the feeder roots have formed and as the new anchor roots start to be produced.

The rationale behind this strategy tends to undermine the move towards dividing and moving clumps of spring-flowering bulbs, particularly snowdrops, 'in the green', from mid-March to mid-April as mentioned earlier. During flowering, the bulbs and corms are using the food reserves to power rapid leaf and flower growth.

In my experience, it is better to divide snowdrops etc. once the leaves have withered and the bulbs have become dormant, in late May to early June, although you will need to mark the clumps well before they die down. Buying bulbs 'in the green' is undoubtedly more successful than buying

A clump of the snowdrop
Galanthus nivalis
'Viridipice'.

dried bulbs, but dividing them repeatedly in this condition checks root growth and filling of the bulb reserves, and tends to slow establishment of the new clumps.

PREPARATION OF THE PLANTING SITE

Most root growth, even with trees, takes place in the upper 20cm or so of the soil, so emphasis should be placed on encouraging horizontal root spread. As a general rule, a planting hole 100 per cent wider than the plant's root system and 50 per cent deeper is appropriate. The aim with planting is to have the plant settled at the appropriate depth in the soil, with the roots able to start growing outwards and downwards as quickly as possible. A large root system will support a large above-ground stem structure, both physically, by providing anchorage, and physiologically, by triggering shoot growth.

On the other hand, for some plants root restriction is actually desirable to minimize shoot growth and maximize flower and fruit development (Chapter 5). Figs fruit best when root spread is restricted, so the planting hole is usually lined with blocks or stones. Other plants which perform best when roots are congested include bay trees, which are best grown in containers, and *Agapanthus*, where the greatest flowering display occurs when large congested clumps are allowed to develop.

Planting Depth

Planting at the wrong depth is one of the most common causes of plant death in a garden. For trees, if not fatal, too-deep planting can inhibit growth for decades.

When planting shrubs, trees and herbaceous perennials, the general guideline is to plant so the soil reaches the same level as in the container or soil. But, as with all guidelines, there are plenty of exceptions. Most grafted plants should be planted with the graft union above the soil level. On the other hand, some grafted plants, like tree paeonies, are recommended to be planted with the graft point 10cm below the soil, so that the scion can root. Herbaceous paeonies, on the other hand, need to be planted with the crown slightly above the soil surface; otherwise they will not flower.

The general rule for planting bulbs or corms is to plant at two to three times the height of the bulb. For example, a bulb measuring 5cm in height should be planted 15cm deep, with 10cm of soil above the top of the bulb. If in doubt with bulbs, it is always sensible to err on the side of greater depth, especially in light soils. Deep planting also protects bulbs from predation by slugs, mice or squirrels, and can protect tender bulbs from frosts.

But how does this happen in the wild? There, new plants of a geophyte will start life from a seed germinating on or near the soil surface. The seedling will eventually produce a bulb, for example, which can then re-position itself deeper by means

Erythronium californicum, another American dog's tooth violet.

A soil profile from a garden showing a layer of dark topsoil, then a lighter-coloured layer of subsoil.

of special contractile roots. In this way, some geo-phytes, like certain lily species, and particularly those producing corms such as *Crocosmia*, *Crocus* and *Erythronium*, can lower their position in the soil to a more appropriate location. *Erythronium* spp. can move down as much as 25cm deep and *Oxalis acetosella* further still, to 60cm. Cells in the cortex of these special contractile roots which develop in spring shorten and become fatter, causing the contraction.

Nerines, *Amaryllis* and *Crinum* and other South African geophytes, on the other hand, can raise their positions. In the garden, these species should be planted with their necks just above soil level to ensure good flowering.

Preparation of Planting Material

Prior to planting in spring, bareroot material (such as roses), bedding plants like wallflowers, and transplanted shrubs and climbers should be root pruned, cutting out damaged roots and cutting back healthy roots by approximately one-third, to encourage the development of new fibrous (feeder) roots.

Recent research from the University of Reading suggests that the roots of container-grown shrubs should be lightly pruned, cutting all the fine roots 10mm from the base of the rootball, rather than teased out, as is usually recommended. It was found that light pruning encouraged root growth, particularly that of lateral roots, and within eight weeks of transplanting produced plants with larger root systems than untreated plants or those where the roots were teased out. After root pruning (and transplanting and division, where roots are lost), leaf and stem material should also be cut back to restore the balance between the root and shoot systems and to reduce water demands due to transpiration, to allow the root system to recover.

Planting and the Use of Soil Amendments

When digging a planting hole, keep any light-col-oured subsoil from deep in the hole separate from the better quality darker topsoil (Chapter 4), by putting them in separate buckets and using mostly the better-quality topsoil to backfill the planting hole. The topsoil is that part of the soil where life tends to go on, in terms of plant roots and soil micro-organisms. A 15–20cm layer of topsoil is acceptable, while 30cm is good. Amendments, like grit, compost and nutrients, can be made to the back-fill soil (Chapter 4).

Another soil amendment which can be used when planting is mycorrhizal fungi. Garden soil will normally contain natural mycorrhizal fungi, but inoculation with commercial preparations can be very beneficial, increasing the uptake of water and nutrients (especially the poorly mobile phos-phorus) and helping to defend the roots against pests and pathogens.

Rose bushes planted into sites where roses have been grown before can suffer from 'rose sickness', possibly as a result of detrimental micro-organisms like nematodes building up in the soil. Inoculation of the root system of the new plant with appropri-ate mycorrhizal fungi has proved to be beneficial.

Generally, endomycorrhizal fungi colonize the roots of herbaceous perennials, while ectomycor-rhizal fungi are associated with the roots of trees and shrubs. A number of commercial mycorrhizal fungus inocula are available, and inoculation is simple. The required weight of inoculum is sprin-kled into the planting hole or onto the roots (if bareroot) so that it is in contact with the plant roots.

Generally, inoculation with mycorrhizal fungi helps the vigour of the inoculated plant both below and above ground. More specifically, mycorrhizal fungi are particularly appropriate for trees, hedges or shrubs which you may not be in a position to water regularly after planting, as inoculation will help the plant access water. Mycorrhized plants are also more efficient at extracting nutrients from soil, so are particularly appropriate where the soil is poor. When the Channel Tunnel was built, mycorrhized trees were used to plant the accompanying roadside verges, constructed from nutrient-poor sub-soil.

Firming In

Firming-in of the soil around the plant is important. Soil water forms a film around soil particles (Chapter 4), and these films need to be continuous to enable the plants to take up moisture. As one drop is taken up by the roots, the film moves towards the root. If the soil is not firmed in, this continuity is broken.

Excessive pressure would be detrimental, squeezing the air out of the soil. Some plants, on the other hand, relish very firm planting. Brassicas, particularly Brussels sprouts, and primroses are prime examples, and firming-in of these species can be best achieved with the aid of the handle of a trowel.

Support Your Plants

For trees over 1.5m tall, staking is usually necessary, at least for the first two years after planting, and particularly for single-trunk trees with a large leaf canopy. The aim is not to put the tree into a straitjacket but to allow it to flex and bend in the wind above the tie, inducing mechanical hardening. The stress associated with flexing of the trunk switches on genes in the trunk cells to mitigate this effect. This process results in some dwarfing and thickening of the trunk and the production of reaction wood which will withstand stress.

Chemical messages from the mechanically hardened stem also allow the root system to develop so that it anchors the tree firmly in place, at which time the stake and support can be removed. In nature, when the wind blows on the leaf canopy of a tree, the trunk of the tree moves in that direction. The corresponding part of the root system is compressed while the root system on the windward side is supporting the tree under tension. The

staking method recommended for garden trees allows this flexing of the trunk and subsequent development of the roots.

The need for a stake again highlights the problems associated with poor root development. Pot-grown trees, in particular, may fail to establish an adequate root system, unlike a tree grown from seed in the open ground. When did you last see a self-sown tree attached to a stake?

The stakes should be removed after one or two years, when the root system is established. Exceptions to this guideline should include trees with naturally small root systems such as fruit trees on dwarfing rootstocks (Chapter 7) like apple cultivars grafted on to 'M9' or 'M27' rootstock, which may need to remain staked for life, while those on semi-dwarfing rootstocks, such as 'M26' or 'MM106' will need staking for the first five years.

Climbers must be placed a suitable distance away from a wall (45cm) or a tree (60cm), so that the roots of the climber can develop fully, and with the stems angled towards it. When planting a climber to grow up another plant as support, always plant the climber on the shady side of the support plant because the climber will grow towards the light.

For the taller and more top-heavy herbaceous perennials, like lupins, dahlias and delphiniums, there is the risk of the flower stems collapsing (lodging), especially under the increasingly wet and windy conditions of summers in western Europe. Stems can be supported by staking, with a wide range of supports available. If set up early enough in the season, with the support downwind of the plant (in terms of the prevailing winds), not only will the supports hold up the plant, but the regular and repeated contact between the stems and the support brings about the natural phenomenon of mechanical hardening mentioned above. Regular bending of the top of the stem causes shortening of the stem and increased stem thickness, reducing the risk of lodging. One inexpensive arrangement I have found useful is split canes or short bamboos holding up a square of green Pea-and-Bean netting through which the shoots can grow, with the netting being moved up the canes if necessary as the plants grow.

CHAPTER 4

Soil, Water and Nutrients

Animals obtain their energy, nutrients and most of their organic chemicals from plants, either by eating plants directly or by consuming animals which have themselves eaten plants. When animals eat, they consume more than they need, in the form of water, proteins, carbohydrates, fats and other chemicals, and wastefully excrete the excess.

Plants, on the other hand, take up what they need in the simplest possible forms from the air (carbon dioxide and oxygen) and soil (nutrients and water) to make the more than 50,000 different organic chemicals they need. They do this by harnessing the energy from sunlight into storable and transportable chemical energy – a far more elegant and sophisticated system. To understand how plants use water and nutrients, and the process of effective watering and feeding, we will take a look at plant physiology, soil science, and some chemistry.

SOIL

An analysis of the soil characteristics of your garden is one of the most useful things you can do as a gardener, as it will provide you with information as to how much nutrient reserves are available, which plants you can grow well and which you cannot, how much watering you will need to do, and how easy the soil will be to work.

A detailed soil analysis includes soil type (how much sand, silt, clay and organic matter is present?), pH (how acidic or alkaline is the soil?)

A fallen sycamore leaf in autumn, showing the yellow carotenoids after degradation of the chlorophylls, which are retained for longest around the veins.

and nutrient content. Home test kits are readily available in garden centres for both pH and nutrients, particularly for the three most important macronutrients ('macro' because they are needed in large amounts). These are nitrogen (denoted on fertilizer packaging by the chemical symbol N), phosphorus (P) and potassium (K). Soil type can also be determined at home.

SOIL TYPE

The physical structure of soil is made up of four components: three are inorganic (clay, silt and sand) and one is organic (organic matter). Inorganic matter comes from non-living sources such as rocks, while organic matter comes from living organisms – the remains of dead plants and animals and their waste products.

Of the three main inorganic structural components, the size of particle increases from clay (the finest) to silt to sand (the coarsest). The characteristics of the soil particles affect how resources such as water, air and nutrients are supplied to the roots. In a soil with an ideal balance of clay, silt and sand, three-quarters of the soil space (the space between the particles) should consist of water while one-quarter (representing approximately 10 per cent of the total soil volume) should consist of air.

The smaller the soil particle, the more tightly they can pack together. This results in more water being trapped as a film around the particles, but less air. Clay-rich soils, with small particles and spaces, therefore, have a high water content but can suffer from poor aeration.

Air is essential for the activity of soil invertebrates,

such as earthworms, which help to further aerate the soil with their tunnelling, and micro-organisms, which help to decompose dead tissue in the soil, returning nutrients to the soil. Roots also need air to grow and to produce the energy needed to take up nutrients from the soil. That explains why lawns go yellow over winter, as waterlogging and low temperatures stop the roots from taking up nitrogen and other nutrients from the soil.

The high water content of clay soils makes them particularly susceptible to the 'heaving' effect following freezing and thawing of the soil. Water expands when it freezes, becoming less dense (which is why icebergs float). Frost heave results in root breakage and plants being lifted out of the soil after heavy frosts, and can be a particular problem with newly planted evergreens.

Sandy soils, at the other extreme, with large particles and large spaces between each particle, are well aerated but contain less water. In the same way, finer sands will hold more water than coarse sands, and silt particles are intermediate in character between clay and sand particles.

Apart from differences in size, the soil particles also differ in their ability to bind soil chemicals including water and nutrients. Clay particles are derived from minerals from rocks, and have negative charges on their surfaces.

As a result of having negative charges, clay particles will bind positively charged chemicals present in the soil, so that water and nutrients such as potassium, magnesium and calcium bind tightly. This means that clay particles act as reserves of such nutrients, as well as increasing the amount of water held in the soil. This binding between clay and water helps explain why soils with lots of clay hold on to water and are slow draining.

The clay-water bond is difficult for roots to break, so some of the water in clay soils can not be taken up by the plants. Sand and silt particles lack these binding sites and so have much smaller nutrient and water reserves than clay particles. On the other hand, most of the water held by silt or sand particles can be taken up by the roots.

Because each soil component has its own strengths and weaknesses, to achieve a good balance between drainage, fertility, water-holding capacity and aeration the ideal soil would be a mix of roughly 40 per cent sand, 40 per cent silt and 20 per cent clay. A lower percentage of clay is needed because it has a disproportionately large effect on soil characteristics. Such a mix is termed a loam. If there is more sand than 40 per cent, it is a sandy loam; if more than 40 per cent silt, it is a silty loam.

'Textural analysis' will give you a good idea of the type of soil you have. It is fairly straightforward to identify the soil type. Take a sample of top soil from the top 10 to 15cm of the soil, because that is the zone where most of the biological activity, including roots, goes on.

With a clean used washing-up liquid bottle, gradually add water a few drops at a time into the soil and let the water be absorbed until it can take no more (do not over-do the water). Gently rub the soil between your thumb and fingers. A gritty feel indicates that sand is dominant; a silky texture indicates silt; while a sticky feel indicates clay. Those who garden on clay soils will know the tenacious way that the soil clings to the spade or your boots. The main texture (gritty, silky or sticky) tells you the dominant component of your soil.

The malleability of the damp soil sample will help you pinpoint the soil type. Try to roll the soil into a ball. If the ball falls apart readily, the soil is predominantly sand. If a ball can be formed, the soil has more silt or clay than sand. If you can roll the ball into a stable sausage shape, but it breaks when you try to bend it into a ring, then the soil is mainly silty. If the sausage can be bent into a ring without breaking, then the soil is clay-rich, as the fine particles pack together so well

WHAT KIND OF SOIL IS IT?

Result when sample rolled	**Type of Soil**
No ball forms	Sand or sandy loam
Ball forms but no sausage	Silt or silty loam
Ball, sausage form but no ring	Silty loam
Ball, sausage and ring form	Clay or clay loam

Organic Matter

If you suspend a sample of dried and sieved soil in water and leave it to settle, the particles will settle out in the order of size: sand after about two minutes, silt after two hours and clay after two days. At that point, you will note that some longer brown particles will stay floating on the top of the water. This material is organic matter, which is usually present at between 1 and 10 per cent of the soil content.

In gardens, organic matter is mostly the decomposed remains of dead plant tissues (including leaves, fruits, roots and petals), plus the remains of the occasional small animal.

These sources of organic matter are acted on by soil invertebrates. Earthworms draw material into the soil, while small creatures, like springtails, millipedes and wood lice reduce it into smaller pieces by feeding. Finally, soil micro-organisms, primarily bacteria, but also fungi, finish the job. The soil organisms remove most of the readily available nutrients from the tissue, leaving the structural remains (mostly cellulose and lignin from plant tissue) in the soil as organic matter or humus. As a result, soil is produced in natural ecosystems at a rate of between 10 and 50g per square metre each year. The same process occurs in compost heaps, with completely rotted compost being well on its way to soil.

The organic matter plays several beneficial roles in the soil. First of all, it is a source of nutrients. Plants take up nutrients from the soil as inorganic forms and convert them into organic forms. As a result, organic matter is a slow-release source of organic plant nutrients, gradually converted by bacteria back into inorganic forms which the plants can take up when soil conditions (temperature, water, air and pH) are suitable.

The nutrients in a soil with a high organic matter content are less likely to be washed away and lost when it rains. This is because organic matter, like clay particles, carry negatively charged sites on their surface which bind positively charged nutrients present in the soil, such as magnesium, calcium, ammonium (another inorganic form of nitrogen) and potassium.

Organic matter also helps to improve the condition of the soil. Almost magically, it can make heavy clay-rich soils freer draining and make light sand-rich soils more water- and nutrient-retentive. In clay soils, organic matter helps the tiny individual clay particles to join together into larger groupings called micelles. This leads to the formation of larger pores between the micelles, and improves soil drainage through these pores as well as increasing the amount of air in the soil.

In a sandy soil, organic matter acts like a sponge, absorbing and holding water. The negative charges on organic matter also help it to bind water. A small increase in the organic matter content of a light soil can have a large effect on the amount of the water the soil can hold. Incorporation of approximately 4kg organic matter per square metre will double the water-holding capacity of most soils. Indeed, increasing the organic matter content of a soil to 5 per cent or more will largely mask any differences in water-holding characteristics caused by the soil components, sand, silt or clay.

As a consequence, the characteristics of soils with organic matter contents of 10 per cent or higher tend to be determined largely by the organic component. Soils with 10–20 per cent organic matter are termed organic soils, followed by peaty loams (20–30 per cent), loamy peats (35–50 per cent) and finally peaty soils (>50 per cent).

For very heavy clay-rich soils, drainage is best improved by incorporation of large particles, namely grit, rather than organic matter, which can sit undecomposed in such soils. For large-scale use, the grade of grit used by local authorities for treating iced roads is effective and more economical, but remember that addition of large amounts of nutrient-free grit will reduce the nutrient content of the soil.

Seaweed meal is another excellent organic soil conditioner. The carbohydrate gels which make damp seaweed slimy to the touch can bind small soil particles together to improve drainage.

The drainage of a clay soil can also be improved by adding calcium compounds such as limestone. The positively charged calcium binds to the negatively charged clay particles, forming larger groupings of clay particles, with larger pores between them. You can see this by adding a few drops of limewater, made by dissolving ground limestone (calcium carbonate) in water, to a suspension of a clay soil. The cloudiness of the suspension will clear quickly as the clay particles connect together or 'flocculate', become heavier and sink to the bottom of the container. However, addition of limestone to soil will raise the pH, making it more alkaline, which may not be desirable. Gypsum, which is calcium sulphate, will improve the soil characteristics without affecting its pH.

SOIL pH

The term pH, from the French term 'puissance d'Hydrogène', meaning 'the power of hydrogen', is a measure of acidity or alkalinity. Values for pH range from 1 (extremely acidic) to 14 (extremely alkaline or basic), with pH 7 being neutral (neither acidic nor alkaline). Most gardens would have soil pH values between 5.5 (moderately acidic) and 7.5 (slightly alkaline or basic). A soil pH of 6.5 is widely considered to be the ideal, especially for vegetable gardens.

Soil pH testing kits are widely available in garden centres and are easy to use. A more indirect indicator of soil pH is the hardness of your water. Water (and soil) with a high pH has a high calcium content and is known as 'hard water'. It is characterized by being difficult to form into a lather with soap and by furring up the electrical element in kettles. In some metropolitan areas, like Birmingham, the water may come from far away and may not be a good indicator of the local soil pH.

The flower colour of hydrangeas in neighbouring gardens is also a useful indicator of local soil pH. If there are pale pink but no blue flowers in the area, it is likely that the soil is alkaline or neutral, whereas if there are blue flowers but no pale pink ones, the soil is acidic (*see* pages 196–7).

Another indicator of a neutral to high-pH soil would be the dominance of snails over slugs. The snail shell is made partly of calcium carbonate, so the animal needs a high-Ca, high-pH soil

Soil pH is measured on a logarithmic scale, which means that a pH difference of 1 unit, say from pH 6 to pH 7, represents a 10-fold difference in acidity, while a pH difference of 2

units represents a 100-fold difference, so do not underestimate the effects of changes in soil pH. The effects of soil pH on plant growth and vigour usually arise because of the effect of pH on the solubility of soil chemicals, so there can be problems of nutrient deficiency or toxicity when the soil is at an inappropriate pH (*see* page 89).

Soil pH is usually regulated by the concentrations of calcium. These bind to the negative charges on clay particles. If most of the charged clay particles bind calcium, then the soil is neutral or alkaline. On the other hand, if they predominantly bind hydrogen, then the soil is acidic.

Alkaline (high pH) soils are common over basic (or alkaline) bedrocks, such as limestone or chalk, which are rich in calcium, and, as a result, alkaline soils are often referred to as lime or chalk soils. Alkaline soils lying over limestone will have a maximum pH of around 8.2, but chalky soils can have even higher pH values.

A chalky soil is a light free-draining soil because the bedrock is porous, letting water through. It usually has a rather shallow topsoil. For gardening, chalky soils have a number of limitations, such as low reserves of water and nutrients as well as low availability of some nutrients such as iron. The free-draining nutrient-poor nature of chalky soils makes them highly suitable for many native plants of the scrub forest biome, particularly those from the Mediterranean region.

Acidic (low pH) soils are common in high-rainfall areas where elements such as calcium and magnesium, which help to keep soil pH high, are washed away. They are also found over acidic bedrocks, such as granite and sandstone, which supply very little calcium. Very acidic soils would have pH values of 4.5–5.0.

Under acidic conditions, bacteria die off, so decomposition of dead plant tissues is very slow, leading to the accumulation of incompletely decomposed plant material. This leads, in extreme cases, to the formation of peat and low levels of soil nutrients such as nitrogen. Plants adapted to such sites have to get their nutrients, particularly nitrogen, from other sources. Nitrogen-fixing plants, insectivorous plants and ericaceous plants with specialized ericoid mycorrhiza all find ways around this problem.

WATER

We all know that plants need water. Water is the most important chemical in a plant, as most of the processes which take place in plants occur in the cell water or cytoplasm (Chapter 1). Water also carries chemicals around the plant and is the principal cooling agent. Water is vital to the most important process in plants, photosynthesis, by which carbon dioxide and water are converted into sugars.

We have all seen non-woody plants become limp when not supplied with enough water. This occurs because water provides physical support to these plants. In plant organs which last for only one season, such as annual plants and the stems of herbaceous perennials, much of the stiffness of the organs is due to water within the cells. The water inside each plant cell presses against the cell wall, like the elastic inner tube of a bicycle tyre pressing against the more rigid outer wall of the tyre. If the plant loses water, this pressure drops and the plant becomes limp.

WATER UPTAKE

By far the main route by which water is taken up by plants is through the root system. The roots of epiphytic orchids, which live on the branches of other plants, have evolved a thick multi-layered epidermis of dead cells called the velamen which acts to absorb water. Leaves can also take up water and the chemicals dissolved in it. This 'foliar treatment' route is a very useful method for feeding plants with rapid effects, such as to overcome some of the symptoms of stress.

Some leaves can readily take up water across the leaf epidermis. On the other hand, species from dry climates have evolved thick waxy cuticles on top of the epidermis, evident as shiny or blue-grey leaf surfaces, to reduce water loss. It is impossible for these leaves to take up water across the leaf epidermis.

An alternative way of taking up water through such leaves is via hydathodes, pores at the edges of leaves which represent the openings of leaf veins. Many leaves with toothed margins trap water from

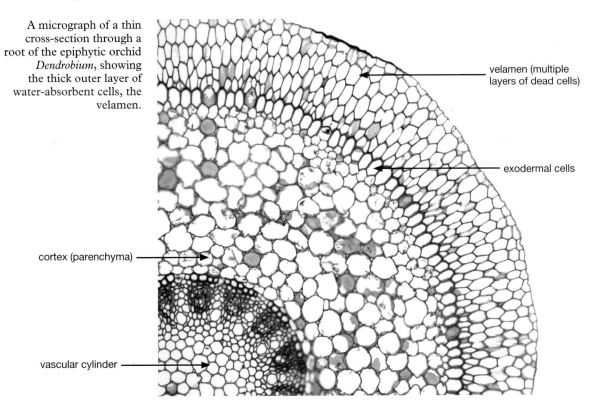

A micrograph of a thin cross-section through a root of the epiphytic orchid *Dendrobium*, showing the thick outer layer of water-absorbent cells, the velamen.

velamen (multiple layers of dead cells)

exodermal cells

cortex (parenchyma)

vascular cylinder

Frost marking out the margins of ivy leaves, resulting from water trapped in margin hairs.

the air and take it in through hydathodes. In cold weather, the frost which forms around the edges of some leaves, like those of ivy, periwinkle etc., is frozen water trapped around the hydathodes. Some plants from dry habitats harvest water efficiently. The concave upper surfaces of hyacinth leaves, for example, channel rainwater to the bulb and roots, an advantage in their home in the eastern Mediterranean and north Africa.

Vascular land plants have evolved a highly efficient system for taking up water from the soil and transporting it from the roots to the topmost part of the plant. This distance can be up to 150m in the tallest trees, the coastal redwoods (*Sequoia giganteum*) of California.

Water in the soil moves through the soil pores from areas of damp soil to drier soil, in the same way as water spreads outwards from a drop placed on absorbent paper. When the root takes up water from the soil, this dries the soil around the root and creates a water gradient, so that water in the soil migrates to the drier region in the root zone. To take up water, the root must break the attraction between water and the soil particles. This is more difficult in clay soils, where the water is actually bound to the clay particles, than in silty or sandy soils.

Water moves from the soil across the root cell membrane into the root (usually via a root hair) by a process known as osmosis. Water can pass in

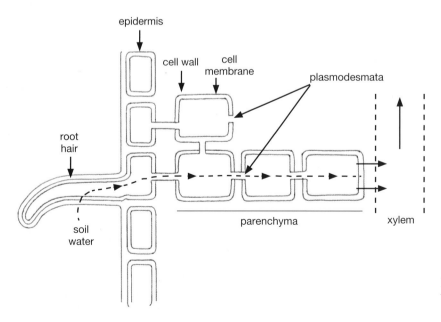

How plant roots take up water.

either direction (soil to root or *vice versa*) through the root cell wall and membrane. Water is the only chemical which moves equally freely via osmosis through a plant membrane in either direction, into or out of the cell, with the dissolved chemicals being kept on either side of the membrane.

With osmosis, water moves from a solution containing a low concentration of dissolved chemicals to one with a high concentration, in order to equalize chemical concentration on either side of the membrane. The chemicals on one side do not have to be the same chemicals as those on the other side. If the concentration of chemicals in the soil water is less than that in the root cell, then water will pass through the membrane into the root cell, resulting in water uptake.

As the soil dries, the decrease in water content means that the concentration of chemicals in the soil water increases, making it more difficult for the plant to maintain the low-to-high chemical gradient from the soil to the root needed to allow water uptake. The resulting reduction in water uptake will result in less water in the cell and therefore a higher chemical concentration in the root cell.

This increased concentration re-establishes the gradient, allowing further water uptake, but there is a limit to how high a chemical concentration a plant cell can endure before it becomes toxic, limiting how much drought a plant can put up with. Plants from dry ecosystems, like the scrub forest or sand dunes, accumulate special non-toxic chemicals called osmoprotectants so that they can continue to take up water from very dry soils.

Addition of high levels of soluble chemicals like table salt, sodium chloride, to the soil causes non-woody plants to wilt because they make it impossible for the roots to establish a gradient to allow the roots to take up water. The Romans took out their vengeance on conquered cities by salting the earth to make it unsuitable for growing crops.

MOVEMENT OF WATER AROUND THE PLANT

Water taken up by the roots enters the xylem part of the vascular system and from there travels around the plant. This process (translocation) is achieved by the water being both pushed and, in particular, pulled up the xylem against the effects of gravity.

Getting water to the top of a 150m sequoia requires a pressure of around 450–500 pounds per square inch (psi). To put this in perspective, a tyre on an average family car is inflated to a pressure of 28–32 psi.

A minor contributor (40–50 psi) to this pressure within the trunk is root pressure. Movement (by osmosis) of water into the root cells builds up pressure in the cell as the water presses against the cell wall, pushing water up the xylem. This process can result in drops of xylem sap being pushed through the hydathodes, a process known as guttation. An obvious example of root pressure would be the drops of water on tips of grass leaves early in the morning; unlike dew, this water comes from the plant itself.

The main source of pressure needed to move water up a plant, however, comes from transpiration, which pulls water up the xylem. The principal function of transpiration is to cool the plant, by allowing water to evaporate from the leaves, similar to perspiration in people. Water molecules form an unbroken column within the xylem cells, from the roots to the leaf cells. Chemical bonds between neighbouring water molecules within the xylem make water able to withstand being stretched, giving water the greatest tensile strength of any liquid. This cohesion between water molecules is also seen if you over-fill a glass with water. The water will form a layer above the glass rim because of surface tension.

When the stomata in the leaf are open, there is a gradient of water concentration between air inside the leaf (high moisture content) and the outside air (low moisture content), so water evaporates from the leaf cells into the surrounding air. As a consequence, when one molecule of water evaporates from a leaf cell and out through a stoma (transpiration), another water molecule is taken up by the root from the soil to replace it.

Water translocation is very rapid, up to 50m per hour in broad-leaved trees. The transpiration pressure is so high that tree trunk diameters in the summer shrink during the day when the stomata

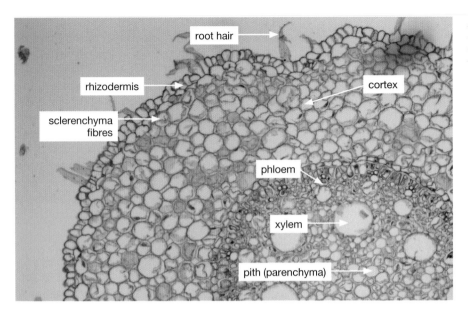

A micrograph of a thin cross-section of root of sweetcorn, showing the vascular system.

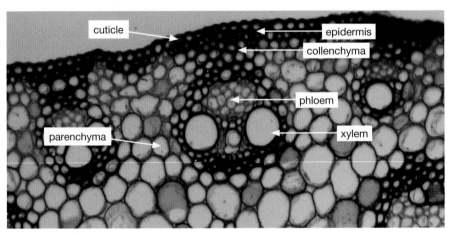

A micrograph of a thin cross-section of stem of sweetcorn, showing the vascular system.

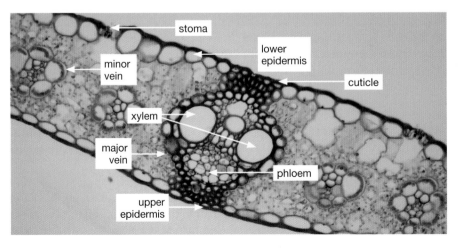

A micrograph of a thin cross-section of leaf of sweetcorn, showing the vascular system. Note the continuity of xylem and phloem from the roots to the leaf.

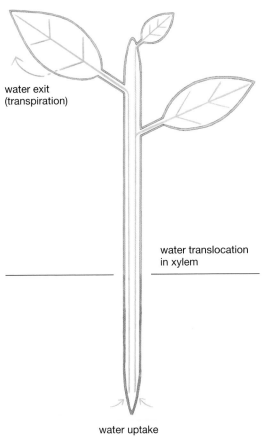

water exit
(transpiration)

water translocation
in xylem

water uptake

How transpiration controls water uptake.

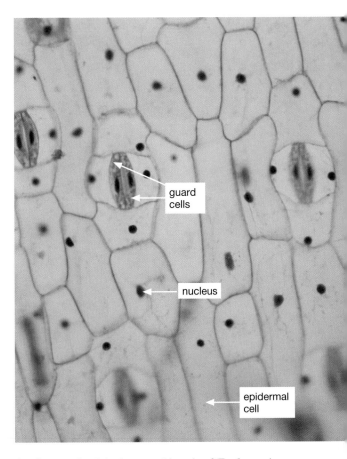

guard
cells

nucleus

epidermal
cell

A micrograph of the lower epidermis of *Tradescantia virginiana*, showing stomata surrounded by kidney-shaped guard cells.

open, when transpiration and translocation take place, then recover at night when the stomata close.

For every gramme of water lost by transpiration, 570 calories of heat energy is also lost, so the plant cools down. The effectiveness of transpiration as a cooling mechanism is illustrated if you walk into your garden in bare feet on a hot sunny day after any dew has evaporated from the lawn. Any paved area will be warm, maybe hot to the touch, but the lawn, exposed to the same conditions as the patio, will be pleasantly cool.

Transpiration cools plants which have plentiful supplies of water, even if the leaf is cooler than the surrounding air. The cooling effect of transpiration is being exploited in buildings with planted roofs (green roofs), where the plants reduce the temperature of the roof by both transpiration and shading. On hot days in Chicago, the temperature on the green roof on the City Hall can be up to 44°C (112°F) lower than that on a conventional roof nearby.

The density of stomata on leaves ranges from 10,000 to 50,000 per cm^2, and they are mostly on the cooler undersurface of leaves. Exceptions include erect leaves like grasses, which have similar stomatal densities on both the upper and lower surfaces, and the leaves of aquatic plants, where all the stomata are on the upper surface.

The method used to re-invigorate a limp butter-head lettuce illustrates how plants take up and lose water through their leaves. If the head of lettuce is immersed for 30–40 minutes in water at room temperature, not cold water as usually recommended,

WATER UPTAKE BY CUT FLOWERS

When picking flowers for the house, it is important to ensure that there are sufficient intact xylem vessels in the stem tissue at the base of the flower to conduct water to the flower. The usual cause of drooping in cut flowers within a day is that, when the stem is cut, the unbroken chain of water molecules is fractured and air enters the xylem at the cut surface, preventing further water uptake and translocation. This is the reason we are encouraged to condition cut flowers by cutting a further 1–2cm from the bottom of each cut stem and immersing it in water, to remove the section where air has entered the xylem.

If wilting occurs 3–4 days after the flowers were put into water, this is usually caused not by air blockages but by bacteria multiplying in the water and blocking the vascular bundles. The water in the vase will usually be cloudy due to the presence of billions of bacteria. Changing the water and adding anti-bacterial agents which can be found in proprietary cut flower foods can extend the life of these flowers.

For many bulbous plants, the apparent 'stalk' of the flower is nothing of the kind. In *Colchicum* and *Crocus*, the 'flower stalk' is the perianth tube, a continuation of the petals (*see* Chapter 1). In the Algerian iris, *Iris unguicularis*, the 'flower stalk' is actually the style of the flower, that part of the female sex organ which connects the ovary to the stigma where the pollen lands, hence the old name *Iris stylosa*.

In these cases, there is no xylem in the 'flower stalk' to conduct water to the petals, so these cut flowers do not last long in water. With the iris, there is a short length of stem (approximately 2cm long) at ground level, but this usually also carries one or two flower buds below the point of attachment of the flower, which must be left so that they develop into flowers in the garden. To cut these iris flowers for the house, part the leaf sheaths, feel for the buds below the open flower and cut the stem above the buds but below the open flower.

it will take up water through the leaf surface and stomata, increasing the pressure within the leaves, which will become turgid. The lettuce should then be transferred to ice-cold water, which will close the leaf stomata to prevent the water being lost.

WATERING PLANTS EFFICIENTLY

Some 98 per cent of water taken up by a plant is lost by transpiration, to achieve uptake and translocation of water and soil nutrients, and to cool plants. A mature broad-leaved tree under sunny but breezy conditions can lose 1,000 litres of water per day, while a modest 100m^2 lawn would use 50,000 litres of water (weighing 50 tonnes) in a year. On a smaller scale, a moderately leafy herbaceous perennial, such as a dahlia, can use 5 litres of water each day over the summer. This underlines the importance of keeping plants well watered, particularly newly planted specimens whose roots may have been damaged (*see* Chapter 3).

The invention of the garden hose some sixty years ago allowed gardeners the luxury of applying water to their gardens with minimal effort. Efficient use of water is becoming increasingly important to conserve limited water resources and to save time and money spent in watering. Inappropriate watering (too much or too little, or at the wrong time or place) can also increase pest and disease problems, reduce flower, fruit and vegetable production (and their quality) and can damage the soil.

What to Water

Only some plants in the garden need to be watered on a regular basis. Generally, lawns with cool-season grasses such as the species of *Lolium* (ryegrasses), *Poa* (meadow grasses) and *Festuca* (fescues) which dominate in gardens in western Europe will turn brown in colour under very dry conditions in Europe and (particularly) North America, but this is dormancy, a strategy for escaping stress, not death.

Dormant growth buds of the grasses under the soil will spring into life when rain occurs. Watering the lawn would prevent the grasses from becoming dormant but is not an effective use of scarce resources. The only exceptions to this guideline are for newly laid or seeded lawns, which could be killed by drought stress. For this reason, autumn is the better time for laying new lawns, as lawns prepared in the spring always require supplemental water.

Most young plants are more drought sensitive than are older plants. Seedlings, newly planted and particularly transplanted or divided specimens may not have developed a sufficiently active root system with which to take up water by the time they need to cope with drought. Handling of the roots will damage the root hairs which contribute so much to the water uptake by young plants (Chapter 3).

Transplanted woody specimens will benefit from watering for up to two years after planting. This is particularly true for evergreens. For sites where regular watering may not be possible, inoculation of the root system with appropriate mycorrhizal fungi can be helpful.

Crops with high water demands include leafy crops (with a high area for transpiration) such as cauliflower, lettuce, celery, coriander, parsley and maincrop potato, and fruit crops like tomato and sweet pepper, as well as soft fruit crops. With crops like tomato and pepper, the number of cells in each fruit is determined at a very early stage, so that mature fruit size is a reflection of the increase in size of each cell, which depends largely on water supply.

Other plant groups which benefit particularly from watering include:

- Plants with shallow root systems: legumes (peas, beans etc.), monocots (ornamental grasses, in particular), and trees and shrubs like cornus, acers, ericaceous shrubs, *Betula* spp. and magnolia;
- Fast-growing ornamentals with large leaves from high rainfall areas: bananas, canna lilies and bamboos;
- Annuals from the scrub forest (hardy annuals), temperate grassland (hardy annuals) and tropical grassland biomes (half-hardy annuals); many of these species will continue to flower until the first

frosts if premature death is not triggered by summer drought as it would be in their native habitat;
- Plants susceptible to powdery mildew: monarda, phlox and asters are vulnerable to this disease, caused by closely related but different pathogens, which is exacerbated by drought;
- Fruit trees grafted on dwarfing rootstocks (Chapter 7): the reduced topgrowth is mirrored in a smaller-than-usual root system, so supplementary watering (and feeding) is necessary;
- Container-grown plants: high plant densities increase water demand, while small containers also have limited water reserves.

On the other hand, woody herbs such as thyme and rosemary from the scrub forest biome (Chapter 2) are effective drought avoiders and have the strongest flavour when 'grown hard', without excessive water or nutrient additions.

When to Water

Evening watering allows the build-up of water reserves before transpiration starts in the morning because stomata are largely closed at night, decreasing transpiration greatly. On the other hand, damp soil and leaves at night encourages slugs and snails, increasing the risk of pest damage. If you are planning to cut flowers, water the plants the evening before, then cut the now-fully hydrated stems in early morning.

For most spring-flowering geophytes, watering triggers growth. Generally, these plants need a dry summer period when they are dormant, then watering from early September onwards as roots start to form.

Source of Water

In areas where the local tapwater is 'hard' (rich in calcium), collected rainwater is particularly appropriate for watering lime-hating species, primarily the members of the heather family (Ericaceae). Rainwater is also preferable to tap water for watering carnivorous plants in all areas because of the detrimental effect on these plants of dissolved minerals in tap water.

On the other hand, stored rainwater should be

avoided when watering seeds or seedlings, as the fungi which cause damping-off disease of seedlings are aquatic and can flourish in still bodies of water like those found in barrels.

Where to Water

To maximize the efficiency of using water, it should be directed to the roots. Placing the plant in a small depression in the soil helps to direct irrigation water (or rainfall) to the roots. Directing water at the roots also avoids wetting the leaves, which would encourage the development of fungal diseases such as downy mildew and potato blight (Chapter 7).

Some plants need water to be applied at other, specific locations. The trunk of tree ferns like *Dicksonia antarctica* is actually a vertical enlarged rhizome known as a caudex. Roots which form in the soil at the base of the caudex have largely an anchoring function, while most of the water- (and nutrient-) absorbing function is carried out by the caudex. It is important therefore to water the trunk of tree ferns, especially in dry weather. Nutrient solution and water can be applied occasionally to the crown at the top of the trunk, but this should not be carried out routinely as it risks rotting the crown.

An understanding of root development and function also allows gardeners to use water more efficiently. The ring culture system for growing crops such as tomatoes and peppers in containers uses two containers, one small bottomless pot (10–14cm diameter) set inside a larger pot (30cm diameter) or Gro-Bag. Because surface fibrous roots take up nutrients while deeper roots, such as taproots, are designed to access water, nutrient solutions are applied to the inner pot while watering is carried out in the outer container. This reduces the amount of nutrients applied and prevents dilution of the nutrient solution by watering.

HOW TO REDUCE WATER LOSSES

Some of the water entering the garden ecosystem is lost by one of three main routes:

- water percolating to levels in the soil below the active root zone of the plants, so that it is not available for uptake;
- water lost by evaporation from soil surfaces;
- water lost by transpiration from the plant.

Each of these can be reduced using simple precautions.

Deep Percolation of Water

Most of the root activity in a garden is in the top 15cm or so of the topsoil. Steps which can be taken to reduce water percolating to below this root zone include increasing the size of the active root zone, by encouraging deep root growth, and increasing the ability of the soil to hold water. A deep root system is encouraged by preparing a good planting hole (Chapter 3) and by watering occasionally but deeply, to a depth of 20–25cm, to encourage roots to move downwards in search of water.

When growing seedlings of shallow-rooted plants like legumes, it is important to encourage downward expansion of the root system. This can be achieved by using deep pots, and by watering the pots from the bottom by using capillary matting to wick water into the lower reaches of the compost. These precautions will give the young plant a good start when transplanted into the open ground.

Because of the positive association between the size of the shoot and root systems of a plant (Chapter 3), raising the cutter height of the lawnmower also increases the size of the root system, so that the grasses are better able to withstand summer drought.

Of the soil characteristics which affect the ability of soil to hold water in a form available to plant roots (particle size, particle charge, organic matter content), only organic matter content of the soil can be readily increased by the gardener. Organic matter in the form of well-composted animal manure, garden compost, municipal composted green waste or spent mushroom compost will add organic matter as well as nutrients, and the effect is greatest on light sand-rich soils. The organic matter should be applied to a depth of 8–10cm over the soil. It can then be incorporated by digging it into the soil, or by leaving it as a surface mulch, from where soil invertebrates, such as earthworms, will incorporate it.

Legumes like beans and peas tend to have shallow root systems, presumably because their ability to fix atmospheric nitrogen, with help from friendly bacteria, means they do not have to scavenge for nitrogen by having large root systems. Addition of organic matter in the form of kitchen waste, even damp newspapers, to the bottom of the planting trench is often recommended for such plants as it serves to increase the water-holding capacity of the soil.

In a new garden with poor soil, where you may not have the opportunity to make much garden compost, a green manure crop can be very useful for increasing the organic matter content. Green manure crops are shallow-rooted, quick-growing plants sown for the sole purpose of being chopped up and dug into the soil before they flower. Species are available which are suitable for spring sowing, such as mustard, or autumn sowing, like rye. In addition, nitrogen-fixing green manures, such as red clover, can be grown which add nitrogen to the soil.

The plant material will decompose to leave organic matter. (There will be no increase in nutrient content of the soil as a result of a green manure crop, except for nitrogen in the case of nitrogen fixers.) Dense sowing of one or two successive green manure crops, particularly rye (not ryegrass), will also help to control weeds in a new garden (Chapter 6).

Evaporation from the Soil Surface

Water evaporates particularly quickly from damp bare soil. The main method for reducing evaporation is the use of surface mulches on the soil to cover any bare soil.

There are two principal classes of mulch available:

- organic mulches: compost, manure, mushroom compost, straw, hay, chipped bark, grass clippings, wood chippings, shredded leaves, cocoa shells;

- inorganic mulches: stones, gravel, slate, grit, glass beads, crushed glass or even crushed CDs.

Although the use of mulches is described here as a way of improving water use efficiency, it is also widely used as a way of controlling annual weeds, to prevent disease infection (Chapter 6), to stabilize soil and to reduce the risks of ground frosts in the winter. Unfortunately, no one mulch can carry out all the beneficial functions listed above, and your choice of material may also be influenced by cost, availability and aesthetics.

Basically, the larger the particles of the mulch, the more air and the less water the spaces between the particles can hold, in the same way as with soil. A fine mulch will have a lot of water between the particles, so that there is a continuous layer of water from soil surface to mulch surface. When water evaporates from the mulch it will drag more moisture up from the soil, so that evaporation losses from the soil are not greatly reduced. With a coarse mulch, on the other hand, there is mostly air between the particles, so that coarse mulches help to reduce evaporation. They also act as a duvet, reducing the risk that the underlying soil will freeze during the winter.

To reduce water evaporation, therefore, organic mulches should be coarse and open. Examples of coarse mulches include cocoa shells, shredded leaves, coarsely chipped bark, chopped straw and hay, though the latter two are of more value in vegetable gardens than ornamental gardens because of their appearance. Coarse mulches are also an effective way of controlling annual weeds, allowing in-soil storage of tender tubers such as dahlia, *Cosmos atrosanguineus*, and tuberous begonias, and keeping winter damp from the collars or crowns of plants.

On the other hand, coarse mulches are ineffective in preventing ground frost damage. The open nature of these mulches prevents conduction of heat from deeper parts of the soil to the mulch surface which could reduce the radiation heat losses associated with ground frost.

Logically enough, fine mulches, which include finely chipped bark, well-rotted composts and manure, and the fine inorganic materials like fine gravel have the opposite characteristics. Fine mulches are particularly effective on sloping sites as they are less likely to be blown or washed away, and will also provide fewer hiding places than open mulches for pests, such as snails and slugs, but more opportunities for annual weed seeds.

All organic mulches absorb water during rainfall or irrigation, reducing the benefits of watering the plants. In the converse of the situation for reducing evaporation, coarse mulches are less efficient than fine mulches at delivering water to the soil underneath. For this reason, mulch must be applied when the soil is damp.

A solution to watering when the mulch is in place is to place open-ended pipes (or plastic bottles with the bottom cut off) through the mulch and into the soil next to particularly drought-vulnerable plants. The pipe directs water to the roots of the plant. (This can also reduce loss by evaporation from non-mulched soil). For similar reasons, the plants should be fed before applying a mulch. Subsequent feeding can be achieved by use of foliar sprays, like seaweed preparations, where nutrients are taken up through the leaves rather than the roots, or by scraping back the mulch, then top-dressing and finally replacing the mulch.

Other factors to be considered for different organic mulches include nutrient content and decomposition rate. Fully decomposed manure and composts, as well as cocoa shells, are mulches which provide low (compost) to high (manure) levels of nutrients. Mulches such as non-composted bark, with very low nitrogen levels but compostable material like carbohydrates, can reduce the amount of soil nitrogen available to plants, resulting in nitrogen theft (*see* page 89). Fine mulches decompose more rapidly than coarse mulches, because the small particles have a larger surface area for decomposers to work on. As a result, finely chipped bark has to be replaced more frequently than coarsely chipped bark.

Inorganic mulches have advantages over organic materials in that they do not absorb water, are usually heavy enough to resist moving or being blown around, and provide an inhospitable home for annual weeds. Light-coloured materials can reflect light and heat, while larger grade gravel can deter cats. Coarser materials, such as 10–20mm gravel, reduce evaporation effectively when used at thicknesses of 5–8cm, while finer gravel is more appropriate for top-dressing spring bulbs and alpines.

Transpiration

The amount of water in a plant is determined by the amount taken up and the amount lost by transpiration. Indeed, as we have seen, losing water is a pre-requisite for taking up water containing nutrients from the soil. The rate of water loss is highest under windy, warm and dry conditions, and precautions need to be taken to minimize transpiration losses, especially from newly planted specimens, where damage to the root system may also limit water uptake.

Evergreen plants are particularly vulnerable to drying out. Although we tend to see hot sunny days as those where plants will be short of water, winter conditions, especially for containerized plants, can also be stressful, with windy weather increasing transpiration while frozen soil reduces water uptake.

A windbreak around recently planted specimens will allow a boundary layer of moist air around the leaves to build up, reducing the moisture gradient between the atmosphere within the leaf and the dry air outside. This reduces the rate of transpiration.

NUTRIENTS

All living organisms, plants, animals and micro-organisms, are composed of a wide range of natural chemicals. These chemicals serve as sources of energy, structural components like cell walls and membranes, enzymes (proteins which speed up biochemical reactions to make more chemicals), growth factors such as hormones, or miscellaneous but important chemicals like the DNA from which genes are made. These chemicals are made up of smaller components known as elements, which we have already encountered, such as nitrogen and potassium.

Nutrition is an aspect over which gardeners have a particular influence by applying nutrient sources, such as garden compost, animal manure or synthetic fertilizers, to the soil. We begin with a description of the various elements used by plants.

MACRO-NUTRIENTS AND MICRO-NUTRIENTS

This planet contains some ninety-two different chemical elements, more than sixty of which have been found in plants. Of these, seventeen are essential to all vascular plants, and they fall into two classes:

- nine macronutrients, which plants need in large amounts: carbon (chemical symbol C), hydrogen (H), nitrogen (N), oxygen (O), potassium (K), phosphorus (P), calcium (Ca), magnesium (Mg), sulphur (S);
- eight micronutrients (or trace elements) which are needed in smaller amounts: molybdenum (Mo), nickel (Ni), copper (Cu), zinc (Zn), manganese (Mn), boron (B), iron (Fe), chlorine (Cl).

Macronutrients are needed in far greater amounts than micronutrients. For example, the nitrogen content of plants is usually more than one million times greater than that for molybdenum, although molybdenum is vital for nitrogen use by plants, being part of the first enzyme that plants use to convert nitrate from the soil into organic nitrogen.

In addition to the eight micronutrients essential to all plants, some other elements are essential for a smaller number of plants. Silica (Si), for example, makes up to 6 per cent of the dry weight of grasses, many times higher than the concentration in dicots. Silica forms bodies called phytoliths (plant stones) which are a major defence component of some grasses. These phytoliths will cut your hand if you run it up the leaf edge of some grasses, and are the main cause of tooth wear in grazing animals. As a result, grazing animals evolved strategies for minimizing this effect, by having teeth which never stop growing, like rabbits, or which have raised crowns which are gradually worn down, as happens in cattle.

Some elements come from rocks and thence from soil, like potassium, phosphorus and calcium (minerals), while other elements, such as carbon, hydrogen, oxygen and nitrogen, come from the air, soil and water.

Organic Compounds

The smallest amount of an element is an atom, and when two or more atoms join together they form a molecule. The gas oxygen (O_2) in the air is an example of a molecule, made up of two oxygen atoms connected together. If there are two or more different atoms in a molecule, it is called a compound, so that carbon dioxide (CO_2) and water (H_2O) are both examples of molecules which are also compounds, whereas oxygen is a molecule but not a compound.

Organic compounds, such as proteins and sugars, are usually defined as those compounds which are made by living organisms, while inorganic compounds are not. This definition is not totally accurate as water, oxygen and carbon dioxide are classified as inorganic molecules but are made by plants as a result of photosynthesis or respiration, but it will do for our purposes.

Functions of Elements in Plants

Of the macronutrients in organic compounds, carbon (C) is the most important, making up some 90 per cent of plant dry matter, that is the plant tissue left after all water has been removed. This figure rises to more than 95 per cent when hydrogen (H), oxygen (O) and nitrogen (N) are also taken into account.

Because macronutrients are needed in such large amounts in plants, an inadequate supply of any one can slow down growth. Of the three macronutrients commonly listed in bought fertilizers – nitrogen (N), phosphorus (P) and potassium (K) – all three are needed for aspects of plant growth and development. In addition, each one encourages, directly or indirectly, particular responses. Nitrogen stimulates vegetative growth, particularly leaves and stems, while phosphorus encourages root development, and high potassium level is associated with flower and fruit development, although potassium is also present in large amounts in leaves and stems.

In addition to their role in plant growth and development, these three macronutrients also have other roles, including stress tolerance and water movement (K), storage of chemical energy (P) and production of chlorophylls, the green pigments central to converting light energy to chemical energy by photosynthesis (N).

Of the other macronutrients, calcium (Ca) is particularly important in the development of plant organs, like leaves, fruits and stems, because it is involved in the jelly-like substance, calcium pectate, which glues together cells in an organ. This is related to the plant compounds which make jam set.

Magnesium (Mg), on the other hand, is best-known for its presence in chlorophyll. The change in colour of green tissues such as peas and runner beans from bright green to grey-green after prolonged boiling is due to the magnesium in chlorophyll being lost and replaced by hydrogen (H). Chlorotic yellowing leaves of plants like hydrangea can be greened up by applying good old Epsom salts, magnesium sulphate, the magnesium being used to produce more chlorophyll.

Sulphur (S) is important in the production of proteins, and is particularly important in members of the Brassicaceae, for synthesis of the defence and taste chemicals of members of the cabbage family. The sulphur smell is familiar to anyone who has eaten overcooked Brussels sprouts.

The functions of micronutrients, on the other hand, have more to do with the activity of specific enzymes. Iron, for example, is associated with enzymes involved in the synthesis of chlorophyll, so iron deficiency results in yellow leaves.

HOW PLANTS TRAP SUNLIGHT: PHOTOSYNTHESIS

Up to the mid-seventeenth century, it was assumed that plants grew as a result of consuming earth and water. Around this time, Jan Baptista van Helmont, a Belgian physician, measured the growth of a willow tree in a pot. After five years, the plant had gained 75kg in weight, but the soil had lost only a few grammes. Van Helmont assumed that the gain in weight of the tree had to be due to water uptake.

By the beginning of the nineteenth century, it had been shown that plants exposed to sunlight took up carbon dioxide from the air and released oxygen, with the amounts of carbon dioxide taken up and oxygen released being exactly the same. We now know that plant dry matter production is carried out by photosynthesis.

Visible light is a component of sunlight and is made of light of different colours and wavelengths which the human eye can detect, as revealed in a rainbow: red–orange–yellow–green–blue–indigo–violet. Leaves trap sunlight energy by using pigments within the chloroplasts (Chapter 1). The main pigments are the green chlorophylls a and b, although yellow and orange carotenoid pigments, which are revealed in the colours of autumn leaves when chlorophyll breaks down, also contribute.

Objects look a particular colour to us because they absorb some colours of visible light but not others, which are reflected or transmitted. The colours of the light reflected give the body its colour. Leaves appear green because they reflect the green light from sunlight to our eyes. Leaves absorb the other colours, with the chlorophylls absorbing mostly blue and red light, which make up about half of the visible light in sunlight, while the carotenoid pigments absorb mostly blue-violet light.

The chlorophylls transfer the energy they get from sunlight to power a series of chemical reactions to split water (H_2O), taken in by the roots, into hydrogen (H) and oxygen (O). Carbon dioxide enters the leaf through stomata. The hydrogen split off from water is transferred to carbon dioxide, to ultimately form the sugar glucose ($C_6H_{12}O_6$), which is a source of chemical energy derived from sunlight energy. The stomata release the oxygen produced from water, which all plants and animals need to live. A large tree produces enough oxygen each day to supply ten people.

In this way, inorganic carbon in the form of carbon dioxide is converted (fixed) into organic carbon, as glucose, by photosynthesis. As a result, the three elements C, H and O are incorporated into organic molecules. The whole complex process can be summarized by a simple equation in which six molecules each of carbon dioxide and water, both inorganic compounds, combine (in

Why leaves look green.

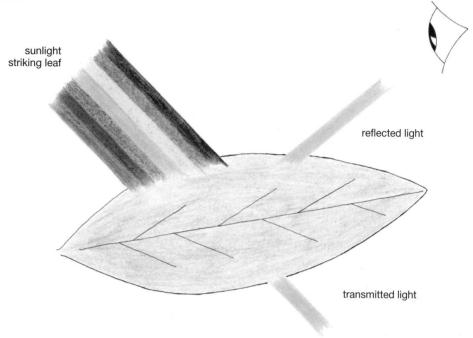

sunlight
striking leaf

reflected light

transmitted light

the presence of sunlight energy) to produce one organic molecule of glucose ($C_6H_{12}O_6$) and six molecules of oxygen:

$$6\ CO_2 + 6\ H_2O + \text{sunlight energy} \rightarrow 1\ C_6H_{12}O_6 + 6\ O_2$$

The two sides of the equation must balance, with the number of atoms of each element (six carbon, twelve hydrogen and eighteen oxygen atoms) being the same on either side. The sunlight energy on the left-hand side of the equation is

Hosta 'Frances Williams', showing orderly leaf variegation.

converted into chemical energy in the glucose on the right-hand side.

Variegated cultivars of garden plants have yellow and green tissues in the same leaf (Chapter 7). The absence of chlorophyll from the yellow tissue means that variegated cultivars grow more slowly than do their all-green counterparts. They also tend to be more cold-sensitive. On the other hand, the slower vegetative growth of the variegated plant means that relatively more assimilates are available for flower production. As a consequence, the variegated tulip tree, *Liriodendron tulipifera* 'Variegata' flowers when it is a younger tree than does the green-leaved cultivar.

The main type of photosynthesis carried out by plants from temperate climates is known as C3 photosynthesis (Chapter 2), because the first organic chemical produced by carbon fixation has three carbon atoms. Globally more than 95 per cent of plants use C3 photosynthesis, but in drier climates plants have adopted different strategies.

In sub-tropical areas of the Americas and Africa, some plants (approximately 3 per cent of the world total) evolved a different form of photosynthesis, known as C4 photosynthesis. Here, the first product of carbon fixation contains four carbon atoms. C4 plants are adapted to conditions with limited water supplies, but also to higher temperatures and light levels, than are encountered in temperate climates.

HOW PLANTS RELEASE CHEMICAL ENERGY: AEROBIC RESPIRATION

When plants need to grow, repair tissue or make new chemicals, they need energy, and they achieve this by releasing the chemical energy stored in the carbohydrates produced by photosynthesis. Basically, aerobic (using air) respiration is the reverse of photosynthesis, except that the energy released by respiration is chemical energy rather than sunlight energy:

$$1 \ C_6H_{12}O_6 + 6 \ O_2 \rightarrow 6 \ H_2O + 6 \ CO_2 + \text{chemical energy}$$

glucose   oxygen   water   carbon
dioxide

The same process occurs in animals as well as plants, with the former using carbohydrates they have obtained from eating plants or animals which have eaten plants. When a lot of people are in a closed room, you will quickly realize that the air gets stuffy as CO_2 from respiration accumulates in the air, and condensation appears on the windows, caused by water vapour released by respiration.

Whereas photosynthesis occurs only in green plant tissues, respiration takes place in all parts of the plant, including non-green tissues such as flowers and roots. These tissues receive sugars from leaves so that they can respire and generate chemical energy.

Usually, 90 per cent of the energy of any fuel ends up as heat when the fuel is used up, but aerobic respiration in plants is remarkably efficient, with 40 per cent of the energy released being retained for use by the plant, and only 60 per cent being lost as heat.

In some plants, a second type of respiration is used in specific organs which is deliberately inefficient, so that extra heat is generated to warm parts of the plant. This so-called 'alternative respiration' is used by plants such as skunk cabbage (*Lysichiton americanum*), our native Lords and Ladies (*Arum maculatum*) and voodoo lily (*Sauromatum guttatum*) to generate warmth in the rod-like spadix part of the flower. In turn, this causes volatile chemicals, which smell of rotting meat, to be released in order to attract flies to pollinate the flowers.

The same method is used by alpine plants which flower at low temperatures, to attract pollinating insects, as in the mountain avens, *Dryas octopetala*. It is also exploited by some spring-flowering alpine plants, such as *Soldanella pusilla*, to allow the flower head to penetrate the snow by melting it.

NUTRIENT UPTAKE FROM THE SOIL AND TRANSPORT

Animals lose 90 per cent of the nutrients they eat as waste. This explains why animal manure is such a good nutrient source for plants. Plants, on the other hand, take from their environment just what they need. (Aristotle was the first to realize this.)

Plants take up nutrients from the soil, air or water in the form of inorganic molecules, which are then used by the plants to make organic compounds. Inorganic nutrients dissolved in soil water move to the roots in the same way as the water does, but the mechanism of nutrient uptake into the root cells is different from water uptake. To understand this, we need to understand a little more about inorganic compounds.

The same plant nutrient can exist in different inorganic compounds. Potassium, for example, occurs as potassium sulphate, potassium nitrate and many other compounds. Similarly, nitrate, the most important form of nitrogen in the soil, can exist as potassium nitrate, ammonium nitrate or calcium nitrate, among others.

We have already seen that elements are made up of atoms. The elements in inorganic compounds exist as charged atoms or ions, so that one molecule of potassium nitrate (KNO_3) consists of one K^+ and one NO_3^- ion. Ions can be positively charged cations, such as potassium (K^+) and calcium (Ca^{2+}) or negatively charged anions, such as nitrate (NO_3^-) and sulphate (SO_4^{2-}).

Most nutrients exist as cations, like potassium as K^+, or magnesium as Mg^{2+}, but some exist as anions, such as sulphur as sulphate (SO_4^{2-}) and nitrogen as nitrate (NO_3^-). Some elements can exist in the form of several different ions. Nitrogen, for example, exists as anions like nitrite (NO_2^-) and nitrate (NO_3^-), and a cation, ammonium (NH_4^+).

Cations and anions are attracted to one another because of their opposite charges. A compound is made up of both cations and anions, with a net charge (when the number of positive and negative charges in the molecule are added together) of zero. To achieve this, the number of positive charges must balance the number of negative ones, so that potassium nitrate is KNO_3 ($1 K^+ + 1 NO_3^-$), whereas potassium sulphate is K_2SO_4 ($2 K^+ + 1$ SO_4^{2-} ions).

When dry, these compounds are solids, and a lot of energy is needed to break them, as you realize when you use a salt grinder to break up crystals of salt, sodium chloride. When added to water,

however, the ions in an inorganic compound separate and water molecules – which have both positive (H^+) and negative charges (OH^-) – bind to them, filling the spaces in between, so that the chemical dissolves in the water. It is in this form that plant roots encounter most inorganic compounds.

The presence of inorganic ions also explains the ability of specific soil particles to bind certain nutrients and water. Clay particles in the soil have negative charges, so that they bind positively charged cations such as potassium (K^+), calcium (Ca^{2+}) and magnesium ($Mg+$) and the water molecule (H_2O), which contains both negative (OH^-) and positive (H^+) ions. Organic matter is also negatively charged, so that it, like clay, can bind cations and act as a reserve of nutrients.

Whereas water moves equally freely across the root cell membrane in either direction, nutrient ions move at different rates. This is because the cell membrane is selectively permeable, allowing more of the ions it wants in large amounts into the cell than those it needs in smaller amounts. When a root encounters potassium chloride (KCl) dissolved in water, it takes up more of the K^+ ion, which it needs more, than of the Cl^- ion.

As a result, nutrient ions are present in plant cells at much higher concentrations than are found in the soil water, with potassium concentrations in plant cells, for example, being fifty to seventy-five times greater than those in the soil.

Some ions are related to one another, like magnesium and calcium, or sodium and potassium. That is why the low-sodium version of table salt (sodium chloride, NaCl) contains about one-third NaCl and two-thirds KCl (potassium chloride). The downside of this relatedness is that plants may have difficulty in distinguishing between these related cations, with plants taking up Na by mistake instead of K which they need in much larger amounts, resulting in sodium toxicity in salty soils.

This movement of nutrients into the root needs energy. Because roots are not green and cannot photosynthesize, sugar is transported to the roots from the leaves. Energy is released by respiration of sugars by the root cells. This explains why plants show nutrient deficiency symptoms, like yellowing

Grass yellowing in a waterlogged lawn, due to lack of oxygen to power nutrient uptake by the roots.

of leaves, when the soil is waterlogged. Flooding drives out oxygen from the soil, without which the roots cannot respire to release energy and thence take up nutrients.

Respiration is also important in balancing the ions in the plant. When a cation, such as K^+, is taken up by the root cell, another cation (usually H^+) has to be released from the cell into the soil to balance it. Similarly, when an anion, such as Cl^-, is taken up, another anion (usually OH^-) is released. These two ions involved in ion exchange are generated from water ($H_2O \rightarrow H^+ + OH^-$), which, in turn, is produced by root respiration.

Transport of nutrients from the root to the rest of the plant occurs through the xylem in water via the transpiration stream, as described earlier.

MOVEMENT OF ASSIMILATES AROUND THE PLANT

All essential elements taken up by the plant, except for potassium and chlorine, are incorporated into organic compounds because they all contain C from CO_2. In this way, more than 50,000 different natural plant chemicals are generated, which are grouped together as 'assimilates'.

Although plants make up only about 1 per cent of the living species on the planet, they produce 85 per cent of the natural organic chemicals. Plants use these chemicals largely to interact with other living organisms, by attracting pollinators and seed dispersal agents (using pigments, scents, flavours) and repelling would-be attackers (deterrent, toxins, pigments, scents, flavours), and to respond to the environment.

Photosynthesis occurs in leaves and some other green organs, such as pea pods. In epiphytic orchids, which grow on tree branches rather than in the soil, such as *Phalaenopsis* (moth orchids), even the roots are green and can photosynthesize, so these plants are often grown in clear pots.

Some of the sugar produced by photosynthesis will be used in the organ that made it, but more will be translocated around the plant to organs which require energy and organic chemicals. Such organs include immature leaves, fruits or storage organs, such as potato or dahlia tubers, and non-green organs such as roots. An organ which exports more sugar than it imports is known as a source, while one which imports more than it exports is a sink.

Movement (translocation) of assimilates occurs in the living part of the vascular bundles, the phloem. The vascular bundles in the leaf are in the leaf veins, which empty into the main rib of the leaf and thence into the vascular system in the leaf stalk and stem. From there on, the phloem (and xylem) form a vascular system connecting all parts of the plant (*see* page 70). The white strings between the skin and the fruit of a banana, for example, are the vascular bundles which transport assimilates from banana leaves to the developing fruit.

In a vascular bundle the phloem is the outer part, with the xylem being the inner part. In broad-leaved trees, the vascular bundles are in a circle just under the bark, with the bark composed largely of squashed phloem.

This arrangement explains how trees can still function when the centre of the trunk, the heartwood – which is dead in mature trees – is rotten, as long as the outer area, the sapwood, containing the vascular bundles, is intact. It also explains how removing even a narrow circle of bark around the trunk of a tree (girdling or ring-barking) will cause the death of that tree. This action will starve the tree by blocking downward movement of assimilates in the phloem to the roots.

Whereas water movement in the xylem can only go upwards from the roots, assimilate transport in the phloem from leaves can move in all directions, such as down to the roots and up to flowers and fruits. Glucose is the sugar which is produced in photosynthesis, but in most plants the form in which sugars are transported in the vascular bundle is sucrose, the sugar found in table sugar. Sucrose is a di-saccharide (two sugars), consisting of one molecule of glucose joined to one molecule of fruit sugar or fructose. Sugars are examples of carbohydrates.

Glucose (and fructose) are examples of monosaccharide (one sugar) sugars. The water containing dissolved assimilates in the phloem is what we refer to as sap. Sap usually contains 2–4 per cent sucrose, but it can be up to 11 per cent, and people of many cultures exploit that by 'tapping' the phloem to release and collect sap which is very sweet, such as maple syrup.

Sucrose travels in the phloem along a sucrose concentration gradient, from high concentration in the source such as a leaf to low concentration in

The trunk of a tree where the heartwood has rotted away, leaving the vascular system under the bark.

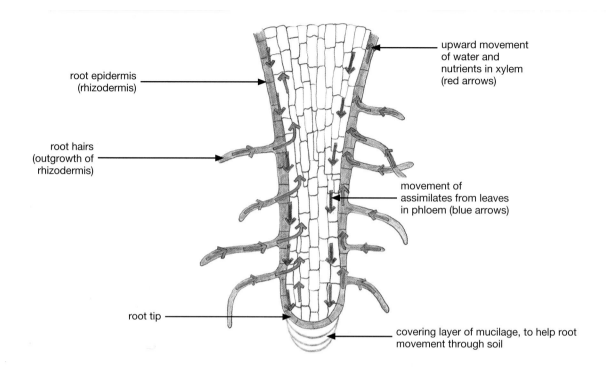

root epidermis (rhizodermis)

root hairs (outgrowth of rhizodermis)

root tip

upward movement of water and nutrients in xylem (red arrows)

movement of assimilates from leaves in phloem (blue arrows)

covering layer of mucilage, to help root movement through soil

Movement of water and assimilates within the root.

the sink, such as a fruit. To maintain the sucrose gradient and hence the flow of sucrose into the sink, the sink must not accumulate sucrose. This can be achieved by the sink using up the sucrose by respiration or by converting it into a different form for storage.

The most common carbohydrate storage form in plants is starch, found in wheat flour and potato tubers, which is created by joining together hundreds of glucose molecules; starch is an example of a polysaccharide (many sugars). When energy is needed, such as when a seed germinates, the starch is converted back to sugars from which the energy can be released by respiration.

The longer leaves stay green on geophytes or herbaceous plants, the more food reserves are built up. That explains why the leaves of geophytes like daffodils must be allowed to die down naturally rather than being cut off or tied into knots, as these acts interfere with the production and translocation of assimilates to the bulbs. It is much better to inter-plant these plants with species which develop

later in the season, so that yellowing foliage is hidden. Daylilies (*Hemerocallis*) are good examples of suitable plants.

Extending the period the leaves stay green is particularly important in kitchen garden crops (Chapter 9). That is why control of diseases and pests late in the season, such as late potato blight, is so important.

Instead of starch, the vegetable crop Jerusalem artichoke stores its carbohydrate in the form of inulin, which the human digestive system, evolved to deal with starch, cannot digest. As a result, inulin reaches the colon of our gut largely undigested, whereupon the gut bacteria attack it, producing un-neighbourly large volumes of gas. Each of us carries around about 2kg of gut bacteria, and the ones which can break down inulin are the friendly bacteria, such as *Bifidibacterium*. Because there is some evidence that these bacteria help to protect us against disease, eating inulin-rich foods like Jerusalem artichoke and florence fennel, can be beneficial to your health.

GROWING A LARGE PUMPKIN

If you want to produce really large pumpkins for Halloween, you can accelerate sucrose translocation to the sink. Make up a strong sucrose solution by dissolving 1 part white table sugar in 4 parts hot water; this high sugar concentration will also stop bugs growing on the sugar solution. Dig a small hole in the soil to support the jar. Thread a darning needle with wool, and thread the wool through the stalk end of the developing pumpkin, keeping the other end of the wool in the sugarwater. The level of sugarwater will need to be kept topped up. By-passing the leaves in this way, large amounts of sucrose will be transported into the pumpkin, which can grow to impressive proportions.

WHY NUTRIENTS ARE NEEDED

In a mature natural ecosystem such as a deciduous woodland, there is little change from year to year in the total nutrient content of the ecosystem, which includes the nutrients present in the plants, animals and the soil. This is because of a process known as nutrient cycling, which operates for each of the individual nutrients. For example, nitrogen levels stay more or less the same because of the nitrogen cycle.

Nitrogen reserves in the soil are largely in the form of organic matter, representing dead animal and plant tissues as well as animal waste such as dung and urine. Such organic nitrogen cannot be taken up by a plant until it is converted into the inorganic form of nitrogen known as nitrate. Most natural soils contain organic nitrogen stores of between 5 and 20 tonnes per hectare. Each year, this is topped up with fresh organic matter, while a small proportion is converted into inorganic nitrogen.

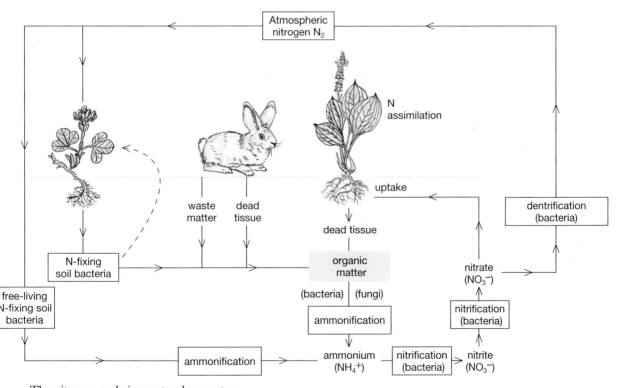

The nitrogen cycle in a natural ecosystem.

This conversion from organic to inorganic nitrogen in the soil is effected by different soil bacteria:

Organic N → ammonium (NH_4+) → nitrite (NO_2^-) → nitrate (NO_3^-)

The nitrate generated is taken up by the plant, which reverses the steps carried out by the bacteria, to produce organic N:

Nitrate → nitrite → ammonium → organic N

The nitrogen is combined with carbon compounds to produce organic nitrogen, in the form of proteins and other N-containing organic molecules such as DNA, chlorophyll and certain defence compounds like nicotine.

Although most of the nitrogen is recycled through the inorganic→organic→inorganic system, some nitrogen is lost from the ecosystem, such as happens when nitrate is washed (leached) beyond the area where plant roots lie. This loss can be balanced by increases in nitrogen content from outside the ecosystem.

Almost four-fifths of the atmosphere consists of nitrogen gas (N_2). Nitrogen gas cannot be used by plants unless it is fixed by soil bacteria into a form the plants can use (Chapter 1). Some nitrogen-fixing bacteria can live in the soil or within the roots or other tissues of specific plants. This plant–bacterium relationship is an example of a mutualism, where both partners benefit, with the plant receiving nitrogen fixed by the bacteria, and the bacteria receiving carbon fixed by the plant as sugars.

The best-known nitrogen-fixing plant species, as a result of mutualisms with bacteria of the genus *Rhizobium*, are the legumes or pea family (Fabaceae), such as peas, beans, clover and lupins, but non-legumes can also be nitrogen fixers. These include the giant rhubarb, *Gunnera tinctoria*, alder and *Elaeagnus umbellata* (autumn olive).

If you cut a leaf stalk of *Gunnera* as closely as possible to the rootstock, the cut end reveals a number of blue-green spots. These are colonies of the nitrogen-fixing cyanobacterium *Nostoc*, which are the sole source of nitrogen for this plant, which helps to power the production of the enormous leaves. *Gunnera* cannot use soil nitrate.

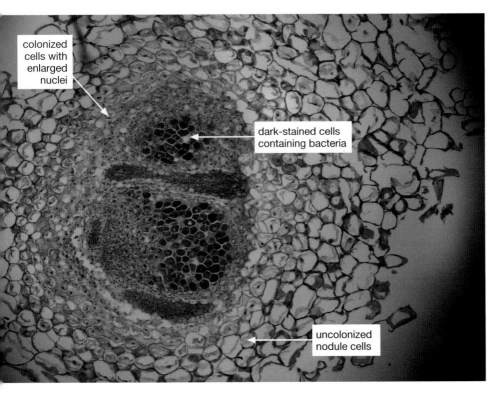

colonized cells with enlarged nuclei

dark-stained cells containing bacteria

uncolonized nodule cells

A micrograph of a thin section through a root nodule involving the roots of a pea plant, containing the nitrogen-fixing bacterium *Rhizobium*.

Part of the rootstock of *Gunnera tinctoria*, colonized by the cyanobacterium *Nostoc*, visible as blue-green colonies.

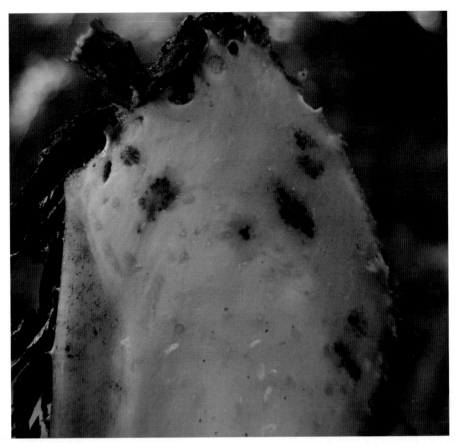

A micrograph (×2000 magnification) of filaments of *Nostoc*, consisting of cells interspersed with the spherical heterocysts where nitrogen fixation takes place.

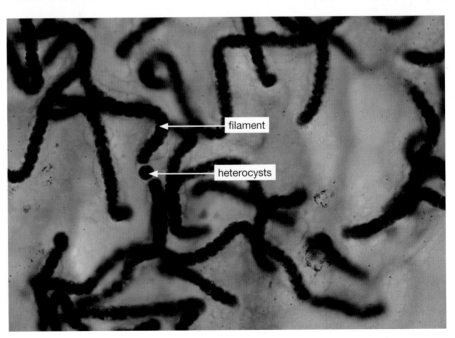

Similar cycles exist for other nutrients. Cycles for the mineral elements (such as potassium, magnesium, calcium and manganese) include increasing levels of these nutrients in the soil by the weathering of the bedrock, say limestone, to release calcium, sometimes phosphorus and magnesium.

Leaching is an important source of loss from an ecosystem for the more water-soluble or mobile elements such as potassium and magnesium, and this is a particular problem on sandy or silty soils, whose particles lack the negative charges that clay particles have, which bind positively charged ions such as K^+. Phosphorus is relatively immobile. On the other hand, not all the phosphorus in organic matter is converted into forms which plants can take up, so that the amount of available phosphorus in an ecosystem can fall slightly from year to year.

Nutrient Levels in Gardens

The consequence of nutrient cycling is that natural ecosystems are 'closed' systems, whereby little or no nutrients are lost from year to year. In managed ecosystems such as gardens, however, nutrient cycling is disturbed, and these ecosystems are 'open' systems with regard to nutrients. The nutrients contained in any plant material removed from the garden ecosystem represent a depletion of the soil's nutrient reserves, be it vegetables from the garden, grass clippings from the lawn, leaves from deciduous trees in autumn, trimmings from hedges or prunings from trees or shrubs, weeds, deadheads, etc.

A potato plot producing 4kg tubers per square metre will have taken a total of 25g N, 10g P and 45g K from that area of soil, in terms of both the tubers and haulm (stems and leaves) produced. For every 30m^2 of lawn, approximately 2kg N, 0.5kg P, 0.8kg Ca and 1.8kg K is taken from the soil in a season in the form of lawn mowings.

In the short term, these losses may not be a problem, in that the soil contains nutrient reserves. But in the medium term, these reserves need to be replenished to replace the nutrients which have been lost.

To mimic nutrient recycling in natural ecosystems, gardeners should compost all waste plant material and re-apply it to the soil. But even if all this plant material is composted and returned to the soil, this will still leave a nutrient shortfall as the recycling of the nutrients will not be 100% efficient. Some N and K will be lost by leaching, while some of the P will not be available to the plants. Furthermore, the nutrients from any of the vegetables and fruit grown in the garden which you eat will be lost into the sewerage system (unless you operate one of the more extreme forms of recycling!).

Physiological Disorders

Garden plants can suffer from nutrient deficiencies or toxicities. These are sometimes termed physiological disorders. Although sandy or chalky soils can be deficient in mobile nutrients such as nitrogen, potassium and some micronutrients as a result of leaching, most garden soils have adequate reserves of individual nutrients.

Most cases of nutrient imbalance in plants result from too little of a nutrient rather than too much. Indeed, such nutrient deficiencies are usually due to the soil conditions being unsuitable for the plant to take up the nutrient, as happens with low pH, drought or waterlogging, rather than that there is not enough of the nutrient in the soil. In western Europe the principal problem for gardeners is with the three main macronutrients (N, P and K), whereas in North America micronutrient deficiencies are a greater problem.

In addition to natural problems of nutrient deficiency or toxicity, we gardeners can also cause problems without knowing it. Because water is vital for the movement of nutrients around the plant, insufficient or irregular water uptake can cause local nutrient deficiencies. Fast-growing organs like fruits have a huge demand for calcium to make calcium pectate which holds together adjacent cells, and they suffer from calcium deficiency when water uptake is inconsistent, resulting in cell death and physiological disorders such as blossom end rot in tomato and bitter pit in apple cultivars, particularly Bramley's Seedling.

Furthermore, because only a proportion of the phosphorus in plants can be used by animals, the remainder is passed through in manure. As a result, excessive application of animal manure can result in problems of phosphorus toxicity in the soil.

Lime-induced chlorosis in raspberry, with the veins staying characteristically green.

One of the most common causes of nitrogen deficiency in recent years is the use of non-composted nitrogen-poor organic mulches such as bark, straw or sawdust. The C in these materials will be degraded by soil micro-organisms but, because there is not enough N in the material to support these bugs, they will take up N from the soil. This results in the nitrogen becoming unavailable to the plants, which can suffer from temporary N deficiency (known as nitrogen theft) until the micro-organisms die and release the nitrogen.

Effects of Soil pH

As soil pH varies, nutrients in the soil become more or less soluble and hence more or less available to the plants. At pH values below 5.5, the availability of many micronutrients – including iron, copper, aluminium, manganese and boron – increases, resulting, for example, in aluminium toxicity at low pH.

At pH values greater than 6.5, the availability of most micronutrients decreases, while that of the macronutrients, as well as the trace element molybdenum, increases. This results, for example, in iron deficiency at high pH. As iron is vital for chlorophyll production, symptoms here are leaf yellowing (lime-induced chlorosis). Alkaline soils can result in manganese deficiency, while acid soils can result in manganese toxicity, symptoms of both conditions being the production of brown spots on plant tissues.

There is an interaction between soil type and soil pH. Sandy soils have only limited reserves of minerals, because they lack the mineral-binding sites found on clay particles and organic matter. As a result, a low-pH sandy soil will release much less aluminium, a principal cause of plant toxicity in acid soils, than will a low-pH clay-rich soil, so low pH is less of a problem with sandy soils than with clay-rich ones.

Some ions can interfere with the uptake of another one. For example, high levels of calcium, as is often found in high-pH soils, inhibit the uptake of iron, leading to lime-induced chlorosis. Similar chlorosis occurs on phosphorus-rich soils, where iron ions bind with phosphate ions (PO_4^{3-}, a form of phosphorus) and results in insoluble forms of iron. This potential antagonism of uptake of two (or more) ions is most serious when the concentration of the two ions is very different. This needs to be taken into account when applying fertilizers to the soil.

Symptoms of Nutrient Deficiencies

When a plant shows nutrient deficiency symptoms, identification of the nutrient in question can be difficult for several reasons. The first signs of nutrient deficiency are stunting of the plant, leaf deformity or a general unthriftiness, but these are all rather general as symptoms go. Most nutrient deficiencies (particularly iron, magnesium or nitrogen) also result in chlorosis, because chlorophyll is not being produced as before, exposing the yellow carotenoids normally associated with autumn leaf colour. Furthermore, the symptoms of nutrient deficiency can vary between plant species.

Although chlorosis is a common non-specific indicator of nutrient deficiency, characteristics of the yellowing can help to distinguish between deficiencies of particular nutrients. If yellowing occurs particularly (or initially) in old leaves, that is those which are lower down the stem, then the deficient nutrient is probably one which is highly mobile within the plant, such as N, K or Mg. In times of nutrient stress, the plant will try to translocate stores of nutrients from old leaves (which therefore become chlorotic) to young leaves which are the priority for the plant.

If yellowing is largely in the young leaves, then the nutrient concerned is very poorly mobile, like Ca, B, S or Fe, because the plant is unable to move reserves from old to young leaves, so the old leaves stay green.

A good strategy when faced with an apparent nutrient deficiency is to apply a general fertilizer containing macronutrients and micronutrients, such as a seaweed extract, Vitax Q4 or Chempak. To speed up the effect and to minimize any interference on nutrient availability from soil factors, such as pH or waterlogging, a foliar spray should be used, as it bypasses the root system.

IDENTIFYING COMMON NUTRIENT DEFICIENCIES

Symptom	Go to Next Symptom/ Deficient Nutrient
1. The leaves are yellow or yellow-green (in part or whole).	2
The leaves are dark green, possibly with purpling of older leaves.	P
2. The first leaves to turn yellow are the young ones.	3
The first leaves to turn yellow are the old ones.	4
3. Young leaves develop twisting, browning around the edges.	Ca (low-pH soils)
No deformities; yellow leaves have green veins.	Fe (high-pH or high-P soils)
No deformities; yellow leaves have yellow veins.	S
4. Yellow leaves have yellow veins, may show purpling.	N (sandy or low-pH soils)
Yellow leaves have green veins.	Mg (low-pH soils)
Yellow leaves show browning of tips, margins.	K (sandy soils), Mn (high pH soils)

FERTILIZERS

To replace the nutrients lost from a garden and/or to provide additional nutrients to maximize performance of garden plants, several different fertilizer sources can be used. Fertilizers can be artificial or natural (such as fish, blood and bone).

Artificial Fertilizers

General features of artificial fertilizers are that they have defined concentrations of the major macronutrients (usually one or more of NPK), but usually lack other macronutrients or any micronutrients, and contribute no organic matter to the soil.

The nutrient content of artificial fertilizers is usually presented on the pack, for example as 10:10:20 or 7:7:7, showing the concentrations of the three major macronutrients NPK as a percentage of fertilizer weight. But, while the concentration of nitrogen in the fertilizer is presented as the percentage of N, for historical reasons the concentration of phosphate is presented on UK products as P_2O_5 (phosphorus pentoxide) while that of K is given as K_2O (potassium oxide).

As a result, a grassland fertilizer described as 10:10:20 contains 10 per cent N, 10 per cent P_2O_5 and 20 per cent K_2O. Because P and K in these forms also contain oxygen, the amount of P and K is actually less than the 10 per cent and 20 per cent, respectively, that you would expect. If you want to calculate the actual amount of P and K in the fertilizer, multiply the percentage of P_2O_5 by 0.44 and the percentage of K_2O by 0.83. In this way, 10:10:20 compound fertilizer contains 10 per cent N, 4.4 per cent P and 16.6 per cent K – quite a different story.

Other benefits of artificial fertilizers include their formulation into products suitable for particular purposes, such as specific fertilizers for orchids, different lawn fertilizers for use in spring (high-N) or autumn (high-K), as well as different formats, like solid, slow-release or liquid fertilizers.

Disadvantages of artificial fertilizers include the fact that N and K, in particular, may be in soluble forms, such as nitrate for N, in these fertilizers, which can readily be leached to below where the roots are, resulting in loss of nutrients. To reduce risks of leaching, try using slower-release formulations of nitrogen. Ammonium salts require bacteria to turn them into nitrate, while urea needs to be converted first to ammonium and then to nitrate, slowing down the release of nitrate. Slow-release pelleted formulations of artificial fertilizers should minimize leaching losses and are particularly appropriate for use in high-rainfall areas, but are expensive.

Natural Fertilizers

Natural, or organic, fertilizers are based on animal tissues or their waste products, or on plant tissues.

The organic fertilizers produced from animal tissues, such as dried blood and bone meal, generally contain one or two macronutrients – dried blood contains 12–14 per cent nitrogen only, and bonemeal has about 8 per cent phosphorus, plus 10 per cent Ca and a little nitrogen (2–4 per cent) – but the nutrient concentrations can vary. Fish meal, for example, can contain 7–14 per cent nitrogen and 4–7 per cent P.

Organic fertilizers containing all three macronutrients (compound fertilizers) can be bought, such as the general purpose preparation fish, blood and bonemeal (5:5:6). You can make your own organic fertilizer by mixing together individual nutrient sources, such as hoof and horn (N), bonemeal (P and small amount of N) and seaweed meal (K plus a small amount of N). Hoof and horn is made up of the protein keratin which makes up our own nails as well as hair, so is a source of N. Note that the high calcium content of bonemeal makes it unsuitable for use on lime-hating ericaceous plants.

Animal-derived organic fertilizers (except manure) generally lack potassium, because potassium is not incorporated into organic molecules. Therefore growers need to turn to plant-derived preparations, such as wood ash (0.1: 0.1: 0.8) and seaweed extracts (approximately 5: 5: 7), to supplement them. Potassium in natural fertilizers is often referred to as potash. Seaweed extracts also contain micronutrients, while some commercial organic fertilizers like bonemeal have micronutrients added. Unfortunately, these organic fertilizers do not contain bulky organic matter, which would act as a soil conditioner.

A major advantage of organic nutrient sources is the slow release of nutrients into the soil in forms which the plants can use. Most of the nutrients are in an organic form which needs to be changed into the inorganic form by soil bacteria before plants can take them up. This characteristic reduces nutrient leaching, and makes organic nutrients particularly suitable for areas where rainfall is high. This is not to say that organic nitrogen sources do not suffer from leaching losses – if applied when plant roots are not present or not working actively, any nitrate generated by bacteria breaking down organic nitrogen can be lost.

Ammonium ions (NH_4^+), on the other hand,

bind to organic matter or clay particles, to resist leaching. The slow-release characteristic of organic fertilizers means that they need only be applied once or twice per year, but the downside is that plant responses to such fertilizers are slow. An exception to this general rule is dried blood, which is a fast-release organic source of N.

MANURES

Manures and composts are derived directly or indirectly from plant material, so contain a wide range of plant macro- and micro-nutrients, though again these are not present in defined proportions. Manures contain more nutrients than composts, particularly nitrogen and phosphorus. Both compost and manure contribute to improved soil condition for both light and heavy soils by including bulky organic matter. These preparations reduce the crusting of soil as a result of rainfall, and increase water- and nutrient-holding capacity of the soil. Repeated application of composts and manures will also lower the soil pH gradually.

The period over which nutrients are released from compost and manures is much longer (1–2 years) than that for other organic nutrient sources. In the past, tenant farmers would claim cash representing 'unexhausted manurial value' from their landlord if they quit the land within two years of applying animal manure.

Manure quality depends on the source (cattle manure is lower in nutrients than that from horses because the former contains more water), age (how completely has the material been composted?), presence and type of bedding incorporated into the manure (bedding helps to absorb urine which is rich in potassium, and straw is preferable to sawdust from a gardening point of view).

The method of storage is also important. If the manure or compost has been stored without being covered, much of the water-soluble nutrients, principally potassium and nitrogen, would have been leached away.

Generally, available NPK concentrations in manure and compost are in the order: N>K>P. The only manure available with clearly defined nutrient content (approximately 4:1:1) is the commercially available pelleted chicken manure, valuable as a general purpose fertilizer, but with high levels of P and relatively low K.

The presence of organic matter in manures means that they are good soil conditioners, improving drainage and workability, but the sheer bulk of manure needed as a fertilizer can be daunting in terms of transport and application. A handful of general purpose 10:5:10 fertilizer used as a spring top-dressing for shrubs or herbaceous perennials would need to be replaced by about one kilogram of well-rotted cow manure.

Fresh animal manure should not be added to the garden as it can be damaging to plants as a result of the amount of ammonia released by bacterial action and the presence of high levels of soluble salts, especially if the animals have been fed a high level of concentrates, as happens with dairy cattle or pigs. Fresh manure should be composted for at least three months (by which time the height of the pile should have been reduced by at least two-thirds), being kept covered with plastic to prevent rain leaching away the water-soluble nutrients.

Dried seaweed collected on the beach at the high-tide mark, though neither a manure nor a compost, will have twice the nutrient content of horse manure and will be an excellent soil conditioner. Salt from seawater will not pose a problem in the use of seaweeds.

GARDEN COMPOST

Garden compost is a valuable soil conditioner, containing 50 per cent organic matter, as opposed to 1–3 per cent in most soils, with some but low nutrient content, maybe 3:0.5:1. By contributing to the natural processes of nutrient cycling, composting also prevents pollution. More than one-fifth of domestic waste is compostable garden and kitchen waste.

What Can Be Composted?

There are two types of garden composting: cold or passive composting (which is the type most gardeners carry out) and hot or active composting. They produce similar end results but, because of

Rose leaves infected by the fungal disease blackspot.

the heat generated, the hot method is faster and can kill pathogens and seeds. The downside of hot composting is that the heap is built all in one go, and the heap should be turned regularly.

Composting is really just the natural process of decay of dead organic materials speeded up by eliminating some of the factors which normally slow it down. The materials which can be put onto a garden compost heap are anything organic (almost always plant-derived) and most are listed below:

- garden waste: lawn mowings, plants, including leaves, garden prunings (chopped or shredded)
- uncooked vegetable and fruit waste, tea bags
- waste from vegetarian pets, such as rabbits or guinea pigs
- waste cotton and wool: including the contents of the vacuum cleaner bag (natural fibre but not synthetic carpets), and the lint trap of the spin drier
- newspaper and cardboard (also a good way of avoiding identity theft by including torn-up bank statements).

With cold composting, be careful not to add diseased plant material, such as blighted potato foliage or rose leaves with blackspot, as it will not kill the pathogens. If you grow your own potatoes, it would be sensible not to compost peel from bought-in potatoes as this may carry surface diseases, such as common or powdery scab, which you will then introduce to your garden when you apply the compost. Similarly, do not include perennial weeds (like creeping buttercup, bindweed or couch grass) or annuals with seeds attached, as the weeds will be spread with the resulting compost. Uncooked food waste should also not be included in domestic compost heaps.

What Happens During Composting?

The material to be composted consists of organic matter which the decomposer organisms, like bacteria, fungi and invertebrates (animals without backbones), need ready-made because they cannot photosynthesize. The natural chemicals in these materials represent energy sources and carbon skeletons for the production of a wide range of chemicals needed by the micro-organisms which live in a compost heap.

A cold compost heap is an ecosystem in which there are many layers of interaction. It is an example of a food web (Chapter 6), where each species feeds on another set of materials or organisms and is, in turn, fed on by a different set of organisms. These include bacteria, fungi and actinomycetes, which are somewhere in evolutionary terms between bacteria and fungi, and invertebrates including earthworms, slugs, millipedes, wood lice, mites and nematodes, which feed on dead tissue. In turn, these are fed on by springtails, predatory mites, nematodes, rotifera and flatworms, which are fed on, in turn, by centipedes, carabid beetles and ants.

Different organic chemicals in the organic matter put into a compost heap will be broken down at different rates. Sugars and proteins from soft green tissues (green material) such as lawn clippings will be readily attacked as they offer a high return in terms of energy and carbon skeletons for the decomposers. Shredded woody tissues, newspaper and dead leaves (brown material), containing hard-to-digest cellulose and lignin but little nitrogen, take longer.

The organisms degrading the organic matter in a compost heap need certain conditions in order to carry out the decomposition. They need a full range of nutrients (similar to the macro- and micro-nutrients needed by plants), particularly carbon and nitrogen. All of these chemicals are present in plant tissues.

Like all organisms, decomposers also need moisture, and, because we are encouraging aerobic respiration, they need air to supply oxygen. Without air in the heap, different organisms will take over and carry out anaerobic respiration, which is less efficient than aerobic respiration and which generates some very smelly by-products, such as hydrogen sulphide which smells of rotten eggs. Decomposers will also work faster as the temperature increases; there will be little microbial decomposition at temperatures below 10°C.

Making a Compost Heap

The larger the compost heap, the better, as the ratio of heap surface area to volume falls, helping to retain the heat and speeding up decomposition. Unless you intend to turn the compost heap regularly, heaps much taller than 1 metre can suffer problems when the extra weight squeezes air out from the organic material.

For cool damp climates like western Europe, a lid or cover is valuable to prevent rain making the heap sodden and anaerobic, and to keep the heap warm. Insulated sides, such as pallets filled with waste expanded polystyrene or with straw or newspaper, and lids will speed up composting, as will building the heap against a wall. Compost heaps are usually hidden away, but should be close to the borders or vegetable beds, reducing the distance to transport garden waste and finished compost. A heap should also be within reach of a tap, as it may need to be watered during dry spells.

Cold composting involves gradual addition of material as and when it becomes available. In the end, the compost consists of incompletely composted plant material, providing the fibrous organic matter, plus the bodies of trillions of dead organisms, with nutrients bound to all this organic matter.

A mixture of waste of the two types, green and brown, is desirable, as each contributes something valuable to the decomposers. Green material provides nitrogen and other nutrients and carbon in the form of readily compostable carbohydrates but has a high moisture content. Brown material has carbon but little nitrogen or moisture. A heap made up solely of green material will pack down tightly, excluding air, and become smelly as anaerobic decomposers set to work. On its own, brown material will decompose very slowly but, mixed carefully with green material, it can absorb excess moisture from the green material, and create pockets of air to maintain the aerobic conditions. Nitrogen from the green material will power decomposition of the brown material.

Mature compost will have a moisture content of about 40 per cent. As lawn clippings and kitchen waste have moisture contents of 80 per cent or higher, it is clear that they must be mixed (in more or less equal volumes) with drier material such as newspaper and dry leaves. This ratio will also give a good mix of green and brown materials. Newspaper should be torn into strips 2–5cm wide before being added to the compost heap. Newspapers tear into strips either vertically or horizontally, depending on the newspaper; trust me, it is quite therapeutic!

TROUBLE SHOOTING FOR COLD COMPOSTING

Any problem with composting will be manifested by a slower-than-normal reduction in the height of the compost heap, as decomposition slows.

Symptoms	Cause	Solution
Smells of rotten eggs (hydrogen sulphide). Presence of small flies (sciarids).	Too wet	Turn the heap. Mix in absorbent brown material. Ensure that bin cover is water-tight.
May contain ants. White fungal growth on outside and inside of heap.	Too dry	Turn compost into adjacent heap, wetting material, or make depression in centre of heap and water it. Reduce water losses through sides and top of heap.
Smells of public toilets (ammonia).	Too much nitrogen	Turn heap. Mix in low-N brown material.
Damp (and warm) only in the centre.	Heap is too small	Increase width, depth of heap. Incorporate insulation into walls of bin.
Heap is moist, no bad smells.	Not enough nitrogen	Turn heap. Mix in high-N green materials, such as lawn clippings, or add high-N activator such as ammonium sulphate, seaweed extract or manure.
Final compost is very fibrous.	Insufficient chopping of material	Remove stems from compost, crush or shred, return to next heap. Next time, shred material before composting.

In cold heaps, waste is usually added to the heap as it becomes available, with lawn clippings being the major source of waste in many gardens over the summer, while teabags seem to dominate our compost heap over the winter. Stockpiling of brown waste, such as dead leaves, dead stems from last year's herbaceous perennials, and newspaper, ideally in the dry and near the compost heap, allows the gardener to add more or less equal volumes of brown and green waste onto the heap.

The compost heap will shrink by 50% in about three weeks in the summer as a result of water loss and the decay and packing-down of compostable material. Many gardening authors recommend that a cold heap should be turned regularly to speed up decomposition, but any benefit from occasionally introducing more air and heating up the heap is temporary. To my mind, the main benefit of turning the heap is to bring the outer layers into the warm centre, where cold composting is fastest, so an emphasis on insulating the walls of the bin is a better option than turning the heap.

When the heap is about 1.5m high, three weeks

or so after adding the latest batch of material, the heap should be closed and any additional material used to build a new heap. Compost is ready for use in the garden when the components are no longer recognizable and the material looks quite uniform.

Finally, when a heap is being turned out for use, retain the top layer (10–15cm deep). This layer is usually incompletely composted, but is a valuable inoculant to start your next heap, introducing beneficial micro-organisms and invertebrates into the waste material.

USING PLANT NUTRIENTS

As with water, effective use of plant nutrients depends on understanding why and when plants need them, and how best to cater for the plants' needs. This will help a gardener produce top-quality plants with the least expense, work and impact on the environment.

Minimize Nutrient Losses

In agro-ecosystems, it is estimated that less than half of the nutrients applied to the soil is used by the plants. This figure should be higher in gardens, where most of the plants are perennials, able to take up nutrients whenever they become available. To ensure that plants benefit as much as possible from the nutrients in the garden, you can minimize losses by increasing the ability of the soil to act as a reservoir for the nutrients and by making them available to the plants.

Increase Nutrient-Holding Capacity of the Soil

Organic matter particles have negative charges on the particle surface, so that they bind positively charged cations (such as NH_4^+ and K^+) but not negatively charged anions (such as NO_3^- or SO_4^{3-}). As a consequence, incorporation of well-rotted organic manure or compost will not only provide more nutrients but also increase the nutrient-binding capacity of the soil. The number of saprophytic soil bacteria, which use dead organic matter as food, will increase when you add their food (manure or compost) to the soil, improving nutrient re-cycling.

Once you have a soil with good characteristics and nutrient reserves, it is important not to waste these nutrients. Digging introduces more air into the soil, which will stimulate the multiplication of soil bacteria, which will convert organic nutrient sources into inorganic forms. As a result, the inorganic N sources become soluble and, if there are no plants to take up the nitrogen, much of this will be leached from the soil.

Ideally, then, digging should be restricted to cool weather when bacterial activity is low, but not when the soil is very cold or frozen, as it can take weeks for the soil temperature to recover if frozen soil is turned in.

Increase Availability of Nutrients

For most nutrients, uptake can occur along the entire length of the root system, although root tips are the most active. A root grows at the tip, and a cap of short-lived cells helps the growing tip to move through the soil. Nutrients are taken up by fibrous root systems of most garden plants, which are mainly distributed in the top 15–20cm of the soil. It is logical then to provide nutrients from the top down, as happens in nature, where dead plant and waste animal matter is decomposed from the surface downwards. Organic matter such as composted animal manure or garden compost, applied as a surface mulch to established plants, will be taken down into the soil by earthworms.

When planting new specimens, particularly trees and shrubs, it is better not to add extra nutrients to the topsoil for backfilling the planting hole (Chapter 3), with the exception of phosphorus, which is relatively immobile, and can be added in slow-release form as bonemeal. In the absence of large nutrient supplies close by, the roots will be encouraged to grow downwards and outwards to access nutrients more efficiently.

Increasing the supply of nutrients to plants can sometimes be achieved by altering soil pH rather than by adding nutrients. A soil pH of around 6.5 is a reasonable compromise between the availability of macronutrients (which increases with pH) and micronutrients (which decreases with pH).

A micrograph showing a root tip, the tip being covered with a cap, which helps the root pass through the soil.

Application of ground limestone (which is largely calcium carbonate) to acid soil will raise the pH effectively but can take several months to have the full effect. More lime will be needed on heavy (clay-rich soils) than on light soils, as the negative charges on clay particles will bind some of the calcium.

Increasing the pH of an acidic soil by liming has a reasonably long-lasting effect because you are adding what is missing. However, lowering the pH of an alkaline soil in order to grow acid-loving plants is a temporary measure only and must be repeated regularly. With an alkaline soil, more and more basic ions (primarily Ca^{2+}) will leach into the soil from the bedrock, raising the pH and undoing the benefits of acidification.

The addition of organic materials such as mature manure and garden compost, composted conifer bark or sawdust, pine needles or leaf mould from oak, beech or pine will all produce organic acids and thus acidify the soil as they break down. Peat was used in the past, but some sources were from environmentally sensitive sites.

Ammonium fertilizers will tend to reduce soil pH because, during the microbial conversion of NH_4^+ (ammonium) ions to NO_3^- (nitrate), H^+ ions are produced which displace Ca^{2+} ions from clay and organic matter particles, making the soil

more acidic. Adding sulphur to the soil will also reduce its pH, as certain primitive soil bacteria use sulphur instead of oxygen in respiration and release H^+ ions, making the soil more acidic. These two methods require microbial activity, so tend to be slower-acting than methods which are purely chemical.

Gardening books will often list pages of plants which 'will not grow on limey soils', but I think this is an exaggeration of the effects of soil pH. There are a limited number of garden plants, referred to as calcifuges, which definitely will not tolerate high-pH high-calcium soils. The most important plants in this group are members of the Ericaceae (heather family), such as most heathers (some, but not all, are calcifuges), pieris, rhododendrons, camellias and azaleas. They are highly adapted to acidic soil conditions, with specialist ericoid mycorrhizal fungi associated with their roots which enable them to access the low levels of soil nutrients available under acidic conditions. These shallow-rooted species will develop severe chlorosis or leaf yellowing under alkaline conditions because the high levels of calcium in these high-pH soils interfere with their ability to take up and utilize iron from the soil.

In the case of most non-ericaceous species, however, the apparent problem with limey soil is not so much soil pH or the associated high levels of calcium, but the associated soil type. High-pH soils tend to be free draining, because the bedrock (limestone) is permeable to water, while bedrocks under acid soils (such as granite) do not allow water to pass through and hence the soils are damper.

If you garden on a high-pH soil and you are trying to grow plants other than ericaceous species which are said not to like lime, the problem may be that the soil drains too quickly, and the plant needs more water and nutrients. Try increasing the water-holding capacity and nutrient content of your soil with additions of well-rotted compost or manure.

USING FERTILIZERS

Although fertilizers can be used to correct nutrient deficiencies in garden plants, their principal function is to maintain or improve plant performance, making the lawn more lush, the bedding plants more floriferous and the vegetable plot more productive. To achieve this, the correct fertilizer needs to be selected, as does the amount, time and method of application, because inappropriate use of fertilizers can be counter-productive.

Choosing the Right Fertilizer

For a seasonal pick-me-up for garden plants, a general-purpose fertilizer with moderate amounts of N, P and K is appropriate. This could be an artificial fertilizer (7:7:7) or an organic fertilizer like pelleted chicken manure or fish, blood and bonemeal. These can be used as a top-dressing to the soil around shrubs and herbaceous perennials in spring, to bulbs after flowering, and to encourage re-growth and flowering after pruning spring-flowering shrubs or cutting back herbaceous perennials (Chapter 5).

Nitrogen

Nitrogen-rich fertilizers encourage growth of leaves and stems, so are particularly appropriate for lawns and for crops like lettuce, spinach, brassicas and celery. Spring lawn fertilizers, say 15:5:10 or 12:2:4, help to colour up the grass after the stresses of the winter, such as cold and waterlogging, where reduced nutrient uptake leads to chlorosis. The natural summer colour of grasses is light green; the dark green colour of lawns in magazine articles is unnatural and results from over-fertilization with N, as happens with sports turf.

The high N content of most spring lawn fertilizers increases grass growth, and so increases the frequency at which the lawn must be mown. A lower-N fertilizer supplemented with iron (needed for increased chlorophyll production) to counteract the chlorosis will result in greening without excessive growth.

High-N fertilizers should not be applied to plants where organs other than leaves, such as flowers or fruits, are the main point. In these circumstances, a high-N fertilizer will encourage leaf growth so that the vegetative tissues become a stronger sink for assimilates (Chapter 5), diverting them away from the more important organs.

Generally, high-N fertilizers result in more leaf but fewer flowers, particularly in plants native to nutrient-poor habitats, like *Cerinthe major* 'Purpurescens' from the scrub forest biome. In sweet peas, application of high levels of N in the spring results in increased competition between the leaves and the flowers later in the season. As a result, some of the flower buds drop off the plant in June. Over-use of N-rich fertilizers on an onion crop increases leaf growth at the expense of the bulb.

There are other situations where over-use of N-rich fertilizers should be avoided. Application of high levels of N to N-fixing plants such as beans and peas can be counterproductive, as this can suppress the ability of the bacteria associated with the plant roots to transform (fix) atmospheric nitrogen gas into a form plants can use.

The faster growth rate of plants over-fertilized with N can also cause problems such as lodging, where the stems collapse, and local deficiencies in nutrients which are poorly mobile within the plant, such as Ca.

In a healthy plant, the nitrogen from fertilizers gets combined with assimilates from photosynthesis to make both primary (carbohydrates, proteins and lipids) and secondary metabolites (everything else, including defence chemicals, flavour compounds and pigments).

The application of high levels of soluble N, in the form of artificial fertilizers or dried blood, tends to divert assimilates away from secondary and towards primary metabolism. As a result, any plant character dependent on secondary metablites is suppressed, including disease resistance, flavour and pigmentation. This phenomenon partly explains the stronger flavour and better disease resistance of organically grown vegetables, which are fertilized with slow-release N sources.

Phosphorus

Phosphorus (P) encourages root growth, so P-rich fertilizers, including superphosphate, are a useful addition to the back-fill soil when planting, particularly transplanting or after division (Chapter 3) where root damage is common. Because P does not move much in the soil, it should be incorporated into the soil rather than used as top-dressing. P-rich formulations are appropriate for autumn lawn fertilizers and for feeding N-fixing plants, such as peas, beans and sweet peas. On fertilizer packaging, P is often referred to as phosphate.

Potassium

Fertilizers which are rich in potassium (K) are used particularly to encourage flowering and fruiting, probably indirectly via an effect on relevant hormones such as ethylene. K-rich artificial fertilizers, such as 18:4:36, are used for containers, Gro-bags and hanging baskets. For annual plants like sweet peas and tomatoes, a high-K fertilizer should be applied regularly from the time the first flower bud is seen. On packaging, K is often refered to as potash, such as sulphate of potash (potassium sulphate K_2SO_4).

K-rich organic fertilizers are based on plant shoots, such as seaweed extracts (commonly marketed as tomato fertilizers), homemade comfrey tea or animal manure. Because K is highly mobile and not incorporated into organic matter, the presence of bedding in manure is a good sign as it soaks up the K-rich urine.

The other main effect of K-rich fertilizers is to

Cerinthe major 'Purpurescens', a scrub forest native, which produces stronger flower colours under low-nutrient dry conditions.

increase tolerance to abiotic stresses such as cold, drought and waterlogging. K is central to the functioning of the stomata and will speed up the closure of stomata in the face of drought. Under these stressful circumstances, a foliar spray with seaweed extract can help the plants cope, as these preparations contain K and osmoprotectants such as betaines, which help plants cope with stresses.

As part of its role in increasing stress tolerance, K is important in regulating cold-hardiness in plants. Autumn lawn fertilizers are usually 4:4:8 or 4:5:15 instead of the 15:5:10 characteristic of spring fertilizers. This autumn feed slows leaf growth (less N), but it encourages root growth (moderate P) and stimulates stress tolerance for the upcoming winter (moderate K). For woody plants, similar precautions should be taken, applying high-K fertilizers after June so that any new wood (especially after pruning) has the opportunity to harden up to tolerate cold weather before the winter.

Other Nutrients

Other nutrients can also be applied as fertilizers. Magnesium is applied to darken the green in foliage in roses and hydrangea, because Mg is a component of the green chlorophyll pigments. Ericaceous plants such as camellia, azalea and rhododendron suffer from lime-induced chlorosis in alkaline soils because the high pH interferes with iron uptake. Chelated iron is a form of iron which these plants can take up, alleviating the chlorosis.

How Much Fertilizer to Apply

The amount of nutrients applied to a particular part of the garden should reflect how much plant material you expect to produce from that site. On this basis, a vegetable garden should receive more nutrients than a herbaceous border, which should in turn receive more nutrients than a lawn. A wildflower meadow will require less than a lawn, while long-flowering annuals should receive less nitrogen (as the aim is to encourage flower production rather than leaves) than herbaceous perennials.

Shade plants and ericaceous plants, which are frequently slow-growing, require little supplementary nutrition. A spring top-dressing with garden compost or well-rotted animal manure, which releases its nutrients slowly, is usually sufficient each year. Most acid-loving species are adapted to and perform best on low-nutrient soils, so need little in the way of fertilizers. Scrub forest plants are also adapted to nutrient-poor conditions. Herbs native to these regions produce the most aromatic foliage under a starvation diet (one application in early summer) and little watering, which encourages high levels of secondary metabolism.

On the other hand, leafy herbs, such as rocket and sorrel, require a general purpose fertilizer to encourage leaf production. Plants such as potatoes, bananas, dahlias, hardy gingers and canna lilies, which produce a very large mass of plant material in a very short time, are examples of gross feeders which need large amounts of nutrient and water, as can be supplied by the liberal use of well-rotted manure. Plants with long flowering periods need lots of nutrients. When grown in containers, these plants may need weekly or fortnightly applications of a liquid fertilizer.

When to Apply

The nutritional demands of a plant varies over the season. With daffodils, for example, flower development requires high-K and low-N nutrition from March to May the year before flowering, before the leaves die down; the roots, requiring a high-P nutrient source, are formed from September the year before flowering to June the next year; and the leaves need high nitrogen levels from April to July. It is important to try to match the nutrients applied with the plant's demands, but for most of us, a general purpose balanced (contains NPK) top-dressing applied around flowering will do the job.

Spring bulbs, including snowdrops, narcissus, crocus and erythroniums, and spring-flowering woodland plants, like hellebores and trilliums, produce immature leaves and flowers for next year in the previous spring and early summer (up to August for snowdrop). We have already described the importance of allowing the foliage of geophytes to die down naturally, but the demand for nutrients continues even when the plants have died down, when other plants are growing around them and competing for nutrients. Fertilizers, particularly those compound fertilizers rich in potassium, or even sulphate of potash (potassium sulphate), applied when the leaves are still green, will produce better displays of flowering next year.

The same general rule (feed early-flowering species for two to three months after flowering) will also benefit early spring-flowering shrubs and trees like flowering cherry, jasmine and daphne, which should be fed with a high-K balanced fertilizer until the July after flowering.

Most of the shrubs and herbaceous perennials which flower later in the season do not develop flower buds until the year they flower, as they need exposure to environmental stimuli such as low temperature and a specific daylength before they make flower buds (Chapter 8). Flower buds in roses develop approximately one week after shoot growth starts in spring and continue for as short a period as two weeks, though the flowers will not expand until much later. It is evident, then, that plants flowering in summer and autumn need to be fed from spring onwards, well before flowers appear, to maximize flowering.

Feeding the plants will also accelerate their growth and development. Bulbs will produce more offsets (which will grow into new plants) when fed, and the time taken for seedlings to reach flowering size can be reduced. Trilliums and hellebores can take four to five years from seed to produce flowers, and this can be reduced to two to three years by judicious use of appropriate fertilizers.

Many gardening books will recommend that some plants, like agapanthus, flower better if starved, by being allowed to become root-bound in containers or in the open ground. To some extent this is true. The plants will have less N, so will produce fewer leaves, so that more energy can be used to produce flowers. But plants also need K for flowering, so these plants need to be fed regularly with K-rich feeds, such as tomato fertilizers, during early summer, when flower buds are forming. General starvation will reduce flowering, as there will not be enough nutrients to support healthy growth.

The slow-release characteristics of balanced organic fertilizers like manure, compost and pelleted chicken manure provide a valuable supply of nutrients to the soil. As the soil warms up, bacterial activity increases, resulting in release of nutrients in a form the plants can use. But this does not necessarily match up with the demands of the plants.

Nitrate released from manure in the spring may be in excess of the capacity of the root systems to take it up, resulting in leaching losses, while potassium release in early summer (to stimulate flower production) or late summer (to induce winter-hardiness in new growth) may be insufficient for these purposes. The flexibility of rapid-release organic (dried blood or seaweed extract) or artificial fertilizers allows nutrients to be made available to the plant when and where they are needed, making these fertilizers valuable tools for the gardener.

How to Apply

Roots are by far the most important route for nutrient uptake, but leaves can also take up nutrients. Foliar application of liquid fertilizers, either organic such as comfrey tea or seaweed extract, or inorganic, achieves some interesting plant responses compared to soil-applied nutrients. Response of the plant is rapid and independent of soil conditions, like pH.

Furthermore, plant stress as a result of transplanting, waterlogging or cold weather can be readily eliminated by foliar application of urea or an inorganic nitrogen source. A potato crop badly attacked by the soil-borne eelworm known as potato cyst nematode suffers as a result of the damaged root system being unable to take up sufficient phosphorus, a relatively immobile nutrient in the soil. Yields can be markedly increased by foliar applications of phosphorus-containing fertilizers.

Nutrient uptake by roots can be ineffective late in the season, as plants start to emphasize storing their food reserves for the winter, and over the winter, when low temperatures or waterlogging slow down root respiration. Under these circumstances, spraying nutrient solutions onto the leaves by-passes the roots and can achieve a quick boost to the nutritional status of the plant. This is particularly useful for helping plants recover from waterlogging, and for encouraging winter-flowering pansies and the like to continue flowering during cold weather.

CHAPTER 5

Pruning and Training Garden Plants

All gardeners are faced at some stage with the need to change the size or shape of some of their plants. This could be trimming a hedge, rejuvenating an overgrown shrub or encouraging a climbing rose to flower at eye level, where the blooms can be enjoyed, rather than twenty feet up in the air. Pruning is one of the topics which gardeners, particularly novices, find most stressing, but a better understanding of how plants grow and develop should take away these concerns and enable you to prune your plants with confidence.

Plants grow and develop very differently from animals. Individuals of a particular animal species have one head and a fixed number of limbs. On the other hand, plants have a more flexible type of organization, as can be seen when you look at different plants of the same species. Individual silver birches, for example, can have one or multiple trunks, each of which will have different numbers of branches. In addition, animals have a fairly defined maximum size, whereas this is less clear-cut for plants.

Similarly, when an animal develops, moving from being a juvenile to a young adult to a mature adult, all parts of the individual will be at the same stage at any one time. With plants, however, part of a plant can be juvenile while another part is adult. In beech trees, for example, the lower part of the tree retains the juvenile characteristic of retaining the brown dead leaves in winter, while the upper part of the same tree is adult and drops its leaves in autumn.

Downward training of a climbing rose, resulting in reduced apical dominance and increased numbers of flowers.

A beech tree in February, with the dead leaves attached to the lower juvenile branches but not the upper adult branches.

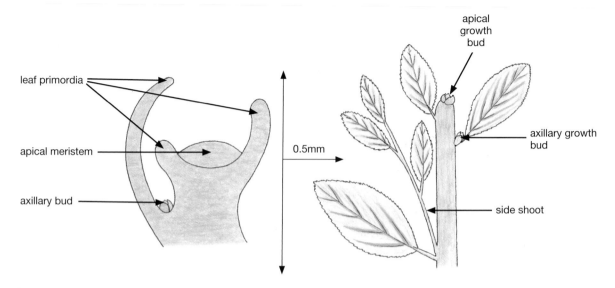

Organization and development of the meristem in a growth bud.

HOW PLANTS GROW

Plants grow in a modular fashion. The basic above-ground growth unit or module is a shoot, comprising at least one leaf attached to a length of stem, and a plant is just a number of these growth units connected together.

When you look at this unit more closely, you can see that each growth unit has a terminal or apical growth bud at the end of the shoot plus one or more lateral (otherwise known as axillary) growth buds. The term axillary underlines that each lateral bud occurs in a leaf axil, where the leaf or leaf stalk meets the stem. A similar organization also occurs with the root system, where there is an inter-connected network of roots, each with apical and axillary buds (in the root tips).

Within each shoot growth bud is a meristem which carries leaf and stem primordia (the immature leaves and stem). The meristem is a dome-shaped body made up of a small number of cells. Some of these cells keep dividing and can become any type of plant cell. In this, they resemble the so-called 'stem cells' in animals. When meristem cells stop dividing, they become specialized, to carry out functions such as photosynthesis or transport. An example of such specialization occurs when clumps

of cells on either side of the dome continue to grow away (by cell division) from the dome to form a leaf.

A good way to visualize the arrangement in a meristem is to remove the leaves in order from a butterhead lettuce, which is basically just an enlarged apical bud. As you remove the leaves from the outside in, from old to young, you will see that the leaves become progressively smaller and are arranged in a spiral arrangement around the stem. When you remove the last leaf, all that is left is a short stem at the tip of which is the meristem, which is usually about 0.2mm across.

When conditions are right, the leaf primordia in apical (or axillary) buds will unfold from the meristem, grow by cell expansion and develop into new leaves held along the new stem. Leaves appear very quickly, such as with deciduous trees in spring, because the increase in size is due simply to the existing cells expanding in size rather than to the production of new cells.

These distinct roles of cell division (to produce more cells) and cell expansion (to produce larger cells) are illustrated in the artificially dwarfed trees known as bonsai. Despite having leaves maybe one-twentieth the size of normal leaves, bonsai trees have leaf cells which are similar in size to normal trees; there are just fewer of them.

A stem apex of coleus, *Solenostemon scutellarioides*, showing the apical meristem, surrounded by leaf primordia, and axillary buds.

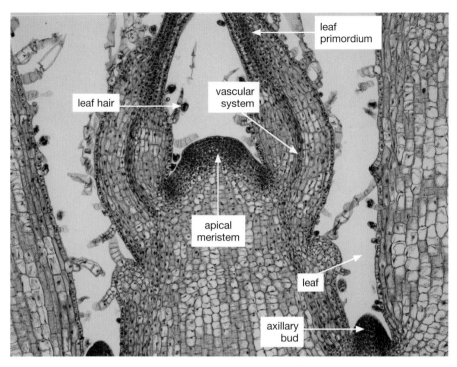

Whereas apical and axillary buds develop in pre-determined positions on the shoot or root, there is a third type of bud, the adventitious bud. 'Adventitious' means that these buds form where

Water shoots developing from adventitious buds following tree surgery.

the organs into which they develop would not normally appear. The roots which help climbing plants like ivy and *Campsis* to grip on to walls or tree bark develop from adventitious buds on climbing stems. Sweetcorn and potato plants also have adventitious roots on the lower part of the stem which help to stablize the plant.

As trees get older, the trunk gets thicker (secondary thickening), and the accumulation of bark can destroy axillary buds which were present when the tree was younger. If a stem with secondary thickening is damaged accidentally or by pruning, shoots which develop will do so from adventitious buds. These include the masses of vertical stems (water shoots) commonly found around the cut surface of pruned tree limbs.

The Roles of Plant Hormones

The growth of shoots from the buds is controlled by natural plant chemicals known as plant hormones. We have already described the two hormones most important in regulating growth, namely the auxins, produced by apical buds on shoots, which increase root growth, and cytokinins, produced by

Apical dominance in a hydrangea shoot, with the apical bud the most advanced, and the axillary buds further from the apex more developed than those closer to the apex.

The excurrent growth habit, where there is a single dominant leader shoot, of conifers, such as *Abies firma*, the Japanese fir.

apical buds on roots, which stimulate shoot growth (Chapter 3). Other hormones include gibberellins, which stimulate flowering and seed germination, abscisic acid, which helps to trigger leaf fall and seed dormancy, and ethylene, which speeds up fruit ripening.

Different concentrations of the same hormone can have very different effects on plant growth and development. At very low concentrations, auxins stimulate root elongation, but at low concentrations they inhibit root elongation but stimulate shoot growth. At moderate auxin concentrations, lateral root formation increases, while at high concentrations, auxins are toxic to plants, particularly dicots. These characteristics are exploited in gardening to make rooting powders, which contain moderate concentrations of auxins (Chapter 7) and lawn herbicides, which contain high concentrations of auxins (Chapter 6).

Auxins produced by the apical shoot bud travel down the phloem in the main stem to stimulate root production. These auxins also inhibit the growth of axillary buds to form sideshoots. This inhibition is known as apical dominance. The closer an axillary bud is to the apical bud, the more apical dominance there is and the less growth of sideshoots occurs. Axillary buds further down the stem, and hence further away from the source of auxins, are less dominated by the apical bud so grow longer sideshoots.

The clearest example of the effect of apical dominance on plant growth is the characteristic A-shape of the Christmas tree and other conifers. In these trees, the apical bud forms the 'leader' shoot which grows vertically, while the axillary buds grow out horizontally. This shape prevents snow accumulating on the branches of conifers in winter and breaking them. Among temperate trees, conifers such as pines exhibit this growth habit, with a single dominant leader shoot and strong apical dominance.

Temperate trees which are flowering plants, such as oak, show a different growth habit with no dominant leader shoot. The lateral shoots

The decurrent growth habit, where there is no single leader shoot, of angiosperm trees.

generally grow out to give a crown with a rounded shape. Some young fruit trees do not exhibit apical dominance, and lateral shoots start to develop from the start.

Palm trees grow from an apical bud at the top of each single stem and produce no growth buds, axillary or adventitious, lower down on the stem, so that, if the apical bud is damaged, the stem dies. A similar situation occurs with tree ferns. That is why it is so important to protect the top of tender palms and tree ferns in the winter in cold regions, by securing an insulating breathable material like straw or dry leaves around the top.

Similar-looking plants such as phormiums, cordylines and yuccas produce leaves in a rosette either at ground level or at the top of a stem, but these plants possess adventitious buds which will form shoots should the apical bud be damaged.

Apical dominance reflects the balance between levels of auxins and cytokinins within the plant and is largely a strategy to allow plants to secure as much light as possible. When the density of plants is high, with neighbouring plants close together, apical dominance is high. All of the assimilates go to the apical bud with little or no sideshoot development. In this way, the plant can grow vertically as quickly as possible to escape shading from its neighbours. An extreme version of this is the etiolated growth of plants grown in the dark (Chapter 9).

In a commercial hardwood forest, the valuable dicot trees are planted with high densities of fast-growing conifers as a so-called 'nurse crop'. The crowded conditions early on mean that outgrowth of axillary buds in the hardwood trees to produce branches is suppressed. This reduces the numbers of knots in the wood, and increases its value.

When plant density is low, as with an isolated specimen tree, apical dominance falls and more sideshoots develop, producing the large rounded leaf canopy characteristic of a single tree growing in isolation.

Apical dominance can be relieved in woody or non-woody plants by damaging the apical bud of the main stem, deliberately, by removing the growing tip, or accidentally, as a result of, say, insect damage. The consequence of this is that the auxin supply is cut off, the auxin:cytokinin ratio falls and axillary buds are no longer inhibited, so that sideshoots grow out, producing a bushier plant. This is the basis of a number of plant manipulations which gardeners use, such as pinching out and pruning.

CHANGING THE SHAPE OF WOODY PLANTS

Pruning is used on woody plants, be they sub-shrubs, shrubs, climbers or trees, grown as individual specimens or grouped together as hedges. Pruning is used to alter plant shape by removing stems and growth buds, resulting, say, in regrowth by axillary and adventitious buds after removal of the apical bud.

Differences in the organization and physiology of different woody plants affects how they respond to pruning. Sub-shrubs from scrub forest biomes, such as lavender and broom, generally do not respond well to hard pruning by cutting back into old wood, which is defined as being older than the current year's wood, although they have the ability to naturally re-sprout from adventitious buds low down on the plant. With these plants, a gentle trimming back of the herbaceous flowering stems immediately after flowering will keep them compact.

We have already seen that dicot trees (or hardwoods) can produce adventitious buds from old wood, resulting in regrowth when branches are cut, but this is not true for most conifers (softwoods) or palms. With most conifers, regrowth will only occur from stems where leaf tissue remains. Exceptions which will respond to cutting into old wood include *Taxus*, *Sequoia* and *Cryptomeria* and (when specimens are young) *Araucaria* and *Metasequoia*.

This information can be exploited when felling a tree. Cutting a conifer to below the lowest branch will kill the tree, but in dicot trees this will cause production of a thicket of water shoots from adventitious buds on the stump.

Formative pruning, to alter the shape of the plant, can be used to ensure you get a single-stemmed or multi-stemmed specimen, to balance out an asymmetrically shaped plant, or to improve the shape of the plant.

For ornamental trees, such as the wedding cake tree, *Cornus controversa* 'Variegata', a single main stem (leader) is usually the most aesthetically pleasing form. Accidental or deliberate damage to an apical bud or leader shoot will result in a reduction in auxin levels and apical dominance. The leader will usually be replaced naturally when the first axillary bud below the original leader moves from its horizontal growth pattern to a vertical one in response to the loss of the apical bud.

Because axillary buds in conifers usually form in a ring around the stem, the loss of the leader will stimulate all axillary buds in the uppermost ring to take over by growing vertically. All bar one of these must be removed to leave a single leader.

Some trees grown for their attractive bark, such as birches like *Betula albosinensis septentrionalis* and *B. ermanii*, *Acer davidii*, *A. catalipes*, *Cornus alternifolia* and ornamental cherries, look particularly good as multi-stemmed trees. This effect can be achieved by pruning a young specimen severely to less than 30cm above the ground. This removes the apical bud and encourages the growth from

near the ground of several shoots from adventitious buds near the base.

The most appropriate shapes for shrubs are vase-shaped for smaller shrubs like roses, and upright for many evergreens. To produce the spreading vase shape, it is best to prune to an outward-pointing bud, in order to avoid a congested centre. Some much-reported data from RHS trials concluded that pruning roses with a hedge trimmer resulted in better flowering than the standard method with secateurs, but the shape of the plants was badly affected.

If the aim is for upright growth habit, then pruning should be carried out to an inward-facing bud, a strategy particularly useful for evergreens such as holly and laurel.

CHANGING THE SHAPE OF NON-WOODY PLANTS

The growth and development of annuals and herbaceous plants can be altered by removal of the apical bud (pinching out) in order to alter hormone levels in the plant, to produce a bushier and usually more floriferous plant.

This involves removal of the apical vegetative bud, enclosed in a tuft of small leaves, at the top of the main stem of a plant. As a result, the sideshoots start to develop to produce a shorter but bushier plant which will have more flowers. This is particularly important in indeterminate plants where the main stem will continue to grow because the apical bud continues to produce leaves and does not flower.

Pinching out, or stopping, is commonly carried out on annuals, such as sweetpeas (at the four- to five-leaf seedling stage) and bedding plants, as well as on container plants, such as pelargonium, agyranthemum and fuchsia (which are pinched out at least once).

Pinching out can also be applied to a flowering stem. With gladiolus, for example, removal of the top two buds of a flower spike will encourage the remaining flower buds to open more or less simultaneously. A secondary benefit is that the flower spike is less likely to bend.

So far, we have dealt with changing the shape of

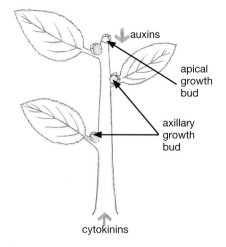

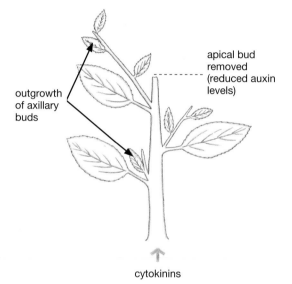

How pinching out produces bushier plants.

plants by physically removing tissues by pruning or pinching out to redistribute hormones, thus altering the way the plant grows. But this is not the only way to alter plant growth and development.

The uppermost bud is automatically the dominant bud in most plants, but the dominance of a particular bud can be altered by raising or lowering parts of the plant. This is an example of training. Two summer-flowering shrubs, bridal wreath, *Spiraea* 'Arguta' and *Exochorda* 'The Bride', form bushes with an attractive cascading shape. The shrub can be made taller by selecting one strong stem and supporting it with a tall stake or cane. By being taller than the rest of the stems, this stem adopts an apically dominant role and becomes a leader shoot, causing the whole plant to grow taller, while retaining the cascade look.

We have already seen how damage to the leader of a conifer will encourage vertical growth of the set of lateral shoots beneath the original leader. To speed up the vertical development of the lateral shoot chosen to be the replacement leader, it can be tied in vertically to a bamboo cane threaded through the centre of the tree, and will take over the role of the leader. When the new leader is growing strongly vertically, the supporting cane can be removed.

Sources and Sinks

So far, in discussing the response of plant growth to the presence or absence of apical buds, we have explained it simply in terms of two groups of plant hormones, namely the cytokinins and auxins. These hormones have both direct and indirect effects on the growth of plant parts.

The indirect effect is caused by the effect of each hormone on the potential size of a plant organ, such as a fruit, flower or leaf. Cytokinins do this by increasing the number of cells in the organ, while auxins work by increasing the size of each cell. For the organ (sink; Chapter 4) to actually increase in size, however, it has to attract more of the assimilates like sugars and other organic molecules from the leaves (sources; Chapter 4).

But how does the plant determine which sinks should be supplied with assimilates from which source? Assimilates can move in all directions in the phloem of the vascular system – up, down, sideways. But the assimilates from a particular leaf prefer to move to a fast-growing sink close to the source, directly above (preferably) or below the source, so that the assimilates can travel along an unbranched strand of phloem.

This arrangement means that there is a steep gradient of sugar concentration from the source (high) to sink (low), so that more assimilates travel to the sink. Fast-growing large sinks have high concentrations of plant hormones, which also help directly to attract more assimilates into that sink

This basic understanding of source–sink interactions will provide you with another tool by which to manipulate the growth of your plants, by increasing the ability of the desirable sinks to attract more of the assimilates.

Disbudding

This method is designed to redirect assimilates away from unwanted sinks (by removing them) and towards desirable sinks, and was developed originally by growers of flowers such as chrysanthemums and sweetpeas for exhibition. To this end, 'disbudding' involves removal of axillary buds so that more assimilates are targeted to the apical bud, resulting in small numbers of large blooms.

Deadheading

Deadheading is one of those garden activities, like turning a compost heap, which is probably talked about more than it is practised. But it is one of the best methods by which the flowering season of a plant can be extended. When a plant starts to set seed, which is its principal purpose, it responds to chemical messages fed back from the developing fruits by reducing or even stopping flowering. This is particularly important for annuals, which will die when they have produced sufficient seed. Busy lizzies (*Impatiens*) need to be dead-headed, as the flowers do not fall off naturally.

Plants which are sterile, as a result of being a hybrid between two related species, such as *Laburnum* × *waterii* 'Vossii' (Chapter 1), or which have the male sex organs (stamens) in the flower turned into extra layers of petals (Chapter 7) as in fully double primroses, do not set seed, so naturally have longer flowering periods.

Removing dead flowers before they produce seeds, therefore, is vital for a prolonged flowering season, by re-directing assimilates from the seeds or seedheads to the rest of the plant, and by preventing the production of the signal which switches off flowering. With indeterminate plants like sweetpeas, where the apical bud stays vegetative, producing leaf and stem tissue, twice-weekly picking or deadheading will markedly prolong flowering. Similarly, for the kitchen garden, it is important to harvest beans, peas and courgettes when they are still small, before the signals are sent to slow down flowering.

With determinate herbaceous perennials (where the apical bud turns from producing leaves to producing flowers, so stopping growth), the

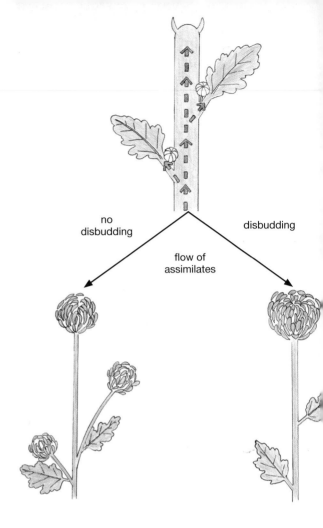

Effect of disbudding on flower number and size in exhibition chrysanthemums.

deadheading method used can vary. Some perennials, like lupin and delphinium, have flowering stems which carry leaves, with axillary buds. In these cases, when the last flower on the spike has faded, cutting off the main spike just below the bottom florets should stimulate the axillary buds to produce flowering sideshoots later in the season.

For herbaceous perennials with a leafless flowering stem and hence no axillary buds, like campanula and *Cirsium*, the spent flowering stem should be cut right back to the base. With plants which produce individual flowers close to the stem, such as daylilies, simply pinch out the faded blooms.

In daffodils, snowdrops and other plants with so-called 'inferior' ovaries (Chapter 1), the ovary is below the petals. In these plants, spent flowers must be removed below the swelling at the back of

When deadheading flowers with an inferior ovary, where the petals attach to the top of the ovary, like daffodil, remove the green swelling (the ovary) to stop seed production.

the flower (which is the ovary), as this will develop into the fruit and seeds.

In some cases, like oriental poppies, pulmonarias and herbaceous salvias, it can be worthwhile cutting back the entire plant (flowering stems, leaves and all) after flowering. This will not only get rid of tatty leaves and dying flower stems but can also result in the regrowth of valuable new plant material. After thorough feeding and watering of the plant (always a good idea after removing any significant amount of tissue), new leaves (oriental poppies, *Alchemilla mollis*, pulmonarias, geraniums, *Euphorbia dulcis* 'Chameleon') and, in some species, new flowers (gypsophilas, salvias, violas and pansies) will form.

The new leaves will usually be free of diseases like mildew which are common in dry summers (*Aster, Acanthus, Pulmonaria*) and will definitely be in better condition, while the resulting plants will be shorter than before and less likely to sprawl (for the more horizontally minded plants, like aubrieta and nepeta) or topple over. Furthermore, removal of the flower stems will reduce self-seeding problems with plants such as aquilegias, *Alchemilla mollis* and red valerian.

With shrubs and trees, deadheading *per se* is rarely carried out. Where deadheading does take place, as little as possible of the parent plant should be removed, cutting to above a strong growth bud. Hydrangea deadheads should be removed with 5–8cm of stem (to avoid removing the flowers developing for next year), while roses should be cut to just above the first leaf with five leaflets. Deadheads of ericaceous plants such as azaleas, camellias and rhododendrons should be removed by hand to avoid damaging buds lower down the stem.

With shrubs like buddleias which produce panicles of flowers, just the panicle should be removed as new flowers may develop from the axillary buds below. Remember not to deadhead those plants where fruits and/or seeds are part of their attraction, such as *Rosa moyesii* or *Iris foetidissima*, or where you want to leave seeds as winter food for the birdlife, such as teasel, which can attract birds like goldfinches.

Cutting Back

Cutting-back herbaceous perennials, by removing part of each stem, resembles pinching out, but the goals are different. In May or June, stems of many herbaceous perennials, such as asters, inulas, phlox, sedums, salvias, rudbeckias, *Verbena bonariensis* and delphiniums, can be cut back by approximately one-half. This removes apical and axillary buds, and regrowth results in shorter and stockier stems, with increased branching in some cases. These plants have little need for support, and flower later than untreated plants. This is sometimes called the 'Chelsea chop', because the traditional time to do it is the week of the Chelsea Flower Show in late May. By cutting back only some of the individual plants or stems in a clump, the flowering season can be extended.

A different approach, halfway between cutting back and dis-budding, is used for herbaceous perennials such as delphinium, where the number of shoots per plant is reduced in spring to five to seven on large plants or three on less vigorous plants. Regrowth is thus directed into a smaller number of shoots (sinks) so that each shoot is stronger, needing less staking, and produces a larger flower spike.

Once you appreciate the capacity of a plant to re-direct its assimilates to a desired sink when the competing sinks are removed, you will be able to improve the performance of many of the non-woody plants in your garden, for example:

- Bring forward the flowering date of oriental hellebores (*Helleborus* x *hybridus*) by removing the leaves in November or December;
- Increase the height of the trunk ('caudex') of the tree fern *Dicksonia antarctica* by removing last year's fronds if you live in mild areas where the fronds survive from year to year;
- Increase the number of flowers of *Nerine bowdenii* by removing the leaves by early July;
- Increase the size of the leaves of *Gunnera tinctoria* by removing the flower heads early on.

PRUNING TO ALTER PLANT SIZE OF WOODY PLANTS

As already mentioned, there is a balance between root and shoot, which ensures that the above- and below-ground parts of the plants are in equilibrium (Chapter 3). Understanding this explains several strategies for controlling the growth of roots or shoots.

Paradoxically, pruning can be used to either increase or decrease plant size in woody plants.

In deciduous trees and shrubs, assimilates produced as a result of photosynthesis during the growing season are moved from the leaves before they die and stored in the roots over the winter, to be transported to the shoots in the spring when growth starts. If your goal is to rejuvenate a plant, winter shoot pruning is the best approach. Hard shoot pruning in the winter (between November and mid-March, when the plants are dormant), cutting back the entire plant to three or four stems, will leave fewer shoot growth buds to be stimulated into growth in the spring by the remobilized food reserves. This will result in increased growth rate and a neater plant structure.

These winter-pruned shrubs can also exhibit highly ornamental modifications, such as spectacularly large leaves in *Tetrapanax papyrifer*, *Lomatia* spp., *Rhus glabra*, *Catalpa bignonioides* 'Aurea', *Toona sinensis*, *Paulownia tomentosa* and *Hydrangea quercifolia*, and larger flower heads in *Buddleja davidii* and *Hydrangea* 'Annabel'. This effect is due, in part, to the re-direction of stored reserves into a limited number of growth buds. But more importantly such development is due to

the increased cytokinin:auxin ratio (which stimulates increased organ size) in the young growth in spring, as a result of the reduced shoot size (which produces auxins) but unchanged root system (which produces cytokinins).

A common problem with shrubs is that growth can be uneven, giving the plant a lop-sided appearance. Although this can be remedied, the first step should be to identify the cause of the uneven growth. If the growth pattern is the result of stress, such as prevailing wind direction, shade or the effect of a wall nearby, then unless this is rectified the problem will recur.

To correct uneven growth, in winter you need to prune the stunted side of the plant more heavily than the strongly growing side. This may seem counter-intuitive but it will result in stronger regrowth on the weaker side of the shrub, because the assimilates from the roots will be channelled towards a smaller number of buds on the pruned side, each of which will grow into a vigorous shoot.

Hard pruning will be stressful for a plant, so it should be fertilized and watered after pruning. If the plant is old, rejuvenation pruning could take place over two or three years, with approximately one-third of the oldest stems being cut down to the ground each year to encourage new growth and reduce stress.

If, on the other hand, you want to restrict the growth of a tree or shrub, then summer shoot pruning may be the answer. By cutting away wood in the summer, you are removing the food reserves which, at this time of the year, are in the above-ground tissue. This results in less vigorous regrowth, and is particularly appropriate for trained fruit trees such as espalier and cordon-trained fruit trees, as it will discourage vegetative growth and encourage flower and fruit production. It is also the most effective way of controlling vertical water shoots which form around the base of trees or at sites of pruning.

An alternative to summer pruning of the stems to reduce above-ground plant vigour is winter root pruning, which will also deplete the food reserves of the plant as well as reducing the supply of root-produced cytokinins necessary to stimulate shoot growth. Root pruning is more drastic than shoot pruning, but is particularly good for re-directing vigour away from vegetative growth. It used to be *de rigeur* for fruit trees but the availability of dwarfing rootstocks (Chapter 7) for grafting has largely eliminated its use. The dwarfing of bonsai trees is achieved as a result of root pruning.

In the same way that shoot growth can be restricted by reducing the size of the root system, you can control the size of the root system by cutting back the shoots. With pollarding, the branches of the tree crown are cut back in winter to a single stump, resulting in a smaller branch canopy in summer. Despite their ugly gnarled crowns in winter, pollarded trees are valuable as street trees or as specimens near houses.

The smaller shoot size results in lower levels of auxins, and hence a parallel decrease in the size of the root system, maintaining the root:shoot ratio. The smaller root system is associated with a reduced demand for water and hence a reduced risk of subsidence in neighbouring houses, particularly on clay soils.

An alternative, if wildly expensive, approach to keeping trees the right size is to replace them. In Moscow's Red Square, when the blue fir trees which surrounded the walls of the Kremlin grew taller than the walls, they used to be replaced overnight with smaller specimens.

UNWANTED SIDE EFFECTS

Frost Sensitivity

So far, the correct time for pruning has been described in terms of plant response, such as winter pruning increases vigour, summer pruning decreases vigour. But there are other factors which need to be borne in mind when selecting the time to prune or cut back.

Time of pruning should be selected to allow any stimulated new growth to survive frosts and drying winds, particularly in evergreens. Winter pruning should be delayed or summer pruning brought forward to allow any stimulated new growth to 'harden' before winter. A high-potassium fertilizer top-dressing, such as wood ash, or seaweed fertilizer should help here, as potassium stimulates stress tolerance in plants (Chapter 4).

Similar points need to be taken into consideration when deciding when to tidy up dead stems of herbaceous perennials at the end of the growing season. The presence of stems in the herbaceous border over winter can provide much-needed structure, and looks particularly well when covered with hoar frost in very cold areas. Seedheads can also provide food for seed-eating birds. In milder damper regions, on the other hand, the stems quickly look unkempt.

A more important consideration, however, is that removal of dead stems encourages early growth of the growth buds once they lose their dormancy after the winter. If stems are cut back in autumn, this can stimulate the production of frost-sensitive young growth in spring, which can result in serious frost damage, especially to half-hardy perennials such as penstemons, fuchsias and melianthus. In cold areas, tidying up of dead stems should be delayed until growth from the buds at the plant base is seen in spring. In areas where frosts are less of a threat, an autumn tidy up should be the guideline for all but the most tender plants.

Along the same lines, there is still controversy about when deadheads of the late-flowering mophead and lacecap hydrangeas should be removed. Late summer or autumn deadheading encourages outgrowth of the axillary buds below the flower early in the spring. Particularly with the less-hardy mopheads, such sideshoots could be killed by frost, so deadheading should be delayed to spring.

Reverting to Original Characters

Sometimes new shoots, particularly those produced after pruning, can be different in character from the rest of the plant. This occurs when a garden plant is made up of two genetically different sets of tissues. There are two principal examples of this: grafted plants and variegated plants with orderly patterns of green and yellow (or white) tissues.

Plants of *Cornus contraversa* 'Variegata' grown on their own roots will be small, because the limited amount of green tissue in the variegated leaves results in low rates of photosynthesis. To produce larger specimens, a scion, or shoot with an apical bud, of the variegated plant is usually grafted onto

All-green suckers forming from the rootstock of a grafted *Cornus contraversa* 'Variegata'.

a rootstock of the green parent, *Cornus contraversa* (Chapter 7). Shoots formed from adventitious buds on the trunk of the rootstock (suckers) will have the less attractive green shoots which, having more chlorophyll, will grow faster than the variegated shoots of the scion parent.

Identification of suckers depends on the plant. The rootstock of grafted hybrid tea roses is usually *Rosa canina* or *R. multiflora*, which have seven leaflets per leaf as opposed to five for hybrid tea roses. The scions generally also have some reddening of the shoots, unlike those of the rootstock species which have apple-green shoots. With tree paeonies, on the other hand, suckers from the rootstock parent (*Paeonia officinalis*) have reddish shoots, unlike those of the scion parent.

Heavy pruning can encourage suckering, especially if it occurs too close to the graft union, a swollen site on the lower part of the stem. Removal of suckers must be carried out as close as possible

to the rootstock to prevent re-growth from adventitious buds on the sucker. This can be done with secateurs, but with woody plants, twisting the sucker around the claw end of a hammer and then tearing away the sucker is effective.

Another source of suckers on grafted plants is adventitious buds on roots of woody plants which spread, such as the coyote willow, *Salix exigua*, and poplars.

The second example where pruning can encourage the production of shoots with different characters occurs with variegated woody dicot plants which show the orderly pattern of green margins and yellow centres, like *Elaeagnus pungens* 'Maculata' or yellow margins and green centres, such as *E. pungens* 'Gilt Edge'. These plants can show 'reversion' to all-green or all-yellow shoots, with the frequency increasing after hard pruning. With variegated conifers, such as *Chamaecyparis lawsoniana* 'Albovariegata', the variegation is less orderly.

To understand how this phenomenon occurs needs a more detailed understanding of the organization of plant organs. A dicot plant shoot or leaf consists of three layers of tissues: Layers L-I, L-II and L-III. L-I is the outer or epidermal layer, with a single layer of cells which lack the chloroplasts containing the green pigments (the chlorophylls) so does not contribute to leaf colour. L-II is approximately 2–4 cell layers thick, while L-III makes up the rest (and in most cases, the bulk) of the organ. Cells in both L-II and L-III contain chloroplasts, so these layers are the ones which are involved in the production of variegated plants.

In variegated plants showing the neat arrangement of different coloured margins and central areas of the leaves, a mutation has occurred in either L-II or L-III, so that the chloroplasts in one of these layers contain no chlorophyll. Only the yellow carotenoid pigments (Chapter 1) are present, so the chloroplasts and cells in this layer are yellow instead of green. Where the variegated tissue is white, there is a block in synthesis of both the chlorophylls and the carotenoids.

This type of plant, with one layer having cells with the gene for green chloroplasts and the other with the gene for yellow (or white) chloroplasts, is an example of a periclinal chimera, because the cells in different layers of the same plant are genetically

Production of a variegated leaf from a periclinal chimera apex in a dicot (GWG).

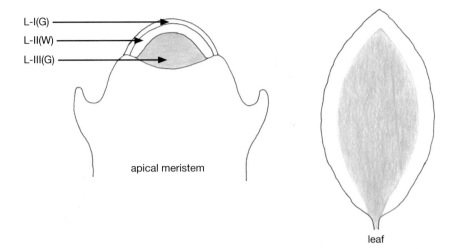

apical meristem

leaf

different. (The original chimera was a creature from Greek mythology with body parts from different animals, such as the goat and the snake.)

To understand why the dicot patterns of variegation arise, imagine that layers II and III are like two transparent but coloured gloves, one inside the other, with L-III on the inside. A variegated plant with leaves with a green centre and white margins would be like having an inner green glove and an outer white glove (white L-II and green L-III). Most of the leaf would appear green, because the inner layer, L-III, is the thicker one, but at the margins (like the fingertips in the glove analogy), one can see only the outer (white) layer. A leaf with a white centre and green margins, on the other hand, would have a white L-III and a green L-II. In both cases, L-I does not contribute to the leaf colour.

In meristems present in apical or axillary buds, the three-layer system is intact, so that shoots growing from apical or axillary buds will result in the same leaf variegation patterns as in the rest of

The 'hand-in-glove' model of a variegated leaf on a periclinal chimera.

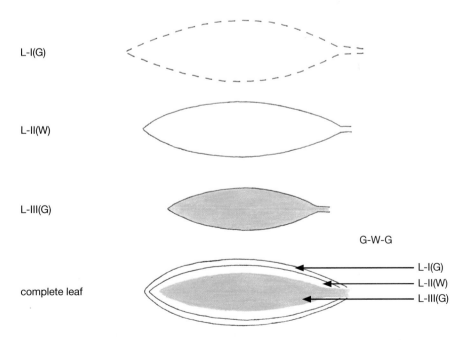

Breakdown (reversion) of the variegated periclinal chimera *Euphorbia characias* 'White Swan' to form all-green shoots.

the plant. With adventitious buds, however, the meristem will usually develop from only one layer, so that all-yellow or all-green shoots can develop, a common enough occurrence with variegated plants. This is particularly common after heavy pruning of shrubs, when regrowth often arises from adventitious buds.

The more important situation is of reversion to all-green shoots, as the higher chlorophyll content of the green leaves means that the revertant shoot will out-photosynthesize and hence out-grow the variegated parental form, taking over from it. Should a revertant shoot or branch develop on a variegated plant, you must remove the offending branch back to the original variegated stem.

JUVENILE AND ADULT TRAITS

Many plants go through a developmental switch from the juvenile phase to the adult phase. In under-storey trees (Chapter 2) the juvenile phase from seed can take between ten (*Davidia involucrata*) and fifteen years (*Magnolia* spp.). In some canopy trees, the juvenile phase can last for more than fifty years. In other plants it can take just a few weeks, until the plant produces a specific number of leaves (around eight for cabbage). Development, like growth, is controlled by plant hormones, and involves switching on or off thousands of genes in each cell. The transition from juvenile to adult in most plants is under the influence of hormones known as the gibberellins, of which more than forty are known.

With most plants, part of a plant may show juvenile traits while the rest shows adult traits. Juvenile traits are usually tied in with protection of the vulnerable young parts of the plant. The dead leaves of beech and scarlet oak on juvenile parts of the tree are retained during the winter, and provide some protection from cold for the growth buds wrapped in the dead leaves. The prickles on the stems of roses tend to be concentrated on the lower, juvenile wood, while the viciously toothed downward pointing leaves of the fierce lancewood (*Pseudopanax ferox*) are juvenile and are soon replaced by more standard adult leaves.

Juvenile shoots in woodland plants usually show traits to help them get to the light in a forest as quickly as possible. Juvenile shoots in many trees grow vertically, whereas adult shoots, particularly in conifers, grow horizontally. Probably the best-known juvenile trait is the ability of ivy (*Hedera helix*) stems to climb the trunks of trees by producing adventitious roots on the stems.

The characteristic appearance of ivy (*Hedera helix*) with the three-lobed leaves is also part of the juvenile phase of the species. If you want to keep the plant climbing, you need to provide it with a solid surface over which it can clamber.

When ivy reaches the top of a tree or wall the new growth of the plant will make the change to the adult phase of growth. Here, the stems lack roots and hang away from their support. These adult leaves lack the lobed appearance characteristic of ivy, and the stems will flower, producing a valuable late summer nectar source for bees and wasps, and an important winter food source for birds in the form of purple-black fruits. In the juvenile phase, ivy is a very useful ground cover plant for dry shade, especially under trees.

The change from juvenile to adult is irreversible in nature. The adult phase will not, under normal conditions, revert to the juvenile phase, although application of gibberellin hormones to an adult ivy plant will produce shoots with juvenile features.

In flowering trees and shrubs, the juvenile parts of a plant are, counter-intuitively, those formed first, on the lower part of the trunk, while the most recently formed and chronologically youngest branches near the top of the plant are adult. The blue gum, *Eucalyptus gunnii*, produces round silvery-blue leaves on juvenile shoots and long narrow green leaves on adult shoots. Similarly, the lower branches of a beech tree are juvenile and retain their dead leaves over the winter, whereas the upper leaves are bare.

The only way to get your adult plant to show its juvenile traits is to cut back to juvenile tissue. Hard pruning into the juvenile tissues in winter or early spring will cause adventitious buds to develop shoots from juvenile tissues. Regular trimming of a hedge tends to encourage the formation of juvenile shoots.

In blue gum, cutting a tree back to the ground (stooling or coppicing) or to a stump (pollarding) results in regrowth with the intensely blue-silver leaves characteristic of the juvenile plant. If your ivy plant develops adult characteristics, the only method for retaining the juvenile characteristics is to hard prune the plant back to the juvenile phase in August, and provide it with further support.

Coppiced or pollarded individuals will be compact with large numbers of shoots which can be of great value in a mixed border, and the height of the plant can be controlled by varying the height to which the plant is pruned. Other attractive changes observed in coppiced plants of trees or shrubs include better leaf characteristics, such as more intense silver coloration in *Buddleja davidii* 'Lochinch', more sun-resistant golden leaves in *Sambucus racemosus* 'Plumosa Aureus' and brighter

An ivy plant showing the juvenile phase (lobed leaves, climbing habit) and the upper adult phase (non-climbing, simple leaves, flowering).

autumn colours in *Cotinus coggyria* 'Royal Purple', as well as more intensely coloured stems of *Cornus sibirica* cultivars or *Salix* spp.

FLOWERING

For gardeners, the most critical aspect of the transition from juvenile to adult plants is that the adult plants can now flower. Once a plant has reached the adult stage, it can respond to environmental factors such as temperature and daylength by producing flowers (Chapter 8).

Flowering occurs when the meristem in the growth bud (apical or axillary) stops producing young leaves and starts to produce young flowers instead. In this way, the bud changes from being vegetative (producing leaves) to being reproductive (producing flowers). This phase change also means that the shoot stops growing, as the meristem has stopped producing stem and leaf tissue.

When an apical bud becomes reproductive, the

main stem will stop growing. Furthermore, apical dominance of the axillary buds on that stem will be relieved because auxin production falls, so that the whole plant stops growing in height but becomes bushier.

Each sideshoot will then grow until the apical bud on that shoot also becomes reproductive. Such a plant is said to be determinate, as in the bush tomato cultivars. Cordon tomato cultivars are said to be indeterminate because the apical bud remains vegetative so that the main shoot keeps growing, while the axillary buds become reproductive, producing flowers and fruits in the leaf axils of the sideshoots. Other examples include bush French bean cultivars (determinate) and climbing French bean cultivars (indeterminate).

The form of the floral primordia (young flower head) can be visualized by looking at a cauliflower head, which is actually an enlarged apical reproductive bud. Four important brassica crops, all varieties of the wild cabbage *Brassica oleracea*, have

evolved over two millennia as a result of selection by early farmers for plants with grossly enlarged growth buds:

- cauliflower, where what we harvest is an enlarged apical reproductive bud;
- cabbage, where it is an enlarged apical vegetative bud;
- calabrese (broccoli), where we harvest the enlarged apical and axillary reproductive buds; and
- Brussels sprouts, where we harvest enlarged axillary vegetative buds.

Flowering is mainly triggered by plant hormones. Once flowering has been initiated by the gibberellins, the levels of these hormones increase even more, stimulating stem extension so that the flowering stem gets taller, so that the flowers are placed high in the air to help pollination and seed dispersal.

In seasonal-flowering roses, where only one flush

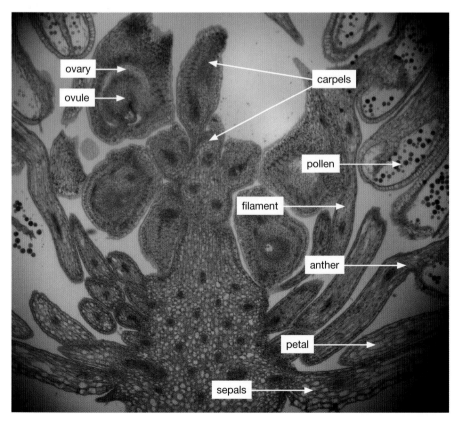

A micrograph of a thin section down a buttercup flower bud, showing a reproductive meristem with floral primordial.

of flowers occurs, the very high increase in gibberellin concentration following flower bud initiation in March inhibits the formation of further flower buds. In repeat-flowering roses, the gibberellin peak can be less than 10 per cent that in seasonal roses, so that inhibition does not occur, allowing these roses to flower throughout the summer. As with auxins, this illustrates how different concentrations of the same hormone can have opposite effects on organ growth and development.

The role of gibberellins in controlling plant height is exploited in the pot plant market, where plants like chrysanthemums and poinsettias are artificially dwarfed by treatment with growth retardants, artificial chemicals which inhibit the production of gibberellins in treated plants. These plants are usually also very floriferous because the reduced stem length means that the stem is a weaker sink for assimilates, leaving more to go to the flower buds. The effect of the plant growth retardant wears off, so if you manage to keep your plant alive till the next year, do not be surprised when it grows much larger.

The dual effects of gibberellins in controlling stem height and flowering date explains the common, though not absolute, association between these two characters, with short cultivars of a garden plant generally flowering earlier than taller cultivars. There are six height classes of bearded iris, for example, ranging from miniature dwarf (20cm, which flower in April to early May) to intermediate (40–70cm, flowering from mid May into early June) and tall (70–120cm, from late May to late June).

Pruning for Better Flowering

The main reason for pruning woody plants like shrubs and climbers is to increase the number of flowering stems and to place the flowers at a reasonable height to be admired. By pruning at the correct time and in the appropriate manner, the flowering of a shrub can be maximized, by re-directing hormones and assimilates.

The correct pruning strategy depends on when the plant flowers, whether flowers form on sideshoots and/or the main shoot, and whether flowers are produced on wood made in the current year (new wood) or the previous year (old wood). If in doubt, pruning should be carried out in early spring (unless the plant is clearly due to flower soon). Most plants will respond well to a light spring trim.

Generally, shrubs which flower early in the season (generally up to June), such as forsythia and ribes, or in early summer like *Philadelphus*, flower on old wood as no new wood will have been produced in time to develop flower buds so early in the season. Those shrubs flowering later in the season (in the second six months) usually do so on new wood, produced in the current year.

When selecting a pruning date, the best guideline is to maximize the period of growth between pruning and flowering. Those shrubs flowering on old wood should be cut back immediately after flowering, but the flowering date determines how that pruning should be conducted. For spring-flowering shrubs, the plant would not have had time to produce any new wood, so all the stems can be cut back hard after flowering. With forsythia, flowers arise on sideshoots, so pruning should be directed to maximize the number of sideshoots.

For early summer-flowering shrubs like *Deutzia*, *Kolkwitzia*, *Weigela* and *Philadelphus*, however, there will already be a mixture of new and old wood. The old stems which flowered this year should be cut back after flowering, leaving the new wood, which will go on to produce the flowers next year. Pinching out the new wood stems will encourage more flowering shoots.

Shrubs flowering on new wood (summer- and autumn-flowering species, such as *Hydrangea paniculata*, buddleia, spiraea, *Fuchsia magellanica* and deciduous ceanothus) are best pruned hard around February or March as this stimulates growth and provides plenty of time for flower formation. Hard pruning of plants like *Escallonia*, for example, also ensures that, by the time the flowers appear, they will be well distributed throughout the shrub, rather than all at the ends of the shoots. Pruning of late-flowering shrubs immediately after flowering would give the plant more time to produce new wood for flowering the next year, but would expose the young growth stimulated by pruning to damage by winter cold, so potassium-rich fertilizers should be applied to increase stress tolerance in the new growth (Chapter 4).

So, the general guideline for pruning shrubs is:

- spring- to early summer-flowering, on old wood: prune after flowering
- mid-summer to winter flowering, on new wood: prune in spring

As with all guidelines, there are exceptions. *Hydrangea macrophylla*, which includes both the mopheads and the lacecaps, flowers in late summer on old wood but is cold sensitive, so should be lightly pruned, actually little more than deadheading, in spring rather than immediately after flowering, to fat buds which will form this year's flowers. *Hydrangea paniculata* and *H.arborescens* 'Annabel' also flower in late summer but on new wood, and respond well to heavy pruning in spring (January or February).

Roses are the garden shrubs where pruning causes most concern. Basically, hybrid tea and floribunda roses flower on new wood so should be pruned in March, while shrub roses flower on old wood so should be pruned just lightly after flowering, although the flowering dates of all the roses are similar.

Many climbers do not require regular pruning. Where pruning is necessary, be it to remove a tangled mass of growth, to increase flowering or to encourage flowering near eye level, the guidelines for climbers are the same as for shrubs:

- flowering on old wood: prune after flowering
- flowering on new wood: prune in spring

The difficulty with climbers, however, is that these guidelines do not necessarily tie in with flowering date, as they do with shrubs. The following all flower on old wood and should be pruned immediately after flowering: winter jasmine (*Jasminum nudiflorum*, flowers in winter), lobster claw (*Clianthus puniceus*, flowers in spring, early summer), honeysuckle (*Lonicera periclymenum*, flowers in early to late summer) and common jasmine (*Jasminum officinale*, flowers in summer and autumn). However trumpet vine (*Campsis grandiflora*, flowers in late summer to autumn) flowers on new wood and should be pruned in spring.

Different *Clematis* species and cultivars flower at different times of the year (from winter to autumn), and on new wood, old wood or both. As a result, different types require different pruning regimes, but for some reason, pruning instructions in gardening books for *Clematis* generally have the impenetrability of some Jesuit treatise. For *Clematis* pruning, all species and cultivars can be classed into one of three groups:

Group 1, the early-flowering clematis (including *C. montana*, *C. armandii*, *C. alpina*, *C. cirrhosa* and *C. macropetala*) flower from late winter to spring on wood produced the previous year. If the larger species (*C. montana* and the evergreen *C. armandii*) need to be pruned at all (largely to keep them in check and to keep flowers near eye level), they should be hard-pruned immediately after flowering in spring, whereas the other, less rampant Group 1 species rarely need pruning.

Group 2 includes all the large-flowered deciduous hybrids. These have two flushes of flowers, the first in early summer from old wood and the second in late summer on new wood. Pruning should take place in late winter or early spring before new growth starts.

Finally Group 3, the late-flowering species, such as *C. viticella*, *C. texensis*, *C. orientalis* and *C. tangutica* flower in late summer on new wood. These should be pruned to about 15cm above the ground when evidence of growth is clear in early spring (February to March), to ensure that flowering is near eye level.

Pruning can be as necessary for keeping the plant tidy and within bounds as for encouraging flowers. An overgrown clematis can be rejuvenated by cutting back hard to the ground just after flowering (Groups 1 and 2) or in spring (Group 3).

Pruning to Eliminate Flowers

Pruning can also be used to prevent flowering, when this is unattractive or when it detracts from the shining glory of the plant. This can be done directly, such as laboriously removing the flowers from *Tanacetum vulgare* 'Isla's Gold', to keep the leaves in good shape, or from *Gunnera manicata*, to redirect assimilates to the leaves which then grow even larger than usual. Alternatively, hard pruning

Santolina in spring, cutting it back to 5cm above the ground when the first shoots appear above the ground, generates new, particularly silver regrowth, and suppresses production of the rather ugly small chrome-yellow buttons of flowers. Hard pruning in spring will similarly stop flowering of *Brachyglottis greyi* and *Phlomis fruticosa*, plants grown primarily for their foliage.

Training to Improve Flower Production

So far, we have seen how pruning can be used to improve flower production by reducing apical dominance so that there is an increased number of flowering sideshoots. But, as mentioned earlier, the dominance of the apical bud is due to its elevated position on the shoot. If it is lowered and tied in to the horizontal, apical dominance disappears, hormone balance and the movement of assimilates change, and sideshoots start to develop, as if the apical bud had been removed. This is the basis of the training of woody plants, primarily climbers, so that flowers develop along the length of the stem (and within reach, for appreciation by the gardener), not just at the top of the plant.

Fruit trees and tomatoes for the small modern garden are frequently trained into shapes where individual stems are at an angle, such as fan (various angles) or cordon (45°), or horizontal, like espalier or stepover cordons, reducing the apical dominance and stimulating axillary growth (Chapter 9). The number of flowering sideshoots (spurs) can then be increased by selective pruning.

A similar approach can be taken with climbing and rambling roses. Left to their own devices, climbers often race up walls and pergolas or into trees, so that flowering occurs too high up to be seen properly. Some roses are naturally arching in habit and these are particularly floriferous; 'Phyllis Bide', for example, can be covered in flowers along the length of the stem. The reason for this, of course, is the reduced apical dominance which encourages axillary bud growth and hence flowering.

With cultivars which are not naturally arching in growth habit, pliable young stems of climbing

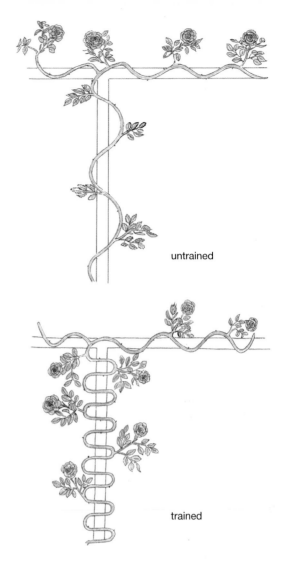

untrained

trained

Effect of training on side shoot growth and flowering in a climbing rose.

roses, produced after pruning out the older more rigid stems, can be wound around and tied in to supports, such as the legs of pergolas, to ensure flowering along the length of the stem. Similarly, old shrub roses can be trained over hooped supports, such as hazel branches, to achieve a similar effect.

Indoor climbers, such as bougainvilleas and jasmines, are usually grown around hooped supports to ensure that the plant does not spread too far and that the flowers are at eye level. These plants flower best if they are untied from their supports and the stems are allowed to sprawl horizontally until flower buds have formed, at which point the stems can be re-attached to the support.

CHAPTER 6

Managing Pests, Diseases and Weeds

The presence of dead trees contributes to the biodiversity of a woodland by supporting the growth of saprophytic fungi, which feed on dead tissues.

A garden is an example of an ecosystem (Chapter 2), albeit an artificial one, with interactions between all the living organisms and between the living (biotic) and non-living elements (abiotic). Some of the biotic interactions are beneficial for the garden plants, such as pollination to get seeds and fruit. Others, on the other hand, are detrimental, such as those involving pests and pathogens, the disease-causing micro-organisms.

To understand how to manage pests and pathogens in the garden with minimal use of chemicals requires an understanding of biotic interactions, involving the physiology of plants, animals and

micro-organisms, as well as an understanding of ecology, to put all these individual interactions into the context of the garden community.

A mature natural ecosystem is very diverse. A deciduous woodland (Chapter 2) can contain more than 300 species of plant and animal, as well as much higher numbers of fungi and bacteria in the soil. This high biodiversity is associated with the presence of a number of different habitats within the ecosystem, each with its own flora and fauna. These include habitats under trees, up trees and between trees (such as in forest clearings), as well as habitat differences between different species of trees, and between dead and living trees. This large number of habitats within the ecosystem provides a home for each of a wide range of species present.

The competitiveness of white clover in a lawn suffering from nitrogen deficiency.

A consequence of this high biodiversity and of the interactions and inter-dependencies between the various species is that an ecosystem is a self-regulating community. The interactions within the ecosystem are based mainly on food supply and demand, in the form of a food chain. Except for the top predator at the top of the food chain, all species within the ecosystem are food for something else.

Food chains have already been touched on with respect to compost heaps (Chapter 4). Here, the food chain involved in an ecosystem like a woodland will be described in a little more detail.

In a food chain, nutrients and chemical energy are passed on from the food item (at one trophic level) to the consumer (at another). Any food chain always starts with a plant, like a grass plant or an oak tree. Plants are known as the 'primary producer', because plants use simple chemicals from the air, soil and water, to make energy and food (Chapter 4). The plants are then fed on by the next trophic level, a herbivore (primary consumer), such as the caterpillar of the oak eggar moth feeding on the oak tree, then to a carnivore (secondary consumer) like the blue tit. The food

chain then continues when the blue tit is eaten by a sparrowhawk or a cat (tertiary consumer).

In a natural ecosystem, food chains can have up to five trophic levels. In reality, food chains are branched rather than linear as different species can feed on any one particular food item, as we have seen. Furthermore, one species can appear at different positions in the food chain. A badger can be a primary consumer, eating blackberries, or a secondary consumer, by eating primary consumers like beetles and mice. As a result of this complexity, the term food web is more appropriate than food chain.

As a consequence of this inter-dependency between species, the size of the population of a food species is regulated by the size of the population of the corresponding predator species, and vice versa. If a particularly mild winter results in more aphids/greenflies surviving the winter, the increased number of aphids (primary consumers) could pose a threat to the plants they feed on in the ecosystem. Instead, the aphids are themselves a food source to other insects which are their predators (secondary consumers) such as ladybirds, hoverfly larvae and ground beetles, or

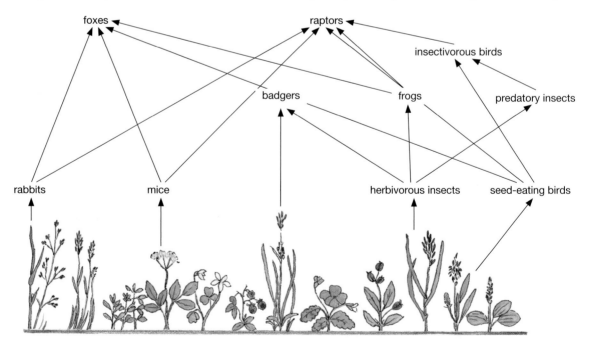

A typical food web.

parasites, which live attached to or inside the host. As a result, the populations of these beneficial insects will increase, reducing the aphid numbers to normal levels and correcting the original disturbance by natural biological control. This is the 'balance of nature'.

If you look at the plants in a natural ecosystem, then, you will find small amounts of disease or pest damage, with usually less than 5 per cent of the plant biomass being consumed each year. Common wild plants are attacked by fungal pathogens such as dandelion rust or groundsel mildew, and by pests like slugs, but the different members of a natural ecosystem are generally in equilibrium.

Man-made ecosystems on the other hand are usually unbalanced and lack the biodiversity and interactions to regulate disturbances, as happens in the woodland. An agroecosystem such as a wheat crop has very few habitats, after elimination of weeds and hedgerows, because every part of the field is dominated by wheat and little else.

The most likely organism to colonize a wheat crop would be one which uses wheat as a food source, in other words a pest like an aphid. The lack of biodiversity makes it highly unlikely that there would be enough beneficial insects to control an aphid outbreak, so farmers depend on pesticides. Despite this, losses due to pests are much higher in agroecosystems than in natural ecosystems.

Gardens are also artificial ecosystems, but are much healthier, in ecological terms, than agroecosystems. Firstly, the biodiversity is much higher, frequently with higher diversity levels than even the tropical rainforest biome (Chapter 2). Secondly, most garden plants, with the exception of those in the vegetable beds, are perennial, providing permanent habitats for beneficial organisms.

GARDEN PESTS AND PATHOGENS

For most gardeners, it is the 'pests' which are our greatest cause for concern. Pests in the garden range from the molluscs like slugs and snails, to insects like aphids and scale insects, and to nematodes or eelworms, and from vertebrates such as birds eating your soft fruit, mice devouring newly planted bulbs, and rabbits laying waste to young trees.

I use the term 'invertebrates' or 'pests' because strictly speaking many of these creatures, including slugs, nematodes and spider mites, are not insects. Pests and pathogens will be dealt with together here, as many of the ecological management strategies are similar.

It is important to realize that most creepy crawlies do not have designs on your plants. Indeed, most plants are completely resistant to the vast majority of bugs. Over the 200 million years that plants and insects have shared the Earth, plants have evolved a tremendous array of physical and chemical defences. Plants are also poor food sources, being at least 85 per cent water and containing less than 3 per cent protein, compared with 20 per cent protein in an average insect, and consisting largely of cellulose, which most organisms cannot use as food.

As a result, most invertebrates eat dead plant tissues (millipedes and wood lice), bacteria (most nematodes) or other live invertebrates (centipedes, ladybirds). Indeed, to achieve biological control of pests an important part of pest management is to encourage in your garden the beneficial invertebrates, such as ladybirds, hoverfly larvae and ground beetles, which feed on those few invertebrates which do eat plants.

Relatively few invertebrate species (approximately 0.1% of the total) feed on living plants. Although one cubic metre (1m x 1m x 1m) of garden soil contains approximately 200 slugs, only four of the 30 slug species found in the UK are pests of garden plants. If you find large slug species in your garden, don't panic. These species feed on decaying plant material, whereas the small species such as the keeled slug, which spends much of its time underground, are the gardener's foe.

Early recognition and identification of pest problems is key to a successful pest management programme. Aphids are sap-suckers and tend to be attracted to yellow tissues, such as old and young leaves. Aphids are easy to see because they commonly aggregate on shoot tips, where the unthickened cells of the young tissues make it easier for

Slugs collected overnight from a single trap.

the insect to get its mouthpart (stylet) into the phloem. Removal of broad bean shoot tips once the plants have started to produce pods helps to control black bean aphids. Scale insects are also sap-suckers, usually found on leaf undersurfaces.

Because sap contains a much higher concentration of sugars than amino acids, the building blocks of proteins, sap-sucking pests like aphids and scale insects must drink a lot of sap to get enough amino acids in their diet. To get rid of the excess sugars and liquid, these pests exude a sugar-rich liquid (honeydew). This can lead to colonization of the leaves by the sooty mould fungus *Cladosporium*, causing large black patches, which can be a useful diagnostic feature for aphids and other sap-suckers such as whitefly.

Certain pests are likely to be a problem in any garden. Slugs and snails will be present in all bar the driest gardens. The soil in most allotments or old vegetable gardens will probably have a population of long-lived and serious soil pests and pathogens, such as potato cyst nematodes or clubroot of brassicas. New lawns planted on what has been old grassland will probably suffer from attack by leatherjackets, the larvae of crane flies (daddy longlegs), which feed on the roots of grasses.

The sight of birds like starlings, rooks and magpies pulling up clumps of lawn early in the morning in late spring or late summer suggests the presence of leatherjackets, which feed near the surface at night. To confirm this, water the area well in the evening, then cover it with black material to keep out the light. In the morning, when you take up the material, large dark brown larvae

(leatherjackets) or fat white grubs (chafergrubs) should be visible. These should be collected and destroyed (or left for the birds).

Plant diseases are caused by pathogens, which are infectious micro-organisms invisible to the naked eye. The devastating effects of crop diseases on society are illustrated by the Great Famine in the 1840s in Ireland, triggered by the spread of the late potato blight fungus, *Phytophthora infestans*. Other potato diseases were regarded as so serious that their common names, like 'scab' and 'blackleg', were used as swear words. On a more trivial level, a disease of coffee plantations disrupted supplies and meant that an alternative hot drink was needed, starting Britain's love affair with tea.

The main disease-causing organisms in gardens in western Europe are fungi, viruses and bacteria, in that order. Bacteria generally need higher temperatures than fungi, so are more common in glasshouses, though climate change has increased the problem of bacterial diseases in field-grown plants. Fireblight is a common garden disease caused by a bacterium which attacks members of the rose family, while bacterial canker is the cause of the shothole effect in purple-leaved cherry.

Fungi can be spread as spores through the soil or through the air, depending on the pathogen, and can infect plants by penetrating through the tissue. Bacteria, on the other hand, need ready-made openings (like wounds or stomata) to achieve entry.

Viruses need another agent (vector) in order to infect a plant. This vector can be mechanical, with the tobacco mosaic virus, TMV, being spread by a gardener handling healthy tomato plants after infected ones. Indeed, smokers have been shown to pass on TMV from their cigarettes to tomato plants they handle. Viruses can also be spread by failing to clean secateurs after cutting out diseased tissue.

The most important living virus vectors are the aphids, although whitefly and thrips can also act as virus vectors. Sap-suckers like aphids spread virus diseases, such as potato virus Y (PVY), by sucking up virus particles in the sap of an infected potato plant through their stylet and introducing them into a healthy plant with their saliva when they feed on the next plant. Once inside the plant, the virus particles can travel systemically in the phloem throughout the plant (Chapter 7).

It is worthwhile keeping a gardening diary, including records of pest and disease problems occurring in different parts of the garden each year, as the organisms concerned will probably overwinter in your soil to cause problems next year unless you take appropriate action.

UNDERSTANDING PESTS AND PATHOGENS

An understanding of garden pests and pathogens can help us develop gardening strategies which shift the balance of power back to the gardener. The fact that nematodes have six lips, honeybees have hairs on their eyes or that intoxicated ants always fall over on their right side may only be of help in table quizzes, but information on the ecology and the life cycle of the pest species is of considerable value to gardeners.

For example, aphid populations can grow very quickly because they produce fifteen or more generations each year and can produce live young, so early identification and treatment of aphid infestations is important.

With some garden plant diseases, symptoms can appear similar, such as the fluffy white pustules on infected leaves associated with mildew diseases of a wide range of plants. But these are symptomatic of two distinct diseases, with different ways of managing them. Powdery mildew produces pustules on the upper and lower leaf surfaces, and is commonly associated with plants growing in dry soils. Downy mildew, on the other hand, has pustules on the lower leaf surface only and is particularly severe under conditions of high humidity.

The feeding habits of pests and pathogens can also be useful to know. Some garden pests are specialists, feeding on only one species or maybe on several closely related species. Potato cyst nematode (PCN) feeds on the roots of potato, tomato and aubergine, all members of the Solanaceae. Specialist pests and pathogens can often be identified by the observation that their common name usually includes the name of the food plant, as in cabbage white butterfly, carrot root fly and rose powdery mildew.

On the other hand, generalists like slugs, snails and vine weevils can attack a wide range of plant species. The main significance of this fact is that

Leaves of *Polygonatum multiflorum* attacked by the Solomon's seal sawfly.

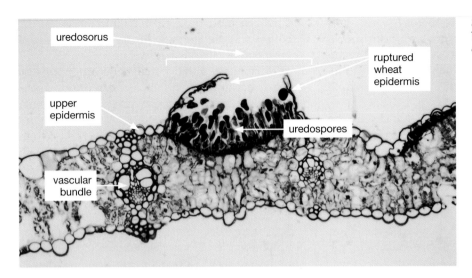

Spores of wheat rust breaking out from the leaf of an infected wheat plant.

crop rotation for management of soil-borne pests and pathogens in the vegetable garden (Chapter 9), by grouping plants from the same family together, is effective only against specialists.

Knowing the host plants of the pest or pathogen you are trying to control can be an important weapon in a gardener's armoury. If you are concerned about an attack of the bacterial disease fireblight on one of your specimen *Pyracantha* shrubs, for example, it is best to be aware that other,

A specialist pest, the caterpillar of the cinnabar moth feeding on the common ragwort, *Senecio jacobaea*.

related plants like roses in your garden can become infected by fireblight and act as a source of infection of your favoured plant. This applies equally to related cultivated and weedy species. Carrot root fly attacks carrot as well as other members of the Apiaceae, such as parsley, and the weeds Queen Ann's lace and cow parsley.

The only situations where a disease can spread from one garden species to another is if the two plant species are closely related, as with late blight attacking both potato (*Solanum tuberosum*) and tomato (*S. lycopersicum*), or where the pathogen is a generalist, such as white rot caused by the fungus *Sclerotinia sclerotiorum*, which can attack carrots, potato, Jerusalem artichokes, brassicas and lettuce, among others.

Most garden pests and pathogens are specialists. Although aphids are among the most common of garden pests, with about one-quarter of all plants being attacked by them, most aphids are specialists, attacking only one or a small number of related species, like the black bean aphid, *Aphis fabae*, on broad beans. There are more than 500 different species of aphid in the UK, but it is rare for one species to be able to spread from one plant species to another. Most specialist pests can attack plants belonging to the same family as the host plant, so that the lily beetle attacks not only lilies but also fritillaries, also members of the Liliaceae.

Specialization is even more pronounced for

plant pathogens, with powdery mildews, downy mildews and rusts each being restricted to a small number of hosts. For example, many unrelated garden plants such as roses, phlox, monarda, sweet peas and asters can suffer from the disease powdery mildew, but the mildew fungus is a specialist and in each case the mildew species is different, so the disease will not spread from, say, aster to rose.

Traditionally in Bordeaux, a red rose was planted at the end of each row of grapevines as an early indicator of powdery mildew, which could devastate the vines. But we now know that the fungus which causes rose mildew (*Podosphaera pannosa*) is completely different from that which attacks grapevine (*Erysiphe necator*). The more likely role of the indicator rose was that all powdery mildews attack when the weather is hot and dry; when the roses succumbed to mildew, the conditions were suitable for vine mildew.

Sometimes, different forms of the same fungus cause disease on two different but related plant species. Wheat powdery mildew is caused by the fungus *Blumeria graminis* f. sp. *tritici*, unlike cocksfoot powdery mildew, where *B. graminis* f. sp. *dactylidis* is responsible. The wheat pathogen will not attack the grass cocksfoot (*Dactylis glomerata*) and vice versa.

MANAGING PLANT PESTS AND PATHOGENS

There are three strategies for managing pests and pathogens of garden plants: help the plant, encourage your pest/pathogen's natural enemies, and ultimately make life impossible for them. Note the use of the word 'manage' rather than control. We are not trying to eradicate the poor misfortune which has evolved to dedicate itself to the destruction of our favourite plants. The aim is not 'scorched earth' but a re-alignment of the balance of power, giving the garden plant (and the gardener) the upper hand.

Help the Plant

Host Plant Resistance

Most garden plants are resistant to the vast majority of pests and pathogens. For example, cabbages are completely resistant to carrot root fly, though they are attacked by cabbage fly. For those plant–pest combinations where the plant can be attacked, like carrots and carrot root fly, or potato and potato cyst nematode, genetic resistance or tolerance may be available in some cultivars of the host plant to minimize the effect.

Hosta sieboldiana 'Elegans' is partially resistant to attack by slugs and snails.

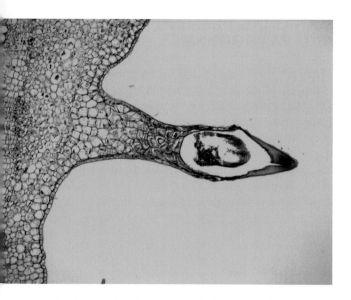

A micrograph of a stinging hair from a nettle stem, showing the silica 'needle'.

For example, rose cultivars resistant to the blackspot fungus include 'Polar Star', 'Congratulations' and 'Sweet Dreams', while potato 'Sarpo Mira' is resistant to the late blight fungus. For asters, powdery mildew can be a real problem among *novae-belgiae* cultivars, so these have been largely replaced by the mildew-resistant *novae-angliae* cultivars or by the more resistant *Aster* cultivars, such as 'Little Carlow'and *A. frikartii* 'Mönch'. Of the clematis cultivars, only *C. viticella* cultivars are reliably resistant to clematis wilt.

Resistance can be physical in nature. Potato cultivars with russet-skinned tubers such as 'Golden Wonder' tend to be moderately slug resistant because the thicker skin provides physical protection. Similarly, partial slug resistance in hostas is associated with the thick-leaved cultivars such as the *sieboldiana*-derived 'Sum and Substance' and 'Snowdon', or tetraploids such as 'Touch of Class', where the extra copies of chromosomes (Chapter 7) make the leaves thicker.

Defence mechanisms can also be chemical in nature. All gardeners are wary of nettles. The stinging hairs on leaves and stems have a hypodermic needle made of silica which injects formic acid (causing the stinging sensation) and histamine (causing the white raised blisters).

Generally, red-leaved brassicas and lettuce tend to be more slug resistant than green-leaved cultivars. This is because the flavonoid chemicals associated with leaf colour are distasteful to generalist pests. Red- or purple-leaved cultivars also tend to be more cold tolerant, as in globe artichokes, a side effect of the same chemicals.

Specialist pests have evolved ways of overcoming their food plant's defences. Ironically, they often use the plant's own defence chemicals as ways of finding their food plants. Pregnant females of the cabbage white butterfly can locate brassica plants partly by the presence in the air of glucosinolates which the plants give off, recognizable as the characteristic sulphury smell of brassicas.

Carrot cultivars such as Flyaway, Sytan and Resistaway bred to be 'resistant' to the specialist pest carrot root fly actually lack the natural chemical, chlorogenic acid, which the pest uses to find its host plant.

There are several types of genetic resistance, but these can be readily grouped into two classes, partial and complete resistance. Surprisingly, complete resistance is usually controlled by a single gene, whereas partial resistance is determined by several different genes working together. Against potato blight, cultivars Sarpo Mira and Sarpo Axona show complete resistance, while cultivars Cara and Maris Peer exhibit partial resistance.

Though complete resistance seems like the better option, there is a disadvantage: resistance controlled by only one gene affects the pest or pathogen at only one target point, whereas that controlled by several genes has several target points. As a result, it is easy for the pest or the pathogen to change through a natural genetic process known as mutation so that the target point is different and the gene for complete resistance is no longer effective.

Because fungi produce so many more offspring than do invertebrates, the chances of this new mutant form (said to be 'virulent') appearing is higher in a pathogen than for a pest. Plants carrying this resistance gene will no longer appear to be resistant wherever this virulent form of the pathogen is present, so complete resistance, particularly against air-borne pathogens, can appear to break

Darmera palmata is a slug-resistant alternative for hosta for a shady site.

down. Examples of resistance breakdown familiar to gardeners include resistance to powdery mildew in *Rosa* 'Super Star' and resistance to late blight in potato 'Santé' and 'Setanta'.

A resistance gene in a plant usually works against only one pest or pathogen. Potato 'Maris Piper', for example, contains a gene for complete resistance to the golden potato cyst nematode (PCN), *Globodera rostochiensis*, but this resistance gene has no effect against the closely related white potato cyst nematode, *Globodera pallida*.

Host Plant Tolerance

Sometimes, a cultivar is said to be 'tolerant of' rather than 'resistant to' a particular pest or pathogen. Maincrop potato 'Cara' is tolerant of attack by PCN. The roots are attacked by the nematodes but, having such a large root system, 'Cara' can withstand this attack without losing too much yield. Unlike PCN-resistant cultivars, such as potato 'Maris Piper', tolerant cultivars increase rather than reduce the size of the pest population, because the pest can feed and multiply, so they can make a bad situation worse. A similar situation can happen with pathogens, with beetroot 'Kestrel' showing increased tolerance to powdery mildew.

Host Plant Escape

Some crop cultivars suffer little or no damage from specific pests or pathogens by escaping their would-be attackers, a strategy similar to stress escape (Chapter 2). For example, first early potato cultivars such as 'Home Guard' and 'Swift' or second earlies like 'Nadine' and 'Kestrel' are usually harvested by late June and hence escape infection by late potato blight.

This fungus cannot infect potatoes until the conditions are mild and humid. Minimum conditions for blight are 48 continuous hours with a minimum temperature of 20°C and a minimum relative humidity of 75 per cent. Such conditions do not normally arise until late July, so, despite the fact that first early cultivars are susceptible to the late blight fungus, they do not succumb in the way that maincrop cultivars do. Similarly, early cultivars escape potato cyst nematode infestation because they are harvested by the end of June, before the nematode has completed its life cycle and multiplied.

In situations where cultivars with resistance to the pest in question are not available, alternative plant choices may be possible. For example, in the presence of heavy slug or snail infestations, the large simple leaves of hosta can be replaced by

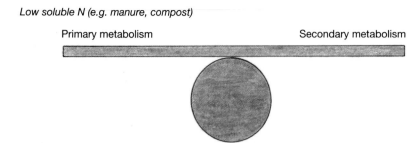

Low soluble N (e.g. manure, compost)

Primary metabolism   Secondary metabolism

Result: high secondary metabolism (high disease-resistance, flavour)

The effect of soluble nitrogen in fertilizers on the balance between primary and secondary metabolism.

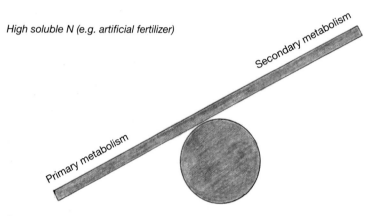

High soluble N (e.g. artificial fertilizer)

Secondary metabolism

Primary metabolism

Result: low secondary metabolism (low disease-resistance, flavour)

slug-resistant foliage species such as *Pulmonaria* spp., *Arum pictum* 'Marmoratum' or 'Primrose Warburg', or *Darmera palmata*. If the flowers and buds of your forsythia are being removed by birds, particularly sparrows, a related species, *Abeliophyllum distichum* would be a bird-resistant alternative.

Environment and Plant Defence

Even if a plant has little resistance to a pest or pathogen, conditions can be modified to increase the level of resistance it shows. The use of slow-release fertilizers which release nitrate slowly (primarily the organic ones like fish, blood and bonemeal, hoof and horn, manure or compost) will result in more secondary metabolism and hence higher levels of defence chemicals (Chapter 4).

The ability of the plant to grow in your garden, and the ability of the pest or pathogen to attack that plant, are both affected by the environment. As a result, it is possible to shift the balance of

power in favour of the plant by modifying the local environment.

Downy mildews prefer damp conditions, so plants like phlox which are particularly prone to infection should be grown in well-drained sites and watering the foliage avoided, while air circulation within the clumps can be improved to reduce humidity by thinning out maybe 30 per cent of the stems in early summer. Clubroot likes heavy soil with a low pH, so brassicas should be grown on well-drained soils, which can be limed if necessary to raise the pH.

Generally, plants growing under appropriate conditions are much healthier than are stressed plants, so selecting the best planting site for that species is important. There is also some evidence that volatile chemicals given off by stressed plants can attract more pests.

My father was a keen rose grower, and his plants rarely suffered from blackspot until Clean Air legislation was introduced to the UK in the 1960s. The reason? The blackspot fungus is sensitive to sulphur dioxide in polluted air. Interestingly, elemental sulphur is a good protectant measure against blackspot, when sprayed onto stems, leaves and the soil (to control overwintering incoculum) before symptoms are evident.

Most diseases and pest attacks cause more damage when the plant is young. As a consequence, it is important to focus plant protection protocols on the young plant. One general way of achieving this is to transplant indoor-grown seedlings into the garden rather than to sow directly in the open ground. By transplanting 3- to 4-week old brassica plants into soil suspected of harbouring clubroot, for example, the larger root system makes the plant more tolerant of subsequent clubroot attack.

Up-Regulating Plant Defences

Unlike mammals, plants have no immune system to protect themselves against would-be attackers, but they have a sophisticated array of chemical defences which can be switched on when they are attacked. The triggers for these defences (elicitors) are small chemicals produced by the pest or pathogen, which the plant recognizes as a sign of attack. Plants can distinguish between elicitors produced by different would-be attackers, so they can switch on the most appropriate defence against pest or pathogen, sap-sucking or chewing pest, and so on.

Signal chemicals then travel systemically around the plant in the phloem, switching on defences even in those parts of the plant which have not been challenged. Some of these signal chemicals are volatile and can travel through the air. One such chemical is methyl jasmonate, one of the main scent chemicals in jasmine, but produced in small amounts by most plants. Remarkably, release of these volatile signals by an attacked plant can warn neighbouring plants of the same species to switch on their own defences.

Unfortunately, these defences are often not switched on quickly enough to protect the plant. A new generation of plant protection chemicals, based on synthetic or natural elicitors, are available for farmers and are slowly entering the market for hobby gardeners. The elicitor has no direct effect on pests or pathogens. Spraying the chemical onto the plant before it is attacked produces a vaccination-like effect, switching on the plant's natural defences.

These elicitors, such as BioFriend Plant Defence and SB Plant Invigorator, increase natural resistance. Products containing potassium phosphite, such as Uncle Tom's Rose Tonic, also have potential as elicitors of systemic resistance. Protection can last up to six weeks, similar to that of a systemic fungicide. Interestingly, unlike conventional resistance genes, this induced partial resistance is active against a wide range of pests and pathogens. Natural elicitor products are usually sold under the general heading of 'bio-stimulants' and include certain seaweed formulations.

Research in my laboratory showed that the natural organic acid oxalic acid, sprayed at low concentrations onto leaves of brassica plants, increased systemic resistance to a wide range of pathogens. Rhubarb tissue, which is rich in oxalic acid, has been used in a number of natural pest and pathogen control methods in brassicas for more than a century. Examples include placing a cube of rhubarb stem or chopped up rhubarb leaves in the bottom of the planting hole to protect against cabbage root fly and clubroot.

ENCOURAGE NATURAL ENEMIES

As we have seen in food webs, every organism is fed on by at least one other organism in the ecosystem. This process of biological control, often shortened to 'biocontrol', is the way in which populations of all plant-eating invertebrates are managed in natural ecosystems. Biocontrol also applies to soil-borne pathogens but less so to air-borne pathogens.

Biocontrol already operates in our gardens, and steps can be taken to increase populations of a pest's natural enemies to increase pest management. There are two main ways by which we can increase the level of biocontrol operating in our gardens: by providing shelter, food and protection for natural enemies (habitat management), or by releasing beneficial organisms purchased from a commercial supplier (augmentative biocontrol).

Habitat Management

The goal of garden habitat management is to increase the number of species (including the numbers of beneficials) visiting or living in the garden. This can be achieved by increasing the range of habitats and food sources present and the degree of permanence of these habitats.

Generally, gardens have very high levels of plant biodiversity and, with the exception of vegetable beds, gardens are largely perennial in nature. Yet the basis of these plant assemblages is aesthetic rather than ecological, with the vast majority of our garden plants being non-native. This lack of balance can result in significant disease and pest problems in our gardens, although these may affect only a small number of the species in the garden.

To maximize biological control, it is important to identify the major pest species and their natural enemies, and to identify the conditions necessary to encourage the latter and discourage the former.

The major garden pests in the UK are slugs, snails, aphids, vine weevil, thrips, caterpillars, scale insects and mites.

Natural enemies of slugs and snails are invertebrates like the devil's coach horse (which also eats leatherjackets) and vertebrates such as thrushes, blackbirds, frogs, toads, ducks and hedgehogs.

To control aphids, ladybirds (adults and larvae), hoverflies (larvae) and ground beetles (which also feed on eggs of cabbage root fly) are useful, while birds like blue, coal and great tits will consume aphids and small caterpillars. The numbers consumed are staggering. A pair of blue tits may need up to 10,000 aphids to raise one brood of young, while one ladybird may eat 1,000 aphids over its short lifetime. There are more than forty species of ladybird and 500 species of hoverfly in the UK.

Unlike pests of garden plants which are mostly specialists, most beneficials found in a garden are generalists, feeding on a wide range of invertebrates. Larvae of the green and the brown lacewing will eat scale insects, mealybugs, thrips, aphids, whiteflies and mites.

Most of us can identify the adults of these beneficials, but often it is the larvae which are the main destroyers of garden pests, so it is important not to think that they are pests. Ladybird larvae have long blue-black bodies with yellow or orange markings. Hoverfly larvae can each eat up to 800 larvae over a 2-week period, and resemble small brown slugs.

Lacewing larvae are ferocious predators of aphids, and are sometimes known as aphid lions. They are brown and quite large, 7–8mm long, with hook-like jaws. To protect themselves against predators like birds, the larvae glue the husks of aphids they have killed to their backs, so that they can look a little like bird droppings.

If you find light brown egg-shaped immobile objects on leaves, these are usually parasitized aphids. A tiny parasitic wasp has laid an egg in an aphid larva. The grub of the young wasp will paralyze the larva and consume it from the inside. A small hole in the parasitized larva indicates that the wasp has hatched out.

The elements of garden habitat which can be manipulated to encourage the beneficials are shelter (for overwintering as well as over the summer) and food. Nest boxes for insect-eating bird species such as blue tits will encourage pairs to take up residence in your garden and to use it as a smorgasbord from which to feed their chicks.

Shelter for surface-dwelling beneficials such as ground beetles, spiders and centipedes during the growing season is provided by hedges, tussock-forming grasses and groundcover plants. Log piles at the back of a border can give shelter over winter to beneficials such as devil's coach horse and stag beetle, while adult ladybirds can overwinter under the dead bark. Tussocky grasses and dead leaves, even bark mulch, can provide over-wintering sites for adult ladybirds and other beneficials.

Unfortunately, such shelter can be as appropriate for pests as for beneficials, with log piles providing wintering sites for slugs and snails, while the space under the lower branches of box hedging is an ideal space for the same pests. The remnants of herbaceous perennials can provide overwintering sites for aphid predators such as lacewings in hollow stems like *Iris* and *Sedum*, but the decision to leave the stems until spring needs to take into account the risk of leaving pests and pathogens among the debris on the soil surface.

A compromise is also needed with respect to soil cultivation. Digging over the soil can improve

The simple open flower of *Convolvulus mauritanicus* is attractive to the adults of the beneficial insect, the hoverfly.

soil conditions, kill soil-dwelling pests, directly or indirectly, by exposing wireworms or leatherjackets to predation by birds, and can bury pathogens. But it can also badly affect beneficial soil dwellers, by killing earthworms, destroying the underground networks of beneficial mycorrhizal fungi and removing shelter for surface-living beneficials like ground beetles. Rotavators are particularly damaging in terms of killing soil flora and fauna.

A sensible compromise is to leave any soil cultivation which must be done to the early winter, by which time beneficials should have moved to permanent overwintering sites. This is also sensible in terms of nutrient use efficiency (Chapter 4).

Unlike the ladybird, where both the adult and larval stages eat invertebrate pests, the adults of most beneficials are not insect predators but need sources of nectar from appropriate flower sources. To produce their eggs, female hoverflies and lacewings need a lot of protein, which they get from the pollen (particularly) and nectar from flowers.

Suitable food plants include those with simple open flowers like *Limnanthes* (poached egg flower), *Phacelia* and *Eschscholtsia* (Californian poppy). Members of the Apiaceae (parsley family, with large flat umbels of tiny flowers such as astrantia, angelica, dill, candytuft) or the Asteraceae (daisy family, such as marigold, asters and coreopsis) are good nectar and pollen sources, and their presence can encourage these beneficials to visit your garden and hopefully lay their eggs.

For most of us, there is not any need to grow specific flowers or leave wild areas to support beneficials, as there will be enough suitable plants in an average garden, although continuity of nectar sources throughout the year is an important consideration.

Most beneficials are good hunters and will locate their food sources readily. Ladybirds lay their eggs in early spring close to where aphid colonies will develop, such as on young shoots. In fact, an increasing number of plants, especially members of the bean family, the Fabaceae, are known to recognize when they are being attacked and to identify the culprit. In response, these plants emit specific mixtures of volatile chemicals. This chemical 'fingerprint' then attracts appropriate beneficials, particularly predatory mites, to the attacked plant. And who said plants were primitive?

Augmentative Biocontrol

If all else fails, gardeners can resort to buying and releasing native beneficials which have been mass-reared artificially (known as augmentative biocontrol). In gardening, this usually involves a single release of large numbers of beneficials, relative to the numbers of the pest, at one time, so that there is a rapid crash of the pest population. Bear in mind that the loss of the food source leads to a corresponding crash of the beneficial population, so that the effect on the pest population is only short term. Biocontrol is only effective when pest populations are low, so the timing of biocontrol applications is important.

Ladybirds can be bought to control aphids, scale insects, thrips and mealybugs, while parasitic wasps can be used to manage thrips or caterpillars. Control of glasshouse whitefly can be achieved by release of the tiny parasitic wasp *Encarsia formosa* when air temperatures are at least 10°C.

To control vine weevil, slugs and leatherjackets, gardeners can buy beneficial nematodes such as *Steinernema* spp. (for control of vine weevil) or *Phasmorhabditis* spp. (control of slugs and leatherjackets) and water them onto the soil. The nematodes enter their host and release specific bacteria from their guts which paralyze the host. After two to three weeks, the nematodes will have multiplied, regained their load of toxic bacteria and burst out of the now-dead host to find a new live one.

The most recent beneficial nematode products are active at soil temperatures as low as 5°C, with control lasting for up to six weeks. Beneficial nematodes are the only product which kills slugs when they are underground, but they are ineffective against snails and less effective against the garden slug (*Arion hortensis*) than against the common grey field slug (*Deroceras reticulatum*).

By far the largest biocontrol product, representing more than 95 per cent of the market, is the bacterial biopesticide Bt, based on the natural soil bacterium *Bacillus thuringiensis*, which is used to control caterpillar pests. The product is available as a dust or a liquid and is applied to the leaves of the plant to be protected. When the caterpillar eats the treated leaves it ingests the toxic bacterium and dies within six to eight days. Widely used in organic farming, when properly applied this product is specific towards pest caterpillars, as only caterpillars which are feeding on the treated plant are killed. Unfortunately, the Bt product breaks down in two to three days in sunlight, so has to be re-applied,

Because there is a single target point in the pest affected by Bt, repeat applications run the risk of selecting for Bt-resistant forms of the caterpillar.

Prevent Survival or Kill It

This part of pest and pathogen management focuses directly on the culprit. Strategies can include preventing the organism from surviving over the winter, or, as a last resort, to killing it with biocidal chemicals.

Prevent overwintering

If your plants suffered from an air-borne pest or pathogen this year, such as the gooseberry sawfly or rose blackspot, simple precautions can reduce the risk of this being repeated next year. Much of the inoculum for such organisms comes from the infected plants. The organism can survive the winter (overwinter) in a dormant form in or on the soil, on infected individuals of the host plant or even on another plant species. Understanding the life cycle of pests and pathogens can allow you to break its life cycle, and so reduce the inoculum for next year.

To overwinter, specialist pathogens and pests move into a different phase of their life cycle, one where a short-lived infective stage that dominated during the growing period of the plant is replaced by a long-lived resting body, such as with blackspot and apple scab. If one of your garden plants has fallen prey to a pathogen which produces such resting bodies, it is vital that in the autumn you gather up and burn (if allowable) or bin any plant residue, such as dead leaves.

Any remaining inoculum needs to be treated, to minimize any risk of it producing infective spores again in the spring. There are two main strategies. One is to turn over the soil, in order to introduce the inoculum to the competitive world where the saprophytes, which feed on dead material like organic matter, will suppress the pathogens.

The second method is to apply a thick mulch of organic matter to the soil surface. This leads to breakdown of some of the resting bodies by the increased numbers of soil micro-organisms, but the mulch also acts to block spore release from the resting bodies. Resting bodies respond to changes in the temperature and daylength in spring by producing infective spores. The mulch layer intercepts this spore release. Rosebeds, for example, should be top-dressed with mulch, compost or farmyard manure in December to help control blackspot.

For airborne pests, overwintering takes place in the soil or on infested tissue, as a dormant form of the active pest. Some pests overwinter in the hollow stems of herbaceous garden plants. Again, as with plant pathogens, clearing away plant residues can reduce inoculum levels.

A small number of pests, particularly aphids, overwinter on what is known as an alternate host, unrelated to the main food plants. The black bean aphid, for example, spends the winter on plants of *Euonymus* spp., particularly the spindle tree *Euonymus alatus* but also on more commonly grown *Euonymus* garden shrubs.

If you intend to grow broad beans, and especially if there is a history of bean aphid infestation in your area, it is a sensible precaution to check the young shoots of any *Euonymus* plants in your garden in spring for signs of black aphids. Similarly, the powdery mildew fungus which

attacks cucumber over the summer overwinters on the unrelated plant groundsel (*Senecio vulgaris*), a common weed.

Chemical and Physical Control Methods

The last method for managing garden plant pests and diseases is to directly kill the organism concerned, using chemical or physical methods.

Some of the terms used for plant protection chemicals can be confusing. Contact chemicals operate on the surface of the plant. Of the contact chemicals, most are preventative, stopping the infection from taking hold, as happens with copper compounds used in the control of potato blight. A few are curative, eliminating an already-established infection. A downside of contact chemicals is that heavy rain and ultraviolet light in sunlight will reduce their effect.

Systemic chemicals, on the other hand, enter the plant and then move through it, in the phloem (in all directions) or the xylem (upwards only). As a result, systemic chemicals provide longer-lasting protection than contact chemicals, lasting up to six weeks. Systemic chemicals can also travel to plant organs which had not been formed at the time

A potato leaf infected by the fungal pathogen *Phytophthora infestans*, the causal agent of late potato blight.

of application and can also control pests which escape contact pesticides by being in inaccessible places. These include thrips in unopened flower buds, leafminers within a leaf and stem-boring caterpillars.

For the organic gardener, there are several contact chemicals available to help control pests and pathogens. Derris dust, containing rotenone, is extracted from the roots of a tropical legume, and is active against caterpillars, aphids and flea beetles, but is rapidly de-activated in sunlight. Pyrethrum is another plant chemical, and is active against aphids, thrips, weevils, capsids and leaf hoppers.

Insecticidal (soft) soaps are effective against soft-bodied insects like aphids, whitefly and red spider mites but need regular re-application (every two weeks). They work by blocking the breathing holes or spiracles in the body of the pest, effectively suffocating it. On the other hand, extracts from the Indian neem tree will not kill pests but will stop many pest species from feeding on the sprayed plants.

Because plants contain such a wealth of defence chemicals, they can be exploited to produce contact pesticides. Rhubarb suffers very little from pest damage because it contains high levels of oxalic acid. A broad-spectrum contact insecticide, capable of killing aphids, mites and caterpillars, can be produced by boiling 50g rhubarb leaves with 100ml water for thirty minutes, and spraying plants with the cooled strained liquid. Other pesticides which can be produced include a nicotine extract from stewing cigarette butts. Both of these extracts are toxic, so use them with care.

For organic disease control, silica is a mineral related to quartz which can be applied as a foliar spray or (more effectively) to the soil as a root drench. The silica forms a physical barrier which helps protect against a range of pathogens. For control of potato blight, copper-based 'bluestone' products are available for organic growers but should be used with care because of their toxicity to soil dwellers like earthworms.

Baking soda can also be used to control powdery mildew and some other diseases on a range of plants at a rate of one tablespoon (about 15g) in four litres of water. For all homemade pest and pathogen control products, addition of half a teaspoon of liquid soap per four litres will help the spray stay on the leaf so that it can be taken up by the plant.

Unlike these natural chemicals, most of the synthetic plant protection chemicals (as well as the biocontrol product Bt) work by affecting a single target point, maybe an enzyme, in the pest or pathogen. The downside of this is that, as with a gene conferring complete disease resistance mentioned earlier, repeated application of such a chemical may select for mutants of the pathogen which are resistant to the chemical. Pesticide-resistant races of late potato blight and aphids have developed and can cause problems for gardeners.

To prevent such races arising in your garden is straightforward: do not use the same chemical time and time again, but alternate with different chemicals which work in different ways, with different target points. In potato blight management, manganese-based chemicals like mancozeb are alternated with chemicals such as cymoxanil, with a different mode of action. Chemicals which do not affect a single target point in the pest, like synthetic contact chemicals, silica and insecticidal soaps, do not run the risk that the pest will evolve resistance.

Most natural and synthetic chemicals are biocidal, in that they act by directly killing the pest or pathogen, but they can also kill species other than the target pest or pathogen, including useful species. Unfortunately, beneficials tend to lay their eggs near pest populations, so spraying with biocides will reduce the numbers of beneficials.

Derris and pyrethrum, like most broad-spectrum or general insecticides, will kill honeybees if sprayed on flowers or flower buds. Negative side effects can be minimized, however. Effects on bees of any chemical can be reduced if spraying is restricted to early morning or late evening, outside the normal flight times of the bees.

Widespread use of broad-spectrum pesticides can also make a pest problem bigger rather than smaller, by killing both pests and the beneficial invertebrates which feed on them, such as ladybirds which feed on aphids, thrips and mites. The problem is that the pests (primary consumers in the food chain) multiply much faster than do the beneficials (secondary consumers), so can recover from the insecticide application much faster.

Within two weeks of a pesticidal spray, the aphid population may have recovered as a result of multiplication of any surviving aphids, whereas the ladybird population may take two years to recover. An aphid colony can go through fifteen generations in one year, whereas beneficials like ladybirds may have only a single generation each year.

Most plant protection chemicals available to gardeners are broad-spectrum, because one product can be used to control a range of pests. More specific chemicals are available, however, like the aphicide pirimicarb which affects only aphids, leaving beneficials well alone.

There are other time-honoured methods. Trapping pests, though more time consuming, will not affect beneficials (nor will the pest adapt to it!). Collection by torchlight of slow-moving pests like slugs and snails at night, especially after rain, is an effective way of reducing the pest population.

'Beer traps', containing beer (or any sweet liquid like milk or sugar solution) to attract slugs and snails, which then drown in the liquid, can be very effective. The container, such as a margarine tub, should be placed in the soil with the rim above soil level to prevent beneficial insects such as ground beetles (which eat aphids, slugs and snails) from coming to a sticky end. Be careful about extended use of beer traps – slugs can follow the scent for almost 200m, so that you could be attracting slugs in from your neighbours' gardens.

Dark 'habitats', such as upturned hollowed-out grapefruit halves for slugs or inverted flower pots stuffed with straw for earwigs, attract nocturnal pests, which can then be collected and disposed of in the morning.

WEEDS

Weeds are more difficult to control than either pests or pathogens, because you are trying to protect one plant at the expense of another. I prefer an ecological approach to the problems of and solutions to garden weeds.

The simplest definition of a weed is 'a plant in a place you don't want it'. That will include wild species, such as chickweed, groundsel and nettles, as well as self-sown garden plants like volunteer potato plants in the vegetable beds.

Weeds can directly reduce the growth of desirable garden plants by competing for resources such as light (particularly the climbers like bindweed), water and nutrients. Others can also introduce natural chemicals, broadly called allelochemicals, into the soil which will inhibit the growth of neighbouring plants. Such allelopathic plants include thistles, euphorbias and many grasses.

The grass root system is a fibrous one, and each root lives for only a short time before dying and being replaced. The living and dying roots release plant-inhibitory chemicals into the soil. This is one of the reasons for keeping a 1m-diameter circle of soil around a tree or shrub planted in your lawn free of grass, particularly in the first few years.

Mainly, however, we want to control weeds in the lawn or herbaceous border for aesthetic reasons.

UNDERSTANDING WEEDS

Different management strategies can be used depending on the main weed species concerned, so it is useful to develop an understanding of the characteristics of weeds.

Have you ever watched a cleared piece of land become re-colonized by plants? Over time, the weeds on the site become taller, but on closer inspection you can see that the change is not because the plants present continue to grow but that different species start to dominate at different stages of the process. What you are watching is secondary succession, the recolonization of a previously vegetated site.

Secondary succession follows a carefully choreographed sequence of the weed species appearing and then being replaced by a more dominant species. The first plants to emerge were already present as seeds in the soil (the seed bank), and the very first plants are termed pioneers. These are annual plants which germinate, grow, flower, set seed and die all within a few weeks. The raison d'être of these plants is to produce as many seeds

The pioneer annual weed meadowgrass, *Poa annua.*

as possible while circumstances are favourable to them.

As a result, pioneer plants like annual meadow-grass (*Poa annua*, the most common plant in the world), shepherd's purse (*Capsella bursa-pastoris*), hairy bittercress (*Cardamine hirsuta*) and chick-weed (*Stellaria media*) put little energy into being competitive. They are small plants, which is fine, because they are the first plants to emerge and, for the first few weeks or months, are the tallest plants around. Each seed produced is very small but there are lots of them, with groundsel producing 1,000 seeds per plant. Pioneers can produce several gen-erations in one year. Some pioneers germinate in autumn or early winter (winter annuals, such as *Arabidopsis thaliana* and *Poa annua*), or in spring (summer annuals, like groundsel, *Senecio vulgaris* and fat hen, *Chenopodium album*), while others can germinate all year round, such as shepherd's purse, hairy bittercress and *Spergula arvensis*.

Another characteristic of these pioneer annual species, the first plants of the succession, is that they can flower at any time of the year, particularly in milder regions. Indeed, it can be difficult to find non-flowering plants of annual meadowgrass.

Tiny seeds have few food reserves for the

seedling, so germination of annual seeds normally only occurs when the seeds are on or close to the soil surface so that the seedling does not have to push its way through the soil. As a result, these seeds need light to trigger germination. In the absence of light, the seeds can remain dormant but alive for many years. When you turn over soil, the buried seeds receive a flash of sunlight, and this triggers the flush of seedlings of annual weeds.

The sequence of plant types which dominate in turn during succession is:

pioneer annual → annual → biennial → non-woody perennial → woody shrub → tree

As succession progresses, the dominant plants become longer-lived. The pioneer annuals are replaced by annuals which have a single gen-eration per year, like the red field poppy, *Papaver rhoeas*. These plants are taller than the pioneers and germinate and flower at specific times of the year (autumn and mid-summer, respectively, for the poppy). Being taller (because they grow for longer), these plants are more competitive than the pioneers, producing even more small seeds per plant, an average of 17,000 seeds per poppy plant and 70,000 for fat hen.

The next group of plants to appear in the site are the biennials, again from the seed bank. These plants, like mulleins, echiums and foxgloves, take two years to produce seeds and then they die. The food reserves stockpiled in the first year are used to fuel the production of a tall flowerhead, attractive to pollinating insects, and well placed to facilitate seed dispersal. Biennials are more competitive than annuals and produce vast numbers of seeds, each of which is small but larger than for most annuals. One self-sown plant of mullein, *Verbascum chaixii* 'Album', in my garden produced more than 800,000 seeds.

After the biennials come the non-woody perennials, which live for several years, re-growing from underground food reserve stores (perennating organs), like rhizomes, corms, bulbs or tubers, and growth buds. With herbaceous perennial weeds, like lesser celandine and Japanese knotweed, at the end of the season the above-ground stems die down and the plant overwinters as vegetative buds. Evergreen non-woody perennial weeds like couch grass, dandelion and docks retain their leaves over the winter. The perennating organs in these weeds double up as means of vegetative reproduction, carrying growth buds from which new individual plants can develop. Because they can regrow from small fragments of root, rhizome and so on, left in the soil, non-woody perennials are among the most difficult weeds to eradicate.

The last group of plants which come to dominate the cleared site during secondary succession are the woody perennials, the shrubs and trees, and will appear only where the previous site was very overgrown. In these plants, stems are retained above-ground from season to season, providing framework for the plant to grow larger and larger over decades. These plants put more of their resources into their above-ground organs than do the non-woody perennials, providing a strong structure so that they can compete for light with the other plants. They also produce fewer seeds, but each is large with a big food reserve and so has a very good chance of developing into a new plant. Seeds of woody weed species will come into the garden as seeds brought by birds, as with bramble, or on the air as with trees like sycamore.

GARDEN WEED MANAGEMENT

The main problem weeds in the garden are annuals (because of sheer numbers) and perennial weeds such as non-woody perennial weeds (docks, bindweeds, nettles, buttercups, etc.) as well as non-woody alien species (Japanese knotweed, winter heliotrope, etc.). An understanding of the ecology and physiology of the target weed species can improve our chances of eradicating the weeds from our gardens.

Weed management methods are fewer than those for control of pests or pathogens. There is little scope for weed resistant cultivars, while biological control of weeds, though possible, is generally outside the realm of amateur gardeners. Weed management strategies therefore usually fall into chemical and cultural methods.

With perennial weeds, the seed bank can still pose a problem but much less so than with annual weeds. Some important perennial weeds, particularly alien species, do not produce seeds, including ground elder, winter heliotrope and Japanese knotweed (*see* Chapter 7). The main problem with perennial weeds is removal of the weeds themselves without leaving behind fragments from which new plants will regenerate.

The Weeding Process

Annual weeds

The most important aspect of annual weed management is to minimize the activity of the seed bank in the soil. With large seed banks in the soil, and each seed being able to live up to fifteen years, it is highly unlikely that the seed bank of annual weeds can be eradicated. Management of annual weeds should therefore focus on not increasing the size of the seed bank – do not allow the weeds to seed or put seeding weed plants on the compost heap – and to minimize germination by reducing soil cultivation. Because pioneer weeds will grow, flower and set seed all year round, it is important to remove these plants even in the winter.

Hand weeding is effective for management of annual weeds on reasonably small areas. Annual weeds usually have limited root systems and are easy to remove by hand weeding. Having no underground food reserves, root fragments left behind in the soil will not regenerate into new plants.

With annuals, weeding needs to take place before the plants have set seed to prevent re-stocking of the seed bank: 'One year's seeding, seven year's weeding'. The plants can be composted but only if they are not in flower or seed.

Hoeing is often recommended for large-scale removal of annual weeds, but can kill self-sown seedlings of garden plants in the ornamental garden and can cause damage to surface roots of plants like raspberries, dahlias and many trees and shrubs. In these situations, mulching would be a more appropriate way of controlling annual weeds (*see* Chapter 4). Hoeing is more appropriate for vegetable beds with plants in rows, but root damage can trigger bolting (premature flowering) in some vegetable plants.

Perennial Weeds

Hand weeding of perennial weeds is less useful, as the tap root (dandelion, dock) or rhizome (couch grass, Japanese knotweed, winter heliotrope) will usually break as the plant is pulled or dug up, leading to re-growth from axillary or adventitious buds. Careful digging out of perennial weeds, supplemented by hand removal of root or rhizome fragments can be partially effective but is very time consuming. The rhizomes of field bindweed, for example, can extend to depths of more than 5m in the soil.

Indeed, digging up weed-infested soil can increase problems of perennial weeds as regenerative fragments can be spread around the garden bed; a piece of Japanese knotweed rhizome as short as 5mm long can regenerate into a new plant. Perennial weeds should not be composted.

Cutting back, strimming or pulling up perennial weeds to weaken them is best carried out several times in the year, particularly in late summer before the food reserves are transported from the shoots to the roots or rhizomes. Be careful: strimmed shoot fragments of weeds like Japanese knotweed can act like cuttings if not disposed of properly, springing up Medusa-like and making the weed

problem much worse. Strimming of certain invasive aliens like old man's beard (*Clematis vitalba*), giant hogweed (*Heracleum mantegazzianum*) and Japanese knotweed should be avoided as the sap sprayed around can cause skin reactions.

Physical Barrier

Suppression of perennial weeds can be achieved using one of a wide range of physical barriers for at least one season, preventing access of weeds to light. Geotextile membrane is widely used as a permanent solution to keeping weeds down around shrubs, as weeds under the membrane cannot penetrate it. But I find that the inability of worms to travel through the membrane results in compacted soil which is not conducive to good plant growth.

For lower-cost control of weeds, particularly perennials, in overgrown sites, overlapping layers of impermeable materials like carpet underlay or black polyethylene, or thick layers (5–10cm) of biodegradable materials such as damp cardboard or newspaper for up to twenty-four months can be very effective. With biodegradable materials, covering them with a mulch of compost or composted bark makes the appearance more attractive and allows for a one-step weed control programme. After the weeds have been controlled, planting can take place directly through the layers.

Mulches (8–10cm deep; Chapter 4) of organic materials like composted bark, cocoa shells, straw, or inorganic materials like gravel, glass or recycled rubber can also hinder germination and growth of annual weed seedlings and make their removal easier. However, they have no effect on perennial weeds.

Competition

Certain plants, like maincrop potato, marrows, squashes and mustard are weed suppressive in their ability to create large light-excluding canopies, and these can be useful weapons in the armoury to manage weeds. When attempting to clean up a newly cultivated piece of land, you can plant a green manure crop like rye or mustard to compete out the weeds.

Rye, being a grass, also has an allelopathic effect

Japanese knotweed controlled by herbicide, followed by competition by grasses and regular mowing. The area to the left was not treated.

on weeds and, when dug into the soil after four to six weeks of growth, will inhibit germination of small seeds, including most annual, biennial and short-lived perennial weeds. If you are planting a vegetable crop after a rye green manure crop, it is important to use a crop with a large propagule such as potato (tuber) or maybe beans (seed), so that the vigorous young plants, powered by the food stores in the propagule, can overcome the allelopathic effect.

If you are faced with a large area infested with pernicious perennial weeds, one useful strategy is to weaken the weeds by cutting them back hard in late spring (to deplete the underground reserves) and autumn (to prevent replenishment of the reserves), or by spraying them with a systemic herbicide. The site should then be raked and perennial ryegrass (not rye) seed sown.

Cool-weather grasses are very competitive, largely by dint of their allelopathic effects, which will gradually suppress the weeds, but ryegrass is particularly effective. Regular mowing of the grass will also inhibit the weeds by removal of the growing points. I have seen this method eradicate winter heliotrope and ground elder in one growing season, and severely restrict Japanese knotweed after two years.

A slow but environmentally friendly weed management method is to eat your problem. Many of our worst alien perennial weeds have been traditionally used as a food source in their native regions. The young leaf stalks of giant rhubarb, *Gunnera tinctoria*, are eaten raw or cooked (as panke) in Patagonia. Ground elder was introduced to Britain as a culinary crop by the Romans, and can be used as a substitute for spinach. Other edible weeds include ransomes (*Allium ursinum*; bulbs and leaves) and Japanese knotweed, where young shoots 15cm long, with the leaves removed, are used as a rhubarb substitute.

Chemicals

As with other plant protection chemicals, an understanding of the terms used with herbicides, and information on their modes of action can be useful to the gardener.

Contact weedkillers, like paraquat and diquat, kill only the green tissues which they hit, while systemic weedkillers are translocated all around the

Japanese knotweed treated with a herbicide, causing epinasty (shoot twisting).

plant in the phloem. Residual weedkillers remain active in the soil for at least six months and contain a mix of herbicides which kill existing weeds (post-emergent herbicides such as linuron and diuron, which are taken up by the roots and translocated in the xylem) or prevent germination of seeds in the soil (pre-emergent herbicides such as trifluralin). These mixed-herbicide products, sometimes also including a phloem-translocated systemic herbicide like glyphosate, are used on paths and other areas which are not intended to be planted that season.

The main benefit of systemic weedkillers like glyphosate and gluphosinate is in the eradication of perennial weeds, like couch grass and Japanese knotweed. During plant growth, the direction of translocation of assimilates in the phloem varies according to which plant organs are the main sinks for assimilates.

Early in the season, most assimilates are translocated to the young leaves, but by late summer perennial plants direct assimilates to the underground food reserves. To kill perennial plants, late-season application of systemic weedkillers is the most appropriate as the herbicide will be translocated to the underground regenerative organs, preventing re-growth.

The speed of action (knock-down rate) of weed-killers varies widely. Contact herbicides which inhibit photosynthesis, such as paraquat and diquat, are fast acting, with some effects in less than one hour. Rapid acting herbicides are appropriate for annual weeds, as slower-acting chemicals may allow these species enough time to produce seeds before dying.

On the other hand, systemic herbicides are slow acting, taking up to four weeks to kill the sprayed plants, although yellowing may be visible after ten days. Most systemic herbicides work by blocking the pathway the plants use to make amino acids, the components of proteins and many other chemicals. Plants sprayed with systemic chemicals like glyphosate or gluphosinate starve slowly as the plant is unable to make all the natural chemicals it usually synthesizes.

The biosynthetic pathway inhibited by glyphosate is branched, so that it produces not only amino acids but also UV protection chemicals, pigments, defence chemicals and lignin, the tissue-strengthening chemical in wood (*see* Chapter 1). If you spray bluebells with glyphosate when the flower buds are just visible, the plant will eventually flower before it dies, and the flowers will be white rather than blue in colour because

Leaf waxes or hairs can cause spray to stay as droplets, limiting their effectiveness. Addition of a small amount of liquid soap or detergent to the spray solution will help uptake into the leaf.

glyphosate inhibits the production of the blue pigment, an anthocyanin (Chapter 8).

Whereas herbicides do not affect biodiversity in the garden in the way that insecticides can, they can be poisonous to humans. Contact herbicides like paraquat are particularly dangerous. Systemic herbicides, on the other hand, inhibit pathways which only exist in plants so are safe to use. Natural herbicides do exist. Fatty acids and organic acids act as contact herbicides, as do salt, bleach or vinegar, while corn meal gluten, a by-product of maize, can work as a pre-emergent herbicide, stopping weed seeds from germinating.

Most natural (fatty acid, organic acid derivatives) and synthetic weedkillers are non-selective, killing all plant species, although selective dicot-only weedkillers are available and are used on lawns.

Many herbicide formulations include detergents (surfactants) to spread the chemical across the leaf surface or to speed up movement across the waxy cuticle on the leaves and stems into the plant. Increased herbicide uptake by waxy perennials like horsetail can be achieved by damaging the weed tissues by raking or rubbing the stems with coarse sandpaper before treatment with the herbicide.

LAWN WEED MANAGEMENT

The single greatest problem gardeners have with their lawns is the presence of weeds. These can be flowering plants like self-heal, white clover and plantain; coarse grasses such as cocksfoot, *Dactylis glomerata*; and mosses. The mixture of grasses and flowering plants is a characteristic of all grassland-dominated vegetation world-wide (Chapter 2). A moderately diverse vegetation, with maybe a dozen different species, is more stable and productive than a less diverse grassland. So, attempting to restrict your lawn to only one or two fine-leaved grass species like perennial ryegrass and red fescue is, literally, going against nature. You are fighting an uphill battle.

Most flowering plants will not survive close grazing/mowing because their upright habit puts their growth buds in danger of damage and death. Pasture dicots and lawn weeds are adapted to close cutting, however, with a prostrate growth habit which protects their growth buds from grazing (in nature) or mowing (in lawns). Despite this, grasses and dicot grassland weeds have different niches (Chapter 2), which enables them to grow together in the long term because they do not exclude one another as a result of competition.

Grasses have relatively shallow roots, while dicots or broad-leaved weeds have deep roots, such as self-heal, *Prunella vulgaris*, or tap roots, as with dandelions and docks. Grasses are particularly tolerant of trampling and respond better to nutrients than do the dicots.

As a result, the two groups of plants mine different parts of the soil horizon for water and nutrients, so that there is no competition. The deeper roots of the dicots means that, in a drought, the weeds stay green as they can access the limited water supplies, while the grasses go dormant and brown.

Ecological Management

A weed-rich lawn suggests that the grasses are not vigorous enough to keep the weeds in check. When growing well and not cut too short, lawn grasses can grow taller than weeds and compete with them for light. Poor grass growth could be due to nutrient deficiency, shade, drought, soil compaction or waterlogging, among other problems. More specifically, some lawn weed species can act as indicators of the overall health of the lawn. If you know the niche of these indicator species, it can help you to pin-point the root cause of the problem.

The presence of white clover is indicative of an alkaline, possibly nitrogen-poor soil, because it is a nitrogen-fixing member of the pea family, the Fabaceae. This trait gives the clovers an advantage over non-fixer species in poor soils. It is also quite shade tolerant. Self-heal, speedwell, annual meadowgrass and buttercup are indicators of damp soils, while mosses indicate a site too shady, wet or acid for good grass growth. Mosses tend to be a problem only in the wetter parts of the year, and they will become dormant in the summer.

On the other hand, yarrow (*Achillea* spp.) and dandelion are indicative of a dry, nutrient-poor soil. Coarse wide-leaved grasses like cocksfoot (*Dactylis glomerata*) and Yorkshire fog (*Holcus mollis*) tend to spread in a lawn where the soil is poor in nitrogen. Other common lawn weeds, like daisy, are not indicator species but opportunists, taking advantage of any gaps in the lawn.

If the weeds and conditions indicate a particular reason for poor grass growth, such as wet soil, treating that problem should reduce the weeds. Grass growth can be encouraged by using a high-N fertilizer and by irrigating in dry spells. The competitive nature of the grasses can be increased by raising the height at which you mow the lawn.

At high levels of soil nitrogen, the ability of white clover to fix nitrogen gas from the air will be suppressed, reducing its competitive advantage over the grasses. If the site is wet, drainage may be necessary. A useful approach to a patchy lawn is to over-seed with grass species better suited to the conditions, like perennial ryegrass for heavy traffic, red fescue for dry or shady sites or meadow grass for a shaded site.

What you are doing in this ecological approach to lawn weed management is shifting the microhabitat of your lawn so that it fits the grass niche better than it does that of the weed species. This will save you time and money and will have a beneficial effect on the biodiversity of the soil and the lawn. Small numbers of weeds are inevitable, and can actually be valuable in terms of improved greenness during summer dry spells.

Chemical Control

The most commonly used weed control strategy for dicot or broad-leaved weeds in lawns is the use of selective herbicides. Selective weedkillers kill most dicots but leave monocots like grasses unharmed, unless excessive amounts of the herbicide are applied. Lawn herbicides are usually a mixture of mecoprop-P, 2,4-D and dicamba, because each chemical has a particular spectrum of dicot weeds which it can control particularly well.

The selectivity towards dicots is largely due to the fact that most grasses are able to de-toxify the selective herbicides. These selective herbicides are systemic and work by acting like the natural growth hormone auxin, so that the plants grow in an unregulated way, exhausting their food reserves and dying. The twisting of the leaves of treated plants is caused by the over-production of another hormone, ethylene.

Unlike natural auxins that the plant breaks down, the synthetic auxins are not metabolized and concentrations stay high. Treated leaves go dark green and the stems twist and coil before the plant dies. As a result, it can take more than ten days before the weeds die. This mode of action explains why it is important that these herbicides are applied when the weeds are growing quickly.

Herbicides should not be applied to lawns in their first year, because plants are most affected by stresses when they are young. In this first year, in particular, it is a good investment to maximize the growth rate of the lawn grasses, because perennial dicots take up to two years to establish and flower.

Broadcasting herbicide or herbicide-fertilizer granules over the entire lawn is inefficient in all bar the weediest situations. Most of the herbicide lands on grasses where it is wasted, while most of the herbicide that hits a dicot leaf falls off, with the exception of the rosette formers, like daisy and plantains. It is more effective to use a liquid preparation, and more efficient to spray the weedy areas only.

Mosses and coarse weedy grasses will not be killed by most lawn herbicides. Mosses, being primitive plants, absorb water and minerals across their entire surface area (Chapter 1), with little regulation of the amount of minerals which they take up.

Moss in a lawn can be killed by watering on iron sulphate at a rate of four heaped tablespoons per standard 10-litre watering can. This concentration is toxic to mosses but not to grasses and other flowering plants which can control the amount of iron (and other elements) which they take up. At a higher concentration, you risk blackening but not killing the grasses. Make sure that the iron sulphate has fully dissolved before applying the solution. Application of iron sulphate to your lawn in spring will also help to green up your lawn after the stresses of the winter.

Circular patches of pale grass in a lawn are usually caused by the large-leaved 'coarse' grasses such as cocksfoot and Yorkshire fog. Characteristically, cocksfoot has flattened 'stems' when you try to roll them between your thumb and forefinger, while Yorkshire fog is softly hairy with red-striped stem bases. Such coarse grasses tend to invade patchy lawns in the winter when fine grasses, like fescues and bents, but not coarse species, stop growing at soil temperatures below 5°C. They can be controlled by using a spade to cut through the crown in two directions. If this is repeated, the grass will weaken and die.

After killing lawn weeds with herbicides, bare earth will be available for colonization. Many general-use seed mixes include seed of grasses like creeping bent which, spread by surface stems or stolons, serve to cover bare patches. Over-seeding should also be considered because it is cheap and effective. Unless you want to repeat the herbicide treatment every year, it is also important to try to correct the conditions (low soil nutrients, too much/little water, too low cutting height) that favoured the weeds in the first place.

CHAPTER 7

Propagating Plants

Genetic variation in date of leaf senescence between individual plants in a beech hedge.

Propagating your own plants is one of the early rites of passage for all gardeners. It can involve taking cuttings from a plant proffered by a friend, dividing your own plants or sowing seeds bought or collected. I still get immense pleasure from seeing the first seedling leaves poking through the soil or the sight of new growth on a cutting.

Basically, propagation methods fall into two categories: seed propagation and vegetative propagation, such as cuttings (using shoots, leaves or roots as source material), division or grafting.

The plants produced by seed or vegetative propagation of the same plant can differ in appearance. Plants produced by vegetative propagation usually come true-to-type, in that they resemble the parent plants (and one another) closely, whereas this is

Clockwise from the top: seeds of climbing French bean, carrot, runner bean, lettuce, pea, pumpkin, spring onion.

rarer for seed-propagated plants. On the other hand, virus-infected plants produce infected offspring via vegetative reproduction but not usually through seed propagation.

To understand how plants can be propagated requires some knowledge of plant physiology, while a grasp of plant genetics helps to understand how characters are passed on from parent to offspring and why some but not all propagation methods result in offspring identical to one another and to the parent plants.

VEGETATIVE PROPAGATION

Vegetative plant propagation takes place in nature primarily as a means of spread, forming a colony of genetically identical individual shoots. An example of such a plant is bracken (*Pteridium aquilinum*), which spreads via rhizomes. Along the rhizome, shoots and roots will develop into new plants (or genets), but all are genetically identical and interconnected with one another to form a clone or ramet. The production of such colonies, where every shoot is genetically identical, is an adaptation to a fairly uniform environment, and permits the plant to dominate a large area. Several invasive alien plant species that have escaped from gardens into the wild in western Europe don't produce seed because they are clones of only one sex of a dioecious species, such as Japanese knotweed (female) and winter heliotrope (male).

One contender for the title of largest plant in the world is Pando (Greek for 'I spread'), which is a male quaking aspen (*Populus tremuloides*) in south-central Utah. Pando consists of 46,000 stems. Each stem was produced from an individual adventitious bud on the roots, all interconnected on a single root system, with an estimated total weight of 6,000 tonnes and covering an area of more than 43 hectares. It is believed to be approximately 8–10,000 years old.

Some vegetative propagation methods use ready-made propagules designed for reproduction by the plant, such as bulbs, corms or tubers. In other cases, such as stem, leaf and root cuttings, the technique involves stimulating plant cells to change from, say, leaf or stem cells into shoot or root cells.

Plants have a much greater potential for regeneration than do animals. Generally with animals, once a cell has differentiated into a specific cell type with a particular task, such as a skin, kidney or eye cell, it cannot be re-programmed to change its role. Some amphibians can re-grow a tail or a leg but that is the limit.

Plant cells, on the other hand, can readily switch from one cell type to another. Indeed, in a laboratory it is possible to take a single cell of some plants, such as a potato, and re-programme it by exposing it to chemical signals to grow into an entire potato plant. These chemical signals include plant hormones, principally cytokinins and auxins. They re-programme plant cells by switching specific genes on and off, so that, say, the stem genes in a cell are switched off and the root genes are switched on, with the result that the stem cells become re-directed to become root cells.

Stem cuttings

A stem cutting contains pre-formed growth buds (apical at the shoot tip and/or axillary at the leaf axils) which will grow out to form shoots, and a cut surface. This cut area will contain juvenile undifferentiated cells known as cambium, which are actively dividing and which generally lie just under the epidermis of the stem, and parenchyma cells. The task of cambium in an intact plant is normally to produce new cells, particularly vascular tissue and bark. In a cutting, the cambium will be involved in producing roots.

Adventitious root development from the cambium cells at the cut surface needs the action of auxins. These chemicals are synthesized in growth buds and then move down the stem accumulating at the cut end. The balance of auxins and cytokinins in the cambium cells will determine which tissues the cambium will develop into.

Initially, cells at the base of the cutting are confused by the change in hormone levels, so they undergo disorganized cell division into an undifferentiated mass of cells known as callus. Callus is commonly associated with tissue injury in intact plants, as seen in the raised collar which forms around the cut surface after a tree limb is removed. Eventually, the auxin levels as the base of a stem cutting trigger the callus to start forming adventitious roots. In turn, these roots produce cytokinins to stimulate outgrowth of the buds already present on the cutting to form shoots.

The cells at the cut surface need moisture, oxygen and energy to produce roots. The rooting medium must be open enough to provide both oxygen and water, and most of the leaves should be removed to reduce water loss by transpiration. This, however, reduces the area for photosynthesis, so most of the energy for rooting has to come from within the cutting itself.

The tissue used for stem cuttings needs to be reasonably large and healthy, so that they can supply enough energy to fuel root development. In appearance, the cutting must also be typical of the parent plant. With variegated plants, for example, it is important that you select tissue with the desired variegation – an all-green cutting will produce an all-green daughter plant.

A collar of callus formed around the cut edges of a branch removed from a magnolia.

The most efficient cutting can vary between different garden plants. A range of different tissue types can be used (softwood, semi-ripe and hardwood tissue, collected at different times of the season) and these can be prepared as different types of cuttings, such as nodal, internodal, basal and heel cuttings.

The best time to collect material for cuttings depends on the plant species, though the sage advice of the late Primrose Warburg ('The right time to take cuttings is when they are offered') should be taken on board. Softwood cuttings are taken from newly formed shoots in May to June. For woody plants, semi-ripe cuttings are taken from August to early October as the new growth starts to stiffen and become woody, while cuttings taken at the end of the season, from October into winter, are less flexible with signs of bark, and are known as hardwood cuttings.

Softwood cuttings tend to root quite easily (being mostly juvenile tissue) but run the greater risk of desiccation and have little food reserves, while cuttings from older wood are more robust with larger food reserves but can be reluctant rooters. As plant tissue ages, its ability to re-programme itself and produce roots from shoot tissue decreases, but cells at the base of a cutting retain juvenility and can root.

The type of stem cutting varies, according to where the bottom cut is taken and where any top cut is made. The most commonly used type of cutting is the nodal cutting, which consists of a small portion of stem which is then trimmed to just below a node. A node is the swollen area on a stem connected to a leaf, with an axillary bud in the angle between the stem and the leaf, which can grow into a shoot. It is via the node that sugars and other assimilates synthesized in the leaf enter the plant's vascular system in the stem, and from where it moves around the plant. Nodes on stems are also particularly rich in auxins (to stimulate root formation) and have large numbers of dividing cambium cells. Nodal cuttings are solid, so are particularly useful for hollow-stemmed plant subjects (whose cuttings can rot). Internodal cuttings are made when the stem is cut about halfway between successive nodes, and are commonly use to propagate large-flowered hybrids of clematis.

With softwood cuttings there is a risk that the very young tissue will rot and the cutting die. To prevent this, basal cuttings should be taken where the young shoot joins the older stem, so that the young shoot has a small length of the older wood at its base. A variant of the basal cutting is the heel cutting, where the side shoot is removed by pulling it downwards so that a small amount (heel) of wood is removed from the older stem and is attached to the base of the cutting. This is commonly used with conifer cuttings. The older wood and the increased area of cambium cells exposed both increase the chances of roots forming.

Rooting powder or liquid is a mixture of synthetic forms of auxin (and usually a fungicide) that have longer-lasting effects than natural auxins (see Chapter 6), as seen for auxin-based selective herbicides, and that are not taken up by the cutting. By dipping the base of a cutting into such a preparation, root formation is encouraged. Softwood cuttings usually do not need such help, but semi-ripe and hardwood cuttings may because of a lack of endogenous auxins and the difficulty in re-programming the cells as the wood becomes less juvenile. Different rooting powders have been developed for particular cutting materials. For hardwood cuttings, Powder No.3 would be the most appropriate.

Most cuttings are stem tip cuttings where the apical bud is left intact and from which the new stem and leaves of shoot development will develop. For plants which root very easily from cuttings, such as sedums, a more productive system involves cutting each stem into short lengths, each with two or three nodes and with the bottom cut on each just below a node. These internodal stem cuttings are then placed with the lower end of the cutting in the rooting medium. Plants can tell which way is up, because higher levels of auxin accumulate lower down a stem, so it is vital that you mark which is the lower end when preparing these cuttings. Roots will not develop if the cutting is inserted upside down.

Root and Leaf Cuttings

Thick-rooted herbaceous perennials like *Verbascum, Phlox, Anchusa, Papaver orientalis, Eryngium, Brunnera, Acanthus, Campanula* and Japanese anemones are difficult to propagate by stem cuttings but are readily propagated by root cuttings. With root cuttings, the cutting is the only source of sugars and energy for the developing plant until leaves are formed. As a result, plants like the above, with thick roots, propagate more readily than do plants with thinner roots, as the former have larger food reserves in the cutting. As with stem cuttings, roots can tell top from bottom so should be placed vertically with the top part of the cutting uppermost. Shoots develop from root cuttings via adventitious buds.

Adventitious buds are often formed after leaf tissue is damaged, and this can be exploited to achieve vegetative propagation from leaf cuttings. Leaf cuttings are commonly used to propagate eucomis, gloxinias, streptocarpus and the foliage begonias, with adventitious buds and thence plantlets forming when major leaf veins are cut and placed in contact with the rooting medium.

Grafting

Some woody plants are propagated by grafting rather than from cuttings because of a problem of growing the plant on its own roots. This could be because it is difficult to induce rooting of cuttings, as happens with many trees, or because the plant is too weak, possibly because of leaf variegation, to produce a large enough root system.

In grafting, the plant to be propagated provides the scion, with apical and/or axillary buds. In budding, as happens with roses, the shoot parent provides an axillary bud only. Most of the above-ground characters of the grafted plant, such as leaf and flower traits, will be determined by the scion parent. The scion will be grafted onto a rootstock of a related plant. The function of the rootstock is to produce a large enough root system for the grafted plant. Subsequently, because of the feed-back mechanism between the root and the shoot (Chapter 3), the vigour of the rootstock parent will affect the above-ground vigour of the grafted plants, as it will supply the cytokinins which help determine shoot growth.

In grafting, the aim is to line up the outer tissues of the cut surfaces of the scion and rootstock, so that the cambium layers just under the epidermis in the two tissues are in contact and can grow together over time.

Advantages of Vegetative Propagation

Most garden plants sold through nurseries or garden centres are propagated vegetatively. The main advantage of vegetative propagation over seed propagation is the production of largely true-to-type daughter plants, which is particularly important for named cultivars of garden plants. But there are other advantages of vegetation propagation.

This propagation method is the only one which can be used on plants which are sterile, such as completely double flowers (Chapter 8) like *Anemone nemorosa* 'Vestal', inter-specific hybrids (Chapter 2) such as the broom *Cytisus* × *kewensis*

The double-flowered *Anemone nemorosa* 'Vestal', which is sterile.

(*C. ardoini* × *C. albus*) and *Clematis* × *jackmannii*, and polyploids like the triploid *Hemerocallis* × *fulva* (Chapter 8).

For perennials, the time to produce a plant capable of flowering can be reduced by vegetative propagation. From seed it can take from one year to many decades to pass from the juvenile to the adult phase, when the plant can flower. It can take four to five years to produce an oriental hellebore, daffodil or trillium to flowering size from seed, but with vegetative propagation such as division, separation of bulb offsets or cormlets (as appropriate) the starting material is more advanced and can lead to the production of a flowering plant within one to three years. With lilies, for example, flowering size plants can be obtained from seed within three years, compared to two years with bulbils.

By starting with one- or two-year-old shoots for cuttings or scion wood for grafting, you have shortened the juvenile period of the resulting plants so that they will flower earlier. Grafting further ages the new plant, as chemical messages from the rootstock contribute to the physiological age of the grafted plant. That is why it is always best to buy plants of, say, wisteria or trumpet vine (*Campsis radicans*) which have been grafted (the swollen graft union is easy to see) rather than seed propagated, as the grafted plants will flower at a much younger age than will the seed-propagated ones, as well as being true-to-type. The juvenile phase for wisteria grown from seed, for example, is around seven years.

Woody garden plants with lower than usual levels of chlorophyll, such as variegated or golden-leaved forms, are usually grafted onto a green-leaved relative in order to produce a more vigorous specimen. The wedding cake tree, *Cornus contraversa* 'Variegata' is grafted onto *Cornus contraversa*, while the golden yew, *Taxus baccata* 'Standishii' is grafted onto *T. baccata*.

Grafting also allows the introduction of altered growth habit, such as standard or weeping habit (by grafting scions of a prostrate cultivar onto a single stem). Other traits which have been introduced by grafting include root characters such as lime tolerance in the Inkarho series of rhododendrons, and resistance to the *Phylloxera* root louse in grapevines, saving the French wine industry. The North American flowering dogwoods, *Cornus florida* or *C. nuttallii*, should always be bought grafted onto *C. kousa* or *C. kousa chinensis*, as these rootstocks make the dogwoods more tolerant of the prevailing climate in western Europe.

Disadvantages of Vegetative Propagation

There is a downside to vegetative propagation. When a virus infects a plant, the virus particles travel around the plant in the phloem (Chapter 4) and hence spread systemically throughout the plant, except for meristems and seeds. As a result, vegetative propagation from a virus-infected plant will involve a plant organ (stem, leaf, tuber, etc.) which contains the virus. The resulting plants will therefore be virus infected if the mother plant was.

As a result, many geophytes, particularly lilies,

Leaf variegation in *Aucuba japonica* 'Variegata' is caused by a beneficial virus.

canna lilies and potatoes, suffer from virus infection, so that the plants lack vigour or exhibit characteristic symptoms. In some cases, so-called beneficial viruses cause desirable traits in garden plants, such as the flower colour breaks in the original Rembrandt tulips and the yellow leaf spotting on leaves of *Abutilon megapotamicum* 'Thompsonii' and *Aucuba japonica* 'Variegata'.

To prevent the spread of viruses, certified tubers of potato cultivars are produced in Scotland and Donegal, because the wet and windy conditions prevent aphids, the main vectors of potato viruses, from flying and spreading the viruses. Viruses can be eliminated from most garden plant stocks by seed propagation. Because of the way the vascular bundle connects to the meristem, viruses do not generally infect seeds. Commercial stocks of lilies, for example, are frequently rejuvenated by passage through a generation of seed propagation.

SEED PROPAGATION

In nature, most plants reproduce via seed, as a result of sexual reproduction. For the plant there are several advantages of seed propagation. The offspring of one plant can differ with respect to height, flowering date, flower colour, and so on. This genetic variation is the basis of natural selection. Individual plants better able to survive ('fitter' plants), so that they will produce more offspring, are said to be 'better adapted' to the local environment. In cold areas, later-flowering individuals are frequently at an advantage because they avoid late frosts and flower at the time when pollinating insects are becoming active.

Another advantage of sexual reproduction involves elimination of infection, especially that caused by viruses. Virus particles spread within the infected plant but generally are not found in the meristematic cells of the flower, so that the virus is generally not spread via seeds. Commercial stocks of many lily species and cultivars, for example, are vegetatively propagated but need to be 'cleaned up', so the virus infections are removed by seed propagation.

In addition, seed reproduction permits the plant to disperse its seeds far and wide, to avoid competition between the daughter plants or between the mother and daughter plants, and to colonize new areas. Seed dispersal can be achieved by wind or by animals, principally vertebrates like birds and mammals but also invertebrates such as ants.

For the gardener, growing plants from seed,

either bought from a commercial seed house or collected by yourself from your own plants or from elsewhere, is an exciting and pleasurable part of gardening. It can be frustrating, however, and a grasp of the factors affecting seed germination can help increase your success rate.

Seed Dormancy

A fully developed seed contains the next generation in miniature, with an embryonic shoot and an embryonic root, plus a food reserve. In temperate plant species, the seed usually abscises from the mother plant and dries within the fruit or seed capsule to 15–20 per cent moisture content, developing a form of dormancy.

In this dry state, the embryo plant in a seed is in a state of suspended animation, when it can withstand unbelievable stresses, such as immersion in liquid nitrogen (at −196°C) or boiling water, or drying to 0.5 per cent moisture content. In this dormant condition, seeds can remain alive in the soil for months, years or decades, depending on species, awaiting the appropriate conditions for germination. They can also survive natural conditions like prolonged drought or fire, which would be lethal to the growing plant.

To some extent the time of the year when the seed will germinate is hard-wired into its genes. Dormancy is designed to prevent the seeds germinating under conditions which would kill the seedlings, which are much less tolerant than an adult plant to stresses such as winter cold for species from temperate woodland or summer drought for species from scrub forest (Chapter 2).

Although the seeds of most garden plants

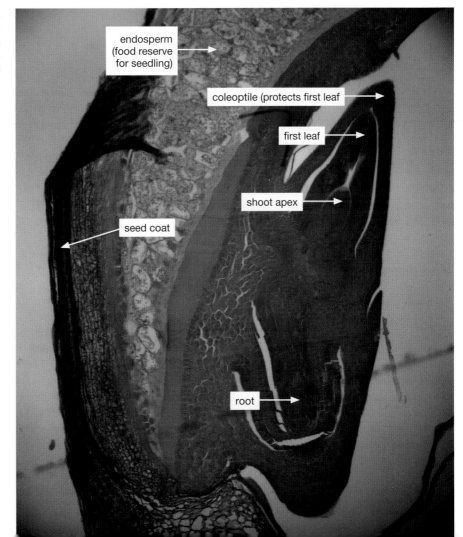

A micrograph of a thin section of a wheat seed, showing the embryo with shoot and root primordia, surrounded by food reserve tissue (endosperm).

endosperm (food reserve for seedling)

coleoptile (protects first leaf

first leaf

shoot apex

seed coat

root

exhibit some dormancy, some do not and will germinate immediately. Annuals, particularly pioneer species, may show little or no dormancy and germinate as soon as they encounter suitable environmental conditions, such as adequate moisture (to raise the ungerminated embryo plant from a moisture content of 10 per cent to a figure nearer the 90 per cent found in growing plants), oxygen, light and suitable temperatures. Seeds of *Nigella damascena* and other winter annuals (Chapter 6) shed in autumn will germinate in profusion almost immediately. Annuals of the Poaceae, Asteraceae and Papaveraceae (poppy family) fall into this category.

Other plants without seed dormancy include temperate species from habitats with very cold winters, such as some alpine species, where the autumn and winter temperatures in their native habitat are too low for germination once the seed has matured, so there is no need to evolve a dormancy period. Fresh seeds of tropical species, particularly rainforest species like coffee and citrus, also germinate without any dormancy, because there is no unfavourable season in their native habitat.

Most other plants, including other annuals (summer annuals; Chapter 6), will germinate the following spring or later, despite the presence of environmental conditions during the autumn which are clearly suitable for germination. This delay in germination occurs in the vast majority of garden plant species and is caused by seeds exhibiting a period of dormancy. This dormancy will dissipate over time, allowing the seeds to germinate at an appropriate season.

Plants have evolved three different strategies for delaying germination of freshly produced seeds until the unfavourable season in their native habitats has passed: physiological, physical and morphological dormancy.

Physiological dormancy

Physiological dormancy is the most important dormancy method among herbaceous perennial and annual garden plants, and among woody plants from dry areas. It is the most advanced of the dormancy strategies. In nature, physiological dormancy is broken by exposure of the seeds to the stress conditions the seedlings aim to avoid, and an understanding of this will help the gardener achieve good seed germination. Plants from temperate areas, where the unfavourable season is in winter, need low-temperature incubation (stratification) to simulate winter before physiological dormancy is broken, whereas plants from temperate areas with an inclement (hot dry) summer, such as scrub forest species, require high-temperature stratification. An example of the latter is the hoop-petticoat daffodil, *Narcissus bulbocodium* from Spain and north-west Africa.

Physical dormancy

Physical dormancy is common in seeds of plants from areas where there are distinct dry and wet seasons, such as the savannah. Such seeds are characterized by having hard seeds which are impermeable to water, so that the seed cannot rehydrate. There are natural openings in the coat which are plugged when the seed is dormant. Gradually, abrasion between the seed coat and soil particles or the action of soil bacteria on the seed coat breaks down this physical barrier so that physical dormancy is eliminated.

Physical dormancy is particularly common among members of the pea family (Fabaceae), like *Gleditsia* and sweet pea, especially tropical species of this family, as well as members of the geranium family.

Morphological dormancy

Here, the embryo in the mature seed is not fully developed. When the shed seed is in contact with moist soil at moderate soil temperatures in late summer and autumn, the embryo will continue to develop until it reaches full size, at which point it will be able to germinate under appropriate conditions, usually in the autumn or spring.

Members of the buttercup family like *Anemone* and *Adonis*, and the lily family, like *Lilium*, *Colchicum* and *Paris*, tend to exhibit this type of dormancy. Many European forest trees also exhibit morphological seed dormancy, including oak, beech, willow, poplar, hazel and horse chestnut. These must be sown immediately they are

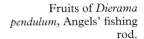

Fruits of *Dierama pendulum*, Angels' fishing rod.

shed, and not allowed to dry out; they will then germinate in the spring.

Breaking Seed Dormancy

When you buy seed, you should get detailed descriptions as to how to store, sow and look after the seed. The seed will have been cleaned to remove debris, weed seeds and so on and should have been checked for germination rate. None of this will be true for home-collected seed, so here are a few words about collecting and storing seeds.

One advantage of collecting your own seed is that you can control when it is harvested. The usual piece of advice given to seed collectors is to harvest the seed at the time the seed is usually shed from the mother plant and to sow it fresh without allowing it to dry, which can induce even deeper forms of dormancy, which are more difficult to break. If not sown fresh, seeds of the Apiaceae, for example, will undergo physiological dormancy, which needs low temperature stratification to relieve.

With some species, if the seed is not sown when fresh, germination can be delayed by one (paeonies or blue poppies) or even two years (hellebores). Sowing of fresh seed works particularly well with members of the Ranunculaceae, Apiaceae and the Asteraceae.

Seed collection is easy with plants whose seeds are held in upright capsules like foxgloves, poppies, alliums, aquilegias and verbascums, but not so easily where the seeds suddenly spill out of their capsule, as with hellebores, or are dispersed explosively, like geraniums and impatiens. In these cases, wrapping the intact seed head in a paper or cellophane bag (not plastic) can be helpful.

The received wisdom is fine, but there are cases where a little knowledge can save you a lot of time waiting for germination. The mature seed of most temperate perennial plants enters a form of dormancy when still within the mother plant, usually physiological dormancy that requires alternating temperatures to break it.

For quite a number of these plants, including primulas, hellebores, crocosmias, zantedeschias, corydalis, hacquetias and trilliums, dormancy is only switched on as the seed matures. If you harvest such seed when the seed capsule is still green, remove surface moisture on absorbent kitchen paper towels and sow the seed immediately; you will then get rapid germination, without the need to break dormancy.

The other plants where seeds should be sown immediately are rainforest plants, such as citrus, which are grown as house or glasshouse plants. When mature, these seeds have a very high moisture content (30–50 per cent) and any drying will kill them, so they should be sown straight away.

Fruits of *Arum maculatum*.

Seeds in fleshy fruits are designed to be dispersed by birds or mammals (Chapter 1), who consume the fruits and spit out or defaecate the seeds. In the presence of the fruit pulp, before the seeds have been ingested, the seeds of many of these species will not germinate. Again, this is a dormancy mechanism which ensures that the seed will not germinate until it has been dispersed. The mode of action of this inhibition varies, but in tomatoes it is known that the pulp prevents the seeds from taking up water. It is vital when collecting such seeds, like tomato, ivy, *Arisaema* spp., *Phytolacca americana*, *Arum italicum* and *Podophyllum hexandrum*, that the seeds are rinsed away from the fruit pulp and the seeds quickly dried on paper towels, before sowing. Failure to remove the fruit pulp in such species can delay seed germination by two years.

Be careful when handling brightly coloured fruits like those of podophyllum and arisaemas. They often evolved to be eaten by birds and can contain toxins active against mammals (Chapter 2), so wear gloves. There is also some evidence that removal of the fleshy elaiosome from ant-dispersed seeds, such as snowdrops and many woodland species, can improve seed germination.

Once you have collected your seeds, if you do not want to sow them immediately, it is important to store them appropriately. Seeds of most temperate plants retain their viability best when cold and dry. However, seeds of plants from the Liliaceae or the Ranunculaceae or others which exhibit morphological dormancy must be treated differently, as drying the seeds will induce prolonged dormancy or could even kill them.

A domestic fridge (not freezer) is suitable for low-temperature storage. To keep the seeds dry, put them in open-topped plastic containers inside a larger sealable container, such as a Kilner jar. Sachets of silica gel salvaged from packaging around computers or sunglasses will keep the atmosphere in the jar dry, but it is best not to allow contact between the seeds and the silica.

Before sowing your seeds, you may want to consider breaking any inherent dormancy. Seeds suspected of exhibiting morphological dormancy should be kept moist. This can be achieved by sowing the seed and keeping it at 15–20°C for four to six weeks to encourage the embryos to develop fully, then transferring them to appropriate germination conditions.

Physiological dormancy tends to disappear after prolonged dry storage of seeds like lettuce at a moderately high temperature (20°C), a process known as 'after ripening'. If this is unsuccessful, you should try appropriate stratification techniques, by incubating the seeds at low or high temperatures. The seeds need to be metabolically active, so they should be incubated in plastic bags with a small amount of damp (not wet) compost or vermiculite. To prevent fungal attack, the compost should be sterilized before use by microwaving thinly spread soil at full power for 90s, or until the compost steams.

Stratification should last for four to six weeks in a refrigerator at 5°C (low) or 20–25°C (high temperature treatments) before being transferred to germination conditions at a temperature of approximately 18°C. Alternatively, for low-temperature stratification of seeds of alpines and hardy trees and shrubs, the pots can be left outdoors in a cold frame in most of western Europe from January, as a temperature between 1°C and 10°C should be adequate.

The standard method of overcoming physical dormancy has been to scarify the seed coat, to breach the barrier of the seed coat. Scarification has been carried out with sandpaper, a blade, boiling water, even concentrated sulphuric acid, and has been part of the routine for sweet pea growers for many years. It is now believed that seeds of modern sweet pea cultivars do not need either these methods or overnight soaking in water to overcome physical dormancy. The most recent research suggests that water uptake is best achieved by removing the natural covers plugging the openings in the seed coat. One scarification method which appears to be effective is the percussive method, where seeds are placed in a glass jar, which is sealed and then shaken for ten minutes to loosen the plugs.

Seed Sowing Conditions

For germination, seeds need to be sown under appropriate light, oxygen and temperature conditions. Generally, the smaller the seed, the earlier in secondary succession the plant appears, and the more likely it is to need light to germinate (Chapter 6).

Fine seeds, such as those from annuals, are sown on the surface of a free-draining seed compost and pressed into the surface to maintain contact between compost and seed. For slow-germinating fine seeds, put the grit on the compost surface, then add the seed. Grit prevents mosses and liverworts from growing on the compost.

Slightly larger seeds can be covered with a thin layer of fine grade vermiculite or fine grit, to maintain moisture but allow light to penetrate. Light can penetrate through 2mm but not 6mm soil, and up to 10mm with larger-particled material like sand. In a study of foxglove germination, more than 70 per cent of the seeds germinated under

10mm sand in the light but only 4 per cent in the dark. Wind-dispersed seeds, like the flattened seeds of lilies, also need light to germinate, so should be sown on the compost surface.

Plants from the South African scrub forest or fynbos are adapted to regular fires, which trigger seed germination of many of the native species. Germination of restios, in particular, is triggered by smoke from the fires, and the germination of these species can be dramatically increased by the use of liquid smoke, using discs impregnated with smoke, which can be purchased from specialist seed suppliers. This development has been a major factor in the greatly increased availability of restios in Europe since 2002.

Generally, the larger the seed, the deeper it should be planted, with flattened seeds like sunflower and pumpkin planted on their edge to minimize rotting. For small-sized seeds, the effect of light on germination can vary, so it is worthwhile leaving some seeds uncovered and some covered. If you need to use artificial light, it is important to use cool white fluorescent tubes, as the light from these contains a large amount of red light, necessary for plant responses to light, especially germination.

Temperature for seed germination again depends on the species. Guidelines are 13–18°C for hardy annual and biennial species, 18–21°C for half-hardy and tender annual seed, 20–21°C for tender perennials (from South Africa, California, Australia) and 24°C for tropical (houseplant) species. Interestingly, the optimum temperatures for germination of plants from the polar climate of the tundra (such as mountain avens, *Dryas octopetala*) are actually higher (more than 20°C) than those of plants from the warmer scrub forest biome, such as cyclamen and tulip, at 10–12°C. Tundra plants must germinate during the brief summer, when the weather is at its warmest, whereas scrub forest plants germinate in the cooler autumn season to avoid the summer drought stress period.

Though supplementary heating can increase germination rate, raising the temperature too high can inhibit germination. With lettuce, for example, temperatures greater than 20°C convince the seeds that the unfavourable summer season in their native scrub forest habitat is about to start, and the seeds will remain dormant until the temperature is lowered. *Meconopsis* spp. also prefer cool conditions for germination.

On a sunny day even in late winter and early spring, unshaded glasshouses can reach temperatures which can cause problems to the germination of the seeds of hardy plants. A cheap and quick method of controlling glasshouse temperature on sunny days is to fill the staging with used potting compost or similar material, and keep it damp; evaporation will very efficiently cool the glasshouse.

A useful list of conditions for germination of seeds of a range of plants is given in *Seeds: The Ultimate Guide to Growing Successfully from Seed* by Jekka McVicar (Kyle Cathie).

The time for germination of seeds varies widely between species, even after dormancy has been overcome, though most annuals will start to appear within three weeks at 18°C. Seeds of some species germinate over a prolonged period, such as those with hard seed coats, such as *Ipomoea* which can germinate over several years, or members of the Apiaceae, like carrot and parsley, where the first-formed seeds (from the primary umbels) have little or no dormancy, whereas the later-formed seeds have prolonged dormancy. These adaptations maximize the chance that some seedlings will survive.

Seeds of some plants, particularly woodland species and largely members of the Liliaceae, may not appear to germinate until two years after planting. This is because of a phenomenon known as double dormancy, where roots and shoots have separate dormancy mechanisms. The roots appear in the first year after sowing and the shoot appears in the second. Examples include *Arisaema* spp., *Paeonia* spp., *Convallaria majalis*, *Polygonatum biflorum*, *Trillium erectum*, *T. grandiflorum*, *Paeonia suffruticosa* and *Uvularia grandiflora*, which naturally show morphological dormancy.

In some lily species, after morphological dormancy has dissipated over the first winter, roots need 3–6 months at a warm temperature, around 20°C, to emerge, while the shoot needs stratification at a low temperature, below 10°C, for six weeks before it will appear in the second spring after sowing.

Seed dormancy is clearly, then, an important characteristic which helps plants to adapt to their environment. To paraphrase the Bard: 'Some seeds are born dormant, some achieve dormancy and some have dormancy thrust upon them' (credit to Professor Philip Wareing, one of the great British plant physiologists, for a memorable quote).

Hardening-Off

Before seedlings are moved outside from the protection of the glasshouse or windowsill, a process known as hardening-off is necessary to acclimatize the seedlings to the colder and more stressful conditions outdoors. The pots should be moved outside during the daytime, then returned under cover (to the glasshouse or, later, the cold frame) during the night. In this way, the seedlings become acclimatized (hardened off) to the colder conditions outside.

The lower temperatures act as a sub-lethal stress, 'immunizing' them against subsequent potentially lethal cold weather. The cold-tolerance genes in the seedlings are switched on by the cold hardening, so that the lipids in the cell membranes change their arrangement, with the result that the seedlings are better able to withstand the cold. Generally, when lipids go cold, they harden, as happens when you put butter in the fridge. Similar changes in cell membranes can cause cell death. Changes in the membrane lipids of cold-hardened seedlings stop that happening so the membranes continue to work well.

Movement of the seedlings by the wind during hardening off will make the plants stockier with thicker stems, by a related acclimatization process known as mechanical hardening (Chapter 3). This effect can be accelerated by shaking the trays or pots of seedlings a couple of dozen times each day when taking the seedlings in and out of the cold. These processes also increase stress tolerance in shaken plants.

PLANT GENETICS

Unlike vegetatively propagated plants, most plants produced from seed look different from one another and from the mother plant. This is particularly true for cultivars of garden plants, while seed progeny from some wild species resemble one another without being identical. To understand why some but not all propagated plants look like the parent plant, we need to refer to plant genetics, the science of how characters (like flower colour) are inherited from parent to offspring.

Any character in a plant species (or other living organism, from human to virus) shows variation between different individuals, like differences in height. Part of this variation is inherited because it is controlled by genes, and the rest is not inherited because it is a response to variations in the environment. Environmental factors affecting plant height would include nitrogen-rich soil, shade or high density of plants, all of which result in taller plants, or exposure to wind, which produces shorter plants.

Genes

Genes are the factors which control all inherited characters, such as flower colour, longevity, height and leaf colour. An average plant species will contain approximately 15,000 genes, which is similar to the figure for animals like flies and nematodes. Each human, however, contains 35,000 genes, but even this figure is put in the shade by rice, the most important crop in the world, which has an estimated 50,000 genes.

The large number of genes in plants reflects their complexity. Plants make all the tens of thousands of chemicals they need from scratch. When faced with stresses like heat or a predator, plants recognize what they are being attacked by (microorganism or animal, sap-sucker or chewer) by identifying chemicals produced, and then switch on the appropriate defence genes. Plants also have a primitive form of colour vision, based on the light receptor phytochrome, can count (Venus' fly trap can count up to two, needing a fly to touch two trigger hairs before closing its trap), and can judge time to within fifteen minutes. All of these complex functions require the plant to have lots of genes.

In fact, every body cell (or somatic cell) of a plant or animal contains the same genes as all the other cells of that organism. The control centre of each cell is the nucleus (Chapter 1), and it is in the nucleus that more than 99 per cent of the genes in a cell are situated. The rest are carried in the cell organelles known as chloroplasts and mitochondria (Chapter 1). The genes are carried on chromosomes, which are complexes of DNA (deoxyribonucleic acid, the chemical from which genes are made) and proteins, all tightly packaged.

Humans have twenty-three pairs of chromosomes, one copy of each chromosome originating

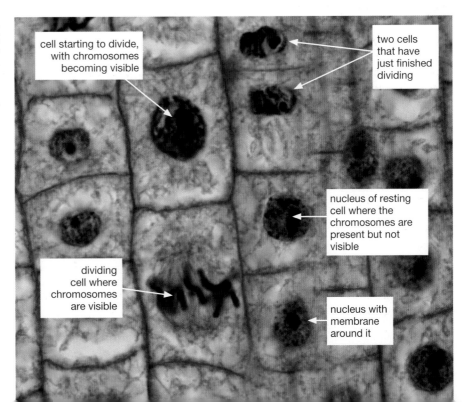

Dividing cells in an onion root tip, showing chromosomes in the nucleus.

cell starting to divide, with chromosomes becoming visible

two cells that have just finished dividing

nucleus of resting cell where the chromosomes are present but not visible

dividing cell where chromosomes are visible

nucleus with membrane around it

from each parent, in each of billions of cells. The DNA in each human cell would stretch to two metres, so that the entire DNA in your body tied end-to-end would stretch to the moon and back more than five times. Plants of the lily family are the world record holders for the amount of DNA in each cell, with each cell of the geophyte *Fritillaria assyriacea* containing more than 60 metres of DNA. (Not all DNA represents genes, so the fritillary is not thirty times more complex than we are.)

Even though every cell in a plant has exactly the same genes as every other cell, they are not all switched on in every cell at the same time. In fact, probably less than 1 per cent of all the genes are 'on' in any particular cell at a particular time. This accounts for why different parts of the plant look different from one another. All plant cells contain the genes to make the green pigment chlorophyll, but the genes are switched on only in leaf and stem tissue exposed to light, which are therefore green in colour. They are 'off', for example, in root and petal cells. Flower colour genes are 'on' in petal cells but 'off' in leaf cells, in root cells and often even in stamen cells which are located close to the petal cells.

How Does a Gene Control a Character?

Despite being so important, DNA is a very simple molecule, consisting of a sugar (deoxyribose), phosphate and four bases, namely adenine (A), thymine (T), guanine (G) and cytosine (C). Each chromosome is one very long molecule of DNA. In turn, each gene is a specific sequence of 1,000 or more DNA bases, such as ACCGTTAGCT...

The linear sequence of bases in a specific gene codes for the production of a specific protein (which is a linear sequence of amino acids), with the order of bases determining the order of amino acids in the protein. In turn, the order of amino acids determines the shape and function of the protein and how well it does its job.

The most common route by which a gene determines a character is that the gene controls production of a specific type of protein known as an enzyme which, in turn, controls a chemical reaction in the cell. In this reaction, one chemical (the substrate) is converted into another, the product, which is a chemical that determines the character. Blue petal colour in bluebell, for example, is controlled by a gene which makes the enzyme dihydroflavonol 4-reductase which makes the blue chemical delphinidin.

But another question is raised. If all plants of one species have the same genes, and genes help to determine the appearance (phenotype) of each plant, how do we get inherited differences between individual plants of the same species? These would include variations (blue, pink, white) in flower colour in the English bluebell *Hyacinthoides*

Genetic variation in white clover leaves, controlled by two alleles of the same gene, producing unmarked (bottom left: recessive allele) or V-marked (centre: dominant allele) leaflets.

marked
leaflets

unmarked
leaflets

non-scripta, or in the presence/absence of V-shaped white leaf markings on white clover, *Trifolium repens,* in your lawn.

In a typical plant, about one-third of all the genes can exist in two or more different forms, known as alleles, with slightly different base sequences as a result of a process known as mutation. The different alleles produce slightly different forms of the same protein with different amino acid sequences, which (usually) generate more or less of the chemical product. For example, the white-flowered form of the bluebell is a natural mutant, where the gene for blue petal pigment has changed (mutated) so that it produces a modified form of the protein which cannot produce any of the delphinidin pigment. Result: no pigment and white flowers.

In humans and nearly all animals, there are two copies of each chromosome and each gene, one inherited from the mother and one from the father. Such species are said to be diploid (two copies, written as 2x). Most plant species, on the other hand, have more than two copies of each chromosome/gene and are said to be polyploid (many copies). Examples of polyploid plants include potato (tetraploid, 4x), wheat (hexaploid, 6x) and strawberry (octaploid, 8x).

How are Characters Inherited?

The simple laws governing how characters are passed on from parent to offspring were discovered in the mid-nineteenth century by an Augustinian monk, Gregor Mendel. It was not until 1900, however, when the scientific paper he wrote on this subject was re-discovered, that the significance of his findings was recognized. In recognition, we now refer to the simple mathematical model which predicts the chance of each offspring individual having a particular appearance, or phenotype, as Mendelian inheritance.

Let us look at bluebell, a diploid plant, so that there are two copies of each gene. In this case, we will consider the character flower colour. If we give the symbol B for the normal (wild-type) allele producing the blue pigment and the symbol b for the mutant allele producing no pigment, then three combinations of alleles (or genotypes) are possible: BB, Bb and bb.

If the two copies of a gene are the same allele, the plant is said to be homozygous for that allele. The individual is said to be a homozygote, either BB (blue flowers) or bb (white flowers). If the two copies are different, then the plant is heterozygous, or to be a heterozygote, Bb. In this example, the Bb heterozygote has blue flowers and is indistinguishable in phenotype from the BB homozygote. One copy of the B allele in bluebell produces enough pigment to give as blue a flower as do two copies, so the phenotypes (flower colour in this case) of the three genotypes are as follows:

Genotype BB Bb bb
Phenotype blue blue white

In the heterozygote, the allele which is expressed (B for blue flowers) is said to be the completely dominant allele and is given the upper case letter, whereas the allele which is not expressed in the heterozygote is termed the recessive allele and given the lower case letter. So, in this case, B is the completely dominant allele, producing blue flowers, while b is the completely recessive allele for white flowers.

In the case of peach, the downy-skinned fruit (peach) is controlled by a dominant gene, while the smooth-skinned form (nectarine) is controlled by the recessive allele. Double flowers in Chinese aster (*Callistephus* spp.) are recessive to single flowers.

With some genes, the heterozygote resembles neither homozygote. The dark purple leaf colour of the cultivar 'Ravenswing' of cow parsley, *Anthriscus sylvestris* is caused by an allele, R, which is incompletely dominant to the recessive allele, r, which produces green leaves in wild-type cow parsley. The heterozygote, Rr, has a phenotype intermediate between those of the two homozygotes, having green leaves with purple splodges:

Genotype RR Rr rr
Phenotype purple green and green
(leaf colour) ('Ravenswing') purple (cow parsley)

Vegetatively Propagated

Vegetative propagation occurs from organs such as stem, leaf and bulb, made up of body or somatic cells. We have already seen that somatic cells in an individual plant are genetically identical. As a consequence, the offspring from vegetative propagation are also genetically identical to one another and to the parent plant. With vegetative propagation, there is only one parent.

In nature or the garden, bluebells can multiply either vegetatively, producing bulb offsets, or by seed. If the parent plant is blue-flowered but genetically heterozygous (Bb), all the offspring produced from offsets will also have the Bb genotype and the blue-flowered phenotype. The same would be true for all other genes in the plant, so the offspring would be identical in appearance (true-to-type) to the parent plant.

Seed Propagated

A seed, on the other hand, arises from fertilization of an ovule by a pollen grain. In a diploid plant, each somatic cell is diploid and contains two copies of each chromosome and gene. But the ovules and pollen are the sex cells or gametes, and contain only one copy of each chromosome and each gene, so are said to be haploid. They fuse together to get back to the diploid state in the fertilized ovule, which will develop into the seed and then the offspring plant.

Each diploid plant contains one copy of each gene from each of its parents. When the plant produces gametes, each gamete receives a unique combination of genes from the two parents of the plant, as a result of re-shuffling of the genes.

According to Mendel's laws of inheritance, you can predict the proportion of the gametes which have each genotype and hence the proportion of the offspring which will have each phenotype, providing you know the genotype of both parents.

If the Bb bluebell plant self-pollinated itself, then it would supply both the pollen and the ovules. So, 50 per cent of the pollen would carry the dominant allele B, while the other 50 per cent would carry the recessive b allele. Similarly, 50 per cent of the ovules would be B, and 50 per cent would be b. If the probability of the pollen being B is ½ and the probability of the ovules being B is ½, then the probability of a B ovule being fertilized by a B pollen is ($½ \times ½$) = ¼.

	B pollen (½)	**b pollen (½)**
B ovules (½)	BB (¼)	Bb (¼)
b ovules (½)	Bb (¼)	bb (¼)

Genotype	BB	Bb	bb
Phenotype	blue	blue	white
Percentages	25%	50%	25%

Because the BB and Bb plants have the same phenotype, there should be, on average, three blue-flowered plants for each white-flowered one. This also shows why plants tend not to come true from seed. From a blue-flowered parent, some of the offspring are white flowered and some are blue. Bluebells, then, like many plants, come true-to-type by vegetative means but not from seed.

This example used self-pollination where the same plant provides both the pollen and the ovules. In most plants, however, a seed is produced by cross-pollination, with fertilization of one ovule on plant A by pollen from a different plant, B, of the same species. Cross-pollination will produce even more variation between individual offspring plants from the same parents than self-pollination.

If you are growing different cultivars of the same cross-pollinated species in your garden, then the parents may be very different in appearance, producing variation in the offspring for a wide range of characters. Seed produced on a plant of *Aquilegia* 'Nora Barlow' may result from fertilization of an ovule of 'Nora Barlow' by pollen from, say, a neighbouring plant of *Aquilegia* 'Ruby Port'. The two parents differ with respect to characters such as petal colour and number, spur length or plant height, so the seed progeny will all differ, carrying different traits from both parents.

When you consider that perhaps 5,000 genes in the aquilegia plant (one third of the 15,000 genes) may exist as two or more different alleles, gene re-shuffling and cross-pollination will result in each individual plant having a unique genotype and phenotype, just as with other 'cross-pollinated' species such as humans, where we all (with the exception of identical twins) have unique genotypes and hence look different.

A section down pin and
thrum flowers of primrose.

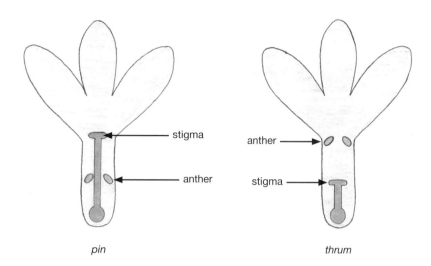

pin

thrum

MECHANISMS FOR POLLINATION

Cross-Pollination

Most plants have flowers with both male (stamens) and female sex organs (carpels) (Chapter 1) and appear capable of self-pollination, but most have evolved mechanisms which promote cross-pollination. In some plants, the stamens ripen, shed pollen and wither before the carpel ripens (protandry), such as with salvias, geraniums, campanulas and saxifrages, while in others, like magnolias, *Helleborus foetidus* and many wind-pollinated species such as grasses, the carpel ripens before the stamens release their pollen (protogyny).

In many *Primula* species, there are two flower forms of each species (pin and thrum), which

Thrum flowers of
primrose, *Primula vulgaris*.

Pin flowers of primrose, *Primula vulgaris*.

cannot self-pollinate. The anthers of the pin form are halfway down the petals with the stigma at the opening to the flower. In the thrum form, the anthers are at the flower opening while the stigma is halfway down. In this way, pollen can be readily transferred from pin to thrum and vice versa, ensuring cross-pollination. A similar mechanism occurs in *Pulmonaria* spp.

The dioecious shrub *Viburnum davidii*.

Pampas grass, where the female plants produce larger plumes.

Another mechanism for promoting cross-pollination is dioecy, where dioecious plants are either male or female, such as holly, pampas grass, aucuba, sea buckthorn, asparagus, *Viburnum davidii* and most skimmias. Often, one sex is more desirable than the other, with male ginkgo (females produce smelly fruits) and female pampas grass (larger flower plumes) being the preferred ones.

Another method is monoecy, where each plant is both male and female, but there are separate male and female flowers on the same plant, such as sweetcorn (female silks in a leaf axil and male tassels at the top of the plant) and many coniferous and flowering plant trees, such as oak and willow.

Many fruit trees, like most apple cultivars, have flowers with both male and female sex organs but are self-incompatible, in that they cannot fertilize themselves (Chapter 9). Common self-incompatible garden plants include members of the poppy, cabbage, rose and aster families.

Most plants are cross-pollinated. As a result, they tend to be heterozygous, and, as we saw with the bluebell example, heterozygous plants produce offspring from seed which are genetically and phenotypically different.

Sweetcorn, showing monoecy, with the male flowers (tassels) at the top and the female flowers (silks) in a leaf axil.

Self-Pollination

A minority of plants, however, employ self-polli-nation to produce seeds, including lettuce, pea, sweet pea, tomato, French bean and some violas.

Pioneer annual weeds like shepherd's purse are also self-pollinated, underlining the goal of these plants to produce as many seeds in as short a time as possible.

The quaking grass *Briza media* is a self-pollinated plant.

Several *Viola* spp. produce distinct self- and cross-pollinated flowers.

Obvious adaptations to self-pollination include flowers which do not open, as with French beans and the grass *Briza*, while many *Viola* spp. produce both open and closed flowers, but at different times of the year, with *V. odorata* producing closed self-pollinated flowers from May to September and open cross-pollinated flowers earlier and later.

An advantage of self-pollination is that seed (and fruit) production are not at the mercy of pollinating insects and hence of the weather. Whereas runner beans (cross-pollinated) do not set fruit well under dry, cold or hot conditions, yield of self-pollinated French beans is more tolerant of climatic extremes.

Self-pollinated plants tend to be homozygous, such as BB or bb. Because one plant provides the pollen and the ovules in a self-pollinated plant, they come true-to-type from seed. Consider the yellow-podded pea cultivar, 'Golden Sweet'. The allele for yellow pod colour, g, is completely recessive to the dominant allele, G, for green pods. Because the trait yellow pods is recessive, only plants homozygous for the g allele (gg) will produce yellow pods. If these plants are self-pollinated, all the ovules and all the pollen will carry the recessive allele (that is, will be g). As a consequence, all the offspring will be gg and will be yellow podded, so the cultivar is true-to-type from seed.

Self-pollinated garden plants tend to come true from seed, but, generally, this is not true because cultivars of cross-pollinated garden plants do not breed true-to-type via seed, although a small number of cultivars such as *Euphorbia dulcis* 'Chameleon' and *Geranium* 'Mrs Kendal Clark' do. For this reason, cultivars should be propagated vegetatively if they are to be sold as the named cultivar.

Inbreeding is a milder version of self-pollination and involves crossing individuals of the same species which look similar, so that the offspring tend to have a similar appearance. In the same way, pedigree dogs or cattle, produced as a result of inbreeding, show strong physical similarities between individuals within a breed, such as golden cocker spaniels. Inbreeding results in largely homozygous plants with the result that the seed offspring appear reasonably similar, as long as the plant is kept separate from close relatives, including other cultivars of the same species.

Many cross-pollinated plant species grown in the garden are sufficiently inbred to breed reasonably true-to-type, such as *Lilium* spp., *Verbena bonariensis* and *Digitalis* × *mertonensis*, especially if the species has been in cultivation for quite a while. Bowles' Golden Grass, *Milium effusum* 'Aurea', also comes true from seed.

Unfortunately, some non-true breeding cultivars are seed propagated for sale, resulting in gardeners buying plants which, when they flower, do not resemble the cultivar they are supposed to be. Examples of this disappointing situation include *Campanula lactiflora* 'Prichard's Variety', *Aquilegia* 'Nora Barlow', *Monarda* 'Cambridge Scarlet' and *Achillea ptarmica* 'The Pearl'. In RHS trials of commercial plants of the latter, which is usually compact with double flowers, many turned out to be seed propagated, with some even having single flowers.

TRUE-TO-TYPE OR NOT?

The general rule is that vegetatively propagated plants are true-to-type, whereas seed-propagated plants (except for self-pollinated species) are not. But exceptions do occur.

Variegated Cultivars

There are several different genetic mechanisms by which leaves (or flowers) can exhibit variegation, the presence of two distinct colours in the same organ. Mechanisms include periclinal chimeras (Chapter 5), beneficial viruses, transposable elements and chloroplast mutations. Each of these mechanisms can only be inherited through a particular type of propagation.

Periclinal Chimeras

The orderly type of variegation, with different-coloured margins and centres of the organ, is caused by a periclinal chimera (Chapter 5), with genetically different cells (green or yellow) in two of the three layers, L-I to L-III. The epidermal layer L-I does not contribute to the green colour of a dicot leaf, so the colour of the margin of the leaf is determined by L-II and the colour of the centre by L-III.

a) *Dicot*, e.g. *Elaegnus pungens* 'Gilt Edge'

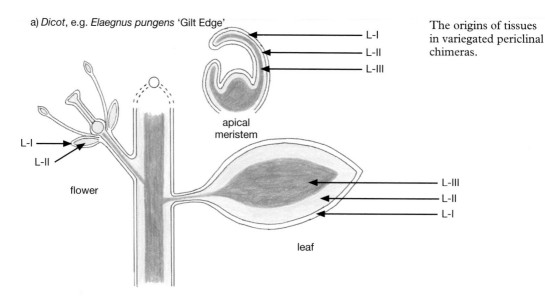

The origins of tissues in variegated periclinal chimeras.

b) *Monocot*, e.g. Hosta sieboldiana *'Frances Williams'*

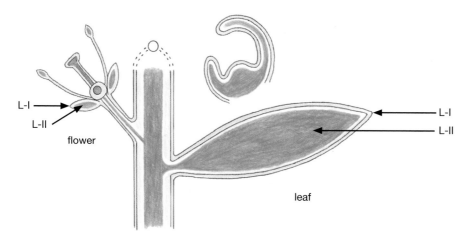

A dicot plant like ivy 'Goldheart', having leaves with a green margin and a yellow centre, will genetically have a green L-II and a yellow L-III layer.

With monocots, the system is slightly different. Here, the L-I layer does contain chloroplasts so can be green or yellow (or white), but layer L-III makes no contribution to leaf colour. The margin of a variegated monocot leaf is controlled by L-I and the centre by L-II. As a result, in hostas, which are monocots, the variegated cultivar 'Frances Williams', with a yellow margin and a green centre of the leaf, has a yellow L-I and a green L-II.

Those variegated monocots with relatively broad leaves, such as hostas, show the typical orderly arrangement of yellow and green tissues. Variegated monocots with more linear leaves, on the other hand, like the variegated lily of the valley *Convallaria majalis* 'Albostriata' or *Iris pallida* 'Argentovariegata', produce irregular patterns of stripes running lengthwise down the leaf.

Periclinal chimeras are also the major cause of orderly floral variegations, such as *Saintpaulia* 'Pinwheel' and *Omphalodes cappadocica* 'Starry Eyes', both flowers with a white margin and a dark centre, and *Myosotis arvensis* 'Star of Zurich', which

Offspring from a variegated dicot periclinal chimera, using different propagation methods.

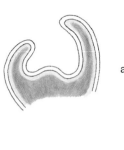

apical meristem

Stem cutting, division, grafting, budding

pre-existing growth bud

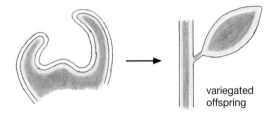

variegated offspring

Root cutting, leaf cutting, layering

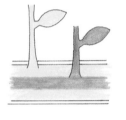

all-green offspring and all-yellow offspring

adventitious bud

Seed (self-pollination)

all-yellow offspring

has flowers with a white central band and a blue margin. Flowers have only two layers, L-I and L-II. Cells in both layers can contain anthocyanin and so can be coloured. 'Starry Eyes' has cyanic (blue, in this case) L-II and acyanic (white) L-I, while 'Star of Zurich' has cyanic L-I and acyanic L-II.

Propagation of a periclinal chimera will be true-to-type with any method which uses pre-formed buds (apical or axillary) with all three layers intact, such as bulbs, tubers, division, grafting, budding or stem cuttings.

Seed propagation of periclinal chimeras in dicots will not produce variegated offspring, because flower tissue develops from only layers L-I and L-II, with gametes being produced by L-II. As a result, all seed offspring will be either all-green or all-yellow. A beneficial side-effect of this is that the white-margined variegated cultivar 'Well Creek' of the invasive willowherb *Epilobium hirsutum* produces all-white seedlings which die soon after germination because they have no chlorophyll.

Propagation methods such as root cuttings, layering and leaf cuttings, however, produce new shoots adventitiously, not from pre-formed buds. Adventitious shoots usually develop from only one layer, so cannot retain the structure of the chimera.

Cultivar A infected with Pelargonium flower break virus

Cultivar B infected with Pelargonium vein-clearing virus

Transmission of beneficial viruses in ivy-leaved pelargoniums by grafting.

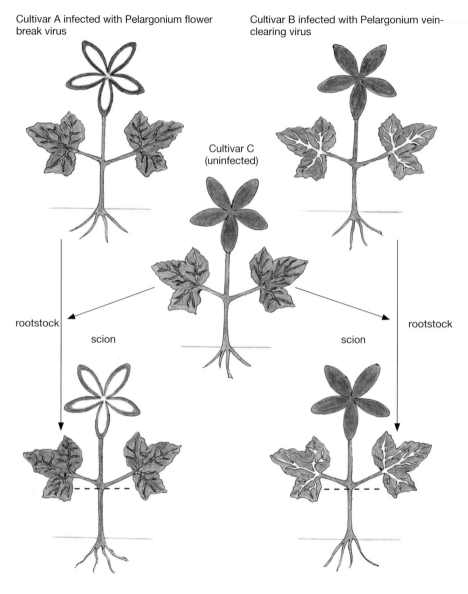

Cultivar C (uninfected)

rootstock

scion

scion

rootstock

As a result, floral and leaf variegation resulting from periclinal chimera will not be inherited using these propagation methods. If the variegated phlox 'Nora Leigh' (white margin, green centre: W-W-G) is propagated via root cuttings, all the offspring have green leaves, as the adventitious buds generally form in L-III.

Beneficial Viruses

There are several classes of leaf or flower variegation which are caused by viruses affecting pigment formation. The yellow mottling of leaves of *Abutilon megapotamicum* 'Thompsonii' is caused by the abutilon mosaic virus, while the golden spots on variegated Japanese laurel, such as *Aucuba japonica* 'Variegata' are also caused by a beneficial virus. The old Rembrandt tulips, with flashes of red or purple on a yellow or white ground are caused by virus particles blocking the production of anthocyanin pigments in the epidermal layer, revealing yellow (carotenoids present in lower petal layers) or white backgrounds (no carotenoids).

The random leaf variegation in nasturtium *Tropaeolum major* 'Alaska' is caused by a jumping gene or transposable element.

Specific viruses cause the variegation brought about by clearing of the leaf veins in *Pelargonium* x *hortorum* 'Crocodile' (Pelargonium vein-clearing virus) and *Lonicera* japonicum 'Aureoreticulata' (honeysuckle yellow vein virus), while a different virus is responsible for the white centres on the deep red petals of *Pelargonium peltatum* 'Mexicana' (Pelargonium petal streak virus).

Virus particles spread systemically in the phloem throughout the infected plant (Chapter 6), with the exception of young growing or flowering buds. As a result, any vegetative propagation method should multiply these plants true-to-type, although they will not come true from seed.

Not only can vegetative propagation produce true-to-type offspring from plants infected by beneficial viruses, but one vegetative method, grafting, can even allow the keen amateur to produce novel variegated cultivars. Alan and Judy Cassells showed that, by grafting a scion from a non-infected pelargonium onto a rootstock of *Pelargonium* 'Crocodile', the virus from 'Crocodile' moved through the graft into the shoots, introducing the vein-clearing variegation into that cultivar. Similarly, when they repeated the experiment with a rootstock of 'Mexicana' and a scion from a cultivar with dark-coloured flowers, the virus passed from the rootstock into the shoots formed from the scion parent, producing flowers identical to those of the second cultivar except for the presence of white centres to the petals.

Random Leaf or Flower Variegation

Unlike the orderly type of variegation associated with periclinal chimeras, some plants exhibit a more irregular distribution of variegated tissues, where white or yellow areas are scattered over the green leaf surface. This type of variegation was memorably referred to by Timothy Walker of the Oxford Botanic Garden as the loose-bowelled pigeon dropping school of leaf variegation. It is usually caused by one of two possible genetic mechanisms: transposable elements or chloroplast mutation.

Usually, each gene has a fixed location or 'locus' on one particular chromosome in every cell of the plant. A transposable element, on the other hand, is a jumping gene which can jump from site to site on chromosomes. In *Nasturtium* 'Alaska', a transposable element normally sits in a gene which makes the green pigment chlorophyll.

Because the transposable element interferes with the proper function of the gene, the chlorophyll gene is switched off and the cells produced from division of that cell will all be white. If, however, the transposable element jumps out of the chlorophyll gene, the gene will be

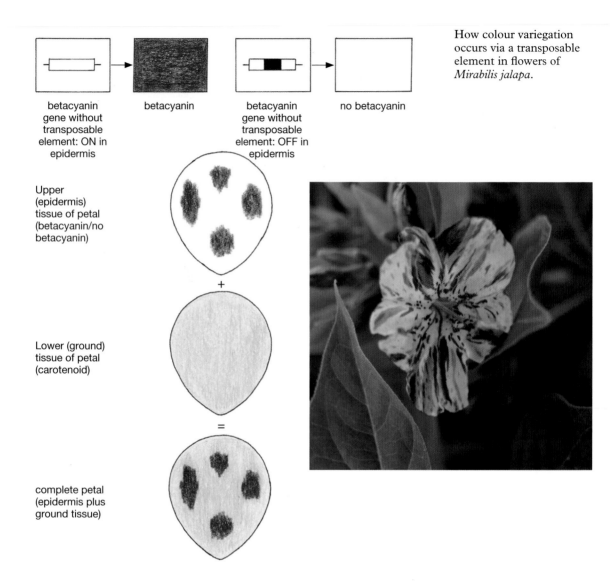

How colour variegation occurs via a transposable element in flowers of *Mirabilis jalapa*.

betacyanin gene without transposable element: ON in epidermis

betacyanin

betacyanin gene without transposable element: OFF in epidermis

no betacyanin

Upper (epidermis) tissue of petal (betacyanin/no betacyanin)

+

Lower (ground) tissue of petal (carotenoid)

=

complete petal (epidermis plus ground tissue)

re-activated and the cell (and its descendants) will be green. This behaviour of a transposable element therefore results in a green leaf with white splashes.

Because the transposable element will be present in the egg, all plants grown from seeds produced from such a variegated plant will also be variegated, so that it comes true-to-type. Other variegated-leaf cultivars caused by transposable elements include the annual variegated hop, the variegated tobacco *Nicotiana langsdorffi* 'Cream Splash' and *Aquilegia vervaeneana* 'Woodside'.

The same phenomenon can also cause splashed colours in flower petals, where a transposable element moves in and out of a gene for anthocyanin production in the epidermal layer. Where the element is present inside the gene, the petal cells will be either yellow, if carotenoids were produced in the petal layers below the epidermis, or white, if they are not. In cells where the transposable element had jumped out of the anthocyanin gene, the blue or red pigment would be produced, resulting in specks of red or blue on a yellow, or white, background. Examples include *Ipomoea* 'Flying

Saucers' (blue streaks on a white background), *Viola soraria* 'Freckles' (blue on white) and *Rosa* 'Anvil Sparks' (red on yellow), among others. The original Rembrandt tulips such as 'Semper August', with colour breaks in the petals caused by beneficial viruses, are now replaced commercially with cultivars with similar colour breaks, caused by transposable elements, to eliminate any risk of virus spread.

The second method of producing random leaf variegation involves a mutation in a gene for chlorophyll synthesis. In this case, the gene concerned is in the chromosome in the chloroplast rather than in the more usual location, the nucleus.

A variegated plant caused by a chloroplast gene mutation will have two kinds of chloroplast, even within one cell. Green chloroplasts will have the normal or wild-type allele while white chloroplasts will have the mutant allele in their DNA. The green chloroplasts will divide to produce more green chloroplasts, while the white chloroplasts will produce more white chloroplasts.

The colour variegation of *Rosa Gallica* 'Versicolor' is caused by a transposable element.

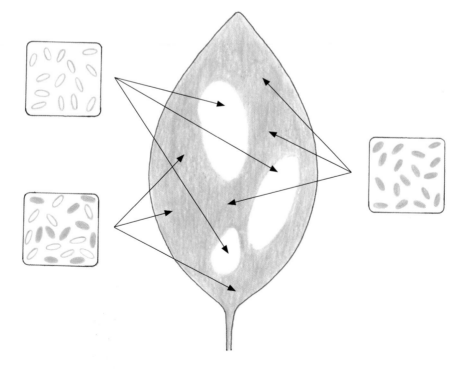

Leaf variegation caused by sorting of green and white chloroplasts.

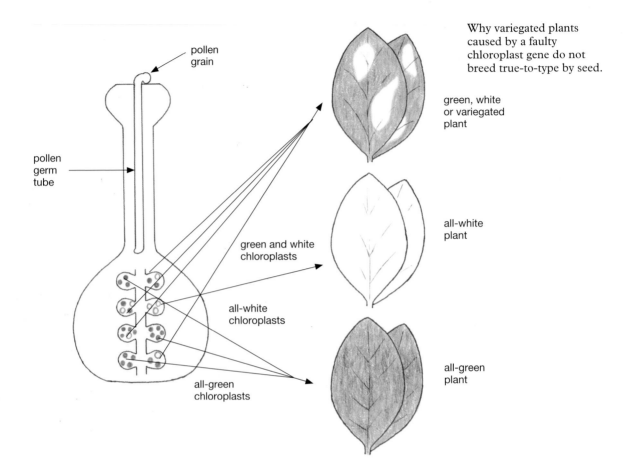

pollen grain

pollen germ tube

Why variegated plants caused by a faulty chloroplast gene do not breed true-to-type by seed.

green, white or variegated plant

all-white plant

all-green plant

green and white chloroplasts

all-white chloroplasts

all-green chloroplasts

Each leaf cell can contain more than 100 chloroplasts. In a variegated plant, the chloroplasts in a single cell can all be green, white or, usually, a mixture of white and green. When a cell divides, the nuclear genes are divided perfectly equally, but the chloroplasts are not. A cell with, say, fifty white and fifty green chloroplasts, may produce a cell with all white chloroplasts (in which case this cell and all of its daughter cells will be white), all green chloroplasts (producing green cells) or a mixture, which can lead to green or white cells. In this way, a plant with a mixture of green and white chloroplasts produces variegated leaves with splashes of green and white tissues.

If a trait is controlled by a nuclear gene, it can be inherited from either the male or the female parent. When the gene concerned is on the chloroplast chromosome, however, it will only be inherited through the female parent. Although the ovule and pollen contribute equally to the nuclear genes in the seed, the ovule contributes all the chloroplasts and hence all the chloroplast genes, because the ovule is so much bigger than the pollen.

As with leaf cells, a variegated plant can produce ovules which have only green chloroplasts, only white chloroplasts or a mixture of both. Regardless of the pollen which fertilizes them, these ovules will produce plants which are all green, all white or a mixture of green, white or variegated, respectively. This is in contrast to random variegation caused by a transposable element, where all the offspring are variegated. In this way, by studying how variegation is inherited, you can distinguish between the different causes.

To summarize, leaf variegation will breed almost 100 per cent true-to-type if it is caused by a transposable element, partially true-to-type if caused by a chloroplast gene, and not at all if due to a periclinal chimera or a virus.

Non-Variegated Periclinal Chimeras

Even some plants not apparently chimeral will produce different-looking daughter plants from vegetative methods involving adventitious buds. Because layer L-I is the outermost epidermal layer of the plant, mutations in L-I result in garden plant cultivars such as thornless blackberry (thornless L-I) and *Ajuga* 'Burgundy Glow' (pink L-I overlayering a green L-II).

The maincrop potato cultivar 'Golden Wonder' is a periclinal chimera of the old cultivar 'Langworthy', due to a mutation in L-I to produce a thick brown russetted tuber surface. To produce plants (and tubers) of 'Langworthy' from 'Golden Wonder', you need to propagate vegetatively from adventitious buds. The 'eyes' from 'Golden Wonder' tubers should be cut out, so that adventitious buds are forced to grow out from single or small groups of cells from one of the deep layers (L-II or L-III). The resulting plants should be identical to 'Langworthy', producing tubers with thin white smooth skin. 'Langworthy' tubers are impossible to purchase, but it would be worthwhile producing your own from 'Golden Wonder' tubers because they give a higher yield and tend to be more floury than 'Golden Wonder'.

Juvenile or Adult Traits

Another situation where vegetative propagation produces true-to-type offspring in contrast to seed propagation is where the desirable form of a garden plant is either the juvenile or adult phase of a plant's life (Chapter 5). The transition from juvenile to adult is caused by a change in gene expression rather than in gene content. The lower, climbing part of an ivy plant is juvenile while the upper flowering part is adult. When the adult phase is propagated from seed, the transition is reversed, with the seedling having juvenile characteristics.

The only way to propagate the adult form of a plant and retain its desired traits is by vegetative propagation. *Hedera helix* 'Poetica Arborea'

Irish yew (*Taxus baccata* 'Fastigiata') is a mutant which retains the upright juvenile growth habit.

is an adult form of ivy which never climbs but forms a dome-shaped free-standing bush which flowers and produces fruits over the winter. In this selected form, the fruits are orange rather than the more usual black.

Some spontaneous 'sports' or mutants retain the juvenile form by failing to make the adult transition. The Irish yew (*Taxus baccata* 'Fastigiata') is a juvenile form of the yew tree, with erect shoots and leaves arranged spirally, in contrast to spreading branches and leaves arranged oppositely in the adult phase. Quite a number of conifer cultivars are juvenile forms, especially those with feathery foliage such as *Thuja occidentalis* 'Rheingold', *Chamaecyparis pisifera* 'Squarrosa Sulphurea' and 'Boulevard' and *C. obtusa* 'Fern Leaf'.

With trees, cuttings from adult material can be difficult to root, unlike that from juvenile tissue such as seedlings. A side-effect can be that cuttings taken from seedlings may stay juvenile, never developing into the adult form. An example of this is the *Cryptomeria japonica* 'Elegans' Group, which has the feathery foliage of the juvenile form.

In addition to the effects of juvenile or adult phase tissue, the characteristics of the tissue used in a hardwood cutting, particularly of conifers, can have a significant effect on the growth habit of the plant produced. As with juvenile vs adult plant forms, the difference is in terms of which genes are being expressed as a result of plant hormone concentrations within the tissues.

Cuttings taken from a leader or other vertical shoots will produce plants with good upright growth, with those from leader shoots usually growing particularly quickly. On the other hand, a plant propagated from a horizontal growing lateral shoot will often have a prostrate growth habit, particularly in genera like *Abies*. Prostrate forms of *Sequoia sempervirens* tend to be generated in this way.

PLANT BREEDING IN YOUR GARDEN

Genetic Variation

Many gardeners dream of producing a unique new plant cultivar. Usually, this thought arises as a result of a chance new plant they find in their garden; maybe a variegated shoot on a green-leaved shrub, or a self-sown seedling with novel appearance. Occasionally, this takes the form of a planned breeding programme on a particular garden plant.

Both can be very satisfying and rewarding hobbies, and it is possible that they could even become financially rewarding. The entire stock (three bulbs) of the 'black' flowered hyacinth cultivar, 'Midnight Mystique' was reportedly sold to Thompson & Morgan in 1999 for £150,000. The most important aspect of any amateur breeding programme, though, is that you enjoy the process.

Breeding work does not have to be large scale. The Reverend William Wilks developed the Shirley Poppy strain from a single seed capsule harvested in his garden at the Shirley Vicarage near Croydon in 1880 from a field poppy flower with a very narrow edge of white around the margin of each petal.

Florence Bellis started the Barnhaven primrose and polyanthus series from her own back garden in Oregon, with the Barnhaven polyanthus series starting with five packets of seed from Sutton's Seeds in 1935. Helen Ballard started the breeding work which resulted in her world-famous Ballard strain of oriental hellebore hybrids with just four plants, two red- and two white-flowered.

The simplest element of plant improvement is to keep your eyes peeled for natural genetic variation, usually resulting from spontaneous mutation. Roland de Boer found more than 800 forms of Solomon's Seal, *Polygonatum multiflorum*, on his travels around Europe, varying in height from 15cm to more than 2m, and exhibiting a range of flower colours.

Variants of British and Irish natives have become good garden plants. The dark-leaved mutant of cow parsley, *Anthriscus sylvestris* 'Ravenswing', the bronze-leaved form of lesser celandine *Ranunculus ficaria* 'Brazen Hussey' collected by Christopher Lloyd, Bowles' golden sedge, *Carex stricta* 'Aurea' found in the wild by E.A. Bowles, and the prostrate form of the western gorse *Ulex gallii* 'Mizen Head' are all garden cultivars of native plants in Britain and Ireland, which were found in the wild. Spontaneous mutants collected from the wild are also the main source of hardy fern cultivars.

In the garden, novel forms of garden plants can arise spontaneously as a result of gene mutation. Spontaneous mutations result in a change in one gene in the parent plant, so that the phenotype of the mutant is different from that of the parent plant. Garden plants cultivars which are mutants (sports) include:

- the Irish yew with an upright juvenile habit, *Taxus baccata* 'Fastigiata' (from *T. baccata*), first found in Co. Fermanagh in 1780;
- the deep mauve *Verbascum* 'Megan's Mauve' (from the copper-pink 'Helen Johnson');
- the variegated myrtle *Luma apiculata* 'Glanleam Gold' (from green-leaved *L. apiculata*);

- the peloric-flowered foxglove, *Digitalis purpurea* var. *gloxinioides* 'The Shirley' (from wild-type flowered *D. purpurea*); and
- *Tulipa* 'Prinses Irene' (from *Tulipa* 'Couleur Cardinal').

Almost 10 per cent of new rose cultivars are spontaneous mutants of existing cultivars, with climbing forms of bush roses being particularly common. In those cases, the gene for climbing delays the apical bud from flowering (changing from the vegetative phase to the reproductive phase), so that the stem grows longer before it starts to flower. The famous hybrid tea rose cultivar 'Peace', released in 1945, has produced at least 21 cultivars as the result of mutations, such as 'Climbing Peace', 'Baby Peace' (a miniature), 'Peaceport' (extra petals per flower) and the colour variants 'Chicago Peace' (pinker petals with a coppery-yellow reverse) and 'Kronenbourg' (deep red petals and an ivory reverse).

Many of the dwarf conifer cultivars were also isolated from the wild, from witches' brooms. Witches' brooms are tightly packed masses of shoots found on branches of conifers and some hardwood trees, particularly silver birch.

Some witches' brooms are caused by damage by mites or pathogens, and are not inherited true-to-type from seed, whereas others appear to be due to mutations and are heritable. Dwarf conifer cultivars developed from witches' brooms include the dwarf spruces *Picea abies* 'Maxwellii', *Picea sylvestris* 'Beauvronensis' and *Picea nigra* 'Hornibrookiana'.

Polyploidy is a type of chromosome mutation which results in a plant with more copies of all chromosomes. Instead of two copies (a diploid, 2x, plant), it could have three copies (triploid, 3x), four copies (tetraploid, 4x), or more. Unlike gene mutations, the efffects of polyploidy on the phenotype, compared to the 2x parent, are fairly predictable:

- **larger organs** such as larger petals (4x daylily *Hemerocallis* 'Strawberry Candy'), thicker petals ('orange peel' petals of 4x evergreen azalea 'Haro-No-Sono') and leaves, and larger fruits such as grape 'Muscat Cannon Hall';
- **slower developing**, resulting in later flowering and fruiting cultivars, as in some of the older autumn raspberries (4x) such as 'Belle de Fontenay' and 'La France';

Witches' brooms on a silver birch.

- **less fertile,** ranging from lower fertility in even-numbered polyploids like 4x pear cultivars to sterility (and seedlessness) in odd-numbered polyploids, such as 3x watermelon cultivars.

The second main way that new phenotypes of a garden plant may appear spontaneously is as a result of segregation. Segregation occurs in cultivars which do not breed true-to-type from seed, when seed propagation re-shuffles the genes from a cultivar and produces a plant with a new combination of alleles (a new genotype) and hence a new combination of characters (phenotype). Examples of new garden cultivars produced by segregation include:

- *Papaver orientalis* 'Royal Chocolate Distinction' is deeper in colour and more fade resistant than 'Patty's Plum';
- *Euphorbia griffithii* 'Dixter' is a segregant selected by Christopher Lloyd from 'Fireglow' for its shorter stature, less spreading habit and slightly different colour;
- *Dierama* 'Merlin' is a seedling selected from seed progeny from 'Blackbird', exhibiting a more purplish tinge to the flower colour;

As can be seen from the examples above, the phenotypic differences between the parent cultivar and the new cultivar by this method are often quite small.

Accidental crossing or deliberate hybridization between two related parents opens up greater scope for genetic variation than does segregation from a single cultivar, as there are two different parent plants contributing genes. Some self-seeding garden plants, like aquilegias and hellebores, are tagged as being 'promiscuous' in that they will readily cross-pollinate with other cultivars of the same species.

Hybridization between related but different species of the same genus produces a much larger gene pool from which the keen gardener can select than can be obtained from hybridization between cultivars of the one species.

Another advantage of inter-specific hybrids (Chapter 1) is that they can be larger and more vigorous (hybrid vigour) than either parent. Examples include the hybrid winter aconite, *Eranthis* × *thunbergii* 'Guinea Gold' (Chapter 1), which has larger leaves and flowers than either parent, and hybrid cane fruits (raspberry × blackberry) such as loganberries, youngberries and tayberries, which have very large fruits. Unfortunately for breeders, many such 'inter-specific' hybrids are sterile (Chapter 1).

The two diploid parents, A and B, of such a hybrid would normally be fertile because each chromosome has a second copy to pair with during

Boysenberries (left) and blackberries (right). Boysenberries are an inter-specific hybrid: raspberry (*Rubus idaeus*) × blackberry (*R. fruticosus*) × loganberry (*R.* × *loganobaccus*). They exhibit larger fruits as a consequence of hybrid vigour.

gamete formation. In the inter-specific hybrid, however, there is only one copy of each chromosome from each parent. Because the corresponding chromosomes from the two parent species do not recognize one another, they do not pair together, so normal viable gametes are not produced and the hybrid is sterile.

Occasionally, a fertile form of a sterile inter-specific hybrid may arise. This occurs because of a spontaneous doubling of the chromosome number in the hybrid. Now, there are two copies of each chromosome from parent A and two from parent B, so each chromosome has a partner to pair with and viable gametes are produced, as with 4x *Digitalis* x *mertonensis*.

Among the finest of the famed blue Himalayan poppies are hybrids between *Meconopsis betonicifolia* and *M. grandis*, such as *Meconopsis* 'Slieve Donard', which are sterile. Spontaneous chromosome doubling in a garden in Cumbria resulted in a fertile hybrid poppy, which is known as *Meconopsis* 'Lingholm'.

The excitement associated with finding a new plant with a novel phenotype highlights the importance of hand weeding in all bar the vegetable garden. By hand weeding, you will learn to recognize seedlings of self-sown garden plants and may see in one of them something worth rescuing.

Developing a Breeding Programme

Possibly the ultimate in getting involved with plants is to try to produce your own cultivars by crossing selected parents and selecting within the offspring. This step usually arises after a gardener has developed a passion for a particular garden species, and wants to produce their own special plants. If you are planning to start out, a more pragmatic approach may be appropriate when selecting the plant you wish to improve, taking into account some of the following parameters:

- The plant should be relatively easy to breed, being capable of both cross- and self-pollination and of vegetative propagation. Lupins, for example, are self-pollinated but are difficult to cross-pollinate, as you need to dissect the flower to access the male and female parts. Hostas are

also self-fertile and easier to hybridize. Daffodils are easy to cross-pollinate as they are protogynous; there is no need to remove anthers from the mother parent. Foxgloves tend to produce fertile inter-specific hybrids.

- The plant should have a short juvenile period, ideally flowering in year 1 (perennial foxgloves) or year 2 from seed (which should have a short dormancy), so that progress can move along swiftly. Many bulbs and other geophytes can take several years to reach flowering size, for example five years in daffodils.
- The plant should ideally be quite small in stature, as large populations may need to be grown to identify the best plants.
- The plant should produce a reasonable amount of seed for segregation studies; you could get over one million seeds per flower from some orchids, rather than the one to five seeds per fruit from hardy geraniums.

It might also be worthwhile focusing on those garden plants which have received little attention from breeders, rather than roses (with more than 13,000 cultivars), hostas, heucheras or hemerocallis.

By focusing on one plant species, you will quickly learn the foibles and eccentricities of that plant. With tulips, for example, crosses between cultivars and wild species are rarely successful, because the hybrids are sterile. Many *Corydalis* species do not set seed in gardens, but this seems to be due to the absence of a suitable pollinator. Manual pollination will result in seed set.

A clear focus is also necessary with respect to the target characters you are aiming to improve. Most successful small-scale breeding programmes have a clear 'search image' in that they are trying to introduce one or a small number of traits. Helen Ballard, in her hellebore breeding programme, selected strongly for outward facing flowers at both the level of the parents and the offspring, while the Reverend Wilks had a very clear picture of what was acceptable for Shirley poppies.

Having said that, one of the joys of plant breeding is that you can never be sure of what you are going to get from a cross. The 'black-flowered' hyacinth 'Midnight Mystique' was achieved by crossing a blue-flowered cultivar with a white-flowered cultivar.

The key area in breeding programmes is hybridization, crossing two plants of the same or related species. Although this can be done in the open garden, protection in the form of a glasshouse or polytunnel makes it better for the plants as well as the breeder.

Your aim is to control the pollination of what will be your female parent. The first step is to prevent either self-pollination or uncontrolled cross-pollination. The latter is achieved by placing a breathable bag over the flower head before the flower opens. Cellophane bags, often sold as dried fruit bags, are useful. If the plant is self-fertile, self-pollination must be prevented by removing all the anthers (emasculation), using tweezers or fine scissors, before any pollen is shed. The stigma surface should then be monitored for the next few days until it becomes receptive to pollen.

At this point, ripe anthers from the male parent are gently rubbed over the stigma of the female parent, and the flower is re-bagged and labelled with the details of the parents and the date. Once the style has shrivelled, the bag can be removed, and the flower checked for signs that the ovary is swelling, confirming that fertilization has occurred. The actual details of hybridization differ from species to species, and you can save yourself a lot of time and effort by reading specialist books and plant society magazines.

The same basic techniques can be used to cross two related species, which can open up new colour combinations in the inter-specific hybrid (Chapter 8). The first recorded artificial crossing of two plant species was in 1691, when Thomas Fairchild crossed a carnation (*Dianthus caryophyllus*) and a sweet william (*Dianthus barbatus*). The result was a large double-flowered sweet william. The hybrid was sterile and known as 'Fairchild's mule', in the same way that sterile inter-specific hybrids between a horse and a donkey or between a canary and a goldfinch are also known as 'mules'. The large-flowered clematis *C.* × *jackmannii*, with blue flowers and maroon bars, is also an artificial inter-specific hybrid, made in 1858 by nurseryman George Jackman, between *C. lanuginosa* (large white flowers) and *C. viticella* (small velvety maroon flowers).

The resulting seedlings from your breeding programme are then grown on and monitored. It is always worthwhile growing on some of the smaller or slower developing seedlings in a batch, because they can be among the more valuable. The double-flowered Barnhaven primroses tend to germinate later than the singles, while *Primula*

Pulmonaria 'Majeste', where the silvering is due to air pockets under the leaf epidermis, a trait believed to help cooling.

vulgaris 'Buxton's Blue', regarded by many as the best double blue primrose ever produced, was one of the weakest seedlings from a batch selected by E.C. Buxton. The most vigorous seedlings from crosses between a wild species and a cultivar tend to resemble the wild parent, with smaller seedlings likely to be more like the cultivar parent.

One useful tip is that some traits are associated with one another, often because one gene can actually have several different effects on the phenotype, a phenomenon known as pleiotropy. Examples include the association between cold tolerance and red foliage in several vegetable crops, red pigmentation of stems and red flower colour in many species, including antirrhinum and busy lizzy, narrow leaves and cold hardiness in *Agapanthus*, and between small stature and both deep flower colour and early flowering in *Campanula lactiflora* and *Agapanthus*. If the associated trait is visible early in the plant's life, you can make your selection earlier, saving time and effort.

The silvering of leaves of plants like *Pulmonaria* is due to the formation of air pockets between the epidermis and the underlying photosynthetic tissue. This is believed to be a cooling mechanism, so pulmonaria plants with more silver on the leaf, like *Pulmonaria* 'Majeste', should be able to withstand high temperatures better.

On the other hand, some valuable traits may not be expressed in young plants. In primroses, the double-flower trait is often not expressed until the second year, so selection for this trait needs to be delayed. Variable expression of the double flower trait is quite common, with the first flush of flowers of *Clematis* cultivars being double while the second flush are frequently singles. These changes are an example of a temporary switching on/off of some genes, known as epigenetics, in response to the external environment, such as temperature, or the internal environment, such as hormone levels, as with the juvenile/adult phase change.

A primrose plant exhibiting an epigenetic effect where some of the flowers (left) have stamens replaced by full-sized petals, whereas other flowers (right) on the same plant have only small extra petals.

CHAPTER 8

Colour in the Ornamental Garden

Colour in the garden can be supplied by flowers, leaves, stems and fruits. An understanding of how colour is determined in these different plant organs, of the factors determining flowering date and how the duration of flowering can be extended involves primarily plant physiology but also elements of plant chemistry. Being able to manipulate these factors will help gardeners to maximize the impact of colour throughout the year.

FLOWER STRUCTURE

Flower Shapes and Components

Flowers are modified flattened shoots, with the different flower components, namely sepals (forming the calyx), petals (the corolla), stamens (each consisting of an anther connected to a filament) and carpel (consisting of stigma, style and ovary), all being modified leaves (Chapter 1).

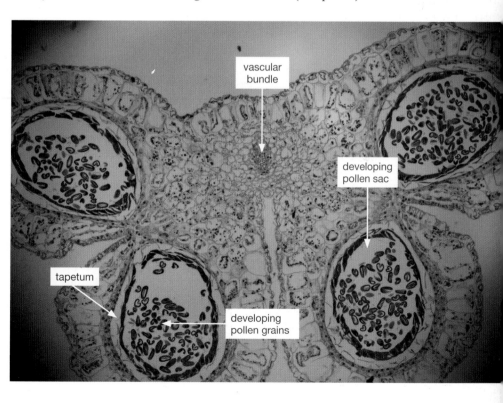

A micrograph of a thin section through a lily anther, containing mature pollen.

vascular bundle

developing pollen sac

tapetum

developing pollen grains

Rosa gallica 'Versicolor' has been cultivated since 1583. The colour stripes are caused by a jumping gene (transposable element).

A tulip flower, such as that of *T. clusiana*, lacks normal green sepals, because they have been converted into petal-like organs (petaloids), with the sepals (outer whorl, pink backs and tips) and petals (inner whorl, no pink) being known collectively as tepals.

Flowers where all four whorls of organs are present are known as complete flowers. In many plants, however, one or more of the organs appears to be missing, because there are fewer than four whorls of organs. Grasses, for example, lack coloured petals so have green flowers, reflecting their adaptation to pollination by the wind so that they do not need to attract pollinating insects.

To identify which whorl is missing, start looking at the whorls from the back of the flower, starting with the sepals. With the tulip, there are no green sepals, but apparently six coloured petals (arranged in two whorls of three each), numerous stamens and a carpel. What has happened in the tulip, lily and many other members of the lily family (Liliaceae), as well as in other relatively primitive plants like magnolias, is that the three sepals are indistinguishable from the three petals. In these cases, where the petals and sepals cannot be told apart, both are termed tepals.

In several members of the buttercup family (Ranunculaceae), like hellebores and anemones, again there only three whorls, but the coloured organs are all in one whorl, indicating that either the petals or the sepals have been lost. Working from the back of the flower, it is apparent that the 'petals' are actually sepals (more accurately, 'petaloids', or petals which used to be a different organ). The whorl of petals has been transformed into a whorl of nectaries, small cups holding nectar to attract pollinating insects.

In other flowers, the sepals and petals are both brightly coloured but are distinct. In the classic *Fuchsia* 'ballerina' flowers, the sepals, identifiable as being the outermost whorl, are the red skirt, while the purple petals are the ballerina.

Another type of modified leaf also forms part of the structure in some flowers. These are known as bracts. Strongly coloured bracts can form the major part of the 'flower', as in the large red or cream 'petals' surrounding the insignificant green flowers of poinsettia (*Euphorbia pulcherrima*), the large white 'petals' of flowering dogwoods, like *Cornus kousa*, and the lower 'petals' of the plants such as monarda, astrantia and hacquetia. The coloured spathe of flowers of aroids like *Anthurium* and *Zantedeschia* are really bracts, which form around the spadix, which in turn carries many tiny flowers.

Changes in Flower Structure

To produce a flower involves hundreds of the 15,000 or so genes found in each cell of a plant (Chapter 7). The vegetative meristem producing shoots and leaves must be converted into a much larger reproductive meristem, forming flowers. Leaves must be converted into one of the four different organs: sepals, petals, stamens, carpel. This change must happen in that precise order to make a perfect flower. There are just three master control (homeotic) genes, A, B and C, which control the functioning of the large number of genes involved in each of these steps:

Genetic control of flower structure.

gene A

gene B

gene C

leaf

gene A
(sepals)

genes A + B
(petals)

genes B + C
(stamens)

gene C
(carpel)

- Gene A 'on' only: sepals
- Genes A and B 'on' together: petals
- Genes B and C 'on' together: stamens
- Gene C 'on' only: carpels

Natural mutations in these master genes upsets the development of a flower, with one or more organ type being lost or even converted into another organ. Similar homeotic genes exist in animals – in fruit flies mutations in these genes result in changes where legs instead of antennae grow out of the head.

Loss of function of the A gene as a result of a natural mutation, for example, produces flowers lacking petals and sepals, so that attraction of pollinators is achieved using masses of coloured stamens (replacing the petals) and carpels (replacing the sepals). This type of flower is common to species from the New World such as the bottle brush plant, hebe and acacia, which are pollinated by mammals such as possums, attracted to feed on the nectar. It also happens in winter-flowering shrubs where individual flowers are small, to prevent damage from wind and rain, and strongly scented, such as *Sarcococca*.

An inflorescence of *Hebe speciosa* where the stamens in each floret take over from the petals in attracting would-be pollinators.

In garden plants, homeotic gene mutations have resulted in unusual flower types which have been selected over the centuries. *Anemone nemorosa* 'Virescens' lacks both genes B and C, so that the flower consists entirely of whorls of green sepals. Lacking both stamens and carpels, these plants are sterile. Cauliflower is a natural homeotic mutant of the wild cabbage, *Brassica oleracea*. Each flower primordium in a *B. oleracea* plant normally changes to produce primordia of the four floral organs, but in cauliflower, each flower primordium produces another, until a 'curd' consisting of 10,000 primordia is formed.

The most common organ-to-organ conversion in garden plants involves transformation of stamens (some or all) and carpels into extra rows of petals (petaloids), resulting in different degrees of flower doubling. The complete inter-conversion of the stamens into petaloids can be due to loss of gene B, where both stamens and carpels are lost, resulting in a sterile fully double flower, as in *Sanguinaria canadensis* 'Snowbunting'. Incompletely or partly double flowers can involve only some whorls of stamens being converted into petals, so the plants are fertile, as with *Narcissus* 'Gay Times'.

In double Lenten roses (*Helleborus* x *hybridus*), it is usually the nectaries, which had evolved from the original petals, which become the extra row of 'petals'. In the anemone-flowered hellebores, the nectaries are enlarged and are often the same colour as the 'petals'.

Petaloids often retain some signs of their previous incarnation. In some double flowers, such

A partially double camellia flower, where some of the stamens have been converted in to petals (petaloids).

as many double roses, the filament of the lost stamens can still be distinguished on the back of the extra petals. In other cases, petaloids formed from stamens are frequently yellow, while petaloids formed from carpels can retain a greenish tinge in the centre of the double flower, as in *Rosa* 'Madame Hardy' and the natural homeotic mutant of lesser celandine, *Ranunculus ficaria* 'Collarette'.

Other garden plants where stamens are converted into petaloids include French lavender, *Lavandula stoechas*, where the tuft at the top of

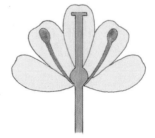
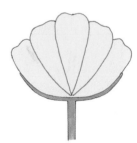

Normal
(wild type)

'Jack-in-the-Green'
(sepals → leaves)

'Hose-in-Hose'
(sepals → petals)

'Double-flowered'
(stamens,
carpel → petals)

Effects of mutations in flower homeotic genes in primrose.

the flower spike is composed of petaloids, and *Paeonia lactiflora* cultivars such as 'Bowl of Beauty' where the centre of the flower is filled with numerous yellow petaloids. Collarette and anemone-flowered dahlia cultivars contain a central mass of petaloids formed from stamens.

Double flowers have a number of advantages as well as disadvantages over the corresponding single flowers. Full doubles, being sterile because the sex organs are converted into petals, do not need deadheading to continue flowering, so generally flower for longer than the corresponding singles. Examples include the semi-double *Camassia leichtlinii* 'SemiPlena' and the double-flowered delphinium 'Alice Artindale'. Each double flower also tends to last longer than the corresponding single-flowered form, as with *Sanguinaria canadensis* 'Snowbunting' and double-flowered paeonies.

Sterility can be advantageous for several reasons. Double-flowered gorse, *Ulex europeaus* 'Flore Plena', for example, is an excellent security hedge, without the problem of producing self-sown gorse seedlings. Double-flowered snowdrops cannot spread by seed, being sterile, but clump up vegetatively more quickly by bulb offsets than do single-flowered cultivars. The double-flowered form of lady's smock, *Cardamine pratensis* 'Flore pleno' is sterile but has evolved a vegetative propagation method, by generating self-rooting leaflets.

Double-flowered lilies are pollen-free, preventing the staining of clothes, a particular problem for florists at weddings. And as a cooking ingredient, the flower buds of double-flowered day lilies are crunchier when stir-fried and eaten than are those of single-flowered cultivars.

On the debit side, however, double flowers of pelargoniums, gardenias and brugsmania tend to stay on the plant and have to be deadheaded when they have turned brown, unlike the self-cleaning singles. The longer flowering period means that double primroses, for example, are gross feeders and need regular feeding and division. They are more prone to rotting of the flowers and crown, and are generally more difficult than the singles to grow well. Being sterile, fully double roses do not produce ornamental rose hips, while double cultivars of *Rosa banksiae* produce much less scent than do the single-flowered cultivars.

A Jack-in-the-Green primrose in which the sepals are converted into leaf-like organs.

Double flowers and other organ-to-organ conversions are reasonably common in *Campanula*, such as the double-flowered *C. persicifolia* 'Wortham Belle' and *C. medium* 'Canterbury Bells' where the calyx is converted into petals.

A Hose-in-Hose primrose, in which the sepals are converted into petals.

Primula, however, takes pride of place in terms of flower organ conversions. Since Elizabethan times, primroses with organ-to-organ conversions such as doubles, Jack-in-the Green, Hose-in-Hose, Gallygaskin, Jackanape and Pantaloon flowers have been collected and valued. In 'Jack-in-the-Green' primroses, such as *Primula* 'Dawn Ansell', the sepals are converted into small leaves. This also happens in *Hydrangea* 'Midoribanaajisai'.

In 'Hose-in-Hose' flowers, the sepals become petals so that a second flower appears to grow out of the centre of the first corolla; hence the name, which refers to the mediaeval style of wearing two sets of stockings (hose) with the outer pair turned down. The Hose-in-Hose trait is also found in *Campanula* ('Canterbury Bells'), lily-of-the-valley (*Convallaria majalis* 'Prolificans'), *Hemerocallis* 'Amethyst Art', some kurume evergreen azaleas such as 'Coral Bells', and *Clematis* 'Odoriba'.

FLOWER COLOURS

Pigments

If people are asked to describe plants in one word, that word is usually 'green'. The leaves of most plants are predominantly green due to the two chlorophyll molecules, the yellow-green chlorophyll a and the grey-green chlorophyll b (Chapter 4) central to photosynthesis. Hidden by the chlorophylls are the yellow-to-orange carotenoids which absorb wavelengths of light which the chlorophylls cannot, preventing damage caused by excess light and heat to the chloroplasts. Parasitic plants like yellowish-red dodder are not green because they do not need to photosynthesize. They steal their sugars and other assimilates from other green plants.

Plants are fantastic natural chemists, however, and use pigments to attract pollinators and seed dispersal agents (Chapter 1), and these colours are central to an ornamental garden.

Apart from chlorophyll in the occasional green-flowered oddity, the pigments in flowers and fruits fall into three main groups: carotenoids, anthocyanins and betalains. Carotenoids are important yellow-orange-red pigments in flowers, leaves (especially visible in autumn leaves of deciduous species), fruits (mango, tomato) and roots and tubers (carrot, sweet potato). Among flowers, carotenoids provide yellow and orange flower colour in garden plants such as daffodil and marigolds, but rarely red, as in pheasant's eye, *Adonis aestivalis*.

The parasitic plant ivy broomrape, *Orobanche hederae*, which lacks chlorophyll because it obtains its organic chemicals not by photosynthesis but by taking them from host ivy plants.

The carotenoids are fat-soluble pigments which are stored in plant cells inside plastids (Chapter 1). In green organs like leaves, the plastids are chloroplasts, whereas in non-green organs, such as flowers and fruits, the plastids are known as chromoplasts. All bar the outermost epidermis cell layer of an organ contains plastids and hence carotenoids.

Most of the reds, blues and purples found in flowers and fruits are caused by a class of plant chemical different from the carotenoids: the anthocyanins. These are water-soluble chemicals. So soluble are anthocyanins that, in auriculas, heavy rain can actually cause the pigments to run. Because they are water soluble, anthocyanins are stored in the aqueous part of the cell, namely the membrane-bound storage organelle known as the vacuole (Chapter 1). Most of the anthocyanins are carried in the outermost, epidermal, cells.

The third class of plant pigment is of a more limited distribution. The betalains are responsible for the colour of beetroot, usually deep red, due to the presence of betacyanins (beetroot = *Beta vulgaris*, hence *Beta*-cyanins) or yellow, due to betaxanthins. In the 'Brite Lites' cultivars of the related vegetable Swiss Chard, the yellow and red leaf mid-ribs are coloured by betalains, while yellow- or red-rooted beetroots are also due to different betalains.

Several plant species also use betalains as red or yellow floral pigments, including carnation, the four o'clock plant *Mirabilis jalapa*, *Amaranthus caudatus* and some cactus (*Mammillaria* spp.) and carnivorous plant species (*Drosera* spp.). Betalains are also water soluble, as evidenced by the 'bleeding' of the pigment in beetroots into the cooking water, and, like the anthocyanins, are stored in the vacuole of the cell.

Functions of Colours

The main function of pigments in non-photosynthetic organs is to attract animals to fruits and flowers. In this way, seed dispersal and pollination, respectively, can be achieved (Chapter 1). Because plants cannot carry out directed movement, they manipulate organisms which can move to do these jobs for them.

Living pollen vectors are usually insects but can include birds and mammals. Bird- and mammal-pollinated flowers are particularly common in the southern hemisphere. The pollinator is attracted by certain flower traits, particularly colour, scent and shape (Chapter 1), and then develops a 'search image' so that it tends to visit flowers of the same species subsequently. The main associations between flower colour and pollinator are:

- red: birds, butterflies
- blue: bees
- yellow: bees, moths, bats
- white, pink: moths and bats

Mammals, apart from humans and other apes, lack colour vision, but because most pollinating

Pigment spots in the throat of the flowers of a *Digitalis* hybrid represent nectar guides for pollinators.

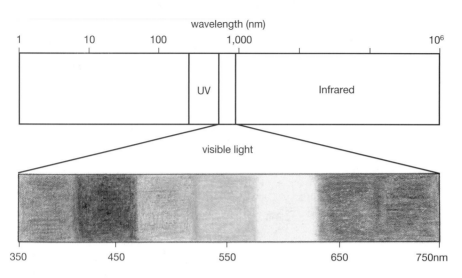

The light spectrum.

mammals are nocturnal, light-coloured flowers which are easily visible at night, such as white, pink or yellow ones, are attractive to them.

Other colours in flowers are used to direct the pollinator to the nectar (nectar guides or honey guides), such as the yellow collar around the blue corolla of forget-me-not, the array of spots in the throat of foxglove flowers and the yellow patch on the 'landing pad' of the snapdragon flower. Bees and some other insects cannot see in the long-wave red end of the spectrum but, in compensation, they (unlike humans) can see ultraviolet light at the other end of the spectrum (280–350nm) in the form of 'bee purple', a mixture of ultraviolet and yellow light. 'Bee flowers' frequently have patches of pigment which absorb ultraviolet light, invisible to us but apparent to bees as dark lines or zones on a bright background.

Hoverflies and other pollinators are attracted to the central area of the flower of lesser celandine, *Ranunculus ficaria*, by the presence of bee purple.

The succulent *Stapelia variegata* produces flowers of the colour and smell of rotting meat to attract flies for pollination.

Scent is also used to increase the specificity of vectors to particular flowers. Birds have no sense of smell, so bird-pollinated flowers are usually unscented. Bees, butterflies and moths are attracted to sweet smells; beetles to spicy scents, such as some *Magnolia* spp.; and flies to smells reminiscent of carrion or dung, as given off by flowers of *Arisaema, Stapelia* and *Arum* spp. Winter-flowering plants, like *Sarcococca* spp. and *Chimonanthus praecox*, depend more on scent than colour for attraction of the rare pollinators around, because large flowers would be damaged by the wind and rain.

Colour is also an important factor in getting seeds dispersed by appropriate animals, and is determined by anthocyanins (most red- to blue-coloured fruits) or carotenoids, which control shades of yellow (such as lutein in sweetcorn) to red (like lycopene in tomatoes). Most of the fruits on garden plants are eaten by birds and, as such, represent a valuable resource, especially in winter, for increasing biodiversity in our gardens. A typical fruit designed to be eaten by birds will be red and scentless, for the same reasons as described for flower characters.

On the other hand, the ornamental value of fruits and berries is lost if the birds strip them too soon. Because birds show preferences for the colour red, garden plant cultivars with yellow-, orange-, pink- or white-coloured variants can retain their fruits longer. Examples of mountain ash species and cultivars which retain their berries for longer than the more usual red-berried species include pink-berried *Sorbus cashmiriana*, *Sorbus* 'Joseph Rock' (yellow) and *Sorbus hupehensis* (pink). There are,

Winter-flowering heavily scented Christmas box, *Sarcococca confusa*, produces flowers with large stamens replacing petals as attractants for pollinators.

The pink fruits of *Sorbus hupehensis* are less attractive to birds than the more common red mountain ash fruits, so last longer on the tree.

however, red-berried trees and shrubs whose fruits are not eaten by birds until late in the season, such as *Berberis prattii* (though a pinky-red), *Skimmia* spp., *Cotoneaster conspicuus* 'Decorus' and some crabapple cultivars.

In several *Paeonia* spp., such as *P. campbessedesii*, the attractiveness of the seeds to birds in the fruit is increased by having the viable blue-black seeds surrounded by red non-viable seeds, when the pod spits open. A similar contrast occurs in the fruits of *Iris foetidissima*.

Where you are growing trees or shrubs for their ornamental fruits, it is important to realize that some of these species are dioecious (Chapter 7), with individuals which are either male or female. Examples include holly, skimmia and *Viburnum davidii*. To produce fruits, it is vital that you plant a female cultivar and that male cultivars, to provide pollen, are in your garden or nearby, within pollen dispersal range.

As named cultivars are vegetatively propagated, all plants of a cultivar will be genetically identical and will be either male or female. Unfortunately, cultivar names are not much help among the hollies, with 'Golden King' being a female while 'Silver Queen' and 'Golden Queen' are both male. Most dioecious woody plants have species or cultivars which are self fertile, producing fruit without the need for a male parent, and these include *Skimmia* x *reevesiana* and holly 'J.C. van Tol'.

Few Pigments Make Many Colours

How do so few pigments produce such a wide range of colours? Frequently, a flower will contain pigments from two of the three pigment groups, producing novel colours, though betalains and anthocyanins (both located in the vacuole of the cell) are never found in the same flower. Carotenoids are found in the deeper layers of the petal tissue, forming the background colour, while the anthocyanins or betalains are concentrated in the outer epidermal layer.

In this way, a genetic block in the pathway making one family of chemicals can reveal a different colour. Carnations can contain both yellow carotenoids and red-purple betalains, so that blocking betalain production reveals the yellow background to the petals, as in the yellow-flowered *Dianthus knappii*. On the other hand, camellias do not produce carotenoids in their petals, so that a mutation blocking anthocyanin synthesis results in white flowers.

Iris 'Katherine Hodgkin' is an inter-specific hybrid between one yellow- and one blue-flowered *Iris* species, and has flowers with a unique combination of colours from the two parents.

Even with a relatively restricted range of foliar pigments (three or four carotenoids, six different anthocyanins and two betalains), plants are capable of producing a dazzling array of flower colours.

Flowers of most wild plant species coloured by anthocyanins contain only one anthocyanin. For example, the electric blue *Salvia patens* contains the anthocyanin delphinidin; the purple species *S. nemorosa* and *S. pratensis* contain malvidin; and the red species *S. coccinea* and *S. splendens* have pelargonidin. Similarly, the blue-flowered species of the borage family (*Pulmonaria, Anchusa, Myosotis*) and of the Iridaceae (*Scilla, Muscari*) all contain just delphinidin.

The advances in breeding of garden plants has led to the development of inter-specific hybrids (Chapter 7) with a greater range of colours. Crossing related species containing different anthocyanins can result in hybrids containing both anthocyanins in the same flower, as with modern-day rose cultivars. The presence or absence of carotenoid pigments in the same flower as an anthocyanin will also affect the shade caused by the anthocyanin. By crossing the primrose-yellow *Iris winogradowii*, containing yellow carotenoids,

with blue *I. histrioides* 'Major', containing the blue anthocyanin delphinidin, the plantsman E.B. Anderson produced the stunning Iris 'Katherine Hodgkin', which has powder blue upper petals (standards) and a lower petal (falls) of the same colour but spotted and lined with darker blue, all against a yellowish background.

But a single anthocyanin pigment can also generate a surprisingly wide range of colours. The blue colour of cornflower (*Centaurea cyanus*) and the red colour of flowers such as field poppy (*Papaver rhoeas*) are both caused by the same pigment, the anthocyanin cyanidin. This discovery was responsible, in part, for Richard Willstätter being awarded the Nobel Prize for Chemistry in 1915. In fruits, cyanidin causes both the black colour of ivy fruits and the red-orange colour of pyracantha fruits. How can one pigment produce so many colours?

Certain metals, particularly magnesium, iron and aluminium, as well as colourless organic chemicals (co-pigments), can bind to anthocyanins in plant cells to change their colour. Cyanidin in cornflower cells binds to iron, magnesium and calcium plus a co-pigment to turn the normally reddish pigment into a striking blue colour.

Colour Variation within the Same Plant

In many plants, the colour of the flower can change through its life, such as pink to blue in *Pulmonaria* and other members of the borage family, presumably to ensure that the pollinator visits the flower when it is at the correct stage for pollen or nectar collection (and, from the plant's point of view, for pollination).

In some flowers, different petals of the same flower can be differently coloured. In sweetpeas, for example, the lateral (wing) petals are frequently a different colour from the keel petals. This is due to the presence of more of the colourless flavonol co-pigments in the wing petals, which interact with the anthocyanin in the same petals, leading to a different colour in the wing tissues compared to the keel tissues.

The environment in which a plant is growing can also affect flower colour. The best-known example is that of soil pH on flower colour in hortensia hydrangeas (*H. macrophylla*). The large-flowered mophead and lacecap hydrangeas produce masses of sterile florets (mopheads) or mixtures of sterile and fertile florets (lacecaps). The apparent petals of the sterile florets are actually sepals.

In acid soils (Chapter 4), with a soil pH of 5.0–5.5, a hydrangea cultivar may have blue sepals, but the same cultivar will have pink or purplish sepals when grown under higher pH conditions. These different colours are all caused by the same pigment, the anthocyanin delphinidin, plus three colourless co-pigments, which would normally result in a pink shade.

In acid soils, the solubility of micronutrients (trace elements) in soil water increases, so the plant takes up more of them. This results in ten times more aluminium and smaller increases in iron in the sepal cells of hydrangea plants grown in acid soils. These metals bind to delphinidin, changing it from the pink colour to an intense blue colour. Pink-flowered cultivars give a better blue than do red-flowered ones.

I remember my father burying old rusty nails and used tea leaves under blue-flowered hydrangea cultivars to make sure that the colour developed properly. In hindsight, I can rationalize this as increasing the level of iron (rusty nails) and flavonoid co-pigments (tea is rich in flavonoids) available to the plant. Recently, British penny coins have found favour in colouring blue-flowered hydrangeas as a result of their high copper content. You can now buy aluminium salts or iron supplements, such

Flowers of most *Pulmonaria* cultivars change from pink in the bud to blue in the mature flower, to attract bees to flowers at the correct stage for pollination.

Purple pigmentation of this fruit of bean 'Viola di Cornetti', caused by anthocyanins, has been blocked in that part of the fruit which had been covered by a leaf.

as Miracid, to water onto the roots of the plants in September to ensure blue flowers. A bonus of using iron is that the leaves of your hydrangea will develop a darker green colour (Chapter 4).

To prevent blueing of a pink-flowered hydrangea in acid soil, addition of lime, to raise the soil pH, or addition of the phosphorus-rich fertilizer superphosphate are both effective. High levels of phosphate react with aluminium in the soil to convert it into insoluble aluminium phosphate, which the plant cannot take up. Remember that a newly planted hydrangea may take several years to adapt to its new environment before it produces its characteristic flower colour.

The woodland hydrangea species *H. asperea*

villosa, on the other hand, retains its lilac-blue colour at all soil pH values.

With flower colours, where the main pigment is an anthocyanin (most flowers in the red/pink/blue/purple spectrum), care should be taken in placing the plant to avoid fading of the flower colour because anthocyanin synthesis needs light. Dark-flowered flowers, such as *Buddleja davidii* 'Black Knight' and *Astrantia* 'Gill Richardson' need to be grown in bright light to maximize colour development. Flowers of *A.* 'Gill Richardson' will become noticeably paler if kept out of the light for as little as twelve hours.

Hot dry conditions can reduce anthocyanin production, turning a dark pink-flowered rhododendron pale pink, while the blue flowers of wisteria will become noticeably paler under dry conditions. Some anthocyanins are prone to bleaching in full sun, as the pigment is concentrated in the outer (epidermal) petal tissue. The pink or purple large-flowered clematis hybrids, such as 'Nelly Moser', should be grown away from direct sun to prevent the colour fading, while the blue-flowered *Phlox paniculata* 'Blue Paradise' can produce pink flowers when grown in full sun.

LEAF COLOURS

Colour in Young Leaves

In some garden and wild plants, colours other than green can be evident in leaves under certain circumstances. The most common leaf colours, other than green, are reds and purples, due to the presence of anthocyanins, although yellow-leaved plants are also familiar.

Many plants produce anthocyanins in young newly emerging leaves, which are therefore red or bronze in colour. Examples include sycamore seedlings and young growth on apple and cherry trees. Selection for particularly strongly coloured young leaves has resulted in the development of many garden-worthy cultivars, including *Pieris forrestii* 'Forest Flame' and *Photinia fraseri* 'Red Robin'.

The anthocyanins are concentrated in the epidermis of the leaf, situated above the layers of tissue containing the chloroplasts. The anthocyanins

This plant of herb robert, *Geranium robertianum*, growing in a wall crevice, is under stress, and responds to it by accumulating anthocyanins so that the leaf and petiole tissue become red.

here are thought to protect the young leaves, where chlorophyll development is not complete, from being damaged by receiving more light than they can tolerate. Anthocyanins can also protect the young leaf cells against ultraviolet light, particularly UV-B, although flavonols, colourless organic chemicals related to anthocyanins, are probably more important in this situation. UV-B is also the main form of ultra-violet light that causes sunburn in gardeners.

Anthocyanins also act as anti-oxidants, protecting the cells from the reactive oxygen species overproduced under a wide range of stresses such as disease, cold and drought. These forms of oxygen are naturally present in plants, but they accumulate when plants are under stress, when they cause damage to cell membranes and important molecules such as DNA. One of the reactive oxygen species is peroxide – think of the effect of hydrogen peroxide in bleaching human hair. Plants of species like dandelion and herb robert growing on walls, which are naturally dry places, often have red-purple leaves and stems, due to accumulation of anthocyanins.

Autumn Leaf Colours

Winter-deciduous trees drop all their leaves in autumn to escape winter stress (Chapter 2). Trees recognize the onset of autumn in response to falls in temperature and the seasonal shortening of the daylength (photoperiod) by becoming dormant (Chapter 2). Some trees rely solely on daylength. When the length of the dark period exceeds a certain value, leaf fall is triggered. As with so many aspects of plant development, leaf fall is controlled by plant hormones. Ethylene and abscisic acid promote leaf fall, while auxin, cytokinin and gibberellins delay it.

Leaf fall is an active process involving specific actions by the plant. If you remove a branch from a deciduous tree, the leaves will die but not fall. Deciduous trees lay down a specialized layer of cells, known as the abscission layer, at the base of the leaf stalk, allowing the leaf to fall. The wound is sealed with the waxy chemical suberin, making sure that water is not lost through it. Before the leaves are shed, however, the stores of nutrients in the leaves must be transferred to the roots to provide food reserves for the upcoming spring growth period. These are primarily reserves of carbon, nitrogen and phosphorus.

Chlorophyll in the chloroplasts is continually being broken down and replaced. If you leave something on the lawn that prevents light from reaching the grass, the grass becomes yellow. In the dark, no chlorophyll can be made, so the green pigment is lost, leaving the yellow carotenoids. Similarly in autumn, chlorophyll synthesis stops in deciduous trees and the green colour dissipates. Exceptions to this general rule do occur. Alder drops green leaves in autumn without depleting

Autumn colour in *Viburnum plicatum* 'mariesii'.

them of food reserves, possibly because it is a nitrogen fixer (Chapter 4).

The loss of the chlorophylls occurs first in the leaves most exposed to sunlight, such as those at the top of the leaf canopy. This process unmasks the yellow carotenoid pigments which were always present in the leaves. In most deciduous trees, the loss of chlorophyll from leaves in the autumn occurs from the margins inwards, with the chlorophyll remaining around the leaf veins until just before leaf fall. In this way, the leaf keeps its transport system (vascular bundles in the leaf veins) active to the end of its life, in order to re-distribute the contents of the leaf to the storage tissues of the plant for the winter.

As the chlorophylls disappear, the amount of sunlight which can be absorbed falls, leading to the excess light heating the leaf up to damaging levels. To prevent this, some trees and shrubs synthesize anthocyanins (primarily the simplest anthocyanin, cyanidin). Anthocyanins appear to act here both as a sunscreen, and as an anti-oxidant, protecting the dying leaves from damage by reactive oxygen species, a mirror image of the situation in young leaves in spring.

The presence of anthocyanins in autumn leaves

is therefore due to their production at this time, rather than merely to their being revealed when the chlorophylls break down, as happens with the carotenoids. Freezing of the leaves, which will stop chemical synthesis, prevents the appearance of anthocyanins in autumn leaves. In the same way, a hard frost may prevent the anthocyanin pigments forming in flowers of the autumn-flowering cherry, *Prunus subhirtella* 'Autumnalis', resulting in white instead of pink flowers.

The red and purple autumn leaf colours found in maples, sumach and ironwood, then, are due to production of anthocyanins. The brown autumn leaf colour characteristic of beech and European oaks is determined by tannins, brown derivatives of anthocyanins. Orange autumn leaf tints are created by mixtures of yellow carotenoids with either red anthocyanins or brown tannins.

Differences in autumn colour have an inherited component as well as a non-inherited element. Trees with the strongest red or purple autumn leaf colours as a result of high levels of anthocyanin are usually native to the temperate deciduous woodland biome (Chapter 2) in North America or Asia rather than in Europe. For example, American red and pin oaks produce scarlet autumn colours compared to the browns associated with European oak species such as pedunculate oak, even when the two groups are grown side by side, showing that the effect is genetic in nature. The autumn light levels in North America are higher than those in Europe, so the American trees produce higher levels of anthocyanins to protect themselves. The young leaves of scarlet oak also take on red colours.

Anthocyanin production is stimulated by environmental factors such as sunlight and by low but above-freezing temperatures. As a result, in addition to their genetic heritage, autumn colour in trees such as liquidamber, sumachs, styrax, enkianthus, ironwood and maples, in which purple, red and orange tints arise, is best in trees grown in brightly lit sites, after long warm summers with cold autumn nights. Even though we can grow deciduous trees from other continents, they will often not perform with quite such spectacular autumn tints as they would in their native habitats, because of the impact of the western European environment. To illustrate the effect of sunlight on anthocyanin production, leaves on the shaded side of a sumach tree (*Rhus typhina*) will produce yellow leaves while those on the sunlit side will develop red tints. If one leaf shades another, you will see the effect of light, with the shaded portion failing to develop the red colours.

Trees like ginkgo (*Ginkgo biloba*), ash (*Fraxinus excelsior*), birches (*Betula* spp.), sycamore (*Acer pseudoplatanus*) and the tulip tree (*Liriodendron tulipifera*), on the other hand, where autumn colour is yellow, show little effect of environment on colour production, which is due to carotenoid levels, as carotenoid production is largely unaffected by environmental factors.

Summer Leaf Colours

So far, we have discussed different leaf colours which occur at specific stages of plant development, either at the beginning or end of leaf life. Many garden plants have been selected for a particular leaf colour which can occur throughout the life of the leaf, such as yellow, green-yellow variegation or blue-grey.

Yellow Leaves

The apparent absence of green colour in leaves (or parts of leaves) suggests the absence of

Young growth of the deciduous scarlet oak, *Quercus coccinea*, is red in colour, due to accumulation of anthocyanins. In autumn, the leaves will also turn red.

chlorophylls, but plants lacking chlorophylls cannot photosynthesize so will die, unless they are parasitic plants like dodder. This means that chlorophylls must be present in plants with wholly or partly yellow leaves, though not necessarily in all cells.

The occurrence of yellow leaves in cultivars is due to a change in the relative production of the carotenoid and chlorophyll pigments in the leaves. Mutations in the genes which control synthesis of these pigments can result in yellow chloroplasts (containing carotenoids but no chlorophylls) or white chloroplasts (no carotenoids or chlorophylls), compared to the normal green chloroplasts, which contain both chlorophylls and carotenoids.

Most all-yellow plants, such as *Milium effusum* 'Aureum' (Bowles' golden grass), *Choisya* 'Sundance' and *Ligustrum ovalifolium* 'Aureum'

Bowles' golden grass, *Milium effusum* 'Aureum'.

(golden privet), produce leaves which are yellow in sun and either green (choisya, golden privet) or a pale, chartreuse green (Bowles' golden grass) in shade.

With the shrubs, a gradient of leaf colours can be found on the same plant, with yellow leaves at the top and green leaves at the shaded base of the choisya or golden privet. Both the yellow and green leaves contain chlorophylls and hence are capable of photosynthesis. Sunlight encourages the leaves to over-produce carotenoids (and under-produce chlorophylls), so that the carotenoids mask the chlorophylls. In shaded areas, the balance of chlorophyll and carotenoids changes so that the leaves are light to medium green.

In many yellow-leaved plants, such as *Choisya* 'Sundance' and *Acer shinosawara* 'Aurea', too much sunlight results in bleaching of the yellow leaves at the top of the plant, which can become white. This occurs because the low levels of the chlorophylls in these plants means that the light cannot be absorbed, resulting in light- and heat-induced damage to the leaf. Varietal differences do occur, however. Of the ornamental golden elders, *Sambucus racemosa* 'Plumosa Aurea' tends to scorch when planted in full sun, but the slightly

This dwarf variegated bamboo, *Pleioblastus viridistriata*, becomes more light green than yellow when grown in the shade.

The leaves of *Choisya ternata* 'Sundance' are yellow in bright light (bleached if too bright) shading to light, and dark green in shade. The all-green shoot (centre) is caused by a genetic process known as somatic recombination.

coarser foliage of *S. racemosa* 'Sutherland Gold' does not.

The effects of light and shade on yellow coloration can also be seen on green-yellow variegated plants. The yellow tissue of all yellow-variegated hostas, such as *Hosta* 'June', one of the most popular hostas in Britain, becomes greenish-yellow when grown under shady conditions, a contrast with the blue-green tissue which is more attractive than that which occurs under brighter conditions. Green-yellow variegated plants which retain their yellow colour in the shade include the ivy *Hedera helix* 'Goldheart', the Japanese grass *Hakonechloa macra* 'Aureola' and the golden laurel, *Aucuba japonica* 'Maculata'.

Those conifers which produce yellow-leaved shoots in spring or winter, which turn green later in the season, such as *Picea orientalis* 'Aurea' and *Pinus sylvestris* 'Gold Coin', contain a gene for chlorophyll production which does not work at low temperatures.

All white- or grey-variegated plants, on the other hand, retain their colour contrast when grown in even the densest shade, such as *Hosta albomarginata* and the ivy *Hedera helix* 'Glacier'.

Blue-Grey, White, Grey or Silver Leaves

Most of these leaf colours are associated with adaptations to dry conditions, and are caused by changes to the leaf surface which reduces the amount of water lost from the leaf (Chapter 2).

Blue-grey or glaucous leaves in grasses like *Helichtotrichon sempervirens* and *Festuca glauca*, and dicots such as *Hosta sieboldiana* 'Elegans' and *Sedum* 'Purple Emperor' are the result of waxes accumulating on the leaf surface or cuticle (epicuticular waxes). To maximize the blue tinge, these plants should be grown under dry conditions. This can be mimicked by growing the glaucous-leaved plants near a wall or under a plant which will reduce water availability to the lower plants. I once grew a cluster of plants of the ornamental grass *Festuca glauca* under a large plant of *Phormium* 'Maori Sunrise', and was amazed at the intensity of the blue colour of the small grass. Glaucous-leafed hostas such as *H. sieboldiana* 'Elegans' show the best blue colours when sheltered from strong sun.

Leaves which are white, grey or silver unrelieved by any green tissue are usually covered with white hairs or surface accretions, such as a flour-like

The silvery patches on leaves of *Brunnera* 'Jack Frost' are caused by air pockets between the epidermis and underlying leaf tissues.

powdery material known as farina (in some primulas) or calcium bicarbonate (related to lime) deposits, exuded from the hydathodes, in silver or kabschia saxifrages. These plants are often grown under glass in alpine houses to prevent damage to these layers. The presence of hairs or lime deposits are adaptations to high-light conditions, such as high-altitude areas. They protect the underlying leaves by reflecting light and heat, while hairs and waxes can also contain organic plant chemicals which absorb ultraviolet light, which is an increasing problem at high altitude. Because hairy-leaved

Damage to this nasturtium leaf is caused by a leafminer burrowing between the epidermis and lower tissues of the leaf, a similar effect to that shown in *Brunnera* 'Jack Frost'.

plants lose sunlight as a result of reflection, they need to be grown in full sun in lowland gardens.

Shade-loving plants with silvery foliage are rare, but include *Astelia chathamica* and the fern *Athyrium nipponicum* 'Pictum', and are adaptations to the dry conditions found under woodland.

Grey/green leaf variegation, as found in *Pulmonaria argentea*, *Brunnera* 'Jack Frost' and 'Langtrees', *Cyclamen hederifolium* 'Nettleton Silver', *Athyrium nipponicum* 'Pictum' and *Asarum magnificum,* are due to the presence of air pockets between the outer epidermal layer and the underlying green tissues. It is sometimes known as 'blister variegation', and can also cause the white veins in leaves of plants such as *Arum italicum* 'Marmoratum'. This effect is similar to the damaging effect caused by the plant pests known as leaf miners, which feed under the epidermis of the leaf, causing white air pockets to develop. This coloration is little affected by the growing conditions, so is a good way of lightening a shady spot in the garden. They will also grow well in sun, without the damage which occurs when white- or yellow-variegated tissue is exposed to sun.

Purple or Red Leaves

The red and purple colours in leaves of some ornamental garden plants like copper beech and *Cotinus coggyria* 'Royal Purple' are caused by the same pigments (anthocyanins) as those found in autumn leaves and are maximized by the same environmental conditions. Although it is important to grow most plants with red- or purple-coloured foliage in bright sites to maximize foliage colour, an exception is the climber *Parthenocissus henryana*. Here the bronze-purple leaves, highlighted by silvery veins, are most colourful when planted in a shady site or on a north-facing wall.

Many evergreen plants such as *Bergenia* 'Ballawley', variegated *Euonymus fortunei* cultivars, purple sage and *Rhododendron praecox* 'Folis Purpurea' show increased reddish colours in leaves and stems in winter. Anthocyanin

The red-purple foliage colour of *Cotinus coggyria* 'Royal Purple' is caused by accumulation of anthocyanins, at its greatest under nutrient-poor conditions and bright light.

Upper surface of leaves of *Parthenocissus henryana* growing in the light (left) or shade (right).

Lower surface of leaves of *Parthenocissus henryana* growing in the light (left) or shade (right). Note the stronger colour in the shade-grown plants.

production is also increased under low soil fertility conditions.

Under high nitrogen conditions, production of secondary plant metabolites, such as pigments, is suppressed (Chapter 4) so maximal leaf colour occurs in plants like *Sedum telephium* 'grown hard', with low nutrients.

Finally, because anthocyanins are also produced in response to stress, you will often see the strongest leaf colours in plants grown under dry conditions, in, say, a gravel garden.

FLOWERING DATE

We have seen (Chapter 7) that, with the exception of tropical species and annual pioneer weeds, plants have adapted their flowering and fruiting season to coincide with the appearance of pollinator animals and seed dispersal agents at particular times of the year. One of the key parts of a plant's life cycle is flowering and fruiting. An understanding of this is of great importance in the ornamental garden, where we aim to have colour in the garden year-round.

Among the plants originating from temperate areas, natives of the deciduous woodland biome flower from spring to autumn, avoiding the winter stress period. In the scrub forest biome, plants flower mainly in winter/spring, such as *Iris unguicularis* and *Grevillea,* or late summer/autumn as with *Schizostylis* and *Nerine,* to miss out the stressful dry summer period. And in the temperate grassland biome, the main flowering period is late summer/autumn, again avoiding the summer drought of their native habitat.

In Britain, the peak month for flowering of wild plants is July, with plenty of pollinators and sufficient time before flowering to build up the plant and after flowering to set seed before winter. Approximately 1,400 wild plant species in Britain have a flowering date in July, compared with 1,000 in June and August, 400 in May and September, and so on, with very few flowering over the winter months.

The distribution of flower colour over the seasons is also interesting, with yellows (pollinated by bees and moths) and whites (flies and moths) predominating in the spring; reds (butterflies), purples (butterflies and flies) and especially blues (bees) in the summer; before returning to yellows (bees) in the autumn. Bees do not become common pollinators until the summer, hence the relative lack of spring-flowering UK native plants with blue flowers.

How do plants identify the appropriate time to flower? The main seasonal factors are temperature, photoperiod and water availability. Because these factors vary between regions, the same plant species can flower at different times of the year in different countries. Linnaeus (Chapter 1) found that the main flowering date of the marsh marigold, *Caltha palustris,* varied from March in the Netherlands, to April/May in Sweden, to as late as June in Lapland.

Temperature Effects

Some plant species need to go through a prolonged low-temperature period each year before responding to environmental factors by flowering. This process is known as vernalization and is meant to signify that the plant has passed through the winter, when it would be dangerous for most plants to flower.

The obvious examples of plants requiring vernalization are biennials, like sweet William, foxglove and forget-me-not, which grow vegetatively, producing leaves in their first year, then flower, set seed and die in their second year. If sown in spring, these young plants will not flower in Year 1 but remain as a rosette of leaves. After their first winter, having passed through their vernalization treatment, however, the flowering stem will elongate and the plant will flower in Year 2. The vernalization response involves plant hormones, including gibberellins (Chapter 5). Application of gibberellins to unvernalized carrots or cabbages will induce flowering.

The vernalization treatment involves being at or below the critical temperature for at least a given unbroken number of days, and the plant must exceed a critical accumulated number of day-degrees before they can be induced to flower. In most species, the critical temperature is around 10°C, with the optimum being around 5°C. The length of the vernalization period can vary from one week (radish) to four weeks (Chinese cabbage) to six weeks (celery) to nine weeks (*Lunaria biennis*).

Vernalization can be accidentally reversed (devernalization) if the plants are exposed to high temperatures (25–30°C) shortly after their vernalization period. Plants vulnerable to devernalization include the brassicas, celery, carrot, regal pelargonium and cineraria.

Early spring-flowering geophyte species such as crocus, narcissus and snowdrop, break dormancy after exposure to low vernalizing temperatures in winter, when roots start to grow. These spring-flowering geophytes start to flower when temperatures increase above 6°C.

As a result of global warming, the flowering date of many spring bulbs in Ireland and Britain has moved earlier by as much as thirty days over the past fifty years, because the critical temperature of 6°C is arriving earlier and earlier. On the other hand, autumn-flowering species, such as colchicum, and very early spring-flowering species like winter aconites are triggered to flower by temperatures falling below a critical value. The flowering date of these species is getting later as autumns get warmer.

The importance of temperature in triggering flowering can be used to 'force' spring-flowering shrubs into flower in early spring for the house. Flower buds of shrubs like forsythia will break dormancy when branches are brought into the warmth. Forcing can be accelerated even further by use of high temperatures. Flower buds of forsythia can be stimulated to flower by exposure to 40–55°C for approximately fifteen seconds.

Photoperiod

Once a plant has passed, if necessary, through the vernalization period, it will then respond to specific environmental factors by flowering. The occurrence of these factors is closely associated with appropriate times of the year. The most accurate indicator of season in western Europe is photoperiod, whereas temperature and water supply can also have a bearing in particular groups of plants.

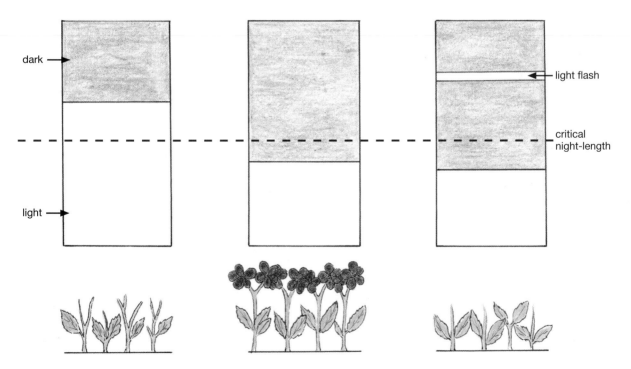

Effects of night-length on flowering of a short-day plant.

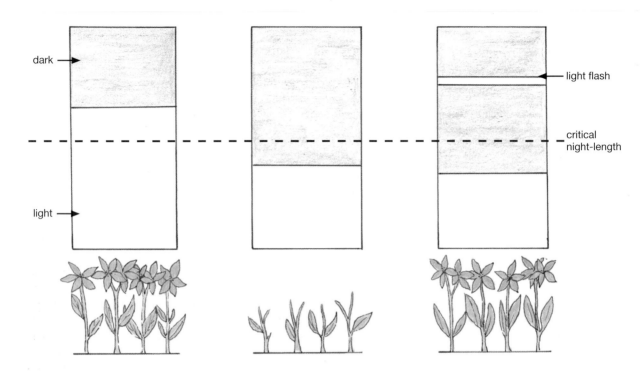

Effects of night-length on flowering of a long-day plant.

The number of hours of daylight in a twenty-four-hour period (photoperiod) is a more reliable indicator of the progression of the seasons in western Europe than temperature, where warm winter spells and early frosts are common. Here, the plants use light, not as a source of light energy as for photosynthesis but as a source of information. Plants detect the appropriate photoperiod via a coloured protein, phytochrome, which acts as a photoreceptor. Phytochrome can also provide information for seed germination (Chapters 6 and 7), leaf fall and bud break in response to light. By using phytochrome, for example, many plants, such as the four o'clock plant, *Mirabilis jalapa*, can tell the time to within fifteen minutes.

Plants fall into one of three broad categories depending on how their flowering responds to a photoperiod. In two of the categories, each species has a critical photoperiod. With short-day species, the plants flower when the photoperiod falls below the critical value for that species, whereas with long-day species, flowering occurs when the photoperiod exceeds the critical value. The critical photoperiod can be the same in both long- and short-day plants. The difference between these two plant categories is how they respond to a photoperiod above the critical value.

There are actually two sub-classes of each of these categories: an 'obligate short day plant', for example, means that the plant will only flower when the daylength is less than the critical value, whereas a 'facultative short day plant' means that the plant will flower sooner when the daylength is less than the critical value.

Long-day plants are temperate plants. They normally flower in summer, and include bedding lobelia, cupid's dart, gazania, poached egg flower, rudbeckia, nigella, dianthus, evening primrose, snapdragon, calendula, eschscholtsia, sunflower, petunia, salvia and cornflower.

Short-day plants, on the other hand, come from more southerly latitudes, and are natives to scrub forest, temperate grassland or sub-tropical areas. Short-day plants flower in late summer and autumn, like chrysanthemum, zinnia, impatiens, celosia, dahlia, cosmos and canna. Occasionally, spring-flowering plants, such as rhododendrons, are short-day plants.

The third category of plants are tropical in origin, and, as such, do not respond to seasonal differences in photoperiod. These species are referred to as day-neutral plants, in that flowering occurs at a fixed number of days (the actual number depending on the temperature) from emergence of shoots or seedlings. Examples of day-neutral plants include black-eyed Susan, sweetcorn, tomato, cucumber, sweet William and rose. Pioneer annual weed species, such as annual meadowgrass and groundsel, are also day-neutral, though temperate in origin, so that they can flower all year round as their goal is to produce as many seeds as possible as quickly as possible (Chapter 6).

The perennial nasturtium *Tropaeolum tuberosum* is a short-day plant flowering late in autumn where it is vulnerable to early frosts, but the cultivar, 'Ken Aslet' is a day-neutral mutant, flowering more than a month earlier.

Actually, the terms 'short-day' and 'long-day' are misnomers, as it is the length of the dark, rather than the light period which determines flowering date. These two categories should really be referred to as 'long-night' and 'short-night' plants, respectively. In other words, short-day plants like chrysanthemums need to receive more than the critical dark period before they will flower.

Knowledge of the dark period is used to manipulate the flowering date of plants like pot chrysanthemums and poinsettias for sale. The critical dark period for flowering in most commercial 'pot mum' chrysanthemum cultivars is about 15 hours. Growers arrange for the light flashes to come on for short periods during the dark period to reduce the length of the dark period to less than the critical value, so that the plants remain vegetative.

When the calendar approaches important days for chrysanthemum sales, such as Mothers' Day, the light flashes are switched off, the plants receive more than the critical dark period and start to flower. The longer the period when the plants receive short night treatments, the larger the plant will be when it flowers.

Photoperiod sensitivity can apply to plant characters other than flowering. Both potato and dahlias are short-day plants, and will only initiate tubers under short days.

Water Supply

While most spring-flowering geophytes have adapted to flower after winter has passed, requiring vernalization and increasing temperatures to trigger flowering, autumn-flowering scrub forest geophytes have adapted to flower after the summer drought has ended.

Flowering in bulbs like *Nerine bowdenii* and *Zephyranthes candida*, the rain lily, is triggered by rainfall in their native habitat or by watering in our gardens. A thorough drenching, with 5–10 litres of water, will stimulate flowering of *Z. candida* to start within two weeks.

Flowering of evergreen woodland plants from the taiga biome such as twinflower (*Linnaea borealis*), bunchberry (*Cornus canadensis*), *Asarum europaeum* and *Hepatica* spp. usually occurs in early summer and is triggered in their native habitat by water availability, as the frozen soil thaws. Poor flowering in these plants in your garden may be because they are planted under trees and are receiving insufficient water to stimulate flowering.

Length of Flowering Period

The duration of the flowering period of a plant can range from less than two weeks in some paeonies through to plants which can flower for months on end, like *Erysimum* 'Bowles' Mauve', sometimes flowering themselves to death. An Irish saying on the long-flowering habit of furze or gorse, *Ulex europaeus*, has it that 'When furze is out of bloom, kissing is out of fashion'.

There are a number of factors commonly associated with species having long flowering seasons. Seed production can switch off the production of more flowers, so anything which stops seed formation should extend flowering. Sterile cultivars, for example, such as double-flowered

ABOVE: A flower head of a lacecap hydrangea. The florets on the outer part of the head appear to have petals but these are sepals which are sterile and so provide the colour. The central florets are fertile but have no sepals.

BELOW: A flower head of *Astrantia* 'Hadspen Blood', showing the small florets surrounded by the coloured bracts.

cultivars or inter-specific hybrids, tend to have longer flowering seasons. The long-lasting flower heads of hydrangeas are made up of sterile flowers (mopheads) or sterile florets surrounding smaller fertile florets (lacecaps). Whereas petals crumple and die, plants where the 'petals' are actually coloured sepals (*Hydrangea, Helleborus*) or leaf-like bracts (*Astrantia* and *Euphorbia* spp.) can last for months.

Day-neutral species, such as bedding plants like *Begonia semperflorens* and *Tagetes patula,* also show long flowering seasons. This trait is particularly pronounced in houseplants such as streptocarpus, African violet and cyclamen. Houseplants are mostly tropical or sub-tropical in origin, flowering regardless of the daylength, so artificial heat ensures that the plants can be in flower indoors for long periods of the year.

Regular feeding and watering are important to counter the drain on the resources of the plant imposed by excessive flower production, while deadheading will extend the flowering season of many plants (Chapter 5), including penstemons, violas, late-flowering salvias and dahlias.

CHAPTER 9

Productivity in the Kitchen Garden

The kitchen garden includes the productive elements of a garden, be it the vegetable plot, a few fruit trees or a herb garden. An average vegetable garden in western Europe can produce almost four times the yield per square metre that an agricultural crop in the same area can. This is because the vegetable plants are arranged to use resources such as light, water and nutrients far more efficiently. To understand the science behind vegetable productivity requires the gardener to look at the plants as a community, an edible ecosystem where the plants interact with one another.

For kitchen gardeners, it is not only the quantity but also the quality of home-grown produce which matters. The quality of the produce – the sweetness of corn-on-the-cob or freshly pulled carrots, or the flavour of tomatoes or new potatoes – depends on the biochemistry of the harvested parts of the plant, the so-called 'economic sinks'.

FRUIT OR VEGETABLE?

A fruit occurs after pollination when the ovules start to develop into seeds, although this may not reach completion, as in seedless cultivars. The ovary in which the ovules are carried grows into an attractive fruit, usually brightly coloured and often fragrant. So any economic sink which develops from a pollinated flower is a fruit. This includes 'classical' fruits such as apples, blackberries, peaches, gooseberries and pears, but also others which, on culinary grounds, would normally be

Herbs grown in a raised bed to mimic the dry native conditions: bronze fennel, mint, golden marjoram, sage, lavender.

dispatched to the vegetable section of the supermarket. Tomatoes, cucumber, chillies, sweetcorn, pumpkins and runner beans are all, botanically speaking, fruits. Nuts are also fruits, albeit dry ones as opposed to the more usual fleshy fruits.

Any food crop which does not come under this definition of 'fruit' is therefore a vegetable. The plant part which is consumed in vegetables varies widely:

- **leaf**: spinach, lettuce
- **leaf base**: spring onion, leek
- **apical vegetative bud**: cabbage
- **axillary vegetative bud**: Brussels sprout
- **leaf stalk:** rhubarb, celery, cardoon, sea kale
- **underground stem (tuber)**: potato, Jerusalem artichoke
- **taproot**: carrot, parsnip
- **stem/root combined**: turnip, beetroot
- **flower bud**: globe artichoke, cauliflower, broccoli

THE VEGETABLE GARDEN

This section deals with the part of the kitchen garden which includes everything bar fruit trees and bushes. Botanically, some of the crops will be fruits, like sweetcorn and tomatoes.

Diversity is essential in the vegetable garden, not only to satisfy the gardener's desire to grow different crops to produce different types of food year round, but also to help maximize productivity and minimize problems with pests and diseases. The key here is to understand how different plants interact with one another and with the local pests and pathogens, to achieve complementarity.

MEASURING PRODUCTIVITY

Productivity is related to how efficiently the plants use the available resources, particularly light but also water and nutrients, and convert them into edible plant organs. Productivity per se is not really that important to the home gardener; the goal is quality and availability of fresh produce, but it can still be enlightening to find out why some crops produce much more food than others. For this, we need to understand a little about crop physiology, the physiology of plants growing as a community rather than as single plants.

The weight of food produced (economic yield) from an area of land can be described by the following formula:

economic yield = total plant biomass × harvest index

Economic Yield

Economic yield is the weight of the economic sink harvested for each 1m × 1m area of land. The economic sink is the plant organ which is harvested as food, such as tubers for potato and cobs for sweetcorn. Economic yields for important garden crops range from around 0.5kg m^{-2} for peas and sweetcorn to approximately 5kg m^{-2} for maincrop potatoes. Differences in economic yield between crops can be traced back to differences in yield components total biomass and/or harvest index.

Total Biomass

Total plant biomass is the weight of the entire crop. Because it is nearly impossible to recover all the roots from the soil, 'plant biomass' always refers to 'plant biomass minus roots', though we ignore the direct and indirect effects of roots at our peril (Chapter 3).

Harvest Index

Harvest index (HI) is the proportion of the total plant biomass which is harvested as food.

Different crops have very different HI values. Crops where the economic sink is the leaves, like lettuce and cabbage, have HI values close to 1.0,

meaning that almost 100 per cent of the biomass is harvested for food. On the other hand, while potatoes and turnips have HIs of about 0.80 and 0.90, respectively, crops where the economic sink is a fruit, such as sweetcorn (0.50) and runner beans (0.50), or seeds, such as peas (0.35) have much lower HI values.

Plant Efficiency

Because more than 90 per cent of plant dry weight (after the water has been removed) is made up of carbon, fixed from the CO_2 in the air as the result of photosynthesis, total biomass is directly related to the ability of the crop to photosynthesize and hence to trap light.

As a single plant, growing in isolation, grows larger, it can trap more and more sunlight and thus carry out more photosynthesis, which powers further growth. The larger the area of leaves on such a plant, the more light could be absorbed and the greater the total plant biomass.

In a crop community, however, the leaves of neighbouring plants of the same crop can block out some of the light which could have been absorbed by that plant. At some point, all of the sunlight will be absorbed, and any more leaves produced will fail to increase the amount of light absorbed or the rate of photosynthesis or the total biomass. You can detect this point by looking directly down on the leaf canopy of your vegetable crop. When you cannot see any soil between the leaves, all the light is being absorbed and the leaf canopy is said to be closed. The ratio of leaf area to soil area is termed the leaf area index (LAI). When the leaf canopy is closed the LAI is said to be at the critical LAI (LAI_C).

You might be thinking that the best arrangement of leaves for a crop plant would be to have large thick horizontal dustbin lid-like leaves which absorb all the sunlight ($LAI_C = 1$). But most of the vegetable plants we grow in temperate gardens exhibit C3 photosynthesis (Chapter 5).

The rate of C3 photosynthesis increases as the light level increases but levels off (saturates) at around one-third of full sunlight, that presents around noon on a cloudless day in mid-summer. So a plant with large flat leaves would only

Effect of leaf area index on biomass production by plants in isolation or in a community.

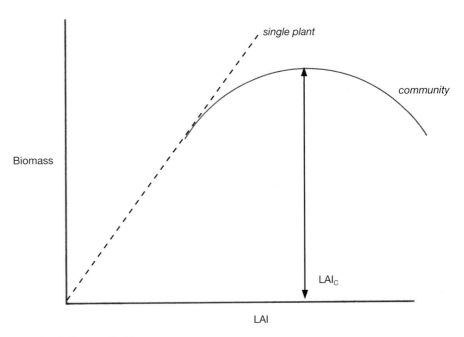

be able to use about one third of the available sunlight, with the remaining two-thirds being wasted, or even becoming dangerous as the leaf heats up.

To increase the efficiency of light absorption, each leaf should be arranged to receive less than the saturating level of light. This is achieved by holding individual leaves at an angle, so that a greater leaf area can be supplied with light. The more erect the leaves, the higher the LAI_C. Potato, with horizontal leaves, has a value of approximately 3.0, compared to sweetcorn, with more erect leaves (6.0). As a consequence, plants with more erect foliage tend to be more efficient at converting light energy into plant biomass than do plants with more horizontal leaves.

The second LAI factor affecting total biomass is how long the foliage stays green and hence productive. The higher this figure, the higher the total biomass which will be produced. Crops with high biomass like potato and turnip tend to have long growing seasons, with the canopy staying green and productive for longer than low-biomass crops like sweetcorn. To maximize the yield from a crop, the period that the leaves are actively trapping sunlight can be extended by starting crops earlier in the season and by controlling leaf diseases late in the season, like potato blight.

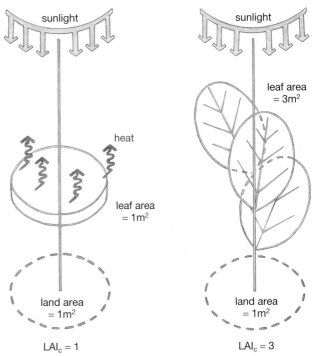

How leaf angle helps a plant use light more efficiently.

ORGANIZING THE VEGETABLE GARDEN

To get the most out of your vegetable garden, you need to consider aspects like which crops and cultivars to grow, how to arrange the planting (considering inter-cropping and crop rotation), how to feed the crops, and how to manage pests and pathogens in the crop.

Which Crops?

You will want to plant those crops which you and your family will eat, those which will grow in your garden (Chapter 2), those which you cannot readily get in the shops and those which taste incomparably better for being eaten shortly after harvesting, like sweetcorn and carrots. Some crops need particular soil conditions (carrots prefer light soils without stones or large lumps of organic matter), while others, such as sweetcorn, will not grow well in the cooler cloudier parts of the country.

If you garden in an area prone to weather extremes, like cold or dry summers, self-pollinated crops like tomatoes, peas and French beans, and seedless crops like cucumbers, tend to have more consistent crops than cross-pollinated crops like runner beans which depend on insect pollinators (Chapter 7). In wet or windy weather, pollinators tend not to fly, while under dry conditions, some cross-pollinated flowers like those of runner beans tend to close, making pollination impossible.

How selective you are going to be is indirectly related to the size of your vegetable garden. Unless you have a sizeable allotment, maincrop potatoes, Jerusalem artichokes and maybe broccoli seem a waste of space. 'New potatoes', in the form of first or second early potato cultivars, or supersweet corn-on-the cob, eaten before the sucrose in the kernels gets a chance to turn back into starch, are a different story altogether.

Which Cultivars?

Selecting the cultivars to be grown depends on personal preferences, the intended uses of the crop, local climatic vagaries and intended harvest date.

Dwarf or Tall

Generally, tall cultivars outyield dwarf cultivars of the same crop because, in the latter, the leaves on a stem are closer together so cause more self shading. Advantages of growing dwarf cultivars are that they tend to produce flowers and fruits earlier than do tall cultivars because the shoot of dwarf cultivars is a weaker sink for attracting assimilates, which is useful where growing seasons are short.

Determinate or Indeterminate

With determinate cultivars of crops, such as bush cultivars of tomato, the apical bud becomes reproductive and the plant stops growing upwards. Instead, the plant starts to grow outwards through development of its axillary buds, becoming bushier.

With indeterminate cultivars, like the cordon cultivars of tomato widely grown in glasshouses, the apical bud remains vegetative, producing more stem and leaf tissue until it is pinched out by the gardener. Generally, indeterminate cultivars have a longer fruiting season than do determinate cultivars, but determinate tomato cultivars are more likely to give you a decent harvest in areas with short growing seasons, such as the north of the UK.

Harvest Date

Cultivars of several vegetable crops are classified into groups according to harvest date, such as cauliflower, where summer and winter cultivars are available. Potato cultivars are categorized into three principal maturity classes: first early (harvested May–June), second early (June–July) and maincrop (September onwards).

The tuber yields are generally in the order maincrop (highest), second early, first early (lowest); but early cultivars are grown mainly for 'new potatoes', where low yields are acceptable as long as the flavour is good. Early-ripening cultivars of many vegetable crops are particularly suitable for gardeners in areas where the growing season is short.

Eating Quality

Cultivars of many crops can be divided into different groups according to their eating characteristics. There are several grades of sweetness among sweetcorn cultivars, such as sweet, tendersweet, sugar enhanced (showing a slower conversion from sucrose to starch once picked) and supersweet, the latter being the sweetest.

Different potato cultivars produce potatoes suitable for different cooking purposes. Floury potato cultivars, such as 'Kerr's Pink' and 'Rooster', are best for mashed, boiled and chipped potatoes; while waxy potatoes, such as 'La Ratte', 'Charlotte' and 'Pink Fir Apple' keep their shape and texture better when boiled and are best used as salad potatoes, because oil-based dressings do not soak into the tubers.

These different purposes are determined by the starch quality of each cultivar. Starch is a polymer made up of hundreds of glucose molecules joined together. There are two types of starch: amylose, where the glucose molecules are arranged in a straight line, and amylopectin, where they have a branched arrangement (Chapter 4). Floury potatoes have more starch than waxy ones and have more amylose than amylopectin in their starch, whereas waxy potatoes have the reverse characteristics.

Immature tubers also tend to be more waxy. 'New potatoes' harvested from early cultivars, for example, tend to be more waxy. 'Jersey Royals' are the immature waxy tubers of the maincrop cultivar 'International Kidney', which are floury in texture. An easy way of distinguishing waxy from floury potatoes before cooking is to put the tubers in a bucket of water: waxy potatoes float, while floury potatoes, with a higher starch content, sink.

Disease Resistance

Most gardeners want to minimize the use of sprays, especially around food plants. To help achieve this, you should select cultivars resistant to the major pests or pathogens in your area (Chapter 6), such as potato 'Sarpo Mira', which shows considerable resistance to late potato blight.

Tomato plants produced by grafting (Chapter 7) tomato cultivar scions onto the rootstock of a wild tomato, *Solanum pimpinellifolium*, are becoming available to the home gardener. These exhibit high levels of resistance to root diseases, such as verticillium wilt, while also being better able to grow in less-than-ideal conditions.

F_1 Hybrids

In seed catalogues, particularly with regard to vegetable seeds but also bedding plants, you will often see the phrase 'F_1 hybrid'. You may wonder what this means and why they are so expensive.

Most vegetable crops are cross-pollinated (Chapter 7). As a consequence, plants grown from seed from a conventional cultivar such as cabbage 'Greyhound' (known as open-pollinated cultivars) will be broadly similar in appearance but will vary in traits such as maturity date, height, head size. In other words, they do not come true-to-type from seed (Chapter 7). These differences in traits are not a problem for kitchen gardeners, but they are for farmers who want to carry out mechanical once-over harvesting of all plants from one field at one time.

To overcome these problems, F_1 hybrids were developed by plant breeders. 'F_1' stands for 'first filial generation', which is the first seed generation from a cross between two parents. In F_1 breeding, the parents are produced by several generations of self-pollination to produce plants which are homozygous for nearly all their genes. These homozygous plants are then crossed to produce the F_1 seed. For this example, consider two parent lines (P1 and P2) and just three genes (such as A), each of which has two alleles, like A and a:

	P1	**P2**
Genotype	AAbbCC	aaBBcc
Gamete	AbC	aBc
F1 genotype	AaBbCc	

All plants of the resulting F_1 cultivar are identical genetically, with the same genotype, AaBbCc. For farmers, this results in a crop which is much more uniform than one from open-pollinated seed. A second advantage is that F_1 hybrids are also higher yielding than open-pollinated cultivars. As you can see, the F_1 hybrid is heterozygous for all the genes where the two parents carried different alleles. In cross-pollinated plants, heterozygosity is very desirable (Chapter 7). F_1 hybrid cultivars, therefore, are much more heterozygous than open-pollinated cultivars and so are much more vigorous and higher-yielding. This phenomenon is known as hybrid vigour.

So F_1 hybrid cultivars give higher yields and are uniform, making them desirable to the farmer. The plant breeder also likes them. With conventional open-pollinated cultivars, the farmer or gardener buys the seed, sows it and harvests the seed. But the seed harvested is more or less identical to that which he bought, so he is entitled to save some of the seed he produced to sow next year (farm-saved seed), saving the farmer money but reducing the sales for the breeder.

The seed produced from an F_1 crop, however, will not be the same as the F_1 seed he bought. The next generation (F_2) will not be uniform, as each plant will have a different genotype as a result of re-shuffling of the genes, nor will they show the high level of heterozygosity and hybrid vigour that the F_1 generation did. The result is that the farmer must buy F_1 seed from the breeder each year. Result: happy farmers and happy plant breeders.

It did not take long for seeds of F_1 vegetable and flower cultivars to become available to the amateur gardener. F_1 hybrid seed for gardeners is produced by hand in countries like India and China where labour costs for hand pollination are low, but the seed cost is still much higher than for open-pollinated cultivars.

But do gardeners need F_1 cultivars? Increased yield is always useful but is not the raison d'être for gardeners. Nor is uniformity. Commercial growers of F_1 cauliflowers will be able to harvest all their plants of F_1 hybrid at the same time, whereas plants of an open-pollinated cultivar can be harvested sporadically over a period of weeks as they reach the desired size. The wider range of maturity dates within an open-pollinated cultivar can actually be desirable for a gardener, avoiding gluts.

Some F_1 hybrids have other desirable characters. Asparagus is naturally dioecious, with separate male and female plants, so that an open-pollinated cultivar like 'Connover's Colossal' will produce similar numbers of the high-yielding males and the less desirable female plants. Asparagus F_1 hybrids

such as 'Theilim', 'Jersey Knight' and 'Backlim' produce more spears (due to hybrid vigour) and all the plants are male. Some F_1 glasshouse cucumber cultivars, such as Pepinex 69 and Passandra, produce plants which are all female, for seedless cucumber production.

PLANTING MATERIAL

The two principal options for planting material are direct sowing of seeds and transplanting of seedlings. The advantage of buying seedlings from a garden centre is convenience, but disadvantages can include introduction of pests and pathogens into your vegetable garden (unless soil-less compost is used), a narrower range of cultivars and problems of the effects of previous stress on the seedlings, such as drought or root compaction (Chapter 3), which can have a permanent detrimental impact on plant performance.

Root problems, the impact of which were highlighted in Chapter 3, can be particularly serious with tap-rooted plants such as squashes, leeks, brassicas, beans, sweetcorn, endives and carrots. If you sow seeds yourself, you can sow directly or transplant, eliminating the problems of bought-in seedlings.

For crops with tap roots or delicate roots, like lettuce, it is best to sow seeds in modules to minimize root disturbance during transplantation. The cardboard tubes in toilet paper or kitchen towel rolls, supported with an elastic band, can be used to provide a suitable compost depth for sowing legumes and leeks. The whole roll, seedling and all, can then be planted into the soil, where the cardboard will disintegrate.

With some crops, seeds are not the only or even the usual planting material. Onion or shallot sets, for example, are immature bulbs that produce harvestable produce more quickly than do plants from seed. Spare cloves of garlic planted from a head you have bought for cooking will grow, but the plant may be of a cultivar not well suited to your growing conditions, and could carry virus (Chapter 6), so it is better to buy garlic cloves intended for planting.

Potato, like garlic, is propagated from vegetative

CHITTING POTATOES

Gardening books usually indicate that you need to allow the tubers to produce shoots before you plant them. This is a process known as chitting and involves storing the tubers, before they start to produce shoots, in a cool but bright place.

But why would you need to do this? First of all, it is useful to get your bearings when looking at a tuber. This is a swollen underground stem, and around the stem are 'eyes', slightly sunken areas from where shoots develop. The 'rose' end is where shoots develop first. The remains of the stolon which attached the tuber to the mother plant may be visible at the other end of the tuber. The rose represents the tip or apical bud of the stem, while those eyes forming around the side of the tuber in a spiral arrangement are the axillary buds. All tubers (except those from first early cultivars) are dormant after being produced and are usually stored at 4°C to slow the dormancy from breaking down until they are to be planted.

Obviously enough, chitting gets the plant growing earlier, but, more importantly, it ages the resulting potato plant so that it produces tubers earlier. Potato tubers are produced when the plants reach a certain age, but this is a physiological age rather than a strictly chronological one.

Once the tubers begin to produce shoots (sprouts), they start to age. The physiological age of a potato plant is calculated as the number of days it is at a temperature above 4°C, so that a chitted tuber which has been stored at 10°C for 30 days will have a physiological age of 30 × [10–4] day-degrees = 180 day-degrees. When a potato plant reaches the critical number of day-degrees for that cultivar (around 1,400 for maincrop cultivars), it will start to produce tubers.

That means that the plant grown from a chitted tuber will start producing tubers earlier than will a plant from an unchitted tuber of the same cultivar. The net result is that chitting allows the grower to harvest potatoes earlier. Combined with early planting and the use of protection with a polytunnel, cloche or horticultural fleece, chitting seed tubers allows the grower to produce new potatoes from early cultivars up to two months earlier than usual.

For the home gardener, early harvesting of new potatoes is the only real benefit of chitting seed tubers. Planting unchitted tubers should give you a somewhat higher but later yield of tubers. By planting some rows to chitted and others to unchitted tubers, you will extend the harvesting period from one cultivar.

By chitting the tuber, you can also control the number of stems which will form from the seed tuber by training the young plant, as described for shrubs in Chapter 5. Each stem from a seed tuber is a more or less independent plant and will produce tubers.

If you want a small number of large tubers to be harvested early, allow only a small number of stems to develop by chitting the seed tuber upright, then placing the tuber upright in the planting trench, with the rose (apical) end uppermost. This will maximize apical dominance, so that shoots will form mostly from the rose end.

Chitting tubers at moderate to high temperatures, around 16–20°C, at least for the first two to three weeks, will also increase the apical dominance of the seed tuber. This will accelerate the breakdown of dormancy, so that the apical shoots will form first and express apical dominance. Any shoots which develop lower down the tuber, from axillary buds, can be removed during chitting by rubbing them off. The chitted tuber should then be placed in the same position in the planting trench.

If, however, you want a large number of small tubers, your aim is for a large number of stems by reducing apical dominance. To achieve this, chit or plant the tubers lying down, so that the apical bud is not above the axillary buds, allowing shoots to develop from the apical buds lower down the tuber. Chitting the tubers at approximately 10°C will help minimize apical dominance. The end result is a higher total yield of potatoes harvested earlier in the season, but with a higher proportion of small tubers.

tissue rather than seed, in this case the tuber which we eat. Again, it is preferable to buy certified disease-free seed potatoes of a known cultivar.

Planting Date

Year-round productivity in the kitchen garden is the goal of many gardeners, and this can be achieved by a combination of successional sowing and the selection of appropriate crops and cultivars. Leeks and cauliflowers, for example, could be available for harvest each month of the year by sowing appropriate cultivars at the correct times.

For early sowing, evidence of weed seed germination in the vegetable beds is a good indicator that the soil temperature is suitable for plant growth. This date can be brought forward by artificially raising the temperature by between 2 and 5°C, using cloches and/or horticultural fleece, up to four weeks before sowing as well as after sowing. Planting under conditions unsuitable for plant growth is rarely successful as plants can take weeks to recover from a growth check brought about by cold stress.

With perennial vegetables, like rhubarb and asparagus, successional sowing is, of course, not possible, so careful choice of cultivars is the only way to spread the availability of fresh produce.

For some crops, planting date is important to ensure or to avoid low temperatures, as plants use such cues to identify the time of the year. Garlic needs to be planted between November and March as a cold spell is vital to break dormancy in the cloves, so that growth starts.

Most vegetable crops are grown as annuals, being sown and harvested in the same year. Many, including cabbage, carrot, fennel, parsnip, lettuce, radish and onion, are naturally biennials (Chapter 8) which we grow as annuals. In nature, these plants store food reserves in swollen stems, roots or leaf bases by the end of Year 1, which are then used to power flowering in Year 2 after the plants have been vernalized after being exposed to low temperatures, signifying winter (Chapter 8). As gardeners we harvest these reserves in Year 1.

With biennial crops, it is important not to plant crops such as beetroot or endive too early,

as exposure to low temperatures could cause vernalization to occur, resulting in the plants flowering (bolting) in Year 1, so that the reserves which we want to harvest are not formed. Some bolting-resistant cultivars with greater vernalization requirements have been bred for early sowings, such as 'Boltardy' and 'Kestrel' beetroot. For salad and herb leaves, like rocket and parsley, regular picking inhibits bolting.

Onions and shallots are also biennials, but are traditionally grown from sets – immature bulbs grown from seed the previous year, which are planted in spring for harvesting in summer. It is important that your onion plants do not bolt, and there are precautions you can take to minimize the risk.

Firstly, vegetative storage organs like bulbs need to be above a certain circumference before they can produce flowers, such as 6–9 cm for tulip and 6–8 cm for hyacinth. To minimize the number of plants which bolt, small onion or shallot sets less than 15mm diameter should be selected.

Secondly, flower formation within a bulb is affected by temperature. For onion, storage of the dormant bulb at 8–12°C is ideal for flower bud initiation. Commercially 'heat-treated' sets do not bolt because they have been stored over the winter at 25–30°C, which prevents the flower primordia from forming.

There is a risk that polytunnels and even simpler forms of protection, such as horticultural fleece, could compromise the low-temperature requirement of crops like garlic (to break dormancy) or purple sprouting broccoli (vernalization, to trigger flowering).

But it is not only low temperatures which can be a problem. Lettuce, radish, spinach, fennel and beetroot are native to places with hot dry Mediterranean-like climates, where germination in summer would be dangerous. As a result, sowing these crops in summer at temperatures above about 20°C can result in very poor germination.

If you want to sow lettuce directly, for example, during the summer, precautions need to be taken to lower the temperature by using shading and by watering the soil before sowing, the water cooling the soil by evaporation. Once they have started to grow, many of these species are at risk of flowering if they undergo a dry spell. Again, this would have been an adaptive response in their native habitat, allowing the plant to escape stress by surviving as seeds.

In many cases, staggering sowing dates in successive sowing results in a less-than-expected delay in harvest date. Sowing some crops under cover in February, then transplanting to the open ground in April will not give harvests much earlier than those achieved from direct sowing in April. Why is that? Many crops only start to produce their economic sink at certain times of the year. Because daylength is a more reliable measure of the seasons than temperature, most crops evolved from temperate wild plants initiate their economic sinks, such as fruits or tubers, in response to photoperiod.

Most vegetables grown for their fruits, like peas and runner beans, are long-day plants (Chapter 8) although many will need to pass through a juvenile period before reacting to changes in daylength. Similarly, onions need long days to stimulate bulb formation. Early sowing under cover of long-day plants will mean that the plants will have a larger LAI by the time they respond to the daylength trigger and so will give higher yields. Early-sown crops with a juvenile phase like broad bean will reach the adult phase earlier in the year, will respond to the critical photoperiod (Chapter 8) sooner and hence will flower and fruit a few weeks earlier.

On the other hand, those long-day crops without a juvenile phase should flower at broadly the same date as plants from seeds sown at the normal time, because both will start to flower when the daylength reaches the critical photoperiod. As a result, there will be little or no harvest date advantage from early sowing of these crops, although they will show the higher yields associated with larger plants.

Potato cultivars initiate tubers in response to short days, so that tubers planted in the open in August or undercover in January will produce a very late or very early crop of potatoes, respectively. To plant in late summer, specially prepared non-dormant tubers will need to be used.

Tomatoes are day neutral (Chapter 8), meaning that they flower and crop at a fixed number of days (depending on temperature) after sowing, regardless of daylength, so early sowing will provide you with early harvests of tomatoes.

PLANTING ARRANGEMENT

Having decided on what you are going to plant in your vegetable garden, it is valuable to consider how you arrange these plants in your beds to maximize yield and minimize pests, weeds and diseases.

Competition within a Crop

Spacing

Competition (for light, nutrients or water) between plants of the same species is the strongest because these plants share exactly the same niche (Chapter 2), with roots at the same depth of soil and leaves at the same height. Traditionally, plants of the same crop have been grown in rows or blocks.

Spacing is usually designed so that the neighbouring plants just touch at maturity. This will minimize competition between plants, although gaps between plants late in the season represent losses in yield as sunlight is not being intercepted by the leaves.

The main resource for which plants compete is light, and this is particularly important for sweetcorn, the only crop plant using the C4 type of photosynthesis (Chapter 4) that European gardeners grow. These plants need high light levels to perform well, but suffer badly when light levels fall. Because sweetcorn plants are among the tallest in the vegetable plot, they suffer particularly from self-shading.

The standard arrangement of plants within a row is that there is a plant at the same position within each row. But this is not an efficient design, and more gardeners are using the offset design where the planting arrangement in consecutive rows is staggered, to reduce competition and make the best use of the sunlight.

If plants between or within rows are too close together, they recognize this using the light receptor phytochrome (Chapter 8). Light reaching the plant having passed through leaves of neighbouring plants will contain less red light (which is absorbed by leaves; Chapter 1) than does pure sunlight. Phytochrome absorbs red light and recognizes the relative lack of red light, triggering the plant to put more emphasis on vertical vegetative growth to out-grow the competition.

This growth spurt can have several detrimental effects for the vegetable gardener. Increased emphasis on shoot growth will delay flowering. Furthermore, the emphasis on the apical bud (to achieve upward growth) is at the expense of the axillary buds, which do not develop because they receive fewer assimilates. This is particularly serious for crops where the economic sink develops from these axillary buds, like sweetcorn, Brussels sprout and peas.

Pollination

Vegetable crops where we harvest the fruit are either self-pollinated, like peas, or cross-pollinated, like runner beans. Here, planting in rows allows for adequate pollination as insects move from plant to plant. Sweetcorn, on the other hand, is cross-pollinated, with pollen being spread by the wind. Here, it is advisable to plant the rows in roughly the same direction as the prevailing winds, which are south-westerly in the UK and Ireland, to blow pollen onto the stigmas of plants downwind.

Inter-cropping

Growing different crops in the same vegetable bed is known as intercropping. It allows you not only to grow many different crops in a limited area of land, but, if care is taken, it can also result in beneficial interactions between the different crops. As a result, yields can be greater than if the different crops were grown in isolation, as in the monocultures so widespread in modern farming.

When the higher yields of beneficial intercrops over monocultures is analyzed, the individual plants with the best yields occur where the two different crops are growing side-by-side. Inter-specific competition (between plants of different species) is usually less than intra-specific competition (between plants of the same species), because the two species have different niches. Inter-cropping reduces competition and increases the efficiency with which nutrients and light are trapped and converted into food.

The structured leaf canopy of an inter-cropped vegetable garden resembles that of a natural ecosystem (*see* page 33) more closely than that of an agricultural crop, and the higher productivity of the vegetable garden reflects the high biomass production of a natural ecosystem.

It is important to know the characteristics of individual crops, so that you can identify appropriate partners. Alternating crops with different characteristics, such as rooting depth, can reduce competition for water and nutrients, although some gardeners prefer to group together vegetable plants with similar requirements, such as heavy watering or feeding, to reduce waste of resources. Crops needing lots of water during the growing season include leafy crops such as potato, brassicas and spinach, root crops like carrot and parsnip, and shallow-rooted crops like sweetcorn, legumes, such as peas and beans, and lettuce.

Competition for light can be reduced by interplanting crops with different leaf canopy characteristics. Plants with horizontal leaves like members of the Cucurbitaceae (cucumber family), such as squash and courgettes, as well as potatoes, are generally better adapted to growing under shady conditions, while plants with upright leaves like leeks, sweetcorn and onions prefer high-light conditions.

To reduce self-shading by neighbouring sweetcorn plants, rows of sweetcorn plants can be alternated on a sunny site with rows of a shade-tolerant crop (characterized by having large horizontal simple leaves; Chapter 2) such as courgette and many salad crops. By increasing the distance between rows of sweetcorn, self-shading is reduced and productivity is increased, while the second-crop benefits from the shade cast by the sweetcorn.

The shallow roots of sweetcorn are also complementary to the larger root system of the dicot courgette. Being a tall narrow plant, sweetcorn is prone to problems with weeds, so a low-growing shade-tolerant crop also helps to control weeds by competing them out. Other compatible tall/short plant combinations include runner beans (growing up supports) and maincrop potatoes. When the two (or more) crops spend most of their life growing together, this is known as row inter-cropping.

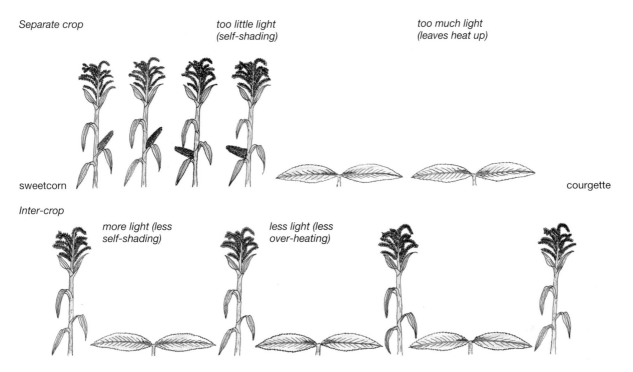

How inter-cropping can increase crop yield in a vegetable garden.

A second type of inter-cropping is relay inter-cropping, where only part of the life cycles of the two crops overlaps. Here, the aim is to 'use' the space around slow-growing crops in their early stages to grow small fast-growing early-maturing crops before the former get too large to compete. Where parsnips can take 14–16 weeks to harvest, radishes sown in the same row will be ready for harvest after four weeks, leaving the parsnips to develop unhindered.

Suitable fast-growing plants for fast relay inter-cropping include spring onions, lettuce ('Little Gem' is faster than butterheads, which are faster than cos), rocket and carrots (for early harvesting), Chinese cabbage and salad crops. Suitable slow-growing crops include plants which cast little shade early on, like sweetcorn, onion, runner beans (on a wigwam, with the other crop planted between or under each wigwam).

The fast-growing crops can also be used as catch crops, to fill in the soil after harvest of one crop and before the planting of the next, such as courgettes after early potatoes. Catch cropping increases the total annual productivity of the vegetable bed by trapping a greater percentage of the sunlight available over the season. It will also stop soluble nitrate, released from the soil organic matter reserves by bacteria (Chapter 4), from being washed away when the bed is empty, as the catch crops will take it up.

When choosing plants to inter-crop, it is important to recognize those plants which are poor competitors. Plants with upright foliage, like onions, or feathery leaves, such as carrots or parsnips, tend not to compete well with other plants.

MAINTENANCE OF VEGETABLE GARDENS

Maintenance of vegetable gardens is similar to that for the rest of the garden, namely feeding, watering (Chapter 4), cutting back (Chapter 5) and the control of pests and pathogens (Chapter 6). Yet, there are different emphases in the vegetable garden, particularly with respect to disease and pest control.

Feeding and Watering

The key here is to provide the amounts and balance of macronutrients (Chapter 4) needed for the different crops. Crops which need to be fed with high levels of nutrients are those with high total biomass and high economic yields, like potatoes and turnips. Leafy plants like potato, courgettes and the brassicas need to be supplied with a high-N fertilizer, while crops where the economic sink is a fruit need a high-K source of nutrients. Legumes, like peas and beans, being N fixers, should not be fed with a high-N artificial fertilizer as this would prevent their association with N-fixing root bacteria from working.

Crops that need to be supplied with lots of water include leafy crops like potatoes, brassicas and members of the cucumber family, like marrows and courgettes, as well as shallow-rooted crops like legumes and sweetcorn. These crops will benefit from a soil with a high organic matter content to retain large volumes of water.

Root crops, on the other hand, like carrots and parsnips, need to avoid planting on soil with high contents of organic matter or stones, as the roots will fork or distort if they encounter such barriers as they grow.

One useful approach to supplying nutrients and water to vegetable crops is to group crops according to their needs. This is an extension of the centuries-old farming practice of crop rotation, which is used primarily to reduce levels of soil-borne pests and pathogens (see below). For a four-year rotation, the usual order is as follows:

A. **root crops**: carrots, parsnips (Apiaceae), also onions, leeks (Alliaceae), beetroot
B. **brassicas**: cabbage, cauliflower, rocket, mizu (Brassicaceae) etc.
C. **legumes**: peas, beans (Fabaceae); also salad crops
D. **potatoes**

A separate permanent bed could also be set aside for perennial crops such as asparagus, strawberries, rhubarb, globe artichokes and herbs.

Crop rotation involves planting similar plants together in each of four (A to D, above) or three separate beds (combining beds B and C). Each year, over a three- or four-year cycle, each group of plants is moved to the next bed until, at year 4 (for a three-year rotation) or year 5 (four-year rotation), each plant group is back in the same bed in which the cycle began.

In a four-year rotation, Year 1 will see the four crop groups planted in beds A to D. In Year 2, the groups will move to the next bed in the rotation (root crops to B, brassicas to C, legumes to D and potatoes to A) and so on.

From a nutritional point of view, the reasoning behind crop rotation is as follows. Potatoes have a very high total biomass and economic yield, so need lots of nutrients and water. Before planting potatoes it is best to add large amounts of well-composted organic matter such as manure and garden compost to the soil, to supply nutrients, increase water-holding capacity and improve soil condition.

After soil has been depleted by a hungry crop like potatoes, a nitrogen-fixing legume crop (Chapter 4) will grow well, because nitrogen fixation is inhibited in nitrogen-rich soils. These crops will enrich the soil to some extent if the roots, containing the nodules where the mutualistic N-fixing bacteria lived, are left in the ground after the crop is harvested. The nitrogen-rich soil left after legumes will benefit leafy crops like members of the cabbage family the next year, as these crops respond well to high nitrogen (Chapter 4).

By Year 4, the compost and manure incorporated in Year 1 will have broken down, allowing the growth of 'root crops' without 'forking'. This term is used to group together crops, other than potatoes, which produce an underground economic sink, although what is harvested may not technically be a root, as with onions, where the bulb is a modified stem.

Pests and Diseases

The management of pests and pathogens in the vegetable garden is a particularly sensitive issue. Everyone wants to minimize the use of plant protection chemicals on food, so there is a greater emphasis on environmentally friendly strategies, such as biological control (Chapter 6).

Biological control harnesses the natural system of beneficial organisms, usually larvae, which use pests as food sources (Chapter 6). To increase the effectiveness of biocontrol, two complementary strategies can be adopted, increasing the population of beneficials and/or reducing the population of the pest.

Increase the Number of Beneficials

Individuals of beneficials such as ladybirds, hoverflies and entomopathogenic nematodes can be bought and released to control particular pests, but it is worthwhile providing habitats to encourage the existing beneficials. These include food sources in the garden in the form of pollen or nectar from plants with simple flowers, for the adult beneficials which usually do not feed on invertebrates (Chapter 6). Other useful features include permanent over-wintering sites like tussocky grasses, which will help to have large populations of beneficials ready in the spring when the pests start to cause damage.

Chapter 6 dealt with pests and their corresponding beneficials which live above ground, but many of the most pernicious pests and pathogens live in the soil. To help combat them, soil-borne beneficials can be recruited by providing them with appropriate food sources.

Parasitic soil organisms, which get their energy and organic chemicals from living plants, are poor competitors for food with saprophytic organisms, which obtain their resources from dead organisms or organic waste material. The simplest way to increase the soil population of general saprophytes is to incorporate their food, organic matter, into the soil. This can be in any form, such as animal manure, garden compost, spent mushroom compost or green manure (Chapter 4).

I remember an old gardener telling me to put lawn clippings into the bottom of the trench for planting seed potatoes in soil infested with potato cyst nematode (PCN). The beneficial effect of adding organic matter to the soil is that it provides food for saprophytes but not pest species, which feed on living plants. In turn, the saprophyte population increases, competing out the pest species.

For more than fifty years, garden compost, particularly that from cold composting (Chapter 4), has been shown to suppress some soil-borne plant pests and pathogens for quite long periods. By adding garden compost to a potting medium or the soil, you are adding organic matter (to encourage saprophytes), plus some competing saprophytes. Pathogens suppressed in particular are those with small spores or resting bodies, and hence small food reserves – such as *Pythium* (responsible for damping-off of direct-sown seeds), *Fusarium* and *Phytophthora* (causes of root rots) – but not those with large resting bodies such as *Sclerotium* or *Plasmodiophora*.

An alternative method is to provide a food source which would encourage a specific beneficial, targeting the pest in question. The eggshells of PCN, for example, contain chitin, the carbohydrate which does for invertebrates what cellulose does for plants. Chitin is also found in the shells of shellfish such as prawns, crab and lobster. If you have PCN in your vegetable plot, the next time you eat any of these shellfish, consider keeping the shells to help control the pest. It is best to break up the shells into small pieces, then incorporate them into the soil from the surface to about 20cm deep, which is the zone where most PCN cysts are found.

Incorporation of chitin into the soil provides a food material for bacteria which can degrade chitin (chitinolytic bacteria). The subsequent increase in their numbers causes damage to PCN eggs, killing the nematodes within the eggs. It would be best not to plant the treated site that year, as by-products of chitin degradation can damage plants.

Prevent Multiplication of the Pest or Pathogen

Most of the pests and micro-organisms which attack garden crops are specialists, feeding on only one crop or on a narrow range of plants from the same family (Chapter 1). The fungal disease potato blight and the pest potato cyst nematode are both specialists, attacking potato and its close relative tomato. This specialization can be their Achilles heel, and gardeners can manipulate the conditions in the vegetable garden to favour the crops.

Earlier in this chapter, crop rotation was described as a method for making feeding and watering of vegetable crops easier. Its main benefit in agriculture, however, is to help reduce the size of populations of specialist pests and pathogens by natural biological control. This is particularly important for crops such as brassicas, carrots, parsnips, onions and potatoes.

Specialists have become adapted to their host plants, and can overcome the defence mechanisms these plants have evolved to keep attackers at bay (Chapter 6). This means that the specialist has little competition from other pests or pathogens which cannot overcome these host defences.

Crop rotation is particularly effective against specialist pests which live in the soil, such as PCN, and pathogens, like clubroot (*Plasmodiophora brassicae*) of brassicas. As 90 per cent of invertebrates spend at least part of their life cycle in the soil, rotation has great potential. Crop rotation works by depriving the specialist of the food plant it needs to feed and multiply.

In a four-year rotation, PCN in a particular bed will multiply in Year 1, under potatoes, but cannot multiply in Years 2–4 because the crops grown are not host plants for PCN. The PCN population will fall by approximately 30 per cent per year for each of those three years, as a result of natural biological control, including predation and parasitism.

By the start of Year 5, the PCN population in the soil to be planted with potato will be less than one-third the population at the end of Year 1. Say the PCN population in Year 1 was 100. A 30 per cent decrease in Year 2 would leave seventy, then a loss of 30 per cent of seventy in Year 3 would leave forty-nine, and so on. Thousands of years ago, the Incas used a seven-year rotation to control 'potato sickness' in their land, presumably PCN.

Related crops are kept in the same bed during crop rotation, because species in the same family can be food plants for the same specialist pest or pathogen. Carrot root fly, for example, attacks carrots, parsley and parsnips, while cabbage white butterfly caterpillars will feed on all brassicas, as well as ornamental members of this family such as nasturtium and wallflowers; these flowers are sometimes used to edge vegetable beds, so consider this before planting them around your cabbages.

Crop rotation does not work against generalist pests or pathogens such as slugs or snails, which have a wide range of food plants, and so will be able to feed on whatever plant is grown in the bed each year.

With air-borne pests, crop rotation is less effective, although growing related plants in the same bed can make pest management easier. Because the carrot root fly is a weak flier, putting a 50cm high wall of 1mm mesh around the bed containing

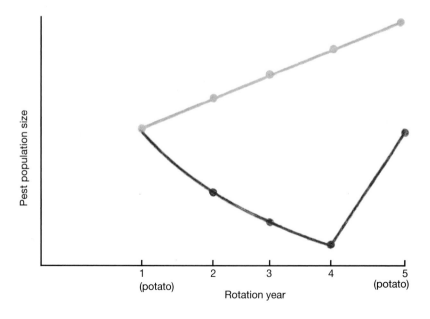

How a four-year crop rotation affects specialist (potato cyst nematode: red) and generalist pests (garden snail: blue).

carrots and parsnips, will protect both crops at the same time. The same trick will work to control cabbage root fly.

Even weeds must be considered when carrying out crop rotation. Pioneer weeds like hairy bittercress (*Cardamine hirsuta*), charlock (*Sinapis arvensis*) and shepherd's purse (*Capsella bursa-pastoris*) are members of the Brassicaceae and also are hosts for clubroot. These weeds must be rigorously eliminated from non-brassica beds in a crop rotation. Similarly, self-sown potatoes from the previous year's crop (volunteers), growing from tubers which were missed during harvesting, will allow PCN to multiply for a second successive year.

Although the principles of crop rotation are sound, this strategy is, to my mind, more appropriate for agricultural fields than for vegetable beds in a garden. Most of us have installed our vegetable beds next to one another, so the risk of pest or pathogen spread from bed to bed is very high, in the form of infected soil on tools, boots and so on. This would nullify any beneficial effects of crop rotation on pest and pathogen management.

The increasing emphasis on high crop diversity, with inter-cropping, companion planting, successional planting of different crops, and green manures, increases the risk of accidentally undermining crop rotation. If you intend to underplant sweetcorn with radishes or cut-and-come-again plants like pak choi, be careful to plant the sweetcorn in the brassicas bed, as radish and pak choi are members of the Brassicaceae. As for green manures, mustard (Brassicaceae) and N-fixers (Fabaceae) should be grown in the appropriate rotation bed, whereas rye (Poaceae) can be grown after any crop of the rotation.

Sweetcorn, spinach, lettuce and members of the cucumber family can be grown with any other of the vegetable groups because they belong to families different from all other vegetables, so will not suffer from the same specialized pests and diseases as the other crops. To avoid their own enemies, they need to be allocated a particular bed in the rotation.

Winter crops of hardy species have the advantage that, at that time of the year, there are very few pests and pathogens around. For example, not only are autumn-sown crops of broad beans

earlier cropping in the following year than spring-sown crops, they also suffer less from black bean aphids. It is still wise, however, to maintain winter crops in the appropriate beds for crop rotation, although most specialist pests become dormant in the winter.

Crop Rotation Plus!

Many of the worst soil-borne pests and pathogens, such as PCN, onion white rot and clubroot can survive, alive but dormant, for more than thirty years in the absence of their food plants. They do this by producing long-lived survival structures like the cysts of PCN and the black sclerotia of the onion white rot fungus. Furthermore, they have evolved to produce the short-lived infective stage only when the host plant is present, by recognizing the presence of chemicals in the soil which only the host plant produces.

Crop rotation will reduce the population but only slowly. The effectiveness of crop rotation can be increased by several strategies whereby the host chemicals are produced in the absence of the host, triggering appearance of the short-lived stage, but the pest or pathogen is not allowed to multiply.

Trap cropping involves planting the host crop in the infested bed, allowing it to grow for no more than four weeks, by which time it will have produced the chemicals to which the pest responds. The crop is then killed with a spray of the fast-acting formulation of glyphosate (Chapter 6). This herbicide will be translocated to the roots, killing them so that they cannot support the multiplication of the pest or pathogen. In the meantime, the pest or pathogen will have emerged from its resting body and will die of starvation if it cannot feed. The host crop should not be planted in that bed that year. With potato trap cropping, the PCN population can be reduced by 90 per cent in one year.

A related strategy involves incorporating kitchen or garden waste from the host plant into the infested soil. Suitable waste includes onion skins and leaves, brassica leaves and stems and potato peelings for onion white rot, clubroot or PCN, respectively, and these can be stored in the freezer until needed. They can then be incorporated into the infested vegetable bed in a year when crops

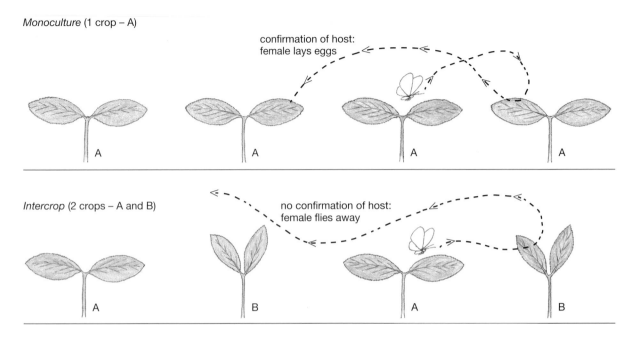

How inter-cropping can protect a crop against a specialist pest.

other than the host plant are to be grown in that bed. There they will be degraded to release their chemicals, triggering emergence of at least part of the pest or pathogen population, which will then starve to death in the absence of the food plant.

Inter-cropping

Inter-crops can help to control crop pests and pathogens. This can be a general effect, a bonus of the extra biodiversity in a vegetable garden, or can be specific, in which case it is sometimes known as companion planting.

Companion planting can encourage beneficials by providing food and shelter, so that biocontrol of specialist and generalist pests is increased. Inclusion of flowering plants designed to attract the adults of beneficials, such as single-flowered nasturtiums, phacelia, calendula to attract hoverflies, should increase the numbers of beneficials within the vegetable bed, with the added advantage of attracting pollinator insects. Planting strong-growing vegetable crops through a layer of the nitrogen-fixer white clover can provide shelter for ground dwelling beneficials such as ground

beetles and reduce infection of plants by pathogens which overwinter in the soil (Chapter 6). The clover can also act as a living mulch, reducing water losses (Chapter 4) and adding to soil nitrogen.

Research on the cabbage/cabbage root fly interaction suggests that inter-crops can also protect against specialist pests by masking the food plant from being identified by the pest by sight or smell. A pregnant adult cabbage root fly identifies the presence of the food plant for her caterpillars initially by detecting in the air the sulphury chemicals (the glucosinolates; Chapter 6) characteristic of brassicas. This causes the insect to stop or 'arrest'. The pest will then fly down and land on anything green. It 'tastes' the leaves, using sensors on its feet, to confirm whether the plant is actually its food plant, cabbage, and then flies a short distance and repeats the process. If the plants keep coming up positive for 'cabbage', the female pest will lay her eggs on one of the plants.

If, however, cabbage is companion planted with an unrelated crop of similar height, say, beetroot, the fly may land onto one cabbage plant and then one beetroot plant. This causes a lack of reinforcement that the pest has found its food plant, so the insect flies off. This may explain why vegetable beds containing several different crops can show less pest damage than do the corresponding monocultures.

Crop Maintenance

Blanching

Perennial crops like celery, cardoon, sea kale and rhubarb, where the part we eat is the leaf stalk or petiole, are often 'blanched' by growing them under a light-proof cover such as an upturned pot or bucket. This has several effects.

Blanching accelerates growth by allowing the stalks to grow under warmer-than-usual conditions, but the main consequence is as a result of the stalks growing in the dark. Without light, chlorophyll cannot be produced so the stalks have no green colour. Rhubarb stems retain anthocyanin which accounts for the pink stem colour; leaves of blanched stems are yellow because carotenoid levels are stable in the dark.

In unblanched stems, the stalks support themselves and the leaves by incorporating the strengthening chemical lignin into the cell walls, especially around the vascular bundles. This leads to the production of the characteristic 'strings' of collenchyma, with their unpleasant mouth-feel, in unblanched celery or rhubarb. In the dark, the plants synthesize less lignin, so that blanched stems are more tender, a desirable quality trait.

Removal of Unwanted Tissue

In vegetable crops, the aim is to develop enough leaves to trap all the available sunlight (to maximize plant biomass) and to direct the assimilates from the leaves to the economic sink, be it cobs in sweetcorn, pods in peas or tubers in potatoes (to maximize harvest index). But the plants will continue to produce non-economic sinks like leaves and stem tissue long after the canopy has closed (when no soil is visible) and all the light hitting the crop has been absorbed. These new leaves and other plant parts will be stealing assimilates away from the economic sink.

Climbing by pea plants is achieved with the aid of tendrils, which are modified leaves.

Flowers and fruits should be discouraged in plants where the economic sink is vegetative, like leaves, roots or tuber. Flowering in these plants is usually a response to a stress like drought (common in lettuce in late July) or root damage (avoid hoeing around shallow-rooted crops like lettuce and asparagus).

Potato cultivars produce pretty little white or purplish flowers resembling those of the closely related tomato around the time tubers start to swell. These are followed by round green fruits like unripe tomatoes. Though they are small, these fruits, by accumulating plant hormones, will attract significant amounts of assimilates away from the growing tubers, and so the flowers should be removed. Similarly, any flowers developing in rhubarb should be removed as soon as they are detected.

Interestingly, a majority of the leaves on a vegetable plant may be unnecessary. Leaves represent both the 'jaws' and the 'claws' of the plant, providing not only the food the plant needs (via photosynthesis) but also its ability to compete with neighbouring plants for resources such as light. As a consequence, most mature plants, particularly in the kitchen garden, have more leaves than they need simply for photosynthesis. Up to two-thirds of the leaves on a climbing runner bean plant, for example, are not needed and could be removed without reducing yield.

Removal of other non-economic sinks can also improve yield. In some climbing crops like peas, the tendrils are photosynthetic but can be removed to give higher yields. If you do this, the plants

need to be attached to their supports with rings. In bush (determinate) tomatoes, no more than five trusses per plant will ripen in southern Britain in an average summer, so excess young flower trusses should be removed.

In crops like peas, runner beans, ridge cucumbers, bush tomatoes and sweetcorn where the economic sink develops from an axillary bud, the leaves closest to the developing economic sink supply most of the assimilates to the economic sink. This is particularly true for those leaves in the axil of which the economic sink forms. The other leaves, particularly the oldest ones at the base of the plant, are of little use and can be removed to improve air circulation and to prevent disease developing on the more important leaves.

In indeterminate cultivars of these crops, it is advisable to remove the apical tip when the plants have reached the top of their support. Not only does this mean that fruits are at an accessible height, but assimilates are re-directed to the axillary buds where the economic sinks are located.

In Brussels sprouts, where the sprouts are enlarged vegetative axillary buds, the apical bud at the top of the stem develops into a loose cabbage-like rosette of leaves. If this rosette is removed when the sprouts are about the size of marbles, the assimilates from the outer leaves tend to move to the axillary buds, resulting in the sprouts developing more uniformly, so that the entire stalk can be harvested at one time. Otherwise, the apical bud can be harvested late in the season and eaten like a cabbage.

Harvest

Sweet-tasting vegetables like carrots, parsnips and sweetcorn need to be harvested at the appropriate stage of development.

With carrots, the central core of a mature carrot is the pith, while the surrounding non-core tissue is the phloem and xylem (Chapter 4). In carrots, the photosynthate is transported as glucose from the leaves to the root via the phloem, so that the outer tissue of the root is sweeter than the core. In young roots up to seven weeks old, the core is very small, but there is little sugar accumulated in the outer part. In older roots, glucose is

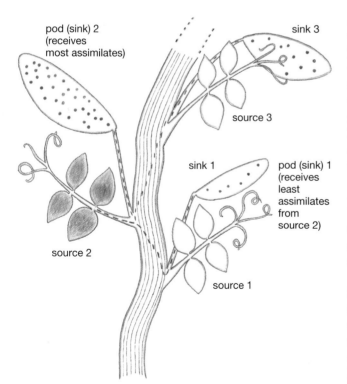

How sugars (indicated in red) move from source 2 to sinks in a pea plant.

transformed to the sugar sucrose, which is sweeter than glucose.

The sweetest carrots are the young mature ones. The diameter of the shoulder of a carrot is a good indication of the size of the core, and hence of whether harvesting should be carried out. Cultivars such as Amsterdam Forcing 2 and Sweetheart produce mature roots with no core, which are sweeter than conventional carrot cultivars.

Onion is a native of areas with hot dry summers, and the dormant bulb is adapted to re-commence growth when the rains start, as with many scrub forest geophytes (Chapter 8). If ripening onion bulbs in the field are dampened by rain for two to three days, this can dramatically shorten the dormancy period once the bulbs are stored, so all efforts must be made to harvest the roots quickly. That is part of the reason for turning over of the tops of the ripening onion plants, as this will accelerate ripening, but be careful not to damage the neck of the bulb as this encourages infection.

With cut-and-come again crops, like rocket, chard and salad leaves, it is important to harvest the topmost leaves to encourage sideshoot formation and to leave a large enough apical bud (at least four leaves) after removing the outer leaves for the table, to allow for re-growth.

The phenomenon of apical dominance (Chapter 5) has applications in the kitchen garden. In many crops, the economic sink is an enlarged apical bud, such as in chicory, Florence fennel, cabbage and Savoy cabbage. With these crops, if a stalk of at least 5cm is left on the plant after harvesting, this will contain axillary buds which will form sideshoots to provide a smaller but welcome late second harvest.

THE FRUIT GARDEN

FRUIT DEVELOPMENT

Fruits start to develop in response to fertilization, with pollen landing on the stigma, germinating and then fusing with the ovule to start seed development.

Fertilization, primarily seed development but also pollination and even unsuccessful pollination in some cases, triggers fruit growth by releasing plant hormones, though the developing seeds are the principal sources of hormones in fruit formation. The hormones involved in fruit development are mainly auxins and gibberellins.

Most fruits develop from the ovary of the flower, which increases dramatically in size as a result of cell expansion rather than the production of new cells. Continued fruit development usually depends on the presence of developing seeds. The development, for example, of small tomato fruits is usually because there are few seeds. Though tomato is self-pollinated (*see* Chapter 7), it still needs visits from bumblebees to vibrate the flowers, releasing pollen. The number of seeds per fruit depends on the number of ovules within each flower, ranging from one seed (e.g. cherry) to eight million (e.g. some orchids) per flower.

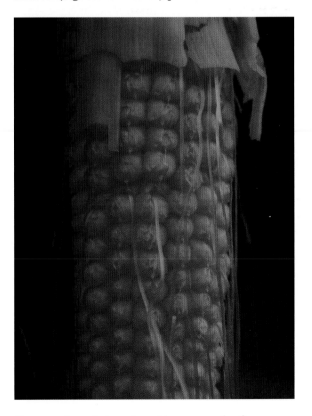

Corn-on-the-cob (sweetcorn) is an example of an aggregate fruit, where each 'kernel' is a fruit. The long threads (silks) are the stigma/style attached to an ovary; each ovary will develop into a fruit after fertilization.

Pineapple is a multiple fruit: there are several flowers, each of which produces a fruit, which merge together to form the pineapple.

Botanically speaking, there are several classes of fruit type, depending on the flower organs which make up the fruit and the number of carpels (female sex organs) which make up each fruit. A berry is a swollen ovary derived from a single carpel, has a thin skin and a soft flesh when mature, and usually contains more than one seed. Tomatoes, grapes, bell peppers, aubergines, bananas and avocados are all berries, while neither strawberries nor raspberries, whose name suggest otherwise, are actually berries. The largest berry in commerce is the papaya, weighing up to 8kg apiece.

Other types of simple fruits include drupes and pomes. A drupe has a single hard seed and develops from flowers with a superior ovary containing a single ovule, and includes stone fruits like peaches, cherries and olives, as well as the less obvious coconut and almond. In pomes, such as apples and pears, the core represents the ovary of the flower, while the remainder of the fruit is an enlarged receptacle, the part of the flower between the ovary and the flower stalk or peduncle (*see* page 15).

The blackberry or raspberry flower contains a cluster of individual carpels, each of which, when pollinated, will form an individual fruitlet. These miniature fruits combine to form an aggregate fruit. The strawberry is another example of an aggregate fruit. In the strawberry, the individual fruitlets are actually what look to be the seeds (achenes) on the outside of the red fruit. These achenes develop from individual carpels attached to a swollen receptacle (Chapter 1).

With the strawberry fruit, it is hormones from the developing achenes which trigger swelling of the receptacle. If you remove achenes from part of the developing fruit, that area will fail to swell, so removing a band of achenes from the central part of the fruit, for example, will produce a strawberry with an hour-glass figure.

Another example of an aggregate fruit is sweetcorn. The silks on the female flower are the carpels. Pollination of each carpel produces a kernel which is a fruitlet, and the corn-on-the-cob is an aggregate of kernels.

Finally, pineapple is a multiple fruit. Several flowers produce fruits which fuse together to form a single (if multiple) fruit.

Seedless Fruits

In most cases, seed formation is a pre-requisite for fruit development, the growing seeds contributing to the hormone increase which triggers swelling of the young fruit. Without adequate seeds as the result of pollination, the developing fruit will die and fall off the plant.

Seedless forms of grapes, watermelon, and cucumber are commonly found in supermarkets, while commercial cultivars of banana and pineapple are always seedless. Seedless fruits are desirable for several reasons. Apart from being more pleasant to eat, they last longer when stored because seeds in a fruit trigger senescence, and they are also less prone to strange shapes.

Because seeds control fruit growth, irregular distribution of seeds within a fruit can stimulate only part of the fruit to swell, producing misshapen fruits in crops like tomato and cucumber. Seedless fruit cultivars are also more likely to produce good crops under less-than-ideal growing conditions as they are not affected by drought, absence of pollinators or extremes of temperature which can affect pollination in normal seeded cultivars.

Seedless fruited cultivars can be produced by one of two mechanisms, parthenocarpy or stenospermocarpy. Parthenocarpic fruits, such as glasshouse cucumbers, are formed without pollination and fertilization; indeed, pollinators need to be excluded from these plants as pollination will result in misshapen cucumbers with seeds.

In sternospermocarpy, as occurs in seedless triploid watermelons, bananas and apple cultivars, both pollination and fertilization occur but the embryos in the developing seeds die so that small empty ovules arise instead of seeds.

CHOICE OF CULTIVAR

Pollinators

Most fruit trees grown in gardens are cross-pollinated and will only produce fruits if fertilized by pollen from a particular type of parent plant. This pre-requisite is the main reason mature fruit trees may fail to produce fruit.

Kiwi fruit plants are naturally dioecious, with separate male and female plants, but self-fertile cultivars such as 'Oriental Delight' and 'Jenny' are available. Fruit trees, such as apple, cherry, plum and pear, exhibit self-incompatibility (Chapter 7). Here, the pollen grains from the anthers in a flower cannot germinate on the stigma of the same flower, or of different flowers on the same plant.

Most of the older cultivars are self-incompatible, including apple 'Cox's Orange Pippin' and pear 'Doyenne du Comice'. To get fruit from a self-incompatible apple, plum, pear or cherry cultivar, you need to plant a second, pollinator cultivar, selected so that the two cultivars are cross-compatible. In this way, each cultivar will act as pollinator for the other one.

The two cultivars need also to flower at the same time, because some fruit trees, like pear 'Doyenne du Comice', have a pollination period as short as two days. The Royal Horticultural Society produces lists, categorizing apple (or pear etc) cultivars according to their ability to pollinate one another and to flower at the same time. Grafted trees (family trees) with branches of two cross-compatible cultivars can also be bought so that each pollinates the other.

In the self-incompatibility mechanism that operates in fruits such as apples, pears and cherries, one gene (S) with multiple different forms or alleles (such as S_1, S_2, etc.) controls self-incompatibility. If the tree is diploid (Chapter 7), then all the plant tissues, including those in the flower, will have two copies of each gene.

If apple cultivar A is heterozygous (Chapter 7) and has one copy of the S_1 allele and one of the S_2, all its diploid cells, including those of the flower such as the stigma, will have the genotype S_1S_2. Pollen has only one copy of each gene (Chapter 7), so half of the pollen from the S_1S_2 flower will contain S_1 and half will contain S_2. If the S allele in the pollen is the same as one of those in the stigma, then no fertilization will take place: self-incompatibility.

Apple cultivar B is used as the pollinator. Again, it is heterozygous, being a cross-pollinated plant, with the genotype S_3S_4. It will not be able to fertilize itself because it is self-incompatible, but the S_3 (or S_4) pollen from plant B will pollinate cultivar A, which in turn will produce S_2 or S pollen to fertilize cultivar B. As a result, these two cultivars are said to be cross-compatible.

Some apple varieties like 'Bramley's Seedling', 'Jonagold' and 'Blenheim Orange' are seedless because they are triploid, 3x, with three copies of

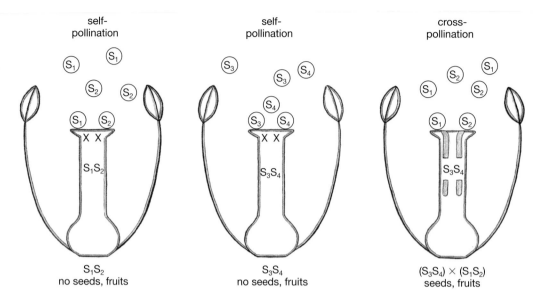

self-pollination	self-pollination	cross-pollination
S_1S_2 no seeds, fruits	S_3S_4 no seeds, fruits	$(S_3S_4) \times (S_1S_2)$ seeds, fruits

How self-incompatibility works in apple flowers.

each chromosome rather than the more usual two copies. Being sterile, these cultivars cannot act as pollinators, so you need to provide two pollinators: one for 'Bramley's Seedling' and one for the pollinator. So, you will need to plant a total of three apple cultivars if one is seedless.

Many modern fruit cultivars are described as being self-compatible or self-fertile. Such cultivars are available for apples ('Greensleeves', 'Falstaff'), pears ('Concorde'), sweet cherry ('Cherokee', 'Sweetheart') plum ('Victoria', 'Czar') and Northern highbush blueberry. This switch from self-incompatible to self-compatible can happen with polyploid cultivars. Though self-compatible cultivars will produce fruit without a pollinator cultivar, more fruit will always be produced if a cross-compatible cultivar is planted alongside.

Flowering Date

Pome fruits, like apples and pears, which contain a core with several seeds, and drupe fruits, such as cherries, nectarines and peaches, with one stone per fruit, flower in spring and have certain temperature requirements for successful fruiting.

Before a tree can flower, it needs to break dormancy and undergo vernalization (Chapter 8)

after exposure to a period of low temperatures. This adaptation ensures that the tree does not produce frost-sensitive flowers until after the risk of cold snaps has receded. Frost kill of the flowers would mean that no fruits would be produced that year.

Cultivars are classified according to the length of the vernalization period (measured in day-degrees) needed to allow flowering, so it is important to pick a cultivar suitable for your local conditions. An early flowering cultivar will have a short vernalization period. Too short a vernalization requirement, as happens with many peach cultivars, and the tree may flower during a frost period. Too long, and a mild winter may fail to provide vernalization, so that the tree does not flower.

Rootstocks

The rootstock onto which top and stone fruit cultivars are grafted will determine the size of the tree (Chapter 3). Apple trees for the smaller garden are usually grafted onto semi-dwarfing (M25 or MM106) or dwarfing rootstocks (M9 or M27) so that the mature tree is small enough to fit into a modern garden and fruit picking can be carried out with ease.

The smaller root system of these trees means, however, that precautions need to be taken to overcome short-comings with regard to poor anchoring (by staking) or poor water and nutrient uptake (by mulching and fertilizing).

A beneficial side-effect of grafting onto a dwarfing or semi-dwarfing rootstock is that the plant will flower several years earlier than the scion parent would on its own roots, because the shoot tissues in the grafted plant are a weaker sink, allowing the flower buds to compete better for assimilates (Chapter 4). It would also flower (and fruit) up to ten years earlier than would a seed–propagated apple because of the age of the scion wood.

Eating Quality

Different cultivars of fruit trees like apple or cherry produce fruits for different purposes, principally dessert (for eating raw) and culinary (for cooking).

With apples, fruits of some cultivars store well into the winter, so careful choice of cultivars can allow you to have fruits ready all year round. Dessert apples, for example, can be eaten between August and early April by mixing cultivars which are early, such as 'Discovery' and late fruiting, like 'Blenheim Orange', with those which are good storers, such as 'Cox' and sterile cultivars such as 'Jonagold', which store particularly well. Early ripening cultivars can be eaten straight from the tree, but the flavour of many, like 'Ellison's Orange', improves with storage.

FRUIT TREE MAINTENANCE

Pest Management

With tall perennials like fruit trees, conventional pest control methods can be difficult to operate, but a knowledge of the pest can help the gardener manage the problem.

Social insects such as aphids communicate with one another via volatile chemicals known as pheromones. Some pheromones warn of danger, others inform of food sources, while still more (sex pheromones) attract males to females. Sex pheromones are used in the management of specific pests, such as the codling moth of apples and

the plum moth. Caterpillars of the codling moth burrow into the young fruits, spoiling their appearance and reducing their storage time.

Pheromone traps, developed to monitor the numbers of moths in a commercial orchard to reduce the number of pesticide sprays, are now available to gardeners. Codling moth pheromone traps are small roofed open-ended boxes containing a sticky base and releasing the appropriate female sex pheromone, and can be bought from garden centres. They are hung in an apple tree after petal fall. The male moths are attracted to the trap, instead of the females, by the pheromones and die on the sticky base. This can greatly reduce the number of eggs laid on the tree.

In the early stages of establishing fruit trees, weed control is important, with the main problem being grass allowed to grow on the soil over the roots. Grass roots, both living and dead, produce allelochemicals which can inhibit the growth of other plants, so a circle approximately 1m across around the tree trunk should be kept grass-free for the first three or four years, and longer for trees on semi-dwarfing or dwarfing rootstocks.

Pruning and Training

For fruit trees, pruning and/or training is important to maximize the number of flowering shoots (Chapter 5). Once the flowers form you can manipulate the number and size of fruits which will form by thinning out the fruit bunches.

Both training and pruning (Chapter 5) of fruit trees involve manipulation of developing buds, controlling their conversion from vegetative buds, producing stems and leaves, to flower buds, producing flowers and fruits. This natural change is controlled by plant hormones (Chapter 5), but the production of these, in turn, can be influenced by environmental factors such as winter cold and daylength, nutrition and stresses. Factors such as high nitrogen levels which encourage vegetative growth do so at the expense of flower buds. Stresses like drought, on other hand, reduce vegetative growth but promote flower buds.

In order to produce good crops of high-quality fruit each year, it is important to achieve a balance between vegetative and reproductive growth.

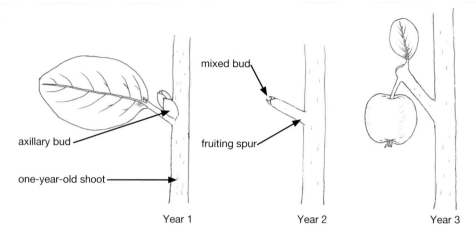

Development of fruiting buds in apple.

Although there is competition between the vegetative and reproductive sinks for assimilates, a large enough vegetative structure must be encouraged to provide enough assimilates (via photosynthesis) to initiate and fill the fruits.

In the early years of the life of a fruit tree, pruning is designed to encourage vegetative growth at the expense of reproductive development, in order to optimize the size and arrangement of the branches on which fruit will eventually develop. This is equally true of standard fruit trees and of trained fruit trees, such as cordons, espaliers and stepovers, for the average garden.

When the tree has reached the desired size and shape, steps can then be taken to control the development of buds into vegetative or reproductive buds. Flower buds are present by October of the year before flowering. Drupe fruit trees, e.g. cherries, produce separate vegetative and flower buds, while pome fruit trees, e.g. apples, produce vegetative and mixed buds, the latter containing both flower and vegetative buds.

Flowers in apples and pears develop from buds on short sideshoots known as spurs, which grow from axillary buds on a one-year-old shoot. In Year 2 a spur is formed with an apical mixed bud, which will produce flowers and fruit in Year 3. Apple and pear trees are pruned to restrict the number of axillary buds which produce spurs. The one-year-old wood is pruned to about five or six axillary buds.

The dominance of the apical bud is due to its elevated position on the shoot (Chapter 5). Training a shoot to the horizontal reduces apical dominance, so that sideshoots start to develop, allowing flowers and fruits to develop along the length of the stem (Chapter 5) and thus facilitating harvest.

Fruit trees for the small modern garden are frequently trained into shapes where individual stems are at an angle, such as fan (various angles) or cordon (45°), or horizontal, like espalier or stepover cordons. These shapes reduce apical dominance and stimulate axillary growth, leading to fruiting spurs. The number of spurs can then be increased by selective pruning.

In some circumstances with trained fruit trees, you may wish to get only one particular bud to grow out but do not want to remove the corresponding apical bud. Because assimilates, including hormones, move up and down the plant via the phloem, a block in the phloem will interrupt hormone distribution and can encourage or prevent the outgrowth of an axillary bud.

The phloem can be blocked by removing a small area of bark. The phloem lies just beneath the bark (Chapter 4) and will be removed with it. Do not remove the bark all around the stem as this will prevent assimilate movement and will kill the stem, a process known as girdling. By removing the bark above the bud in question (notching), auxin movement to this bud is interrupted, but not

Effects of notching or
nicking on bud growth.

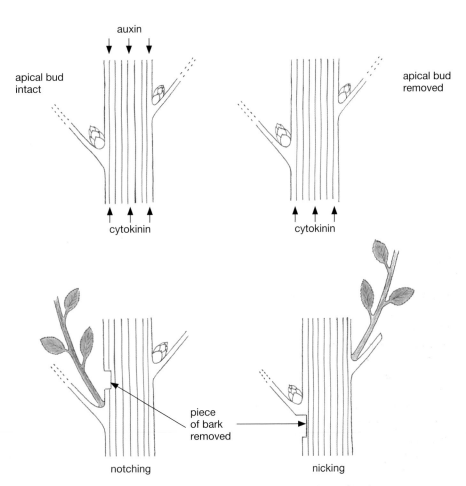

cytokinin flow from the roots to the bud. Result: outgrowth of the bud.

The opposite involves removal of the bark below the bud (nicking). Here, cytokinin but not auxin supply is interrupted to the bud, which will fail to grow out even under circumstances where it would be expected to do so, as in fan-trained apple trees.

Competition between developing fruit within a truss on an apple tree will result in the youngest apple(s), the weakest sinks with the lowest hormone content, attracting the fewest assimilates and falling off the tree in early summer (the June drop). This is yet another phenomenon the plant controls via hormones. The remaining fruits will increase in size up to maturity. If you want larger fruit, you will need to remove another one or two fruits per truss when they are immature, so that the assimilates go to fewer fruits.

With crops like plums, which produce fruits singly, thin the fruits to approximately 8cm apart so that the reduced number will grow to full size. With cluster fruits like dessert grapes, to increase the size of individual berries, remove half the bunches and remove half the developing berries on each of the remaining bunches.

STORING AND USING PRODUCE

STORAGE

In crops harvested as immature fruits, like peas and sweetcorn kernels, sucrose accumulates before it is transformed to starch as the fruit matures. Immature fruits like peas are growing and metabolizing rapidly and will react to being harvested by trying to convert the sucrose into starch. To get the sweetest flavour, it follows that it is best to eat the produce of these crops as soon as possible, ideally straight away, or to freeze them, to prevent the sucrose-to-starch conversion.

Blanching vegetables, by brief immersion in boiling water prior to storage (not to be confused with blanching in the dark – *see* page 229), prevents the sugar-to-starch conversion by killing the enzymes involved. With fruits, e.g. tomato, cherry and apple, the opposite situation happens. As the fruit ripens, the sugar levels increase to attract an animal which will eat the fruit and disperse the seeds (Chapter 1).

Fruits are divided into two groups on the basis of how they ripen: climacteric and non-climacteric. Climacteric fruits – such as apples, pears, tomatoes, plums, bananas, peaches, melon and kiwi fruits – produce a hormone, the gas ethylene, as they ripen. In turn, ethylene naturally accelerates ripening in climacteric fruits. As a result, climacteric fruits can be picked unripe and then allowed to ripen at room temperature.

Some imported climacteric fruits such as apples, kiwis, plums, tomatoes, mango and avocado are harvested before they are ripe for ease of transport, and can be ripened by storage at room temperature, when more sugars form. An understanding of the role of ethylene in fruit ripening enables the domestic gardener to ripen fruit which has had to be picked when immature at the end of the season.

The climacteric fruit to be ripened should be placed in a tied paper bag with a rich source of ethylene, such as a ripe apple, banana or kiwi fruit. Ethylene production is increased if the fruit producing the ethylene is damaged. To maximize flavour, green tomatoes need to be at the mature green stage when picked; any younger and the fruits will turn red but have less flavour. Pears improve on storage if picked fully mature but not ripe.

Non-climacteric fruits, like raspberries, strawberries and cherries, must be harvested ripe and will not benefit from further storage. As a result, they have a short shelf-life.

In crops where the economic sinks are vegetative and are harvested when mature in autumn, such as Brussels sprouts and many root crops, these organs are near-dormant and can be left in the garden for long periods, up to the spring.

In many mature vegetable crops, reserves of starch can be converted into sugars if the sinks are exposed to frost. Studies indicate, however, that soil temperatures down to 1°C, but not freezing, stimulate sugar build-up in parsnips, up to a concentration of 45% sugar, which is higher than that in sugarbeet. These temperatures would be achieved during the winter under snow cover. The water-soluble sugars formed may act as an antifreeze to help tissue prevent freezing damage. Not only is *in situ* storage a convenient way of storing produce over the winter, the sweetening is also a sought-after improvement in crops like parsnips, turnips, celeriac, salsify, cabbages, leeks, Brussels sprouts, Jerusalem artichoke and kale.

Care should be taken, however, with *in situ* storage of some other vegetables over winter. With non-root crops like cabbages stored into spring in this way, the winter weather provides the plants with the vernalization stimulus to trigger flowering in springtime. With root crops like carrots and beets, winter storage in the ground will stimulate re-growth of the foliage. Production of either leaves or flowers will start to use up the food reserves the gardener wants to eat.

Harvested plant organs, particularly fruits, are still alive, albeit severed from their life-support system. A green pepper, for example, left at room temperature in the light will continue to ripen, taking on shades of yellow and red. As a result, fruits, for example, can suffer from stress if not treated properly.

In the refrigerator ripe fruit and roots from temperate climates, such as apples and carrots, will survive for up to one month. On the other hand, ripe fruits from sub-tropical and tropical climates will be subjected to chilling stress if stored at temperatures below 10°C, such as in a domestic refrigerator (at 2–4°C). The door is the warmest location in a fridge (at approximately 6–8°C), while the back is the coldest part (1–2°C); the crisper is the most humid section.

The refrigerator is too cold for ripe fruits of

pineapple, watermelon, honeydew melon, mango, papaya and cucumber, which should all be stored at temperatures above 10°C, and bananas should be stored at temperatures greater than 14°C. Stored in the fridge, chilling damage causes banana skins to quickly blacken, although the fruit inside will still be acceptable for eating. Though from a tropical region, tomato is native to high-altitude sites which may explain its apparent ability to withstand storage at low temperatures. On the other hand, refrigeration of tomatoes affects flavour badly.

Fruits which can be safely stored in a refrigerator include apples, grapes, kiwi and cantaloupe melon, while lettuce and other leafy vegetables can also be refrigerated as long as humidity is kept high.

Another concern with storing fruit in a domestic refrigerator is that ethylene from ripening fruits can accumulate in the sealed refrigerator, causing damage in vegetables stored in the same fridge, such as bitterness in carrots, brown spots on lettuce, yellowing of broccoli and sprouting of potatoes.

The refrigerator is not a place for garlic and onions, both geophytes from the scrub forest. Dormancy of the storage organs in both species is lifted by low temperature, so storage in the refrigerator can be counter-productive as it can trigger sprouting. This is particularly true for home-grown produce.

COOKING WITH GARDEN PRODUCE

Pigments are often affected badly by cooking. They can leach out of the plant tissue and/or they can be degraded or otherwise damaged by aspects of the cooking process.

Most fruits are coloured with anthocyanins, though sweet peppers and tomatoes contain carotenoid pigments. Purple- or red-coloured (cyanic) forms exist of many vegetables that are usually white or green, including broccoli, onions, cauliflower, cabbage and runner beans.

A proportion of the water-soluble pigments such as anthocyanins (in purple French or runner beans, potatoes and asparagus) and betalains (in beetroot) is released into the cooking water as a result of heat damage to the plant cells during

cooking and lost. In some crops, the cooked tissue retains its colour, such as with red cabbage, aubergine, purple cauliflower, red Brussels sprouts, purple asparagus, rhubarb and red onion, while in others, including purple French beans, radicchio, and purple sprouting broccoli, the cooked plant tissue is dark green.

Loss of water-soluble pigments is greatest following boiling, whereas greater colour retention can occur following cooking methods which involve little or no water, such as microwaving, roasting, steaming or stir-frying. Roasting young beetroots or boiling coloured-flesh potatoes, such as 'Highland Burgundy Red' and 'Salad Blue', whole and unpeeled helps to retain the pigmentation.

In cyanic vegetables like red cabbage and red onions, colour is retained after cooking, but it may not be the one you started with. This is because the colour of anthocyanins is greatly affected by pH (the amount of acidity and alkalinity) and the presence of metals (Chapter 8). Generally, the anthocyanins in most vegetables are red under acid conditions, light violet at neutral pH, and blue or green-yellow under alkaline conditions. As a consequence, the colour of plant tissues pigmented by anthocyanins can change during cooking as alkaline conditions tend to arise.

Blackcurrants and blueberries turn green when baked into scones and muffins as a result of the effect of the alkaline chemical baking soda. Red cabbage turns blue when cooked in water, because the anthocyanin loses hydrogen (H^+) ions at high pH. This explains why red cabbage is often cooked with acidic cooking apples or vinegar, to retain the purplish-red colour. Cooking with metal utensils can also modify the colour of anthocyanins to green or grey shades, because the H^+ ions are replaced by metal ions like Al^{2+}, as seen earlier with hydrangea flowers (Chapter 8).

The water-insoluble plant chemicals, the chlorophylls and carotenoids, are bound to the cell membranes so are all retained to a large extent in plant tissues following cooking, As a result, carrots and yellow French beans (beta-carotene, lutein), green broccoli (chlorophylls), saffron (crocetin), and tomatoes and red peppers (lycopene) retain their familiar colour on cooking. Carrots become more yellowish and red peppers more orangeish when cooked for too long or at too-high temperatures (as in pressure cooking), as a result of changes in the molecular structure of the pigment.

Over-cooking of green vegetables used to be *de rigeur*, especially in school dinners, where vegetables were regarded as the enemy, to be subdued at all costs. The familiar greyish-green of overcooked runner beans and other green vegetables is due to the replacement of the magnesium ion in the centre of the chlorophyll molecule by a hydrogen ion, with the green chlorophylls being converted into olive-green phaeophytin. This occurs as a result of heat in an acid environment. Cooking the vegetables in a large volume of water will reduce the concentration of acidic components which leach out of the tissues.

If your tap water is naturally acidic, it will often have higher than usual levels of soluble metals such as zinc, copper or aluminium, because acid conditions increase the solubility of metals (Chapter 4). Under these conditions you may not suffer from 'grey greens' because the magnesium atom will be replaced by a metal ion rather than a hydrogen ion, so that the vegetables remain bright green in colour. Similarly, if your water is hard (alkaline), then the magnesium may not be stripped from the chlorophyll molecule as there will be magnesium ions in the cooking water.

Health Benefits of Garden Produce

Many of the pigments found in plants are known as nutraceuticals when included in our diet, because they have health-supporting properties over and above their nutritional value.

Anthocyanins are the active components in many so-called superfoods such as blueberries, acai berries, blackcurrants and pomegranates, which protect us from damage associated with ageing or pollution. Anthocyanins act as anti-oxidants in both plants and humans, quenching the reactive oxygen species generated during stress, so that the cells are not damaged.

Several carotenoids (including astaxanthin, lycopene, lutein and beta-carotene) also act as anti-oxidants. Lycopene from tomatoes is reported to reduce the risk of several cancers, while lutein and beta-carotene have also been implicated in treatments for macular degeneration, an age-related condition affecting eyesight.

Because the chlorophylls mask the presence of carotenoids in green leaves, it is not possible to identify directly plants which are rich sources of the carotenoids lutein and beta-carotene. There is a fairly constant carotenoid to chlorophyll ratio (approximately 1:4) in green tissues, to ensure that photosynthesis takes place efficiently. As a consequence, dark green leaves containing lots of chlorophyll, such as kale and York cabbage (particularly the darker outer leaves), will be rich sources of beta-carotene and lutein. Interestingly, free-range chickens eat green plants, with the plant carotenoids imparting the strong orange-yellow colour to the yolks of the eggs they lay.

One thing to be aware of, however, is that the presence *per se* in plants of any of these nutraceuticals is not enough to prove that eating that plant material will be beneficial to your health. The key word here is bioavailability, the ability of the chemical to be taken up through our gut and into our bloodstream.

Water-soluble nutraceuticals such as anthocyanins generally have a high bioavailability, but fat-soluble chemicals, such as carotenoids, must be packaged by the body into special units before they can be taken up effectively. This packaging can vary between sources. Lycopene, for example, has no bioavailability from raw tomatoes or red peppers, so has no value to us but is moderately bioavailable from raw watermelon or pink grapefruits. To benefit from the lycopene content of tomatoes, you should eat them with some plant oils, such as olive oil but not sunflower oil (to help with dissolving the fat-soluble lycopene), cook them or slice them very finely. Any of these steps will increase the bioavailability of this powerful anti-oxidant.

Glossary

Abscission Deliberate separation of an organ, such as leaves, flowers or fruits, from the plant. An active process, in which specialized layers of cells (abscission layers) are produced to aid abscission and prevent water loss through the site of abscission, controlled in part by the plant hormone abscisic acid.

Acid soil Soil with a pH less than 7, usually pH 5.5–6.5, low in calcium ions, high availability of micronutrients such as aluminium. Ericaceous plants are mostly adapted to acid soils. Soils less than pH 5.0 are low in soil bacteria, so are nitrogen poor.

Adventitious buds Buds which form shoots or roots from tissues which do not usually form these organs, such as adventitious roots on climbing stems of ivy, and on stem nodes of maize. Can be exploited in vegetative propagation, such as roots from stem cuttings, shoots and roots from leaf cuttings.

Alkaline soils Opposite to acid soils. Soil with a pH greater than 7. Usually pH 7.5–8.5. High in calcium ions. Generally free-draining soils. Include chalk soils. Will cause lime-induced chlorosis in ericaceous plants.

Allele Different forms of the same gene, resulting in different forms of the same character, such as blue- or white-flowered bluebells.

Alpines Plants adapted to high-altitude (above the tree-line) or high-latitude conditions. Spend winter at above-freezing, reasonably dry conditions under snow cover. Characterized by small stature but large flowers, with silvery or white leaf components to protect from UV.

Anions Negatively charged ions, such as Cl⁻ (chloride anion) and NO_3^- (nitrate anion). Combine with cations.

Annual Plants which germinate, set seed and die within one year. Produce moderate numbers of small seeds which need light to germinate. Subdivided into winter annuals, summer annuals and pioneers, the first plants to colonize a cleared site (*see* **succession**). Garden annuals are largely natives of scrub forest habitats.

Anthocyanins A group of water-soluble pigments present in the vacuole of cells, primarily of the epidermis. Present in petals (cornflower, poppy), fruit tissue (raspberry, blackberry), as well as some autumn leaves (*Parrotia*). Provide most of the colours in the red-to-blue colour spectrum.

Anti-oxidants Natural organic plant chemicals produced to control the level of reactive oxygen species in plants such as peroxide and hydroxyl. Include anthocyanins and carotenoids. Has same function in human diet.

Apical dominance Ability of apical growth bud to prevent outgrowth of axillary growth buds on the same stem. Caused by a high auxin:cytokinin ratio.

Assimilates Natural organic chemicals made as a result of photosynthesis and other synthesis pathways. Include carbohydrates and proteins, as well as defence and pigment chemicals. Transported around the plant in the phloem.

Augmentative biocontrol Biological control achieved by releasing mass-reared native beneficial organisms, such as beneficial nematodes, to control native pests.

Auxins Natural plant hormones which control plant growth (by affecting cell expansion) and apical dominance. Produced in shoot apical growth buds. Synthetic auxins are used in rooting powders and selective weedkillers.

Beneficial The natural enemy of a pest species, which can be exploited to effect biological control, e.g. hoverfly larvae as a natural enemy of aphids (greenfly).

Biennial A plant which lives for two years before flowering and dying, such as the wild foxglove, *Digitalis purpurea*. At the end of the first year, the plant will have built up a store of food reserves. Exposure to low temperatures (meant to signify passing through winter: vernalization) means that the plant will mobilize its food reserves in Year 2, flower, set seed and die. Many vegetable crops are biennials grown as annuals where we harvest the food reserves, as with carrots, cabbages and parsnips.

Binomial So-called 'Latin name' for plants (and all living organisms), presented in italics. System developed by Linnaeus. Two names, comprising of genus (e.g. *Primula*) and species (e.g. *vulgaris*), such as *Primula vulgaris* (common primrose). Additional names include subspecies, form, variety and cultivar.

Biological control Using one living organism to control another, particularly to control invertebrate pests. Often condensed to 'biocontrol'. Can provide short-term (augmentative biocontrol) or long-term (habitat management) management of pest populations, but cannot eliminate the pest.

Biomass The total weight of living tissue. In crop physiology, economic yield = total crop biomass × harvest index.

Biome Geographically separate regions with similar seasonal distribution of precipitation and temperature and similar types of plants: tundra, taiga, temperate deciduous woodland, temperate grassland, scrub forest, tropical grassland, tropical rainforest, desert. Examples of the same biome, with similar types of plants, are found at the same latitude.

Blanching (1) Growing crop plant where the economic sink is leaf stalk (petiole) e.g. celery or rhubarb, in the dark to produce longer stalks, earlier and with fewer collenchyma strings; (2). Short-term immersion of vegetables in boiling water to kill enzymes which convert sugars to starch.

Bracts Large modified, often coloured, leaves surrounding flowers to attract pollinators. Examples include *Cornus kousa*, *Euphorbia* spp. and *Davidia involucrata*.

Bulb An underground storage organ consisting of a compressed stem with food reserves and growth buds which will develop into the next year's flowers, leaves and stems, e.g. tulip or daffodil, surrounded by fleshy leaves and dry scale leaves. Produced by geophytes.

C3 photosynthesis Adapted to temperate conditions (moderate light, temperature, adequate moisture). Reaches maximum speed at about one-third full sunlight. Synonymous with 'cool-season' in grasses. 95+ per cent of plants use this type of photosynthesis.

C4 photosynthesis Adapted to sites with low water availability, high light, temperature, such as maize (sweetcorn). More efficient than C3, so can close stomata, saving water. Continues to increase at light levels above full sunlight. Synonymous with 'warm-season' in grasses; needs higher temperature for germination than C3 grasses.

Canopy trees In woodlands, the tallest, most competitive plants.

Carbohydrate One of the primary metabolites (along with proteins and lipids). Includes sugars like glucose and sucrose, cellulose (providing strength to plant cell wall) and starch. First product of photosynthesis (glucose).

Carotenoid A group of yellow-to-orange-to-red fat-soluble pigments which give colour to roots (carrots), tubers (sweet potatoes), fruits (tomato, mango), flowers (*Adonis* spp.) and autumn leaves of some trees (ash, tulip tree). Present in the plastids in the parenchyma, below the epidermis, of leaves (chloroplasts) and fruits, flowers and roots (chromoplasts). Includes beta-carotene (in carrots), lutein (in sweetcorn) and lycopene (tomato). In the leaves, carotenoids assist chlorophylls to absorb light of different wavelengths.

Carpel The female sex organ of flowers, consisting of the stigma (where the pollen lands and germinates), the style and the ovary, containing the ovules and eggs. Known as the pistil in the US.

Cations Positively charged ions, such as Na^+ (sodium cation) and Ca^{2+} (calcium cation). Combine with anions.

Cell   The basic building unit of plants. Differs from an animal cell in having a cell wall, plastids and a vacuole.

Cellulose   The main strengthening chemical of cell walls. A carbohydrate, the most prevalent chemical in the natural world. Combines with lignin in wood to form lignocellulose.

Chitin   The insect equivalent of cellulose. A carbohydrate, very similar in structure to cellulose, providing the outside skeleton (exoskeleton) of invertebrates.

Chitting   Incubation of non-dormant potato tubers under bright cool conditions to induce sprout formation, and the early production of tubers. Causes physiological ageing of the potato plant.

Chlorophyll   Two fat-soluble green-coloured plant pigments (chlorophyll a and chlorophyll b) which are involved in trapping light energy in photosynthesis. Present in chloroplasts in all bar epidermal tissues in the leaves. Contains one atom of magnesium per molecule of chlorophyll.

Chloroplast   A form of plastid involved in photosynthesis in green-coloured organs such as leaves, stems and pea pods. Up to 100 chloroplasts per leaf cell. Contain their own DNA, chromosome and genes as a result of evolution from a cyanobacterium.

Chlorosis   Yellowing of leaf tissue, usually as a result of a nutrient deficiency, such as magnesium or iron, due to reduced chlorophyll synthesis. Some species, particularly ericaceous species, exhibit lime-induced chlorosis when grown on alkaline soils.

Chromosome   The genes, the factors controlling inherited traits, are carried in the nucleus of each plant cell on chromosomes. Smaller numbers of genes are also found on chromosome in chloroplasts or mitochondria. Each gene has a fixed location on a particular chromosome. Each chromosome is a piece of DNA (linear in nuclear chromosomes, circular in chloroplast or mitochondrial chromosomes).

Clay   The smallest of the three inorganic components of soil (clay, silt, sand). Carries negative charges, so can bind cations like Ca^{2+}, and water. Clay-rich soils contain large reserves of nutrients and water, although some of the water is bound and cannot be taken up by plant roots.

Clone   In most vegetative propagation methods, the offspring are genetically identical to one another and to the parent plant. The offspring from one plant is known as a clone.

Collenchyma   One of the three plant cell types: parenchyma, collenchyma and sclerenchyma. Collenchyma is a thicker-walled cell type used to provide additional support for living tissues and organs such as leaf stalks.

Companion planting   A form of inter-cropping, whereby two (or more) crops are grown together in order to achieve management of pest and/or pathogen populations.

Coppicing   Involves cutting back a tree to near ground level in winter. Results in rapid re-growth (root food reserves channelled into a smaller number of surviving growth buds) and larger-than-usual leaves (high cytokinin: auxin ratio). Because re-growth occurs from the juvenile part of the tree, the new growth will show juvenile traits, such as the round blue-grey foliage of *Eucalyptus gunnii*.

Corm   An underground storage organ, like bulb, but consists almost entirely of stem tissue surrounded by scale leaves with no fleshy leaves. Flower shoots develop in axils of scale leaves, e.g. crocus, crocosmia. Produced by geophytes.

Crop rotation   Planting sets of crops in a series of beds in a vegetable garden, each set related or having similar characteristics, e.g. root crops, brassicas, legumes, potatoes, and then rotating them in successive years. Advantages are that the plants in each bed have similar food and water requirements and are attacked by the same organisms. Crop rotation (three- or four-year rotations) can help to manage soil-borne specialist pests (e.g. potato cyst nematode) and pathogens (e.g. clubroot) by preventing multiplication and encouraging natural biocontrol.

Cross-pollination   Where seeds are produced when the ovule of one flower is fertilized by pollen from a flower of the same species from a separate plant. Seed progeny are usually different in appearance from each other and the parent (not true-to-type).

Cultivar   Short for 'cultivated variety'. Written

as 'cv.' or with the name in single inverted commas, such as *Rosa* cv. Peace or 'Peace'.

Cuticle The layer of water-repellent waxes which coats the outer layer of cells (epidermis) of above-ground plant organs. Reduces loss of water from these organs, and can impart a blue-grey or silvery colouring, and/or a shiny surface to leaves. The chemical nature of the waxes determines their shape (crystal, rods, plates) which, in turn, determines the leaf colour. Found in particular in plants from dry habitats, such as scrub forest and under-storey of woodland.

Cutting A piece of tissue (stem, root, leaf) used in vegetative propagation, in which the new organs (roots or roots and shoots) develop from apical buds (stems) or adventitious buds (root or leaf).

Cutting back Removing part of stems of herbaceous perennials in May–June to produce stockier, shorter, later-flowering plants which do not need support. Can also be used to refer to removing flowering stems and leaves of plants like oriental poppies and *Alchemilla mollis* after flowering, to stimulate production of new better quality leaves and possibly a second flush of flowers.

Cyanobacterium One of the earliest groups of photosynthetic organisms. Can also fix atmospheric nitrogen gas into a form plants can use. Some, e.g. *Nostoc*, have developed mutualistic relationships with flowering plants, living within the plant organs, such as *Gunnera*, where the cyanobacterium provides fixed N and receives fixed C, as sugars, from the plant. Used to be known as blue-green algae.

Cytokinins Natural plant hormones which control plant growth (by affecting cell division) and apical dominance. Produced in roots. Can delay senescence of leaf tissues.

Day-neutral plants Plants which flower a certain number of days from germination, regardless of daylength.

Deadheading Removal of spent flowers to encourage the production of more flowers. Otherwise, seed and fruit formation can inhibit further flowering. Flowers should be removed so that the ovary is taken off. With flowering stems

carrying leaves, removal of the dead flowers above axillary buds can encourage new flowers to form.

Deciduous Woody plants which lose all their leaves in autumn in order to escape the stresses of the winter. The trigger for leaf abscission is shortening daylength and/or falling temperature, depending on the species. Prior to abscission, the chlorophyll in the leaves breaks down and bright colours can develop, ranging from yellow (as carotenoids are revealed) to reds and purples (as anthocyanins are synthesized to protect the leaves). *See* **evergreen**.

Deciduous woodland The terrestrial biome characteristic of areas where the winters are mild to severe, summer rainfall is adequate and the soil is quite rich in nutrients. Found in locations such as western Europe, eastern seaboard of the US and coastal regions of Japan and China.

Determinate A plant, particularly in the vegetable garden, where the apical growth bud eventually becomes reproductive, producing flowers instead of shoot and leaf organs. As a result the plant grows to a fixed height. Bush cultivars of tomato are determinate, for example. Opposite of **indeterminate**.

Dicotyledon The most common (compared to monocotyledon) and probably the original form of the flowering plants. Broad-leaved plants, characterized by having two seed leaves, a net-like (reticulate) vein arrangement in leaves, and flower parts (e.g. petals, anthers) in 4s or 5s, or multiples of either number. Usually abbreviated to 'dicot'.

Dioecious Plants which have separate male and female plants. A strategy to ensure cross-pollination. Only the female cultivars will produce fruits, e.g. holly, but need the nearby presence of a male plant to supply pollen. Examples include pampas grass (females produce larger plumes) and asparagus (males are preferred) (*see* **monoecious**).

Diploid Where there are two copies of each chromosome (and gene) in each cell, one copy from each parent. Symbolized as 2x, e.g. sweetcorn is 2x=20: a diploid species with two copies of 10 (=x) different chromosomes. Nearly all animals are diploid, but only about 20 per cent plant species. Most plants are polyploids (more than two copies of each chromosome).

Disbudding Removal of unwanted growth buds to re-direct assimilates to the desired part of the plant. In chrysanthemums, sweetpeas and dahlias grown for exhibition, the axillary buds (unwanted sinks) are removed so that they do not produce flowers. As a result, more assimilates are translocated to the apical flower bud, producing a larger flower. Also used to limit the number of trusses produced on cordon (indeterminate) tomatoes.

DNA Deoxyribonucleic acid. Each chromosome consists of one molecule of DNA, with each gene being a particular stretch of that DNA.

Dominant In a diploid plant, if a gene exists as two different forms (alleles), the genotype of a single plant can be AA (homozygous for allele A), aa (homozygous for allele a) or Aa (heterozygous). If the appearance (phenotype) of a plant with an Aa genotype is the same as that of a plant with an AA genotype, then the A allele is said to be completely dominant to the a allele (the recessive allele). The dominant allele is depicted by an upper case letter. If the phenotype of the heterozygote is intermediate between the two homozygotes, then allele A is incompletely dominant to allele a.

Dormancy A method for surviving stressful conditions. Can apply to entire plants, which die back to seeds (annual species), or to underground (herbaceous perennials) or above-ground growth buds (deciduous woody plants) in the winter (e.g. plants of the deciduous woodland biome) or summer (e.g. plants of the scrub forest biome). Dormancy is triggered by season-specific environmental factors such as temperature extremes, daylength or drought. Dormant plants or organs can still recognize and respond to environmental conditions. *See* **seed dormancy**.

Ecology The interaction between living and non-living components of the environment.

Economic sink Applies to plants in the kitchen garden. The economic sink is that part of the plant which is harvested and eaten, such as the fruit of apple and the tubers of potato.

Ecosystem An abbreviation of 'ecological system'. A system involving interactions between the community of living organisms and the non-living components such as soil, water and air. Examples include a forest or a sand dune.

Egg Contained within the ovule inside the ovary of the flower. Fertilization of an egg nucleus in the ovule by a pollen nucleus results in seed (and then fruit) formation.

Epidermis The outermost tissue, one cell thick, of all plant organs. In leaves, epidermal cells contain no chloroplasts (except for the guard cells of stomata, mostly on the undersurface of the leaf) but are often the layer containing anthocyanin. Outgrowths of the epidermal cells include root hairs (on the root epidermis or rhizodermis), leaf hairs and stem prickles, including the stinging hairs of nettles. Covered with a waxy cuticle to reduce water loss.

Evergreen Woody plants which do not lose all their leaves at any one time. Adapted to stressful environments (e.g. understorey shrubs of deciduous woodland, shrubs of scrub forest) and those where the growing season is short (e.g. conifers of the taiga and alpine plants). Leaves on a woody evergreen do lose their leaves, e.g. in spring in bamboos, but not all at the same time, and the effect is hidden by the remaining leaves.

F$_1$ hybrid Seed-propagated cultivar of cross-pollinated plants which comes true-to-type. Advantages include uniformity and hybrid vigour, but seed is expensive.

Family Related plants in different genera are placed in the same family. *Helleborus*, *Clematis* and *Ranunculus* are all members of the buttercup family, Ranunculaceae. Family names are not written in italics, and all end in the suffix –aceae.

Flowering plants The most advanced plants in plant evolution; includes both the monocotyledons and the dicotyledons.

Food chain Nutrients and chemical energy pass along a chain from a plant (primary producer) to a herbivore (primary consumer) and thence to one or more carnivores (secondary, tertiary etc. consumers). Each member of the chain is termed a trophic level. Transfer of energy and nutrients from one trophic level to another is inefficient, with approximately 90 per cent being lost at each transfer.

Food web Within an ecosystem, food chains (see above) are more complex, with many species capable of consuming more than one organism, which may be at a different trophic level. A badger can eat blackberries (is a primary consumer) and earthworms (is a secondary consumer). These more complex interactions result in food webs.

Fruit Botanically, the result of the pollination (successful or unsuccessful) of a flower. Apples, tomatoes and sweet peppers are all fruits, while rhubarb is not.

Fungi Non-photosynthetic organisms which generally obtain their food, chemicals and chemical energy by decomposing organic matter (saprophytes), by infecting living organisms (pathogens) or by entering into a mutually beneficial association (mutualism) with plant roots (mycorrhiza).

Gene The factor which controls inherited traits like flower colour. Carried on chromosomes in the nucleus (most genes), chloroplast or mitochondrion of every cell.

Generalist A pest or pathogen which attacks a wide range of unrelated plant species. The garden snail (*Arion hortense*) is a generalist pest, while grey mould (*Botrytis cinerea*) is a generalist pathogen.

Genotype The collection of genes in a plant. For a gene with two forms or alleles, A and a, in a diploid plant there are three possible genotypes: AA, Aa and aa.

Genus The first name in a plant's binomial, e.g. *Clematis* or *Rosa*. Plural form is 'genera'.

Geophyte Plant which survives the stress period in the form of an underground storage body with food reserves and immature flowers, leaves and stems, such as a bulb, corm, tuber or rhizome. Adapted to a short growing season, e.g. spring-flowering bulb like bluebell from the deciduous woodland, and autumn-flowering bulb, such as nerine from the scrub forest biome

Gibberellins A family of at least 40 natural plant hormones. Involved in triggering flowering, stem extension and seed germination.

Grafting Connecting the tissues of two plants, the rootstock and the scion wood, so that they will grow into one another, producing a plant with traits from each. The scion parent, a piece of shoot with apical and axillary buds, will determine most of the above-ground characters, like flower colour, fruit characters, leaf variegation. The rootstock parent determines root traits like resistance to soil-borne pests, and tolerance to extreme soil pH, but also determines how big the grafted plant will grow, because the root system controls shoot growth.

Green manure Plants which are grown specifically to be dug into the soil after a few weeks' growth, to increase the organic matter content of the soil. Include mustard, rye and red clover (also increases soil nitrogen content, because it is a N fixer). Soil can be planted 2–3 weeks after the green manure has been incorporated.

Growth bud Can be present at the end of a shoot (apical growth bud) or in the leaf axil (axillary growth bud). Contains meristem including immature shoot and leaves. Under appropriate environmental conditions, the growth bud can change from vegetative to reproductive, with the meristem producing flower primordia instead of leaf primordia.

Habitat management Modification of characteristics of the garden, particularly the vegetable garden, to encourage beneficials, to achieve increased biological control of the pests. Involves attracting female beneficials with flowers to provide food in the form of pollen and nectar, so that they will lay eggs. Also provides shelter, particular permanent areas, to provide habitat and over-wintering sites for beneficials.

Hardening off The mechanism by which seedlings grown indoors are gradually acclimatized to the cold before they can be transplanted outdoors. Seedlings are moved outside during the day then brought in at night, then left out in cold frames, to allow the induction of genes involved in cold tolerance (acclimation).

Hardwood A tree which is a dicotyledonous flowering plant, such as oak or sycamore (cf. softwood from conifers). A misnomer because the softest wood, balsa, comes from a hardwood tree (*see* **softwood**).

Harvest index That proportion of the total plant biomass which is harvested and eaten (*see* **economic sink**).

Herbaceous perennial Non-woody plants which die down above-ground in autumn, surviving over the winter as underground growth buds and food reserves.

Heterozygote Consider a diploid plant and a gene with two alleles, A and a. If the two copies of the gene in each cell are different alleles (the genotype is Aa), the plant is a heterozygote ('hetero-' means different, '-zygote' means fertilized egg), and is heterozygous for that gene.

Homeotic gene One master gene which controls a large number of genes affecting part of plant development such as flower formation. A mutation in a homeotic gene results in one flower organ being replaced by another (organ-to-organ conversion), as in the Jack-in-the-Green mutant, Primula 'Dawn Ansell', where the sepals are converted into leaves.

Homozygote Consider a diploid plant and a gene with two alleles, A and a. If the two copies of the gene in each cell are the same allele (the genotype is AA or aa), the plant is a homozygote ('homo-' means same, '-zygote' means fertilized egg), and is homozygous for that gene.

Hormones Natural plant chemicals which control most aspects of plant growth and development by switching specific genes on and off. The five main plant hormones are auxins, cytokinins, gibberellins, ethylene and abscisic acid.

Host plant The plant being attacked by a pest or pathogen.

Hydathodes Pores at the edge of the leaf which allow water in and out of the leaf. Early in the morning, water droplets form from the hydathodes (guttation) of some plants. Some plants trap water by use of small hairs around the leaf edge and this water is taken up through hydathodes. This is the source of the frost around leaf edges.

Indeterminate A plant, particularly in the vegetable garden, where the apical growth bud remains vegetative, producing more shoot and leaf tissue, and does not become reproductive. As a result the plant continues to grow upwards unless pinched out, by removing the apical growth bud. Cordon cultivars of tomato are indeterminate, for example. Opposite of **determinate**.

Inorganic Inorganic nutrients do not contain carbon. Mineral forms of nutrients, such as potassium sulphate, K_2SO_4, are inorganic. Inorganic sources of nitrogen, for example, are nitrate and ammonium ions, whereas urea and hoof and horn (contains protein) contain carbon and are organic.

Inter-cropping Growing two or more crops together in the vegetable garden in such a way that competition is minimized and complementarity is maximized. Beneficial effects of inter-cropping include more efficient use of natural resources such as light, water and nutrients, and better pest management (*see* **companion planting**).

Inter-generic hybrid A plant obtained by crossing plants of two related genera from the same family, e.g. *Fatsia × Hedera* (both members of the Araliaceae family) to produce × *Fatshedera*. The '×' before the generic names indicates an inter-generic hybrid. Almost always sterile.

Inter-specific hybrid A plant obtained by crossing plants of two species of the same genus, e.g. *Digitalis × mertonensis* = *D. purpurea* × *D. grandiflora*. The '×' before the species name indicates an inter-specific hybrid. Often but not always sterile.

Invertebrates Animals without backbones. Includes insects, but many other invertebrates which are important (as friends or enemies) to gardeners are not insects, such as slugs, nematodes and mites.

Ions Charged atoms of elements. Can be positively charged (cations), e.g. calcium Ca^{2+} or negatively charged (anions), e.g. sulphate SO_4^{2-}.

Juvenile phase A condition caused by an irreversible change in gene expression, which many plants (woody and non-woody) need to pass through before they can respond to environmental factors and start to flower. The same plant can be part juvenile and part adult, with the juvenile part being close to the base of the trunk in woody species. Some juvenile traits can be attractive, such as the climbing habit and lobed leaves of ivy.

Leaching The washing-out from the root zone of the soil of mobile ions such as potassium (K^+) and nitrate (NO_3^-). Leached nutrients cannot be taken up by the plants and are lost to the ecosystem, as well as posing a risk of pollution to groundwater.

Leaf Area Index (LAI) The leaf area of the vegetable crop per squared metre of land. For a single plant, total plant biomass increases as LAI increases as more light is being absorbed. For a crop community, however, the amount of light absorbed will increase until all the sunlight hitting the leaf canopy of the crop is absorbed (the leaf canopy is 'closed') and no soil will be visible when you look vertically down on the canopy. At this point, the LAI becomes the critical LAI (LAI_c). Production of more leaves when the canopy is closed is counter productive.

Legume A plant belonging to the pea family, Fabaceae (previously known as the Leguminosae). Includes pea, beans, clover, lupin etc. All can fix atmospheric nitrogen into a form plants can use with the help of mutualistic N-fixing bacteria (*Rhizobium*) living within the root cells in a root nodule. The flower is characteristically pea shaped.

Lignocellulose A complex of lignin and cellulose in cell walls which provides considerable tensile strength to trees and other woody plants.

Meristem The basic unit of plant growth, present in each vegetative growth bud. Consists of apical meristem and leaf primordia, with axillary meristems in the axils of the leaf primordia. Tends to be virus free in infected plants.

Mitochondrion An organelle within all plant cells. Releases chemical energy from assimilates, primarily sugars from photosynthesis, by aerobic respiration. Contains genes on a circular chromosome. Plural: mitochondria.

Monocotyledon Seedling produces one seed leaf. Includes the grasses and most geophytes. Characterized by parallel leaf veination and flower parts in threes or multiples thereof. Usually abbreviated to 'monocot'. The less common form of flowering plant (*see* **dicotyledon**).

Monoecious Refers to plants where there are separate male (staminate) and female (pistillate) flowers on the same plant, as with sweetcorn and cucumber. A strategy to increase cross-pollination (*see* **dioecious**).

Mulching Covering soil with an organic material (usually), such as chipped bark, cocoa shells or compost, although inorganic materials like gravel or crushed glass can be used. Reduces water loss by evaporation. Can also reduce the risk of ground frost and help manage annual weeds.

Mutant A spontaneous heritable change (sport), due to a mistake in one gene (gene mutation) or in one or more chromosomes (chromosome mutation). One of the major sources of new cultivars of garden plants.

Mutualism An association between plants and another organism where both parties benefit. Plants usually supply sugars and other assimilates. Examples of benefits to the plant include nitrogen fixation (by bacteria), increased water and phosphate uptake (mycorrhizal fungi), pollination (mostly insects) and seed dispersal (mostly birds).

Mycorrhiza A mutualistic relationship between the roots of most plants and a beneficial fungus. Two main types: endomycorrhiza, where the fungus lives within the plant cell (mostly non-woody plants) and ectomycorrhiza, where the fungus lives partly inside the root but outside the cells and produces a sheath around the root (mostly trees). Most woodland mushrooms and toadstools are the fruiting bodies of ectomycorrhizal fungi. Specialist mycorrhiza are also known for ericaceous plants and for orchids. In addition to increasing uptake of water and less mobile elements, such as phosphorus, from the soil, mycorrhizal fungi can also protect the roots from pest or pathogen attack.

Niche The conditions under which a particular plant lives within an ecosystem. The fundamental niche represents the potential range of conditions under which the plant can live, such as soil pH, light levels and temperature extremes. But the plant will have to share the ecosystem with other plant species, and their fundamental niches will overlap to some extent. Because no two species can occupy exactly the same niche in the same ecosystem for long (one will always compete out the other), the species will each reduce their realized (or actual) niche until there is no competition.

Nicking Removing a piece of bark below an axillary bud, interrupting cytokinin but not auxin supply to the bud, which will fail to grow out even under circumstances where it would be expected to do so, as in fan-trained apple trees (*see* **notching**).

Nitrogen fixation Plants cannot use nitrogen gas, N_2, as a form of nitrogen. Certain micro-organisms can fix nitrogen gas into ammonium and have adopted a mutualism with specific plants, which supply sugars to the bacteria. Examples include *Rhizobium* bacteria and legumes, and *Nostoc* cyanobacteria and *Gunnera*.

Notching Encouraging growth of a bud on a shoot by removing the bark above the bud, interrupting auxin movement, but not cytokinin flow from the roots to the bud.

Nucleus The control centre of each cell, containing the genes which determine the functions of the cell. All cells of a plant contain the same genes, but different genes are switched on or off in different cells.

Nutrient cycle The sequence of nutrients taken up by plants, animal and micro-organisms in a natural ecosystem. The amounts of individual nutrients stay more or less the same from year to year because they are returned to the ecosystem when the organisms die or produce waste material, which is decomposed by bacteria and fungi. Each nutrient has a separate cycle, such as the nitrogen cycle.

Organ Part of the plant, made up of the three tissue types, epidermis, vascular tissue and ground tissue. Organs include stem, leaf, flower, root and fruit.

Organelle Small membrane-bound body within the cell which carries out a particular function, such as the nucleus (control of the cell), chloroplasts (photosynthesis) and mitochondria (respiration).

Organic Any chemical containing carbon which is synthesized by a living organism (*see* **inorganic**).

Organic matter The material left after decomposition of waste from a living organism, either dead tissue or dung. Contains negatively charged components, which bind cations and water, so that it increases the water-holding capacity of the soil and acts as a nutrient reserve, particularly on light, sand-rich soils. Can also bind to clay particles to increase pore size, improving drainage on heavy soils.

Osmoprotectant A natural chemical which helps plants survive stressful conditions. All abiotic (non-living) stresses, except for waterlogging, cause osmotic stress as a component. Drought, heat and salinity stress, for example, all result in increases in the salt content of root cells, which maintains the gradient from the soil to the inside of the root, so that water uptake is maintained. Prolonged exposure to high salt concentrations is damaging, so plants adapted to stressful conditions, such as the coastal shoreline, accumulate osmoprotectants such as proline or glycinebetaine, to maintain water uptake even under very dry conditions.

Parenchyma The most widespread of the three cell types. The least specialized, their main function is metabolic, carrying out biochemical reactions such as photosynthesis and nitrogen assimilation, and storing the products. The mesophyll cells which make up most of a leaf are parenchyma (*see* **sclerenchyma** and **collenchyma**).

Pathogens Disease-causing micro-organisms, such as fungi (the most common plant pathogens in western Europe), bacteria (the least common) and viruses. Can be specialists, such as *Phytophthora infestans*, the cause of potato light blight, or generalists, like *Botrytis cinerea*, the fungus producing grey mould. Some pathogens, such as *Blumeria graminis* f. sp. *tritici*, the causative organism of wheat powdery mildew, infect only living tissues and keep them alive (obligate biotrophs). Grey mould (a necrotroph) attacks moribund tissue and causes its death.

Periclinal chimera A plant in which a mutation occurs in one of the layers, so that the layers are genetically different in the same plant, whereas in most plants the cells in all three layers of the organs are genetically identical. Traits which arise as a result of a periclinal chimera include orderly leaf variegation, e.g. *Hosta sieboldiana*

'Frances Williams' or petal variegation, e.g. African violet 'Pinwheel', and surface traits such as thornless blackberry or russetted potato tubers, e.g. potato 'Golden Wonder'.

Pests Usually invertebrates which attack (garden) plants, including insects (aphids, lily beetle), molluscs (slugs and snails), mites (red spider mite) and nematodes (potato cyst nematode). Some vertebrates can be pests, including pigeons (especially on young brassica plants), mice (bulbs in containers) and rabbits, which can kill young trees by nibbling off the bark (and the underlying phloem).

Petal The main flower organ designed to attract pollinators as a result of appropriate colours. All the petals combined make up the corolla.

Petaloids Extra petals within a flower which have been converted into petals from other flower organs by homeotic gene mutations. Often yellow in colour when derived from stamens, while those from modified carpels tend to be green.

pH A measure of how acid or alkaline something is. Ranges from pH 1 (extremely acidic) to pH 14 (extremely alkaline), with pH 7 being regarded as neutral. Soil pH in most gardens ranges from approximately 5.5 to 7.5. Soil pH can limit which plants can be grown, with ericaceous plants generally not tolerating alkaline soils.

Phenotype The combination of traits shown by a particular plant, caused in part by genes and in part by environmental factors. Only the genetic component can be inherited.

Phloem That part of the vascular system which transports assimilates all around the plant, composed of live cells. In vascular bundles, the phloem is to the outside and the xylem (which transports water and dissolved nutrients from the soil) is to the inside. In woody species, the phloem is just under the bark, so removal of the bark will disrupt movement of assimilates, causing death (girdling) or affecting apical dominance (nicking or notching).

Photoperiod Number of hours of light in a twenty-four-hour period. Detected by phytochrome. Used by temperate plants as indicator of season, triggering responses like flowering, leaf fall and dormancy.

Photosynthesis The process by which the energy in sunlight, absorbed by chlorophylls in the leaf chloroplasts, is used to 'fix' the carbon in CO_2 into the organic molecule, glucose. The chemical energy in photosynthesis can be released by aerobic respiration in mitochondria.

Physiological disorder Symptoms caused by a deficiency or excess of a nutrient in a plant, such as brown dead tissue around the leaf margins of calcium-deficient plants or purpling of leaves in phosphorus-deficient plants.

Phytochrome A protein which acts as a photoreceptor within plant tissues such as seeds, leaves and growth buds, allowing the plant to respond to presence or absence of light, to different times of day or to seasonal differences in daylength.

Pinching out Removing the apical growth bud from the shoot. This prevents auxin flow from the apical bud to the lower, axillary buds which would normally be stopped from growing out (apical dominance). Pinching out therefore encourages the axillary buds to form side shoots, so the plant becomes shorter but bushier. Otherwise known as 'stopping'.

Pioneer Plants which colonize bare soil from which the vegetation has been removed. In a garden, the first weeds to appear are the pioneer annual weeds like hairy bittercress and annual meadowgrass, programmed to produce seeds as quickly as possible. The seeds are very small and need light to germinate. A pioneer can produce seeds within two months of germinating, then dies, but can produce several generations in one year. Most pioneers are day-neutral, flowering whenever the temperature is above 6°C. Pioneer trees which colonize gaps in woodland include birches, which are fast-growing but relatively short lived, with an upright habit.

Plastids A range of related membrane-bound organelles within plant cells. Include green chloroplasts (containing chlorophylls) in leaves, yellow or red chromoplasts in fruits (tomato, red pepper) and petals, and colourless amyloplasts, which store starch (potato tubers).

Pollarding Cutting branches back to the crown of the tree trunk in winter, to limit the size of the tree canopy. The root:shoot balance means that pollarded trees also have smaller-than-usual root systems so pollarding is commonly carried out on street trees.

Pollen   The male sex cell (gamete) in the sexual reproduction (via seeds) of plants. Produced by anthers, pollen grains have to germinate on the stigma of a compatible flower so that the pollen nucleus can fuse with an egg cell (the female sex cell) in an ovule in the ovary of the flower.

Polyploid   A plant where there are more than two copies of each chromosome in each cell, such as 3x (triploid, 3 copies) apple Bramley's Seedling, 4x (tetraploid) potato, 8x (octaploid) strawberry. Probably 80 per cent of plants are polyploids or were polyploid during their evolution. Polyploidy results in useful traits such as larger and thicker organs like leaves and petals, seedlessness (in odd-numbered polyploids, such as 3x and 5x) and late flowering and fruiting.

Protein   One of the three classes of primary metabolites (others are carbohydrates and lipids). Organic molecules containing nitrogen. Main function of a protein is to act as an enzyme, which controls a specific biochemical reaction in the cell. Each enzyme is, in turn, produced by a specific gene.

Pruning   Removing shoots or parts of shoots to make woody plants larger or smaller, to change the shape of the plant, to encourage flowering or to produce more spectacular leaves. The effect of pruning depends on which season it is carried out, whether part or all of the shoot is removed and how many shoots are pruned.

Recessive   In a diploid plant, if a gene exists as two different forms (alleles), the genotype can be AA (homozygous for allele A), aa (homozygous for allele a) or Aa (heterozygous). If the appearance (phenotype) of a plant with an Aa genotype is the same as that of a plant with an AA genotype, then the a allele is said to be completely recessive to the dominant A allele. The recessive allele is depicted by a lower case letter. If the phenotype of the heterozygote is intermediate between the two homozygotes, then allele a is incompletely recessive to allele A (*see* **dominant**).

Respiration   Biological process in mitochondria by which chemical energy in assimilates like sugars is released. Aerobic respiration requires oxygen, anaerobic respiration does not.

Resting bodies   Many pests and pathogens produce two types of offspring: short-lived infective offspring and long-lived resting bodies. The resting bodies, such as chlamydospores of clubroot or cysts of potato cyst nematodes, enable the organism to survive stressful winter periods in the absence of the host plant. In specialist pests and pathogens, the organism will remain dormant in resting bodies for years until it detects the presence of the host plant (usually in the form of host chemicals).

Reversion   Occurs when a plant exhibiting an orderly leaf variegation produces a shoot with all-green leaves. Particularly common after heavy pruning when new shoots arise from adventitious rather than pre-formed axillary buds.

Rhizome   An underground stem which looks like a thick root but is a storage organ. New shoots can occur along the length of each rhizome as a result of vegetative reproduction, e.g. the fern bracken, so that all the plants are clonal and genetically identical (from 'rhizo' meaning 'root').

Root hairs   Small short-lived outgrowths of the root epidermis just behind the root tip which greatly increase the ability of the root to take up water and nutrients from the soil.

Sand   The largest of the three types of soil particle. A sandy soil is free-draining but has limited reserves of nutrients and water.

Saprophytes   Micro-organisms (fungi, bacteria) which obtain their nutrients and chemical energy by decomposition of dead or waste organic matter in the soil.

Sclerenchyma   A cell type which provides support and rigidity to plant parts which have stopped growing. The cells have thick walls which are stiffened by inclusion of lignocellulose. Sclerenchyma cells eventually die but this does not affect their ability to provide support.

Scrub forest   The smallest terrestrial biome, but second only to tropical rainforest in terms of the number of plant species present. Characterized by mild to cool winters but hot dry summers (Mediterranean-type climate) which are the principal stress period, along with regular fires.

Vegetation is sparse and dominated by evergreen shrubs, with small or leathery leaves. Also contains large numbers of geophytes as well as annuals. This biome is found in California, the Mediterranean, South Africa and Chile.

Secondary metabolites Whereas primary metabolites are carbohydrates, proteins and fats, secondary metabolites are a much wider range of plant chemicals, including defence chemicals, pigments, DNA, hormones, etc. High levels of nitrate, as produced when synthetic fertilizers are used, increases primary metabolism at the expense of secondary metabolism, so that plant defences are suppressed.

Seed dormancy Many seeds, when produced in late summer or autumn, will not germinate even when provided with ideal conditions. This is an adaptation (dormancy) so that seedlings do not have to live under unfavourable conditions in the winter. The three types of seed dormancy are physiological seed dormancy, where a hormone-based dormancy gradually wears off over time; physical seed dormancy, where the barrier to water entry into the dry dormant seeds is gradually worn away in the soil; and morphological seed dormancy, where the embryo in the seed continues to develop after the seeds are shed, until it is mature enough to germinate.

Seed propagation Usually sexual reproduction, following seed production via cross- or self-pollination. The offspring from seed propagation do not usually come true-to-type.

Selective weedkillers Lawn herbicides which kill dicot weeds but not the monocots, such as the lawn grasses, because the enzyme inhibited by the herbicide in dicots is absent from the monocots.

Self-incompatibility Where pollen from a flower cannot germinate on the stigma of the same or a different flower from the same plant, maximizing cross-pollination. Because of this, most fruit trees, such as apples, need to be planted alongside a compatible pollinator tree.

Self-pollination Reproductive method of plants where seeds are produced following fertilization of ovules by pollen from the same flower or from a different flower on the same plant. Results in less variation, more homozygosity. Examples include tomato, French beans, etc.

Sepals The green organs in the outermost whorl of the floral structure, which protect the flower in the bud stage from factors such as frost. Together, the sepals form the calyx.

Short-day plants Term for plants which will flower only when the actual daylength is below the critical daylength (though it is actually the length of the dark period which controls flowering).

Silt The mid-sized of the three types of soil particle.

Sink A plant organ which receives more sugars from other organs than it produces (i.e. a net receiver), e.g. a root (*see* **source**).

Softwood A conifer tree, like a pine or fir.

Source A plant organ which produces more sugars than it receives (i.e. a net producer) from other organs, e.g. a full-sized leaf (*see* **sink**).

Specialist Pest or pathogen attacking only one or a small number of related species, such as potato cyst nematode and late potato blight which attack potato and its close relative tomato. Most important crop pests are specialists, but their populations can be managed by crop rotation and other strategies.

Species 1. The second name (e.g. *vulgaris* in *Primula vulgaris*) in the binomial of a plant. There can be different species in the same genus, such as the foxgloves *Digitalis purpurea*, *D. lanata*, *D. ambigua*, *D. grandiflora* etc.; 2. Used to denote the individual plant, e.g. 'The woolly foxglove, *D. lanata*, is a common European plant, and this species is used to produce digoxin…'; 3. Also used to refer to any living organism, e.g. humans, elephants, dandelions. Plural: species.

Sport (*see* **mutant**)

Stamen The stamen is the male part of the flower, consisting of an anther, which produces pollen, attached to the flower by a thread, the filament.

Stomata Controllable pores in the upper and (mostly) lower epidermis of the leaf through which CO_2, O_2 and water can pass in and out. The opening of the stoma is controlled by two kidney-shaped guard cells on either side of the pore. For every molecule of CO_2 which enters a leaf (for photosynthesis) through a stoma,

200 molecules of water vapour leave, so there are many plant adaptations to minimize water loss and increase water use efficiency, such as sunken stomata, inrolled leaves and leaf hairs. Singular: stoma.

Sub-shrub Plant native to the scrub forest biome with a woody framework plus herbaceous current year's growth. Includes lavender, *Cytisus* (broom) and *Zauschneria*. Best kept compact by pruning back current year's growth after flowering.

Subspecies Distinct populations of the same species which are separated by long distances. Two subspecies can still cross to produce fully fertile hybrids.

Succession Process by which bare soil becomes colonized by plants. The first species are pioneers, short-lived annuals, followed by annuals, biennials, non-woody perennials, shrubs and trees. Strictly speaking this is secondary succession, whereas colonization of a site which has never had plants on it before, such as a wall or a volcanic island, is known as primary succession.

Systemic Spreading throughout the plant, used of chemicals, whether a herbicide or a fungicide, which travel in the phloem.

Taiga The largest of the terrestrial biomes, covering Northern Canada, Northern Europe and Siberia, dominated by conifers, which are evergreen, so that they can take advantage of the short growing season, drought avoiding and cold escaping. Also includes drought- and shade-tolerant evergreen plants from the under-storey flora.

Taxonomy The science of identifying the relatedness between plant species.

Temperate grassland A biome found in the interior of continents, where the summers are hot and dry, and the winters cold to very cold, such as the US Midwest (prairie), Russia (steppe) and Argentina (pampas). Dominant plant types include grasses (shorter species in the drier areas), both cool-season and warm-season species, and late-flowering dicots, particularly members of the daisy family, the Asteraceae.

Tepal Term used to describe both the petals and sepals of a flower in plants where they are indistinguishable, as in tulips.

Tissue Formed by two or more of the three cell types (parenchyma, collenchyma and sclerenchyma) combined together to create a specialized tissue with a particular function. The three major tissue types are the outer epidermal tissue (protective function), the vascular tissue (transport function) and the ground tissue which makes up the bulk of the plant.

Tolerance Ability of a plant to withstand stresses. When exposed to the stress it suffers far less than does a non-tolerant species.

Training Changing the shape of the plant and its floriferousness, not by pruning but by physically changing the habit of the plant. For example by supporting the main stem of the plant in a vertical arrangement, apical dominance can be increased, resulting in a taller plant, while the opposite, in which the main shoot is tied to the horizontal or at an angle, reduces apical dominance so that axillary buds grow out into side shoots.

Translocation The movement of dissolved nutrients or assimilates around the plant in the vascular system.

Transpiration Evaporation of water vapour through the stomata of the leaf, resulting in cooling of leaves and the plant. Because there are continuous columns of water from the site of uptake in the xylem of the root to the leaf, transpiration also results in the uptake of water (and dissolved nutrients), and is the major contributor of water uptake.

Transposable element A jumping gene, which can change its location on the same or different chromosomes in the nucleus. When the transposable element is integrated into a gene, the gene is switched off. When it jumps out of the gene, the gene is switched back on again. Transposable elements integrated into pigment genes will produce irregular patterns of variegation on leaves and flowers, such as nasturtium 'Alaska'.

Trap crops Crops used to reduce populations of soil-borne specialist pests and pathogens by triggering emergence but preventing multiplication of the organism.

True-to-type Plants which are exactly like their parents. Generally, seed propagation produces offspring plants which are different from one another; in other words they do not breed true-to-type.

Tuber An enlarged underground stem which contains growth buds and a food reserve, as with potato and *Cyclamen hederifolium*.

Under-storey trees Species in deciduous woodland with broad spreading canopies and shorter than the canopy trees, such as magnolia, silverbells and *Amelanchier*.

Vacuole Membrane-bound sac unique to plant cells, used to store chemicals, particularly defence chemicals which are released when the cell is damaged.

Variegation Usually refers to green/white colour variation in leaves, but can also occur in flowers. Orderly leaf variegation is caused by a periclinal chimera, which is not inherited via seed, while the more 'splashed' type of variegation can be caused by a mutation in chloroplasts (produces different proportions of green, white and variegated offspring) or by a transposable element (produces almost all variegated offspring).

Vascular system A tissue system which runs throughout the plant, from roots to stem to the veins in the leaves, consisting of the xylem, which transports water and dissolved nutrients taken up by the roots upwards, and the phloem which transports assimilates like sugars, proteins and secondary metabolites in all directions.

Vegetative propagation Propagation involving somatic cells, like stem, leaf or root, rather than seed. Because only one parent plant is involved and all somatic cells in a plant are genetically identical, all the offspring are usually identical to the parent and one another (true-to-type) and represent a clone, although some characters are not inherited by certain vegetative propagation methods.

Vernalization A period of exposure to low temperatures, which is needed before many species can respond to environmental factors like lengthening days and rising temperatures by flowering. This adaptation prevents plants from flowering under stressful winter conditions.

Water-holding capacity The amount of water which a soil can hold and make available to plant roots. Clay soils hold more water than silty soils which hold more than sandy soils, but some of the water in clay soils is bound to the clay particles and cannot be taken up by roots, whereas all of the water in sandy soils is available to roots. The amount of water held by a soil can be increased markedly by adding organic matter like garden compost, well-rotted animal manure or a green manure.

Xylem That part of the vascular system which transports water and dissolved nutrients from the soil up the plant. Xylem cells die but still function, while also providing some support for the plant. In vascular bundles, the phloem is to the outside and the xylem is to the inside.

Index

abscisic acid 106
acidic soil 66, 89, 97, 100, 214
adult phase 103, 116–8, 177–8, 221
adventitious bud 105, 107, 114 116, 150, 152, 171–2, 241
after ripening 158–9
algae 8
alkaline soil 66, 89, 97, 100, 241
allele 163, 175, 241
allelochemicals 36, 139, 142–3, 235
alpine 41–42, 156, 241
alternate host 137
altitude 41
anion 81–2, 96, 241
annual 36, 38, 53, 140, 141–2, 241
anther 15, 187–8
anthocyanin 9, 190–1, 197–200, 239, 241
anti-oxidant 240, 241
aphid 124–6, 134–7
apical bud 104–9, 111, 118, 121, 171, 216, 230
apical dominance 106–7, 109, 118, 121, 219, 221–2, 231, 236, 242
assimilates 13, 82–85, 109, 241
atom 77, 81
augmentative biocontrol 135–6, 241
autumn leaf colour 198–200
auxin 51, 105–7, 109, 112–3, 146, 153
avoidance (tress) 42
axillary bud 104–9, 111, 118, 121, 171, 230–1, 236

bareroot plants 53, 57
beneficial
    insect i25, 133–6, 241
    virus 154, 172–3
berry 231–2
betalain 190–1, 239
biennial 140–1, 242
binomial 17–23, 242
bioavailability 240
biological control (biocontrol) 242
    augmentative 133–5
    habitat management 133–135, 224–5
biomass 214, 223, 242
biome 30–43
    deciduous woodland 29, 30, 31, 32–5, 206, 244
    scrub forest 31, 32, 35–40, 57, 73, 206, 209, 251
    taiga 30–31, 32, 40–44, 57, 253
    temperate grassland 30–33, 40–41, 57, 253
    tropical grassland 42–3
    tropical rainforest 42
biostimulant 133
blanching
    cooking 237–8, 242
    growing 228–9, 242
bolting 142, 220
bonemeal 91, 96
bract 186, 242
breeding 178–83
broad–spectrum (plant protection) chemical 138–9
brown material (composting) 94–5
bud 104–5, 245
    adventitious 105
    apical 104–5
    axillary 104–5

reproductive 118, 186
vegetative 118, 186
bulb 53–6, 57, 59, 242

calcium (Ca) 64, 66, 77, 78
canopy tree 32–3, 242
carbohydrate 242
carbon 77–8
    carbon dioxide (CO_2) 36–7, 78–9, 80
    carbon skeletons 93
carotenoid 9, 78, 190–1, 199–200, 201, 239, 240, 242
carpel 15, 186–8, 231, 242
catch crop 223
cation 81–2, 96, 241
cell 8–12, 242–3
cell wall 8
chalk soil 66, 97
chicken (poultry) manure 92
chimera (periclinal) 114, 169, 176–7, 249
chitting 219, 242
chlorophyll 9, 78, 198–200, 201, 239, 240, 243
chloroplast 9, 12–3, 161, 173–7, 243
chlorosis 89–90, 99, 100, 243
chromoplast 9, 191
chromosome 9, 161, 243
clay 63–4, 81, 89, 243
climate 29–30, 45–7
    macroclimate 29–30
    microclimate 47–8
collenchyma 10, 11, 13, 229, 243
colour
    flower 190–7
    fruit 193–4, 195, 197
    leaf 197–206
companion planting 227–8, 243
competition 29, 41, 142, 221–3
    competitive ability 29, 41, 142
    intra-specific competition 221–3
    inter-specific competition 221–3
compost 92
    composting 93–6
    disease–suppressive compost 225
compound 77–81
conifer 7, 8, 42, 43
contact (plant protection) chemical 137, 138
container–grown plants 53
cooking 237–8, 239–40, 242
cooling 71–2
co-pigment 195, 196
coppicing 112, 117, 243
corm 53–6, 57, 59, 243
crop rotation 224, 226–7, 243
cross pollination 216, 243
cultivar 22–3, 216, 233–4, 243
cuticle 14, 244
cutting 178, 244
    hardwood 150–2
    leaf 152
    root 152
    semi-ripe 150–2
    softwood 150–2
cutting back 111, 244
cyanobacteria 7, 12, 86–88, 244
cytokinin 51, 105, 107, 109, 112–3, 150, 236–7

day-neutral plant 208–9, 211, 221, 244, 250
deadheading 110, 211, 244
deciduous woodland 29–30, 31, 32–5, 206, 244
determinate 110, 216, 244
dicotyledon (dicot) 25, 244
digging 134–6
dioecious (dioecy) 167, 244
diploid 163, 164, 179–80, 244
disbudding 110, 244
disease 93, 126–7, 224–8
division 57–9
DNA (deoxyribonucleic acid) 162, 244
dominant 163, 245
dormancy
    plant 28, 36, 47, 53, 57, 73
    seed 154–9, 245
double flowers 189

ecology 28, 245
economic sink 213, 245
economic yield 214, 223
ecosystem 28, 30, 32, 85, 123–5, 245
elaiosome 158
element 77–8, 81
elicitor 133
emasculation 182
epidermis 8, 11, 14, 245
escape (stress) 28, 40
evergreen 33, 35, 36, 38, 44, 57, 73, 245
evolution 7–8

family 23–5, 78, 128, 224, 225–7, 245
feeding 223–4
fern 8, 34
fertilizer 90–2, 98–101
    artificial 91
    natural 91–2, 98–100
flower 15–7
    cut flower 72
    colour 190–3, 194–6
    scent 193
    structure 15–7, 185–90
flowering 118–121
    flowering date 38, 141, 206–9, 234
    flowering duration 39, 100, 209–11
foliar feeding 67, 90, 101
food chain 94, 124, 245
food web 124, 245
frost 47, 48, 113
    frost pocket 49
fruit 16–7, 213, 231–2, 246
    colour 193–4
    ripening 238–9
    seedless 232–3
    storage 237–9
    thinning 237
    type (berry, drupe, aggregate) 232
fungi 246
    mycorrhizal 13, 32, 51–3, 60–1, 248
    pathogenic 125, 126–7, 132, 249
    saprophytic (decomposer) 85, 136, 225
fungicide 137–9
    contact 137–8
    systemic 137–8

gamete 164
gene 9, 12, 161–3, 246

generalist 127–8, 134
genetics 160–4
genotype 163–4, 246
genus 18–20, 23, 246
geophyte 29, 34, 35, 36, 38–40, 53–6, 57, 84, 100, 246
    bulb 53–6, 57, 59, 242
    corm 53–6, 57, 59, 243
    rhizome 53–6, 57, 251
    tuber 53–6, 57, 219, 253
gibberellin 106, 118–9, 206, 231, 246
glucose 78–80, 82–4, 237–8
grafting 113, 152, 173, 246
    rootstock 152, 153
    scion 152, 153
grasses 40
    cool-season 73
    warm-season 40–1, 73
    green manure 75, 112
green material (composting) 94–5, 246
groundflora 34
group 23
guard cell 14
Gulf Stream 46

habitat management 133–5, 224–5, 246
hardening 100, 246
    hardening off (cold hardening) 46–7, 160
    mechanical hardening 61
harvest 230–1, 237–8
harvest index 214, 246
herbaceous perennial 35, 36, 38, 41, 58, 141, 246
herbicide 106, 143–5
    contact 143–4
    residual 143–4
    selective 146–7
    systemic 144–5
herbs 38, 44
heterozygous (heterozygote) 163–4, 167, 217–8, 233, 246
homeotic gene 186–8, 246
homozygous (homozygote) 163–4, 169, 217–8, 247
hoof and horn 91
hormone 51, 105, 107, 109, 112–3, 146, 150, 231, 236–7
    abscisic acid 106
    auxin 51, 105–7, 109, 112–3, 146, 150, 231, 236–7
    cytokinin 51, 105, 107, 109, 112–3, 150, 236–7
    ethylene 106, 238, 239
    gibberellin 106. 118–9, 206, 231
    hormone weedkiller 106
hose-in-hose 188–190
host disease escape 131
host disease resistance 129–130, 132, 133, 217
host disease tolerance 131
hybrid 20
    inter-generic hybrid 21
    inter-specific hybrid 20, 21, 180–1, 182
    F_1 hybrid 217, 218, 245
hybridization 180–3
hydathodes 67–8, 70

in-the-green 56, 58–9
inbreeding 169

indeterminate 108, 110, 216, 231, 247
inorganic 77, 91, 247
insecticide 137–9
  contact 137–8
  systemic 137–8
inter-cropping 222–3, 227–8, 247
inter-generic hybrid 21, 247
inter-specific hybrid 20–21, 247
invertebrate 125–7, 248
ion 81, 248
  anion 81–2, 96, 241
  cation 81–2, 96, 242

Jack-in-the-Green 188, 190
jumping gene 173–5, 221, 253
juvenile phase 101, 116–8, 150–1, 153,
  177–8, 221, 248

K (potassium) 77–8, 88, 99–100

layers (L–I, L–II, L–III) 114–5, 169–172
lawn weeds 145–7
leaching 88, 91–2, 96, 248
leaf 36–8, 44
  leaf hairs 37–8, 44–45, 203
  leaf rolling 36–8, 44
  leaf waxes 36–7, 44, 203
Leaf Area Index (LAI) 214–5, 247
  critical LAI (LAI$_c$) 214–5
leaf colour 197–206
  autumn leaves 198–200
  blue, grey, silver, white: 202–4
  purple, red 204–6
  summer leaves 200–206
  yellow 201–2
  young leaves 197–8
legume 24, 32, 248
light 78–9, 86–7, 146, 223–4
  spectrum 78, 192–3
  colour development 197, 204–5
  germination 159–60
lignin 10
lignocellulose 10, 248
lime 65–66, 96–7, 197
lime-induced chlorosis 89–90
loam 64
long-day plant 221

macronutrient 77–8, 88, 91, 92, 96
manure
  animal manure 92, 98
  green manure, 75, 142
Mendelian inheritance 163–4
meristem 104, 186, 248
metabolism
  primary
  secondary 131–2
microclimate 47–8
micronutrient 77–8, 88, 91, 92, 96
mitochondrion 9, 12–13, 161, 248
molecule 77, 78–9
monocotyledon (monocot) 25, 248
monoecy (monoecious) 167, 248
moss 8, 34, 147
mulch 75–6, 136, 142, 248
mutant 163, 178–80, 248
  chloroplast mutant 114, 169–70, 175–7
  periclinal chimera 114, 169, 176–7,
    249
mutualism 12–3, 32, 86, 248
mycorrhiza 13, 32, 51–3, 60–1, 248
  ectomycorrhiza 52–3, 60
  endomycorrhiza 52–3, 60

N (nitrogen) 77–8, 85–8, 98–9, 223
  nitrogen cycle 85–8
  nitrogen fixation 24, 32, 86–7, 146,
    223–4, 248–9
  nitrogen theft 26, 89
nectar
  nectar guide 191–2
  nectar plant 225
niche 28, 248
  fundamental 28–9
  realised 29, 145
nicking 236–7, 248

nitrogen 77–8, 85–8, 98–9, 223
notching 235, 249
nucleus 9, 161, 249
nutrient 64, 76–101
  macronutrient 77–8, 88, 91, 92, 96
  micronutrient 77–8, 88, 91
  uptake 81–2
  nutrient cycle 85, 88, 249
nutrient deficiency 88–9

organ 11–2, 15, 186–90, 249
organelle 9, 12–3, 249
organic 77, 85–6, 94, 249
organic matter 65–66, 75, 85, 91, 96–7,
  249
osmoprotectant 69, 249
ovary 15, 231–2
overwintering 136–7
ovule 15, 176, 231–2
oxygen 8, 78–9, 80, 94–5

P (phosphorus) 88, 99, 197, 211, 221, 250
parenchyma 8, 10, 11, 13, 14, 249
parthenocarpy 233
partitioning 109, 229–30
pathogen 125, 126–7, 132, 249
  generalist 128
  specialist 128, 136
perennial 141
periclinal chimera 114, 169, 176–7, 249
pest 125, 224–8, 235, 249
  generalist 127–8
  specialist 127–8, 136
pesticide
pesticide resistance 136, 138
petal 15, 185–90, 250
petaloid 186, 187–90, 250
pH 66, 249
  cell pH 239
  soil pH 66, 96–98, 196–7
phenotype 163–4, 250
pheromone 235
phloem 13, 14, 70, 83–4, 137, 236, 250
phosphorus 88, 99, 197, 211, 221, 250
photoperiod 207–9
  day-neutral plant 208–9, 211, 221, 250
  long-day plant 208, 221
  short-day plant 207–8, 221
photosynthesis 7–8, 40, 78–80, 82, 250
  C3 40, 80, 242
  C4 40–41, 80, 221, 242
physiological disorder 88–90, 250
phytochrome 208, 221, 250
pigment 190–91, 194–6
  flower 190–3, 194–6
  fruit 193–4
  leaf 197–206
pinching out 108, 250
pioneer 250
  tree 34
  weed 139–40, 209
planting 53, 59–61, 218–223
planting date 57, 218–221
plant protection chemical 137–9
  synthetic 137–9
  natural 137–9
plastid 9, 12–3, 161, 170, 173–7, 191,
  243, 250
pollen 15, 185, 250
pollination 16, 191–3, 233–4
  cross-pollination 164, 165–7, 182, 216,
    222
  self-pollination 164, 168–9, 182, 216,
    222
pollarding 113, 117, 250
pollinator 16, 191–3, 233–4
polyploid 163, 179–180, 250
potassium (K) 77–8, 88, 99–100
potato
  chitting 219
  early 216, 217
  maincrop 216, 250
primary producer 124
propagation 149–60
  seed 154–60, 164
  vegetative 149–154, 163–4

pruning 107–8, 112–5, 235–6, 251
  altered flowering 119–20, 235–6
  altered plant size 112–3
  bigger leaves 112
  formative pruning 108
  pruning date 119–121
  root pruning 112–3
  summer 112
  winter 112
receptacle 15, 232
recessive 163, 251
respiration 80, 82, 251
  aerobic 80
  alternative 80
  anaerobic 94
reversion 113–6, 251
rhizodermis 51–2, 84
rhizome 53–6, 57, 251
ripening 238
root 51–3, 59, 251
  root hair
  root: shoot balance 51, 74
rooting powder 106, 151–2
rootstock 61, 234

sand 63–4, 251
scarification 159
scion 61, 153, 234
sclerenchyma 10, 13, 251
scrub forest 31–2, 35–40, 57, 73, 206,
  209, 251
seaweed 92
  extract 91, 99
  meal 65
seed 154–60, 139–42, 232–3
seed bank 140–1
seed dispersal 17
seed dormancy 154–60, 251–2
  breaking 157–9
  morphological 156
  physical 156
  physiological 156
seed germination 38, 140, 159–60
seedless fruit 232–3
  parthenocarpy 233
  stenospermocarpy 233
segregation 180
self-incompatibility 167, 233–4, 252
self pollination 168–9, 252
sepal 15, 185–90, 252
short-day plant 207–8, 221, 252
silt 63–4, 252
sink 83, 109, 110, 11–2, 252
  economic sink 214, 222, 229–30
slug 125–6, 134, 136
snail 125–6, 134, 136
soil 60, 63–66
  chalky 66, 97
  clay 63–65, 81, 89, 243
  organic 53–5
  sandy 63–5
  silty 63–5
soil pH 66
  flower colour 196–7
  nutrient availability 89, 96–7, 196–7
soil moisture 63, 64, 74–6
soil type (textural analysis) 63–66
source 83, 109, 229–30, 252
sowing seed 159–60, 218, 220–1
  successional 220–1
  temperature 159–60
spacing 36, 40, 42, 221–2
specialist 127–9, 134, 252
species 18–19, 23, 252
sport 163, 178–80, 248
staking 61
stamen 15, 252
starch 84, 217, 237–8
stenospermocarpy 232–3
sterility 21. 110, 152–3, 233–5
  double flower 110, 152–3
  inter-specific hybrid 21, 110,
    152–3
  polyploidy 233
stigma 15, 165–6, 231, 234

stomata 14, 36–8, 71–2, 78, 252
storage 237–9
  in situ 238
  low-temperature 237–9
stratification 158–9
stress 28. 38, 40, 198, 206
  avoidance 28, 40, 42, 198, 206
  escape 28, 40
  tolerance 28, 40, 160
style 15, 165–6, 231–234
sub-shrub 36, 107–8, 252
sub-species 21–22, 252
succession 139–41, 252–3
sucker 113–4
sucrose 82–4, 230
sugar 82–3, 230, 238
superphosphate 99, 197
surfactant 138, 145
systemic 82–4, 137, 143–4, 253

taiga 30, 31, 42–3, 209, 253
tannin 199
taxonomy 7, 17–25, 253
temperate grassland 30–1, 32, 40–1,
  57, 253
tepal, 186, 253
tidying up 113
tissue 11, 253
tolerance 28, 40, 160, 253
top dressing 113
training 109, 121, 236–7, 253
translocation 69–72, 82–84, 109, 253
transpiration 37–38, 60, 70–72, 76,
  253
transplanting 57–9
transposable element 173–5
trap cropping 227, 253
triploid 179–80
trophic level 124
tropical grassland 42–3
tropical rainforest 42
true-to-type 149, 152, 160, 164, 169–78,
  253
tuber 53–6, 57, 219, 253
tundra 30, 31, 41

ultraviolet (UV) light 8, 41, 192–3, 198
under-storey trees 33, 34 253

vacuole 9, 191, 253
variegation 79–80, 114–6, 169–172, 173–6,
  202, 253–4
variety 22, 23
vascular
  vascular bundle 13, 70–73, 83
  vascular plant 13
  vascular system 11, 83, 253
vegetable 213–239
vernalization 206–7, 234, 254
virulence 130
virus
  beneficial virus 154, 172–3
  virus disease 56, 127, 153–4, 218

water 67
  soil water 64, 68, 74–6
  water loss 36–8, 40, 42, 74–6
  water uptake 67–69, 72
watering 72–4
water shoots 105, 112
waxes 36–7, 44, 202
weed 139–41, 226
  pioneer 139–40
  annual 141–2, 156
  perennial 142
weedkiller (herbicide) 106, 143–5
weed management 141–7
  chemical control 143–5
  ecological 146
  hand weeding 141–2
  hoeing 141–2
  mulching 142
witches' broom 179
wood ash 91, 99

xylem 13–4, 70–1, 83, 137, 254